The Short Oxford History of Italy

Italy in the Age of the Renaissance

The Short Oxford History of Italy

General Editor: John A. Davis

Italy in the Early Middle Ages
edited by Cristina La Rocca

Italy in the Central Middle Ages
edited by David Abulafia

Italy in the Age of the Renaissance
edited by John M. Najemy

Early Modern Italy
edited by John Marino

Italy in the Nineteenth Century
edited by John A. Davis

Liberal and Fascist Italy
edited by Adrian Lyttelton

Italy since 1945
edited by Patrick McCarthy

The Short Oxford History of Italy

General Editor: John A. Davis

Italy in the Age of the Renaissance

1300–1550

Edited by John M. Najemy

OXFORD
UNIVERSITY PRESS

OXFORD
UNIVERSITY PRESS

Great Clarendon Street, Oxford OX2 6DP

Oxford University Press is a department of the University of Oxford.
It furthers the University's objective of excellence in research, scholarship,
and education by publishing worldwide in

Oxford New York

Auckland Cape Town Dar es Salaam Hong Kong Karachi Kuala Lumpur
Madrid Melbourne Mexico City Nairobi New Delhi Shanghai Taipei Toronto

With offices in

Argentina Austria Brazil Chile Czech Republic France Greece
Guatemala Hungary Italy Japan South Korea Poland Portugal
Singapore Switzerland Thailand Turkey Ukraine Vietnam

Oxford is a registered trade mark of Oxford University Press
in the UK and in certain other countries

Published in the United States
by Oxford University Press Inc., New York

© Oxford University Press, 2004

British Library Cataloguing in Publication Data
Data available

Library of Congress Cataloging in Publication Data
Data available

ISBN 0-19-870040-7 (pbk)
ISBN 0-19-870039-3 (hbk)

Typeset in Minion
by RefineCatch Limited, Bungay, Suffolk
Printed in Great Britain
on acid-free paper by
Biddles Ltd., King's Lynn, Norfolk

General Editor's Preface

Over the last three decades historians have begun to interpret Europe's past in new ways. In part this reflects changes within Europe itself, the declining importance of the individual European states in an increasingly global world, the moves towards closer political and economic integration amongst the European states, and Europe's rapidly changing relations with the non-European world. It also reflects broader intellectual changes rooted in the experience of the twentieth century that have brought new fields of historical inquiry into prominence and have radically changed the ways in which historians approach the past.

The new *Short Oxford History of Europe* series, of which this *Short Oxford History of Italy* is part, offers an important and timely opportunity to explore how the histories of the contemporary European national communities are being rewritten. Covering a chronological span from late antiquity to the present, the *Short Oxford History of Italy* is organized in seven volumes, to which over seventy specialists in different fields and periods of Italian history have contributed. Each volume provides clear and concise accounts of how each period of Italy's history is currently being redefined, and their collective purpose is to show how an older perspective that reduced Italy's past to the quest of a nation for statehood and independence has now been displaced by different and new perspectives.

The fact that Italy's history has long been dominated by the modern nation-state and its origins simply reflects one particular variant on a pattern evident throughout Europe. When from the eighteenth century onwards Italian writers turned to the past to retrace the origins of their nation and its quest for independent nationhood, they were doing the same as their counterparts elsewhere in Europe. But their search for the nation imposed a periodization on Italy's past that has survived to the present, even if the original intent has been lost or redefined. Focusing their attention on those periods—the Middle Ages, the Renaissance, the *Risorgimento*—that seemed to anticipate the modern, they carefully averted their gaze from those that did not, the Dark Ages, and the centuries of foreign occupation and conquest after the Sack of Rome in 1527.

Paradoxically, this search for unity segmented Italy's past both chronologically and geographically, since those regions (notably the South) deemed to have contributed less to the quest for nationhood were also ignored. It also accentuated the discontinuities of Italian history caused by foreign conquest and invasion, so that Italy's successive rebirths—the Renaissance and the *Risorgimento*—came to symbolize all that was distinctive and exceptional in Italian history. Fascism then carried the cycle of triumph and disaster forward into the twentieth century, thereby adding to the conviction that Italy's history was exceptional, the belief that it was in some essential sense also deeply flawed. Post-war historians redrew Italy's past in bleaker terms, but used the same retrospective logic as before to link Fascism to failings deeply rooted in Italy's recent and more distant past.

Seen from the end of the twentieth century this heavily retrospective reasoning appears anachronistic and inadequate. But although these older perspectives continue to find an afterlife in countless textbooks, they have been displaced by a more contemporary awareness that in both the present and the past the different European national communities have no single history, but instead many different histories.

The volumes in the *Short Oxford History of Italy* will show how Italy's history too is being rethought in these terms. Its new histories are being constructed around the political, cultural, religious, and economic institutions from which Italy's history has drawn continuities that have outlasted changing fortunes of foreign conquest and invasion. In each period their focus is the peoples and societies that have inhabited the Italian peninsula, on the ways in which political organization, economic activity, social identities, and organization were shaped in the contexts and meanings of their own age.

These perspectives make possible a more comparative history, one that shows more clearly how Italy's history has been distinctive without being exceptional. They also enable us to write a history of Italians that is fuller and more continuous, recovering the previously 'forgotten' centuries and geographical regions while revising our understanding of those that are more familiar. In each period Italy's many different histories can also be positioned more closely in the constantly changing European and Mediterranean worlds of which Italians have always been part.

John A. Davis

Acknowledgements

With gratitude and pleasure I acknowledge here the help I received in the preparation of this book. John Davis, General Editor of the series, gave wise guidance and showed infinite patience with a project that took much longer than either of us imagined. David Peterson, Edward Muir, Julius Kirshner, and David Abulafia responded generously to my requests for advice and suggestions. I thank the editors at Oxford University Press, in particular Fiona Kinnear and Matthew Cotton, for accepting the many delays with such good grace and smoothing the way through a variety of problems. I am most grateful to Greg Tremblay for help with the maps. Finally, many and warm thanks to Amy Bloch for her time and help in choosing the cover illustration, for expert assistance with art historical matters, and much appreciated general encouragement.

John M. Najemy

Cornell University

Contents

List of contributors

DAVID ABULAFIA is professor of Mediterranean history at Cambridge University and a Fellow of Gonville and Caius College. His books have a southern Italian flavour and include *The Two Italies* (1977), *Frederick II* (1988), and *The Western Mediterranean Kingdoms, 1200–1500* (1997), all of which have also appeared in Italian. The President of Italy appointed him Commendatore dell'Ordine della Stella della Solidarietà Italiana in 2003.

ROBERT BLACK is professor of Renaissance history at the University of Leeds. His books include *Benedetto Accolti and the Florentine Renaissance* (1985), *Romance and Humanism in Sienese Comedy*, with Louise George Clubb (1993), *Studio e scuola in Arezzo durante il medioevo e il Rinascimento* (1996), *Boethius's* Consolation of Philosopy *in Italian Medieval and Renaissance Education*, with Gabriella Pomaro (2000), and *Humanism and Education in Medieval and Renaissance Italy* (2001).

ALISON BROWN, emerita professor of Italian Renaissance history at Royal Holloway, the University of London, is the author of *Bartolomeo Scala, 1430–1497, Chancellor of Florence: The Humanist as Bureaucrat* (1979), and *The Medici in Florence: The Exercise and Language of Power* (1992). She has edited *The Humanistic and Political Writings of Bartolomeo Scala* (1997) and *Language and Images of Renaissance Italy* (1995). In recent essays, including 'Lucretius and the Epicureans in the Social and Political Context of Renaissance Florence', *I Tatti Studies* (2001) and 'Lorenzo de' Medici's New Men', *Renaissance Studies* (2002), she has begun an investigation of changing mores in Renaissance Florence.

FRANCO FRANCESCHI teaches medieval history in the University of Siena's branch in Arezzo. His publications include the book *Oltre il 'Tumulto'. I lavoratori fiorentini dell'Arte della Lana fra Tre e Quattrocento* (1993) and many articles on labourers, guilds, economic policies, and the culture of the working classes between the thirteenth and sixteenth centuries. He is co-editor of the volumes *Il Quattrocento* and *Il Cinquecento* in the series on the history of the

Florentine guilds, *Arti fiorentine: La grande storia dell'artigianato* (1999–2000), and a member of the advisory board of the project *Il Rinascimento italiano e l'Europa* of the Fondazione Cassamarca of Treviso.

DIANE OWEN HUGHES is professor of history at the University of Michigan and the author of many articles on the social history of late medieval and Renaissance Italy, with a particular focus on Genoa. Among the best known are 'From brideprice to dowry in Mediterranean Europe', *Journal of Family History* (1978) and 'Distinguishing signs: ear-rings, Jews and Franciscan rhetoric in the Italian Renaissance city', *Past and Present* (1986). She has also edited, with Thomas R. Trautmann, the volume *Time: Histories and Ethnologies* (Ann Arbor, 1995).

DALE KENT is professor of history, University of California at Riverside, and author of *The Rise of the Medici: Faction in Florence 1426–1434* (1978), *Neighbours and Neighbourhood in Renaissance Florence: The District of the Red Lion in the Fifteenth Century*, with F. W. Kent (1982), and *Cosimo de' Medici and the Florentine Renaissance: The Patron's Oeuvre* (2000). She is currently preparing a study of society, culture and politics entitled *Fathers and Friends: Patronage and Patriarchy in Early Medicean Florence*.

JULIUS KIRSHNER, emeritus professor of history, University of Chicago, is the author of numerous studies of the legal and social history of the Italian Renaissance, including a *A Grammar of Signs: Bartolo of Sassoferrato's 'Tract on Insignia and Coats of Arms'*, with Osvaldo Cavallar and Susanne Degenring (1994). He is the editor of *The Origins of the State in Italy, 1300–1600* (1995) and *Legal Consulting in the Civil Law Tradition*, with Mario Ascheri and Ingrid Baumgärtner (1999).

EDWARD MUIR is professor of history at Northwestern University. He is the author of *Civic Ritual in Renaissance Venice* (1981), *Mad Blood Stirring: Vendetta in Renaissance Italy* (1993), and *Ritual in Early Modern Europe* (1997). He is also co-author with Brian Levack, Michael Maas, and Meredith Veldman of *The West: Encounters and Transformations* (2004).

JOHN M. NAJEMY, professor of history at Cornell University, is the author of *Corporatism and Consensus in Florentine Electoral Politics, 1280–1400* (1982), *Between Friends: Discourses of Power and Desire in the Machiavelli–Vettori Letters of 1513–1515* (1993), and numerous essays on Florentine history and Renaissance political thought. He is currently writing a history of Florence from the thirteenth to the sixteenth century.

DAVID S. PETERSON is associate professor of history at Washington and Lee University. He has published numerous articles on religion, politics, and the Church in Renaissance Florence, including 'Conciliarism, republicanism and corporatism: the 1415–1420 Constitution of the Florentine clergy', *Renaissance Quarterly* (1989) and 'State-building, church reform, and the politics of legitimacy in Florence, 1375–1460', in W. J. Connell and A. Zorzi (eds.), *Florentine Tuscany: Structures and Practices of Power* (2000).

CAROL EVERHART QUILLEN is associate professor of history at Rice University. She is the author of *Rereading the Renaissance: Petrarch, Augustine and the Language of Humanism* (1998) and articles on humanism and feminist theory. She has recently translated *The Secret* by Francesco Petrarch (2003). Her current work analyses the boundary between the human and the non-human in Italian humanist writing from Petrarch to Machiavelli.

ANDREA ZORZI is associate professor of medieval history at the University of Florence. He is the author of: *L'amministrazione della giustizia penale nella Repubblica fiorentina: aspetti e problemi* (1988) and co-editor of the following books: *Florentine Tuscany: Structures and Practices of Power*, with W. J. Connell (2000); *Criminalità e giustizia in Germania e in Italia: pratiche giudiziarie e linguaggi giuridici tra tardo medioevo ed età moderna*, with M. Bellabarba and G. Schwerhoff (2001): and *Le storie e la memoria. In onore di Arnold Esch*, with R. Delle Donne (2002). His articles have appeared in *Annales E.S.C., Crime, History and Society*, and other international journals and collaborative volumes.

Introduction: Italy and the Renaissance

John M. Najemy

Italian history between 1300 and 1550 is ineluctably tied to the Renaissance. Yet each is in a sense larger than the other. Italy's history encompasses more than the cultural Renaissance, and the Renaissance similarly extends beyond Italy in its ramifications and influences. But neither can be understood without the other. The chronological parameters of this volume coincide with a broad definition of the Renaissance in Italy, and one of our purposes is to raise the question of how the one is related to the other. In introducing the politics, society, religion, culture, economy, and intellectual history of Italy in these centuries, we seek to depict the environment in which the Renaissance occurred and some of its chief manifestations. But this is a history of Italy in the period of the Renaissance, not a history of the Renaissance. Knowing however that many readers will come to these pages from an interest in the Renaissance, it seems appropriate in this introduction to sketch a broad interpretation of the larger connections between Italian history and the Renaissance over these two and a half centuries.

The period encompasses a particular phase in the history of Italy's relationship to the rest of Europe: one of relative autonomy between two eras in which Italian politics and culture were heavily conditioned by influences from outside the peninsula, before 1300 from Germany and France, and after 1530 from Spain. North-central Italy was part of the Holy Roman Empire, and from the mid twelfth to the mid thirteenth century, Italian history was dominated by the ambitions, first of Emperor Frederick I ('Barbarossa') Hohenstaufen, who waged a thirty years' war from the 1150s to the 1180s to subdue the cities of northern Italy, and then by his grandson Frederick II, born in Italy and based in Sicily, who repeated the effort on a more grandiose scale between the 1220s and the 1250s. The dynasty's final defeat in the 1260s put an end to a century-long struggle that profoundly affected Italian society by dividing its cities and elites into warring camps of pro-imperial Ghibellines and anti-imperial, pro-papal Guelfs. The opposition was led by the papacy, which forged a coalition of Guelf parties in central and northern Italy with Charles of Anjou, brother of Louis IX of France. With loans advanced by Florentine Guelf bankers, Charles assembled an army, crushed the Hohenstaufen at Benevento in 1266, and created the Angevin kingdom of Sicily and Naples. Charles's power extended to the centre and north through the network of Guelf parties, and for the next generation Italian politics and culture developed in an Angevin–French orbit.

After the 1282 revolt in Sicily (the 'Sicilian Vespers') against French rule, Charles and his successors retreated from wider ambitions to concentrate on the kingdom of Naples, and under Robert (r. 1309–43) Angevin rule gradually ceased to be a foreign implant. By the 1330s France itself was engulfed in war with England and turned its attention away from Italy. Imperial power faded as well. In 1310–13 Emperor Henry VII tried to revive imperial claims in Italy, but he was no match for the combined forces of the Angevins and the Guelf cities, now at the peak of their wealth and power. His failure made it evident that the empire was no longer a serious factor in Italy. Even the popes left Italy. In 1309, a French pope, Clement V, transferred the papacy from turbulent Rome to Avignon in what is today the south of France. For nearly seventy years French popes governed the Church from outside Italy. After about 1310, therefore, Italy was freer to give shape and direction to its social, political, and intellectual life than it had previously been. Autonomy was of course not isolation. Cultural and economic ties with the rest of Europe and the Mediterranean never abated. If anything, they intensified, but now on terms decided as much by the Italians as by their neighbours. The only major intrusion of foreign power into Italy between the Angevins in the 1260s and the crisis that opened in 1494 occurred again in the South. In the 1430s Alfonso of Aragon invaded the Neapolitan kingdom and by 1442 replaced the Angevins. But the new dynasty soon became integrated into the Italian political and cultural world. The relative freedom from foreign influences provides one justification for treating these two centuries as a discrete phase of Italian history.

At the other end of the period, between 1494 and the middle of the sixteenth century, Italy's political independence collapsed under a seemingly endless succession of foreign invasions. France and Spain, asserting conflicting dynastic claims to portions of Italy, contended for supremacy on the peninsula in a long and costly struggle that divided the Italians, ultimately took Naples and Milan into the Spanish empire, and established Spanish hegemony even in places, like Tuscany, that remained nominally independent. In the mid sixteenth century, the Church undertook a radical restructuring of its relationship to lay society that gave it far more power in Italy than ever before. These developments changed Italy in profound and lasting ways that also transformed the cultural Renaissance whose contours had been moulded by the autonomy of the preceding two centuries.

A world of cities

Autonomy meant more than the simple absence of foreign armies and princes. It also ensured the survival of the multiplicity of political entities that is the most characteristic feature of Italy's political life in the Renaissance. Contemporaries and modern historians were and are divided in assessing this reality. Some decried Italy's political fragmentation as the cause of endemic conflicts in what could and should have been a united province under imperial overlordship; others celebrated the preservation of the vital and distinct cultures of the city–states. Just after 1300, Dante condemned the self-declared autonomy of the cities as a debilitating failure to recognize the only legitimate sovereignty, that of the empire. A century later, Florentine humanists lauded the preservation of 'liberty' in Florence's resistance to the expansionist 'tyranny' of Milan. Still another century later, Machiavelli blamed the Church for keeping Italy divided. However varied the judgements about the existence of so many self-governing entities, it was a reality that nothing came close to changing, not even the expansionist tendencies of the fifteenth-century territorial states. Even as smaller cities were absorbed into these regional states, local autonomies, institutions, laws, jurisdictions, religious observances, civic rituals, and a fierce sense of local pride and dignity persisted. Modern observers who assume the nation state as the obvious goal of progressive politics typically see these local autonomies as somehow backward, as the expression of an exaggerated provincialism that prevented Italy's emergence as a 'modern' state. But such assumptions obscure the understanding that most contemporaries had of the political culture of Renaissance Italy, in particular the aspirations and values associated with the 'free' city.

By 1300 the independence of Italy's many cities made them workshops of politics and government, engines of wealth, and innovative centres of culture as no European cities had been since antiquity. The north and centre were home to a remarkable number of cities that counted among Europe's largest. Before the plagues drastically reduced populations beginning with the Black Death of 1348, Italy had four of Europe's five largest cities (Venice, Milan, Genoa, and Florence), all with populations over 100,000, and several dozen cities between 20,000 and 50,000, several as large as any (except Paris) in northern Europe. Their de facto independence from superior powers meant that each city was a political battleground, a locus for the exercise and contestation of power, in which more was at stake in the control of its government and economy, not only for its own inhabitants, but also for its hinterland (*contado*), than would have been the case had they been governed by a larger sovereign authority. Each city embodied a civic identity, tradition, and historical memory whose distinctiveness was jealously safeguarded. Even small cities loomed large, both as sites of power and as 'states of mind',[1] or collective consciousness. Italians identified themselves as the children or artifacts of their cities. In Dante's *Purgatorio* (v.133–4), a Sienese woman identifies herself only with her given name and her city: 'I am Pia; Siena made me.' Italians of this age were more likely to identify with those who lived centuries earlier in their own cities than with contemporaries even fifty miles away. Again in the *Purgatorio* (vi.70–81), Dante dramatizes the profound bonds linking inhabitants of the same city across a divide of many centuries when he and Virgil, who was born in Mantua, meet the thirteenth-century Mantuan poet

[1] 'La città come stato d'animo', in R. S. Lopez and M. Berengo, *Intervista sulla città medievale* (Bari, 1984), p. 3.

Sordello, who asks the two wayfarers whence they come. Virgil manages to utter only the word 'Mantua' before Sordello, knowing nothing else about him, rises, embraces Virgil, and proclaims 'O Mantuan, I am Sordello, from your own city.' The mere fact of being Mantuan suffices to establish a common identity, before names are spoken, across the thirteen centuries that separated Dante from ancient Italy. Dante comments that the 'sweet sound' of the name 'of his city' prompts Sordello to give such warm welcome to his 'fellow-citizen'. The idea that cities generated and preserved identities was not new in the Italy of 1300, but the political autonomy of the next two centuries kept it alive and powerful and made Italians even more self-consciously aware of it.

This was a culture that idealized cities, citizens, and the norms of civility that emerged from assumptions about cities. In this respect it was unlike any European culture since antiquity. The 'civilizing process' was under way in and through Italy's cities long before it was translated to Europe's courts. Praise of cities as the incubators of a superior civility and the unique locus in which citizens could fulfil their intellectual and ethical potential pervaded Italian culture from Dante to Machiavelli. Panegyrics to cities were legion. In *On the Marvels of the City of Milan* of 1288, Bonvesin da la Riva sang the praises of Milan's population, wealth, social services, the prosperity and productivity of the surrounding territories, and the 'dignity' of its people: 'on festive days, one looks at the merry crowds of dignified men, both of the nobility and of the people', and 'the comely gatherings . . . of [married] ladies and [unmarried] virgins going back and forth or standing on the doorsteps [of their homes], as dignified as if they were daughters of kings.'[2] A famous visual analogue to Bonvesin's praise of Milan is the depiction of the effects of good government in Siena by Ambrogio Lorenzetti in the 1330s: idealized representations of the city's splendid architecture, its myriad trades and economic activities, teachers instructing students, and young people dancing. The chronicler Giovanni Villani likewise inserted into his massive civic history of Florence a celebration of the city's great wealth and the ways it served the common good through education, hospital services, and the distribution of wages paid to thousands of workers

---

[2] *De magnalibus Mediolani*, ed. M. Corti (Milan, 1974), p. 104; trans. R. S. Lopez and I. W. Raymond, *Medieval Trade in the Mediterranean World* (New York, 1968), p. 69.

in the textile industry. Even Dante, despite his passionate belief in the divinely instituted empire, has his ancestor Cacciaguida speak lyrically (*Paradiso* xv.130–2) of having been born in 'so peaceful, so fine a community of citizens, such a devoted citizenry, such a sweet dwelling'.

Humanists praised free cities as moral civic spheres in which the virtues could be perfected. In 1377 the Florentine chancellor Coluccio Salutati urged the people of Bologna to reject papal rule and embrace a republic, in which 'merchants and guildsmen' would take turns in office, as the only form of government in which liberty, peace, equality, and justice could be realized. Leonardo Bruni, also a chancellor, made the Florentines the perfect heirs of Rome in his *Panegyric to the City of Florence* of *c.*1406, and in Milan the humanist Pier Candido Decembrio countered Bruni's claims for Florence in his own *Panegyric of the City of the Milanese* of 1435–6. The praises of Naples were sung in 1471 by a courtier, Loise de Rosa, who underscored the excellence of the city's nobility, its hospitals, schools, and churches; and he was followed by others, including the humanist Giovanni Pontano, who lauded Naples for producing so many learned men. In his *Florentine Histories* of the 1520s, Machiavelli made the physical city itself a repository of memory and an agent in the preservation of liberty. In relating how the Florentines invited the foreign nobleman Walter of Brienne to assume the reins of government in the military and fiscal emergency of the 1340s, and how they quickly became alarmed by his attempt to make himself permanent lord of Florence, Machiavelli conveys the protests of the Florentines in a long invented speech spoken to Brienne by an elected official who tries to persuade him that his ambition will necessarily fail because of the love of liberty that cities inspire and protect: 'It is most certain that time does not suffice to suppress the desire for liberty, because in cities one often sees it resurrected by those who have never known it', either because of the memory of it left by their fathers, or because, 'even if their fathers do not recall it, the public buildings, the offices of the magistrates, the banners of free institutions will recall it.'[3] Public buildings and insignia here become the bearers and preservers of collective historical memory.

[3] *Istorie fiorentine* ii.34, in Niccolò Machiavelli, *Tutte le opere*, ed. M. Martelli (Florence, 1971), p. 682. My translation.

Culture and class

These idealizations obviously took little account of the reality of conflict and inequality that characterized every city to one degree or another. But they were not simply naive expressions of local patriotism. Their historical importance lay, especially in the early Renaissance, in their role as a normative and implicitly polemical discourse through which the urban middle classes (the 'popolo') expressed aspirations and grievances against the powerful elites of merchants, bankers, and landed nobles. In the thirteenth century the population and wealth of Italy's cities exploded with immigration from the countryside, rapid commercial growth, banking, manufacturing, scores of skilled and specialized trades in the textile, provisioning, and building industries, and expanding numbers of shopkeepers, retailers, teachers, lawyers, and notaries. New categories of urban dwellers, indeed new classes, grew in numbers and strength unprecedented and unparalleled in other areas of Europe. Each economic, artisan, and professional category formed itself into its own self-governing association, or guild, with written statutes, elected consuls, and legislative councils that mirrored the republican constitutions of the communes. These merchants, shopkeepers, notaries, and artisans, organized in and represented by their guilds (and not to be confused with the labouring classes), were the literate, educated, politically engaged, professional, sometimes (but not always) wealthy, guildsmen who did *not* come from elite families. These were the groups in Italian urban society who most fully embraced the civic ethos and fashioned a culture and a political ideology representing their vision of communal society. Civic ideology first emerged from the challenge of these middle ranks of society to elite power. Indeed, a second consequence of the cities' political autonomy, one closely related to the kind of culture they produced, was the constant tension between the popolo and the elites with whom they contended for power. If the prevalence of self-governing, powerful, and wealthy cities was the distinctive political feature of Italian society in the late Middle Ages and the Renaissance, its inseparable social corollary was the constant tension between the elites of great families and the popolo in its guilds.

The absence (except in the South) of an overarching monarchical authority deprived Italy's elites of the protection that landed nobles enjoyed in feudal monarchies elsewhere in Europe (including Naples), where royal power depended on the cooperation of the nobility and in turn respected and defended noble privileges. Indeed, the popolo's challenge to entrenched elites would not have been possible under a monarchy inclined, as most were, to limit urban autonomies and guild associations. The elites of north-central Italy thus had to face the challenges of the popolo without such support and protection. This was not, however, a straightforward competition between the urban popolo and rural nobles. The great landed families of most regions had established a prominent and even dominant presence in cities from as early as the twelfth century. With the exception of Venice, built on islands in its lagoon and with a ruling class that for many centuries looked outwards to its maritime empire, until the thirteenth century Italy's landed nobilities controlled both the cities and the countrysides. Elite families in Milan, Verona, and Padua, in Mantua and Ferrara, Florence and Siena, Rome and Naples all had strong ties to the countryside and large estates from which they assembled private military forces. For as long as these powerful landed families dominated cities and urban politics, social conflicts were muted. But by the late thirteenth century the popolo's challenge was at its peak.

With each city's elite confronting the popolo on its own, the results varied. In some cities the popolo succeeded in subduing and transforming the elites; in others long struggles ended in compromise; and in some places the popolo was weak. But almost everywhere between about 1250 and 1400 the challenge occurred, as elite families that were powers in both city and countryside had to contend with the competing economic and political interests and military power of the popolo. Nor did social mobility blur the distinction between the classes. Although wealthier members of the popolo emulated the elites by buying land, they always lacked the feudal ties to the countryside and the large clan-like families and agnatic lineages that made elites so powerful. No one from the popolo, no matter how wealthy, could assemble a private army from, or exercise jurisdiction in, rural lands. The popolo was thus fearful and suspicious of elites that were able to do these things and used whatever control of urban institutions it achieved to rein in these overmighty citizens. In city after city, through its guilds and federations of guilds and neighbourhood militias, the popolo established itself as an alternative government. The initial expansion of city power into the countryside occurred largely under the influence of the popolo and was an attempt to limit the power, especially the private armies and factions, of the elite classes.

The popolo did not succeed everywhere, or permanently in any city or region, in displacing, much less dispossessing, the elites. The other side of this story is the tenacious resistance and recovery of elites under the *signorie* and oligarchic republics of the fifteenth century. The popolo did not overthrow Italy's elites. What it did was perhaps less dramatic but more profound: over two or three centuries, but with particular intensity between the mid thirteenth and the end of the fourteenth century, it engaged in a constant competition with the elites, a dialogue of power whose cultural consequences continued into the fifteenth century and changed Italy's elites into something quite different from what they had been at the beginning of the period. Actual popular governments may not have lasted long, but the civic, cultural, and intellectual achievement of the popolo had an overwhelming long-term impact.

In his *Discourses on Livy*, Machiavelli explained (i.55) the political geography of Italy as a function of the varying degrees of survival of powerful landed elites in different regions. In those areas in which landed 'gentlemen' lived from the rents of their estates without engaging in economically productive activities, and exercised military command and jurisdiction over populations 'who obey them' (he mentions the kingdom of Naples, the area around Rome, the Romagna region in the north-east corner of the papal state, and Lombardy), the social inequality inherent in the privileges and power of such 'gentlemen and lords' precluded the establishment or survival of republics. By contrast, in Tuscany, where there were 'no lords of castles and no gentlemen, or very few', social equality permitted free republics to flourish. Machiavelli knew that Tuscany too had once had such 'gentlemen and lords' but that their power had been drastically curtailed by the popolo. Every republic, he explains in the *Discourses* (i.4), has 'two different humors', the 'popolo' and the 'grandi', and in the *Florentine Histories* (iii.1) he evaluated the consequences of the 'grave and natural enmities' between Florence's 'nobles' and its popolo. The latter deprived the nobles of political offices and military power, and the nobles, if they wished to regain political rights, found it necessary 'not only to be, but to appear, similar to the popolo in their behavior, their spirit, and their way of life', which resulted in 'the changes in coats of arms and family names that the nobles adopted in order to seem like the popolo'. Where it happened, the real victory of the popolo consisted in 'civilizing' these formerly unruly elites.

Both republicanism and humanism were in a sense the products of this competition between the classes. Especially in its first century, humanism was far more a product and expression of the popolo than of the elites. This culture was defined and promoted by the laity, even in its religious dimensions, characterized by civic and urban values, hostile to the inherited privileges of elites and to the notion that 'nobility' resided in blood, and sufficiently secular to appropriate republican (indeed pagan) Rome as a political and cultural model. Early humanism and the turn to antiquity provided the popolo with the ideological justification and historical legitimacy it needed to mount its challenge against Italy's elite classes. The principles of good government and virtuous citizenship that humanists, notaries, chron-iclers, and lawyers found in Roman history, law, and literature served, not only as a statement of the popolo's ideals of civility and govern-ance, but indeed as an implicit critique of the misrule of turbulent and fractious elites. The idealization of cities in these terms came largely, almost exclusively, from the popolo, at least until the fifteenth century, as did most of the early humanists and political thinkers who fashioned the culture of the early Renaissance. Literacy was universal among the men of the popolo, and nearly so among its women. The huge numbers of notaries, trained in legal Latin and Roman law and self-taught in ancient literature, brought Roman history and letters into the chanceries of government and into their own households. Humanism began in the enthusiasm of this class for the implications that ancient Rome held for the popolo's vision of communal society and politics. In the thirteenth century, the Florentine notary and chancellor Brunetto Latini (whose hero was Cicero) praised govern-ment through law and the participation of ordinary citizens and penned a long poem about the re-education and domestication of the warrior nobility. In the early fourteenth century, the Paduan notary, poet, and historian Albertino Mussato wrote a play celebrating com-munal liberties. Cola di Rienzo, who inspired the Roman revolution of 1347, was a notary from humble origins; Petrarch's father was a notary who read Virgil and Cicero. Salutati, who transmitted Petrarch's legacy to Florence and into the chancery, was likewise a notary. Giovanni Boccaccio was the son of a middle-class merchant from the Florentine *contado*. The Florentine chroniclers Compagni, the Villani brothers, Stefani, Dati, and the civic humanist Palmieri were merchants from non-elite families. Milan's Bonvesin da la Riva was an elementary Latin teacher and a member of the third order of the mendicant Humiliati. Early humanists in the princely courts, like Giovanni Conversini in Padua, were from the middle ranks of urban society, as were the humanist teachers Gasparino Barzizza, Vittorino da Feltre, and Guarino da Verona. And the list could be much longer. In the fourteenth century, the social elites of Florence, Venice, and Milan showed little interest in the nascent cult of antiquity or the new directions of political thought that were the foundations of Renaissance culture.

Around 1400, however, the phase of direct confrontation between elites and popolo gradually ended. New socio-political relationships emerged, as *signorie* in the north and oligarchies in the republics became more firmly established. For the next century, oligarchic republicanism rested on the (sometimes grudging) acquiescence of the popolo. This happened for two reasons. The first was that both classes were frightened by the radicalism of insurrectionary movements, particularly in Tuscany, in which workers and artisans sought a place in government, sometimes by violent means. The historic weakness of the popolo was that it feared the lower classes as much, or more, as it mistrusted the elites, and the spectacle of angry workers sitting in the councils of government persuaded middle-class guildsmen to make their peace with the elites they had so long opposed. The second reason for the relative docility of the popolo in the fifteenth century was war. Between the 1370s and 1400, the papacy, Milan, Florence, Naples, and Venice all embarked on policies of territorial expansion that soon collided. Thus began a series of major wars among these states that lasted, with some interruptions, until the mid-1450s. Only after seventy-five years of steady and costly conflicts did they finally come to an accommodation that acknowledged their respective spheres of influence and limited conflicts for the next forty years until 1494. This long period of warfare transformed attitudes and state finances, and thus the configuration of power and political culture in each state. Governments now depended as never before on the wealthy to finance wars, and political power and influence inexorably gravitated toward the source of such wealth. In the republics, official ideologies proclaiming the citizen's overriding duty to his government discouraged dissent and masked upper class hegemony in the language of patriotism. In these circumstances, the popolo found it ever more difficult to voice opposition.

In the republics, elites and popolo tacitly agreed to a social compact in which the former ruled and the latter accepted a share of offices, but without real power or systematic representation of its interests. The numbers of office-holders in Florence increased, as did the size of Venice's Great Council. In Genoa, *popolari* were guaranteed a certain proportion of seats in legislative and consultative assemblies. Yet oligarchies recruited from the social elites controlled policy almost everywhere after 1400. In Florence the rule of elite families led to the dominance of one, the Medici, who for sixty years from 1434 to 1494 exercised unprecedented power even as they had neither title nor office. With their wealth, and the extensive local and international patronage network created by that wealth, they seized behind-the-scenes control of elections, finances, and foreign policy. No single family was permitted to lift itself above the others in this manner in Venice, but an ever narrower oligarchy within the Senate monopolized power. The principalities were also more solidly established by 1400, as ruling lords gained titles, legitimacy, and undisputed dynastic succession. Occasional conspiracies and assassinations came not from the popolo, but from disaffected elite families. The most famous were the assassination of Milan's duke Galeazzo Maria Sforza in 1476, the Pazzi revolt against the Medici in 1478, and the uprising of provincial nobles (the 'barons') against the king of Naples in the 1480s. But such attacks, however dramatic, did not disrupt basic configurations of power. By comparison with the fourteenth century, and despite tensions that simmered beneath the surface, this was an age of socio-political consensus. As the popolo accepted elite leadership in the republics, so also in the *signorie* it acquiesced in the social pre-eminence of courtly elites as the latter in turn acquiesced in the domination of a single family. The popolo's political voice lost strength and consistency and its expressions were restricted to moments in which oligarchic or signorial government collapsed, as when the last Visconti duke died without an heir in 1447 and the ensuing struggle for control of Milan opened the door to a republican revival, or when the Medici regime collapsed in 1494 under pressure from internal opponents and foreign invasion and led to a more broadly based government—a sequence repeated in 1527 with the expulsion of another generation of Medici and the institution of yet another republic, the last and most radical of all Florentine popular governments. Apart from such exceptional circumstances, however, elites regained and maintained power almost everywhere in the fifteenth and sixteenth centuries.

But the popolo's objectives were not entirely thwarted. After almost two centuries of challenges, including actual popular governments in the republican, or sometimes republican, cities of Bologna, Genoa, Padua, Florence, Siena, Perugia, Rome, and others, and a century of conditioning by the constraints of princely power in the *signorie*, Italy's elites had undergone a remarkable metamorphosis. Although still tied to the land, they were no longer a warrior class and, except for the Neapolitan barons, rarely commanded private armies or led factional battles in the cities. Less inclined, and less able, to disrupt their cities with factional violence, and with declining opportunities for the exercise of private power or military strength in the expanding territorial states of both republics and *signorie*, once unruly elites became domesticated aristocracies. The phenomenon took two forms. In the republics, but chiefly in Florence and Venice, the elites adopted much of the civic ethos and culture of the popolo. Where once they had scorned the merchant and his account books, great families promoted an economic image of themselves as bankers, long-distance traders, and manufacturers, thus accepting the discipline of commercial law and custom. And having long and contemptuously dismissed civic institutions, laws, and courts, by the fifteenth century republican elites became self-declared defenders of constitutional government (in Florence against what many perceived as the tyranny of the Medici). In the *signorie* the domestication of elites was the work of the courts, those enclosed theatres of privilege, manners, and ritualized sophistication. In the great courts of Milan, Mantua, Ferrara, Urbino, and Naples, and a host of smaller ones that emulated them, semi-feudal elites learned a courtly discipline that was not unlike the civic discipline of their republican counterparts. They became paragons of cultivated sophistication and stylized elegance defined by courtly rituals. And in both republics and *signorie* they finally embraced the educational and cultural programme of humanism. The difference between the Italian elites of 1300 and those of 1550 is a measure of the political and cultural impact of the popolo. Although historians have no doubt claimed too many 'firsts' for Renaissance Italy, it can be argued that this was the first sustained challenge against an elite class in European history that actually succeeded in transforming the elite's culture, norms, and mores.

As class relationships changed, so did the relationship of class to culture. Nobles substituted eloquence and literature for martial pursuits. Great Florentine, Venetian, and Sienese families began to produce humanists and literati as steeped in Latin and classical culture as the intellectual leaders of the popolo had been for two centuries. Applying their wealth to such interests, they also became consumers and patrons of art and literature and builders of sumptuous private palaces, thus creating the demand for art that lay behind the fifteenth-century artistic Renaissance. Learning, literature, and antiquity became signifiers of social status, patronage of art and music the signs of civility. Although many humanists still came from non-elite origins (and the majority of artists from artisan backgrounds), they now increasingly served oligarchies and courtly aristocracies. The Florentine humanist chancellors (Bruni, Poggio Bracciolini, Bartolomeo Scala), the Medicean court poet Angelo Poliziano, the Platonist Marsilio Ficino, Venetian humanists Pier Paolo Vergerio and Giovanni Caldiera, the Neapolitan humanist Giovanni Pontano, and the irreverent poet and playwright Pietro Aretino all came from modest backgrounds but worked for princes and elites. And the social elites now joined this cultural elite. In Florence, the humanist and architect Leon Battista Alberti, the humanist Alamanno Rinuccini, and the historian Francesco Guicciardini; in Venice, the humanists Francesco and Ermolao Barbaro, Bernardo Giustiniani, Gasparo Contarini, chief fashioner of the myth of Venice, and the poet Pietro Bembo; Aeneas Sylvius Piccolomini, the humanist pope from Siena; the philosopher Giovanni Pico della Mirandola; Baldassare Castiglione, the author of *The Courtier*; and the poet Vittoria Colonna—all were from distinguished patrician or noble families. Italy's elites had finally let themselves be drawn to a culture first defined by the popolo in an effort to tame those very elites. As they embraced humanism and Renaissance culture, the elites also changed it by making it serve oligarchic and princely interests. In

Florence and Venice civic humanists adapted the old language of republicanism to the needs of consensus politics by imbuing the model citizen with a dutiful passivity that made loyalty to paternalistic (and oligarchic) government the test of virtue. In Lorenzo de' Medici's Florence humanism became less political, more philosophical, theological, esoteric, and even mystical. In Milan and Naples humanists turned historiography into praise of princes and moral philosophy into a codification of their ideal virtues. And Roman humanism supported the Renaissance papacy's appropriation of ancient imperial grandeur.

Culture and crisis

Two centuries of Italian autonomy came to an end with the foreign invasions. If not with the first French invasion of 1494, then certainly with the second of 1499 and the subsequent intervention of Spain into the expanding wars on the peninsula, Italians gradually realized they were no longer masters of their own house. Regimes and governments fell: the Medici were driven from Florence (as was the republic that succeeded them), the Aragonese from Naples, the Sforza from Milan. Only Venice and the papacy experienced no overthrow of government, although both suffered devastating blows from foreign armies. The fate of each state depended in large part on its relationship to the conquering foreign powers and their rivalries. In the end, Spain won the struggle with France and by the 1530s became the arbiter of politics and culture throughout the peninsula, except in Venice. Here and there, in the interstices of the collisions among foreign powers, the old social struggles were replayed, sometimes with heightened intensity, as in Genoa in 1506–7 when a revolt against French rule spilled over into a brief seizure of power from the nobles by the popolo, or in Florence's last republic. But both were snuffed out by overwhelming external force. Foreign rulers now determined both the constitutional and social configurations of power. Spanish hegemony rested on an alliance with Italy's elites, now politically emasculated, but confirmed in their wealth and prestige as reward for their cooperation. The elites entered a long golden twilight of several centuries in which they enjoyed the protection of kings, emperors, and popes and no longer needed to fear the popolo.

The first thirty years of the crisis were a time of unparalleled intellectual and artistic freedom in Italy, the result of the Church's alliance with humanism, the development of print technology, and toleration by governments, especially in Venice where so much of the publishing industry was concentrated and heterodox religious ideas were protected. A cardinal of the Church, Bernardo Dovizi da Bibbiena, wrote a racy play about cross-dressing and the ambiguities of gender and had it performed not only in Urbino but also in papal Rome. The brilliant and scurrilous Pietro Aretino wrote poems, plays, and dialogues full of explicit sexuality. This freedom also permitted inquiries into the causes of the political and military disaster and directed a critical eye toward elites whose leadership had proved wanting. Except in Venice, where the proud myth of the republic's political stability and social harmony reached its apogee, much of the culture of this generation took aim at the failures of princes and ruling classes. Guicciardini structured his great history of Italy around the melancholy awareness that Italy's rulers, in particular the ecclesiastical hierarchy, had been fatally complicit in allowing foreign armies to enter and ravage the country. Castiglione's interlocutors in *The Courtier* speak out painful admissions of the military inadequacies and the idle, corrupting elegance of the courts. The poet Lodovico Ariosto lampooned the chivalric daydreams of the courts and castigated poets and humanists for their too easy willingness to serve power. And Machiavelli reprised two centuries of the popolo's critique of elites with an indictment of their factionalism, pursuit of private and family interests, and lust for power that weakened the Italian states and rendered them vulnerable.

After the Sack of Rome in 1527, the fall of the Florentine republic and establishment of the Medicean principate in 1530, the consolidation of Spanish imperial hegemony throughout the peninsula, and the Church's decision in the early 1540s to combat heresy with the sterner methods of prohibiting books and intimidating authors and readers, the intellectual climate changed. The monarchical and authoritarian regimes supported by Spanish power cooperated in the enforcement of restrictions and censorship, and the Council of Trent imposed intellectual, social, devotional, and psychological forms of discipline that would have been unacceptable in the preceding two centuries. The achievements of the Renaissance did not disappear with these developments; if anything, the study of ancient letters and history, philological scholarship, and historiography reached new levels of sophistication. But it was now an academic culture no longer nourished by the relationship to politics and the contest for power between social classes that had generated it.

Education and the emergence of a literate society

Robert Black

Literacy and the rise of the vernacular

Literacy was remarkably widespread in north-central Italy during the fourteenth and fifteenth centuries. In 1288 Bonvesin da la Riva declared that, in his native city of Milan, 'there were more than 70 elementary masters teaching reading and writing'.[1] Giovanni Villani, writing at the end of the 1330s, said that '8000 to 10,000 boys and girls' were 'learning to read' in Florence.[2] According to one estimate, this means that 'Florence had a male schooling rate of 67 to 83 percent'.[3] Although the accuracy of Villani's figures has been doubted, they tally with the picture of literacy disclosed by the Florentine tax records (Catasto) of 1427. Each head of household was obliged to submit a declaration copied in his own hand. The vast majority of householders complied, and roughly 20 percent had to have their submissions written by a relative, notary, or friend because they were illiterate, which confirms an overall male literacy rate of about 80 percent for the city. This explosion of literacy in Italy seems to have been largely an urban phenomenon. The Catasto embraced not

[1] Bonvesin da la Riva, *De magnalibus urbis Mediolani*, ed. F. Novati, in *Bullettino dell'Istituto Storico Italiano*, 20 (1898), p. 87.

[2] Giovanni Villani, *Nuova Cronica* 12.94, ed. G. Porta (Parma, 1991), vol. iii, p. 198.

[3] P. Grendler, *Schooling in Renaissance Italy* (Baltimore, 1989), p. 72.

only the city of Florence, but also its ancient countryside (*contado*) and its more recent territorial acquisitions in Tuscany (*distretto*). There is a notable divergence between the rural and urban returns from the Florentine *distretto*. Tax submissions from its cities and towns resemble those of Florence: heads of households wrote their own returns, and each volume contains a multiplicity of hands. In the volumes from the rural areas, however, the returns tended to be written by just a few hands, chiefly a local notary, a contrast suggesting a lower level of literacy in rural localities.

The expansion of literacy reflected, and was in part the cause of, a vast growth in Italian vernacular literature from the later thirteenth century. Vernacular literature was already flourishing in France and Spain during the eleventh and twelfth centuries, but of the Romance languages Italian was the closest to Latin, and so Italy found it difficult to cast off the literary monopoly of Latin. Although vernaculars had been spoken in Italy since at least the eighth century, Italian writers continued to employ Latin exclusively until the thirteenth century. The amazing development of Italian vernacular literature from the late thirteenth century—from the *stilnovisti* poets to Dante —is well known, but corresponding to this burgeoning of literary Italian was the remarkable emergence of vernaculars for everyday purposes, particularly sermons, business letters, family correspondence, political chronicles, and account books, especially in Tuscany, where the genre of the business diary developed into full-scale personal, family, and civic memoirs (*ricordi* or *ricordanze*). Italian vernacular production, both literary and practical, continued to thrive in the fifteenth century, to such an extent that Italian began to replace Latin as the language of official political documents in the later 1400s. In this climate, it is hardly surprising that, of all the Western European countries, Italy emerged as the most prolific font of vernacular printing in the last three decades of the fifteenth century.

Primary and secondary education

The widespread literacy implied by this extensive written and printed culture was supported by a highly developed education system. By the end of the thirteenth century, a new class of specialist elementary teachers (*doctores puerorum*) was emerging, as elementary and secondary education became more differentiated. This specialization held true for private tutors as well as public elementary and grammar schools. Towns usually employed one type of teacher for elementary reading and writing and a real grammarian for Latin at the secondary level. Elementary teachers were men (occasionally women) of little education, drawn from the artisan class, who seem to have known little or no Latin. They usually took pupils from their ABCs up to 'Donatus', the most basic Latin grammar. Curriculum outlines reveal that the basic textbooks of elementary education were the *tavola*, *salterio*, and *donato* or *donadello*. *Tavola* was a sheet of parchment or paper, which began with the alphabet and concluded with syllables to sound out. The next stage consisted of learning words and phrases by reading the psalter or other religious texts. By the sixteenth century common prayers and devotional texts had replaced the psalms.

A curious fact in the history of Italian pre-university education in the thirteenth and fourteenth centuries is that the vernacular was not used at what must seem—given widespread literacy in the vernacular—the most obvious point in the curriculum: the elementary stages of learning to read. The first reading texts were in Latin. It may have been problematic, if not impossible, to teach basic reading technique in a language—like the pre-modern Italian vernaculars—without fixed orthography. Indeed, in the Middle Ages and early Renaissance, Latin was regarded as an artificial, created, unchanging language, an *ars* (skill or discipline) suitable for teaching, whereas the vernaculars were considered changeable and unstable, learnt naturally but formally unteachable; only with the triumph in the sixteenth century of the humanist view of Latin as itself a natural, historically changing language did it become conceivable to teach fundamental language skills in the vernacular. A significant indication of exclusively Latinate elementary education is the progressive structure of the elementary curriculum. Curriculum outlines throughout Italy specify a similar syllabus progressing from table to psalter to 'Donatus'. Until the advent of printing, the *donato* or *donadello*, a manual spuriously attributed to the late Roman grammarian Donatus and christened *Ianua*—or gateway, after the first word of its verse prologue—was exclusively in Latin. The elementary curriculum would make little sense if vernacular devotional texts—for example, the seven penitential psalms—had been inserted as a preparation for reading a demanding elementary Latin work like *Ianua*. The purpose of *Ianua* in its full, early form was to provide a solid grounding for pupils who, it was assumed, would progress further in the study of Latin language and literature and who would spend possibly years memorizing a long text on the parts of speech to give them a thorough grounding in Latin morphology and the terminology necessary for later literary comment and analysis. The early text of *Ianua* was not a quick route to Latinity.

Secondary education in Italy was also traditionally dominated by Latin. At this level the main concern was sentence construction and syntax. The seminal textbooks here were two northern French verse grammars, Alexander of Villedieu's *Doctrinale* and Evrard of Béthune's *Graecismus*, dating from the turn of the thirteenth century and widely circulating in Italy throughout the later medieval and Renaissance periods. Although their verse format implies memorization, in Italy this was not the paramount teaching technique at this level. Italian masters quickly produced a series of alternative secondary grammars, whose significance for the curriculum is that they were prose works not to be memorized by pupils, who generally bought or wrote their own copies. Several were known as *summe*, the standard university term for textbook; not surprisingly, the educational practices used to train professionals at universities eventually prevailed in the preparatory schools run by grammar teachers. In the increasingly secularized and urbanized society of thirteenth- and fourteenth-century Italy, there was an ever-growing demand for rapid educational results: hence, the emergence of the pupil-owned prose textbook.

Continued pressure for mass literacy produced extensive modifications in the elementary and secondary curricula during the fourteenth century. One important development was the abbreviation of *Ianua*: only shortened versions appear among later manuscript copies and early printed editions. It may have taken as long as a century for the condensed version to establish itself and prevail over the traditional versions. The shortening of *Ianua* suggests the work's changing function in the classroom. Its abbreviation coincides with new educational aims and the new class of specialist elementary masters whose aims were not to give a full course in Latin grammar but only to teach elementary reading and writing, as is clear from surviving education contracts of the period. The abbreviated *Ianua* became the standard version of 'Donatus' used in elementary education throughout Italy in the fourteenth and fifteenth centuries.

Teachers went yet further in their endeavours to satisfy the demand for rapid literacy. A two-tiered system of learning *Ianua* emerged, enabling the vast majority of pupils to gain only generalized skills of reading (applicable to either Latin or vernacular texts) and reserving a deeper and fuller knowledge of Latin grammatical forms for the few who would progress beyond elementary reading to the genuine study of Latin. This teaching system is evident in the distinction frequently made between reading 'Donato per lo testo'—phonetic reading—and 'per lo senno'—with meaning or comprehension. Elementary teachers initially had their pupils simply sound out and read the words of *Ianua* directly from a written text, either copied onto a waxed tablet or from a copy owned by the pupil. At this stage, pupils were hardly yet learning Latin; the emphasis was on phonetic technique, on reading skills, rather than on Latin itself. If pupils progressed to the next level, 'per lo senno', the emphasis was on comprehension and memory. *Ianua* must have been memorized at this stage by boys learning Latin, because there was no other manual in the grammar curriculum that included full declensions of nouns and pronouns and complete conjugations of regular and irregular verbs. The secondary curriculum was also adapted in response to demands for increasing and ever more rapid literacy. Before the end of the thirteenth century, theoretical grammar books had been in Latin. The most important way in which masters popularized Latin was to use the vernacular as a learning aid, introducing it into the teaching of grammar and prose composition. Although the vernacular was not employed at the elementary stage where basic Latin morphology was learnt through the study of *Ianua*, at the secondary level it was increasingly brought into the syllabus until extended prose composition was studied on the basis of full-scale translation exercises from the vernacular into Latin.

A second major innovation was the establishment of a syllabus specifically designed to teach techniques needed for business. The commercial revolution that overwhelmed north and central Italy during the twelfth and thirteenth centuries put an ever-increasing premium on the acquisition of business skills. Schools had traditionally emphasized literacy, not numeracy, but educators soon developed a syllabus of commercial arithmetic to be taught in new institutions called abacus schools. The earliest abacus treatises were in Latin, but before long they were written almost exclusively in the vernacular. The hub of this development, and one of the great centres of the commercial revolution, was Tuscany and especially Florence. Sometimes these abacus schools provided a form of tertiary education, which pupils followed after having learned elementary reading and writing from a *doctor puerorum* and Latin grammar from a *magister grammatice*. But by the fourteenth century many pupils went to an abacus teacher immediately after elementary school. From a relatively small number in the thirteenth century, the abacus schools mushroomed rapidly in the fourteenth, until, at least in Florence but possibly elsewhere in Tuscany as well, they became the predominant form of secondary education. The result was that in Florence an educational syllabus was developed that tended to sidestep Latin. Elementary reading and writing may have been taught through the medium of Latin, but pupils gained reading skills without understanding the Latin texts they were using and then proceeded to abacus school where they finished their secondary education in the vernacular.

On an institutional level, the demands of Italian society for mass literacy produced a rapid and powerful growth in publicly sponsored education. Some towns (for example Montagnana, near Padua) gave licensed teachers a monopoly of instruction; others exempted them from military service (Brescia, Ferrara, Parma, Genoa); Palermo even bestowed citizenship on foreign grammar teachers. Free housing was provided as an inducement to teachers in Verona, Vigevano, and Cuneo. Even more importantly, communes began to pay salaries to teachers: Ivrea (from 1308); San Gimignano (1314); Treviso (1316); Turin (1327); Pistoia (1332); Savona (1339); Lucca (1348); Bassano (1349); Feltre (1364); Vigevano (1377); Sarzana (1396); Modena (1397); Udine (1400); Faenza (1410); Novara (1412); Bergamo (1430); and Brescia (1432). By the mid fifteenth century, publicly appointed and salaried teachers were omnipresent from Lombardy to Sicily. A further strategy to enhance access to education came in the form of capping the fees that private teachers exacted: scales of approved charges for the different levels of education became common. Eventually, free education for the children of all communal taxpayers became standard practice in many Italian cities, including Turin, Lucca, Modena, Siena, San Gimignano, Arezzo, Colle Valdelsa, Prato, and Pistoia.

Although communally sponsored education became the norm throughout Italy, there were two important exceptions: Venice and Florence. Here private teachers remained the overwhelming preference among elite families. The antipathy to public education among elite circles in Venice and Florence may be reflected in the kind of snobbery evinced by the Dominican preacher, Giovanni Dominici, who was born and raised in Florence but who had just spent twelve years in Venice when, around 1400, he penned these remarks about communal education: 'Send your son to the commune's school where there is gathered a multitude of ill-disciplined, vicious and troublesome boys inclined to bad behaviour and immune to good conduct, and I fear he will throw away in one year whatever he has learned in seven.'[4]

Latin and vernacular education

Most urban Italians sought literacy for practical motives. They needed to keep business accounts, have some understanding of legal documents written in Latin by notaries, and on occasion even write Latin business letters. Thus, a Genoese boy was to be instructed in Latin 'so that he could know how to read adequately and to write his accounts'; another Genoese teaching contract stipulated that a pupil was to learn Latin 'only insofar as it pertained to merchants'; and a third similarly laid down that 'reading, writing and Latin composition were to be taught as relevant to the work of a merchant' and 'letter writing was to be learned adequately for the purposes of Genoese commerce'.[5] Given such aims, it is not surprising that in some great commercial cities Latin remained the main subject of secondary education. In Venice, Latin grammatical education predominated until at least the second half of the fifteenth century. The Venetians were slow to develop a strong vernacular literature—in contrast to the people of Florence and Tuscany—and were equally conservative in their educational habits, preferring traditional

---

[4] Giovanni Dominici, *Regola del governo di cura familiare*, ed. D. Salvi (Florence, 1860), p. 134.

[5] G. Gorrini, 'L'istruzione elementare in Genova durante il medio evo', *Giornale storico e letterario della Liguria*, n. s., 7 (1931–2), pp. 269–70.

Latinate grammar schools to newer vernacular abacus instruction, which was being imported from Tuscany and Florence in the form of both treatises and teachers. Indeed, the most radical response to the demands of a mass literate society took place in Florence. This is already apparent in the contrast between the accounts of Bonvesin da la Riva and Giovanni Villani. Although both suggest that by far the largest sector of education was elementary reading and writing, Bonvesin claims Milan had eight large grammar or Latin schools, while Villani says there were only four in Florence. Moreover, according to Bonvesin, Latin was the only form of secondary education available in Milan, whereas Villani reports that in Florence the abacus schools boasted twice as many pupils as Florence's grammar schools.

This contrast in secondary education between Florence and the rest of Italy became more pronounced as the fourteenth century progressed. Family diaries mention few pupils learning Latin in the fourteenth century and even fewer in the first half of the fifteenth. The normal pattern of education was simple instruction in reading and writing, followed by abacus training as a preparation for entry into the world of commerce and industry. It is clear that for most Florentine families the aim of education was utilitarian: reading prepared for abacus school, which in turn led to the family business or trade, as was explicitly stated in the case of two orphans from the Michi family, whose educational fare consisted of 'enough reading and writing to go to abacus school'.[6] The weakness of Florentine commitment to Latin education, suggested by the *ricordanze*, is substantiated by the Catasto: the largest sector of pre-university education was the reading school, followed by the abacus; Latin learning was hardly pursued by the population at large.

The waning of indigenous Florentine grammatical study between 1350 and 1450 may seem paradoxical. But since the early fourteenth century Florentines had conducted their business affairs mainly in the vernacular: hence the proliferation of vernacular account books, so numerous in Florence as early as 1300, but much less common outside Tuscany. In Florence and Tuscany, there was a notable decline in Latin business contracts as formalized by notaries, whose records were increasingly dominated by property transactions, marriage

---

[6] Florence, Archivio di Stato (henceforth ASF), Manoscritti 82, fol. 66v (12 November 1416): 'leggere et scrivere a soficenza d'andare all'abacho'.

contracts, and wills. Some Florentines of course entered the professions of notaries, physicians, and lawyers and hence studied Latin. This was the irreducible minimum of Latin education found in every Italian city. But there seems not to have been much additional Latin study beyond this minimum. Indeed, there is evidence that Florence was producing an insufficient number of native-born professionals in the early fifteenth century. 'The question arises of how to explain the presence of so many outsiders among the lawyers in the guild . . . [T]he figures at hand indicate that there was a shortage of lawyers in Florence during the second half of the fourteenth century and up to about the 1430s.'[7] A similar pattern holds true for physicians: 'the decades after 1348 saw the virtual collapse of the native Florentine medical profession . . . [as] their places were filled by immigrant doctors from the countryside and other, smaller towns.'[8] The same was probably true for the clergy, given the establishment of two large church schools in the mid fifteenth century at San Lorenzo and the Cathedral, explicitly founded to augment the number of clerks competent in Latin.

Indeed antipathy to useless Latin learning was an attitude common among the Florentine elite in the early fifteenth century. What was desired for scions of many mercantile families was enough literacy and numeracy to carry on the family business, to maintain and improve the family patrimony. For them, as Alberti has the humanist character Lionardo lament in the dialogues *Della famiglia*, 'it is enough to know how to write your name and how to add up how much you are owed'.[9] It was along these lines that Bernardo Manetti provided for the education of his son Giannozzo: 'At a young age, he sent him, according to the custom of the city, to learn to read and write. When, in a brief time, the boy had mastered the learning necessary to become a merchant, his father took him away from elementary school and sent him to abacus school, where in a few months he learned enough to work as a merchant. At the age of ten he went into a bank.' Only subsequently and on his own did Giannozzo Manetti acquire the knowledge of Latin and Latin literature that

[7] L. Martines, *Lawyers and Statecraft in Renaissance Florence* (Princeton, 1968), p. 73.

[8] K. Park, *Doctors and Medicine in Early Renaissance Florence* (Princeton, 1985), pp. 7, 42–6, 76–82.

[9] Leon Battista Alberti, *I libri della famiglia*, in *Opere volgari*, ed. C. Grayson (Bari, 1960), vol. i, p. 68.

permitted him to become a leading humanist. His father, a man 'who was, in accordance with the city's customs, more given to earning than to learning',[10] refused to support his son's classical studies, which Giannozzo therefore began only at the age of twenty-five. Another Florentine, from an ancient feudal family, Messer Andrea de' Pazzi, offered his son Piero little encouragement to pursue his education: 'Being the son of Messer Andrea and a young man of handsome appearance, devoted to the delights and pleasures of the world, Piero gave little thought to the study of Latin letters: indeed, his father was a merchant and, like those who have little education themselves, he had scant regard for learning nor did he think his son would show much inclination in that direction.'[11] The disinterested study of Latin was rare in early fifteenth-century Florence: 'very few men in that period took up Latin—or were made to take it up', wrote Antonio Manetti in his *Life of Brunelleschi*, 'unless they expected to become a physician, notary or priest'.[12]

The decline of grammar education seems to have been a phenomenon peculiar to Florence. Venice maintained a commitment to Latinity, and the same was true of the university town of Bologna, where the number of grammarians employed by the university grew from four in the mid fifteenth century to fifteen at the end of the century.[13] Rome too had thirteen communally appointed grammar teachers by the turn of the sixteenth century. The reinforcement of Latinity and the humanities as the backbone of the curriculum was also characteristic of Tuscany outside Florence, where instruction in classical authors was the culmination of a thorough grammatical training. Famous Tuscan teachers were mostly non-Florentines like Convenevole da Prato, Francesco da Buti, Mattia Lupi, and Domenico di Bandino. The main area of difference among Tuscan communal schools in the fifteenth century was the provision of abacus teaching. In Arezzo abacus teachers were rare before the mid fifteenth century, and regular appointments began only at the end of the century; in contrast, Lucca employed abacus teachers regularly from the mid

[10] Vespasiano da Bisticci, *Le vite*, ed. A. Greco (2 vols., Florence, 1970–6), vol. ii, p. 519.
[11] Ibid., p. 309.
[12] Antonio Manetti, *The Life of Brunelleschi*, ed. H. Saalman (University Park, Pa., 1970), p. 38.
[13] Grendler, *Schooling*, p. 26.

fourteenth century. A commitment to public abacus teaching was a feature of several Tuscan towns, including Pisa, Pistoia, and especially Prato. But other cities, notably Arezzo, maintained a more exclusively grammatical–humanist emphasis. San Gimignano and Colle Valdelsa appointed few abacus teachers, as did Sansepolcro—despite the fact that both Piero della Francesca and Luca Pacioli, authors of important abacus treatises, were native citizens. Outside Tuscany 'communal [abacus] appointments were sporadic and tended to lack continuity. Verona, for example, hired an abacist in 1284 (the earliest known appointment), but the next abacist certain to have received a salary there appears only in 1424.'[14] This contrast between Florence, with its emphasis on abacus schools, and the *distretto*, with its preference for Latin education, is further substantiated by an examination of 324 manuscript Latin schoolbooks surviving in Florentine libraries. A number of them were produced in association with teachers, including books copied and signed by teachers themselves or by pupils identifying themselves as learning in a school under a teacher. They yield the names of 34 teachers, 17 from Tuscany, but only one from Florence: Maestro Spigliato da Firenze, a teacher in Prato and Florence in the 1380s.

In these circumstances, it is not surprising to find a number of contemporaries who despaired of Latinity's fortunes in mid fifteenth-century Florence. The philosopher Marsilio Ficino lamented the status of grammar teachers and private tutors, declaring that they were regarded as lower than table servants,[15] while the humanist Alamanno Rinuccini complained in 1474 of how difficult it was to organize classes for the study of Latin literature.[16] Even more germane are Vespasiano da Bisticci's imprecations to parents to move beyond the traditional commercially oriented school curriculum and provide a humanist education for their children: 'When your sons are born, you Florentine citizens send them to abacus schools; other forms of learning you do not esteem, because they are unfamiliar to you.'[17] 'Let

---

[14] P. Denley, 'Governments and schools in late medieval Italy', in *City and Countryside in Late Medieval and Renaissance Italy: Essays Presented to Philip Jones*, eds. T. Dean and C. Wickham (London, 1990), p. 101.

[15] A. Della Torre, *Storia dell'Accademia platonica di Firenze* (Florence, 1902), p. 495; P. O. Kristeller, *Supplementum Ficinianum* (Florence, 1937), vol. ii, p. 182.

[16] Alamanno Rinuccini, *Lettere ed orazioni*, ed. V. Giustiniani (Florence, 1953), p. 101.

[17] Vespasiano, *Vite*, vol. ii, p. 507.

fathers with sons have them learn something besides the abacus', he implored.[18] Leonardo Bruni's *Dialogues*, written at the beginning of the fifteenth century, reflect the reality of Florentine culture: Niccolò Niccoli's antipathy to vernacular culture voiced genuine distress at the weakness of Florentine Latinity.

The revival of Latin, and humanist education

This decline of Latin inevitably produced a reaction among professional humanists and within the Florentine social elite which was eager, in the years of oligarchic consolidation after the popular government of 1378–82, to set itself apart from the middle and lower classes. For men such as Palla Strozzi, Niccolò Niccoli, Roberto Rossi, Antonio Corbinelli, and Agnolo Pandolfini, classical learning was an essential ingredient of gentility, a necessary qualification for membership in the social elite—a view they derived from the study of the ancients themselves. The classical texts that provide the most compelling portrait of the ideal Roman gentleman—Cicero's *Orator* and *De oratore* and Quintilian's *Institutio*—were studied with renewed vigour at the turn of the fifteenth century; from such sources the Florentine avant-garde was confirmed in its view that no one without a classical education should command a high social position or rightfully call himself a gentleman or be considered qualified to rule. Such ideas were at the core of the first and most influential of all humanist educational treatises, the Venetian Pier Paolo Vergerio's *De ingenuis moribus*, written around 1402 after the author's stay in Florence and his association with Coluccio Salutati's circle as a pupil of the Byzantine teacher of Greek, Manuel Chrysoloras. Vergerio's work aimed to guide the education of society's leaders, whether citizens, princes, or courtiers; it established classical learning as an essential qualification to merit or retain political power and social leadership. The greatest humanist teacher, Guarino da Verona, was likewise soon advertising the humanist claims to educate society's rulers, as in this letter to a *podestà* of Bologna in 1419:

---

[18] Ibid., p. 543.

I understand that when civil disorder recently aroused the people of Bologna to armed conflict you showed the bravery and eloquence of a soldier as well as you had previously meted out a judge's just sentence . . . You therefore owe no small thanks to the Muses with whom you have been on intimate terms since your boyhood, and by whom you were brought up. They taught you how to carry out your tasks in society. Hence you are living proof that the Muses rule not only musical instruments but also public affairs.[19]

The result of this new educational ideology was the emergence of amateur humanism, particularly in Florence, from the end of the fourteenth to the middle of the fifteenth century. One study lists over forty Florentines in this period who were educated in their native city, pursued humanist studies, and hence knew Latin well.[20] But only one of them adopted humanism as a profession (Lapo da Castiglionchio), and only a handful wrote extended Latin compositions (Giannozzo Manetti, Lapo da Castiglionchio, Matteo Palmieri, Alamanno Rinuccini, and Donato Acciaiuoli). The striking fact is that almost all the leading professional humanists in Florence at this time were non-Florentines: some from Tuscany, including the chancellors Salutati, Bruni, Poggio Bracciolini, Carlo Marsuppini, Benedetto Accolti, and Bartolomeo Scala, and still others like Cristoforo Landino, Ficino, and Poliziano; some from outside Tuscany, like Ambrogio Traversari, Francesco Filelfo, and Guarino; and a few non-Italians, including Chrysoloras and John Argyropulos. Alberti was a Florentine exile, while Manetti is the proverbial exception proving the rule, given his father's opposition to his humanist education. A similar story emerges for clerks, lawyers, and physicians: foreigners, and especially citizens of Florence's subject towns, were filling the gap left by Florentines. The weakness of native Florentine humanism and Latinity is demonstrated by a comparison with the town of Arezzo, which had only a tenth of Florence's population in 1427. The list of famous humanists educated there from the end of the fourteenth to the mid fifteenth century includes Bruni, Poggio, Marsuppini, Giovanni Tortelli, Francesco Griffolini, Girolamo Aliotti, and Benedetto and Francesco Accolti: eloquent testimony to the relative weakness of Latin culture in the city of Florence before the later fifteenth century.

[19] Cited from A. Grafton and L. Jardine, *From Humanism to the Humanities* (Cambridge, Mass., 1986), p. 2.

[20] L. Martines, *The Social World of the Florentine Humanists, 1390–1460* (Princeton, 1963), pp. 105–44, 147–91, 306–50.

Florence may have been the cradle of humanism in the late four-teenth and early fifteenth century, but that humanism was not the creation of Florentines themselves.

Venice is famous for its antipathy to humanism: according to Paolo de Bernardo, a Venetian follower of Petrarch, writing shortly after the latter's death in 1374, 'In my own city—I say it unwillingly—nothing is less appreciated than the study of [Latin] literature.'[21] And yet, in 'contrast to Florence, where the local leaders of the [humanist] movement were scholars like Bruni and Poggio who came from Florentine territories, in Venice the leadership [of the humanist movement] was largely in the hands of patricians from the city, one of whom, Francesco Barbaro, almost rivalled the two Florentines in fame.'[22] Indigenous Venetian humanism was building on the founda-tions laid by teachers such as Giovanni Conversini, Gasparino Barzizza, Guarino, and Vittorino da Feltre, who in turn relied on the traditional commitment to Latin characteristic of Venetian secondary schools.

By the turn of the fifteenth century, north-central Italy was a mass literate society, its needs and demands provoking a veritable revolu-tion in education. The progress of this revolution was uneven, but in its most extreme manifestation in Florence it meant a decline of popular Latinity between about 1350 and 1450. It is against this back-ground that the achievements of the Renaissance humanists in the field of education have to be considered. In one sense, humanist educators like Guarino and Niccolò Perotti were no innovators at all. Fourteenth-century grammar teachers had given definitive shape to the secondary prose textbook—it lasted throughout the Quattrocento and beyond. There is little justification for dividing the fifteenth from the fourteenth century as a new period in the history of secondary Latin grammar teaching. In terms of theory and content, the two most popular and influential grammars—by Guarino and Perotti— are essentially indistinguishable from those of their Trecento pre-decessors. A few fifteenth-century teachers—such as Sozomeno da Pistoia and Gaspare da Verona—tried to introduce humanist elements into their formal grammar teaching, as did Perotti in his

---

[21] Cited from F. Gilbert, 'Humanism in Venice', in S. Bertelli et al. (eds.), *Florence and Venice: Comparisons and Relations* (2 vols., Florence, 1979, 1980), vol. i, p. 13.

[22] R. Witt, *In the Footsteps of the Ancients* (Leiden, 2000), pp. 455–6.

1468 *Rudimenta grammatices,* which became the most popular secondary grammar after *Doctrinale* and *Graecismus* at the turn of the thirteenth century. Like Sozomeno and Gaspare, Perotti evidently disliked the non-classical practice of introducing mnemonic verse into grammar teaching, and he too sometimes cited ancient authors and texts to illustrate grammatical points.

Despite these glimmers of change, however, the Italian Quattrocento must remain, in the history of secondary grammar, a period of tradition and superficial reform, which witnessed Guarino's conservatism and the largely ineffectual innovations of Sozomeno, Gaspare, Perotti, and the Roman humanist Pomponio Leto, who, despite his radicalism, was unable completely to set aside tradition and whose school-level grammar treatises languish in a handful of manuscripts and only one printed edition. Even in a negative sense, the humanists did not succeed in banishing medieval grammatical 'ignorance' and 'barbarity'—to repeat Lorenzo Valla's condemnation —from the schoolroom. Until the advent of printing, medieval grammars continued in wide use; medieval dictionaries happily survived the coming of the press; and attempts to replace or correct *Doctrinale* failed in Italy until the mid sixteenth century. It is a bizarre fact that, among all Western European countries, it was in Italy, the cradle of humanism, that Alexander of Villedieu remained strongest. In the history of grammatical education, what the Quattrocento created was not tangible innovation—no genuinely new and successful methods or textbooks—but rather a revolutionary social ideology for education. The aim may have been to replace medieval linguistic terminology and theory, medieval verse grammars and prose textbooks, but humanist school grammarians did not yet know how or with what.

The educational momentum inherited by the fifteenth-century Renaissance from the later Middle Ages was considerable. The system of teaching elementary reading through phonetics, followed by memorization, had evolved over many centuries; the streamlining of this technique that occurred in the thirteenth and fourteenth centuries made possible an explosion of literacy in the Italian urban population. The extensive penetration of the vernacular into Latin education, not as a system for learning to read, but rather as a tool to simplify the understanding of Latin texts and to ease the learning of Latin composition, facilitated the burgeoning of the Latin-educated professional classes which is such a prominent feature of Italian civic life from the thirteenth to the fifteenth centuries. What is sometimes overlooked about Renaissance humanists—particularly as schoolmasters—is their essential pragmatism and flexibility. They were able to enjoy many benefits from a medieval heritage that allowed widespread literacy among the urban masses as well as basic Latinity for the professional classes.

The triumph of humanist education

The *studia humanitatis*, embracing the study of classical language and literature at an elevated level, were largely an elitist pursuit during this period. But humanists did have an important social influence in one respect: they eventually succeeded in reversing the decline of popular Latinity which had been occurring, especially in Florence, since the mid 1300s. The Renaissance finally reached the Florentine schoolroom in the last quarter of the fifteenth century. In this period, the numbers of pupils studying grammar, according to the *ricordanze*, significantly exceeded those at abacus school. There is also unambiguous evidence of humanist influence on the grammar curriculum. Before about 1475, schoolbooks mentioned in the *ricordanze* were traditional. However, on 8 July 1477 Bartolomeo Sassetti entered in his diary a payment of one florin, three soldi for 'for the cost of one book of Cicero's *Epistolae familiares* which I bought for [my son] Gentile'.[23] Cicero's familiar letters, rediscovered in 1392, had never formed part of the traditional medieval grammar syllabus, but by the later fifteenth century they were being used as stylistic models by some humanist teachers and became widely diffused in the Florentine classroom. On 2 August 1477, less than a month later, Bartolomeo spent one florin for a copy of 'a book which is called the *Elegancies* of Lorenzo Valla'.[24] Valla's *Elegantiae* were rather too advanced for the schoolroom, and humanist teachers normally preferred Agostino Dati's *Elegantiolae*; but Sassetti's intention was clear, and it was an attitude now shared by other elite families. The most concrete sign of

---

[23] ASF, Carte Strozziane V, 1751, fol. 132r: 'per costo di uno libro dell'epistole di Tulio familiari comperai per Gentile, Fl. 1 S. 3'.

[24] Ibid.: 'uno libro che si chiama *Le eleganzie* di Lorenzo Valla'.

this new fashion for humanist textbooks in the Florentine schoolroom at the end of the fifteenth century is the fortune of Perotti's
Rudimenta. First printed in the early 1470s, his new grammar became
a best-seller in Florentine schools. The Florentines now had some
reason to feel that they had fulfilled the new definition of a gentleman
as laid down by Alberti's Lionardo:

And who does not know that the first thing useful for children are (Latin)
letters? This is so important that someone unlettered, however much a
gentleman, will be considered nothing but a country bumpkin. And I should
like to see young noblemen with a book in hand more frequently than with a
hawk . . . If there is anything which goes beautifully with gentility or which
gives the greatest distinction to human life or adds grace, authority and name
to a family, it is surely letters, without which no one can be reputed to possess
true gentility.[25]

Alberti, who wrote *Della famiglia* in the 1430s, was criticizing
Florentine attitudes similarly denounced by the lawyer Otto Niccolini
at a Florentine meeting of 1460 convened to discuss the future of
Florence's university:

This city, indeed from its very origins, has been dedicated to commerce and
manufacturing, to which it has always devoted all its energies and efforts.
Florentines believe that these activities are entirely responsible for sustaining
and enhancing their republic, for ensuring the prosperity and the notable
enrichment of private citizens, convinced that wealth has led to the growth of
its reputation and authority. Putting other occupations to one side, they have
always dedicated themselves especially to business, and the result has been
that the pursuit of learning has been less prized, nor have scholars and
students commanded the same respect in Florence as elsewhere. Indeed, they
are held in contempt by Florentines, who shun their company and show
them little regard; understanding the situation here and aware of how different things are elsewhere, men of learning are unwilling to come to Florence
or, if by some chance they happen to arrive here, they are desperate to get
away.[26]

But by the end of the fifteenth century the Renaissance had changed
the character of Florentine education, and in particular the status of
Latin, at least among the upper classes. Native Florentines now made

---

[25] Grayson (ed.), *Opere volgari*, pp. 68, 70.
[26] Cited from G. Brucker, 'A civic debate on Florentine higher education (1460)',
Renaissance Quarterly, 34 (1981), pp. 531–2.

their presence felt more forcefully in the professions, and not only in law where there was a great increase in Florentine lawyers after 1480, but also in humanism and in the university: with the likes of Marcello Virgilio Adriani and Piero Vettori, it was no longer necessary to import a Poliziano from Montepulciano, a Landino from Pratovecchio, or a Marsuppini from Arezzo to teach rhetoric and poetry in Florence.

By 1500 humanism had become a peninsula-wide phenomenon: there were no longer pockets where Latinity failed to penetrate the upper classes. And corresponding to this spread of Latinity among the Italian social elites, and in part preceding it, was widespread popular literacy in the vernacular, strengthened at the level of secondary education in abacus schools, and manifested in business accounts and letters, in popular religious devotional writings and sermons, and in the vast diffusion of vernacular literature disseminated in manuscript and then in print. But now in Venice and particularly in Florence, the elite's disinclination toward communal schools gave rise to a new social hierarchy of education: with Latinity available overwhelmingly from private schools and expensive private tutors, a humanist education became the hallmark of the social elite. In Florence a private classical education became a status symbol, one further sign—like wealth, ancient lineage, public office, and prestigious marriages—of a family's high social position. This type of education provided upper-class Florentines with a particularly effective means of distinguishing themselves and their children from the middle and artisan classes whose education was limited to basic reading, writing, and commercial arithmetic.

In smaller Italian towns, on the other hand, Latinity was more widely diffused through public education, and all the more so when this began to be provided free of charge from the second half of the fifteenth century. Lesser centres had good practical motives for encouraging Latin education. Arezzo, for example, was a city in severe economic decline under Florentine rule. The city's poverty was frequently noted, and not just by Aretines in the hope of mitigating financial demands from their own local government or from Florence. In these dire circumstances, Aretines particularly valued education and learning, arguing that 'the only glory left to the impoverished city of Arezzo is intellectual excellence, which cannot be achieved except through letters and the diligent work of a good grammar teacher'. They had no real hope of giving their sons a start in the commercial world because 'Aretine citizens are not rich enough to make their sons into merchants'. It was through grammatical training, which led to the professions, that Aretines could acquire 'fame, honours and riches . . . You know how important a grammar teacher is to your commune, because at least, if you cannot leave riches and possessions to your children, you are able to bequeath to them the virtues' which are gained through education.[27] In the absence of commercial opportunities and the political advantages unavailable to citizens of subject cities, professional advancement through education was the main course open to Aretines. Similarly, in sixteenth-century Volterra the city council asserted that 'in our city, which lacks business opportunities available to others, there is no better way to gain benefit and honour than through the acquisition of Latin learning, an extremely useful introduction especially to those who are later to go on to higher education in the public universities'.[28] And the Pistoiese likewise declared in 1473 that their city was 'remotely situated for trans-Italian traffic; little commerce and trade are exercised there because of its citizens' poverty . . . For Pistoia all hope of remedy is excluded, except through learning.'[29] A final example comes from San Miniato in 1452, where it was agreed that the city was in a state of ruin, with public and private buildings in collapse and depopulation threatening; the only hope for renewal was through education: 'this place cannot be revived unless it is done through the exercise of public grammar schools and teachers, providing more able pupils with access to higher education and to degrees'.[30]

---

[27] R. Black, 'Humanism and education in Renaissance Arezzo', *I Tatti Studies*, 2 (1987), pp. 214–15.

[28] M. Battistini, *Il pubblico insegnamento in Volterra dal secolo XIV al secolo XVIII* (Volterra, 1919), p. 62.

[29] A. Zanelli, *Del pubblico insegnamento in Pistoia dal XIV al XVI secolo* (Rome, 1900), p. 61.

[30] M. Battistini, 'Taddeo da Pescia maestro di grammatica del sec. XV', *Bullettino storico pistoiese*, 31 (1929), p. 92.

Humanism and the lure of antiquity

Carol Everhart Quillen

The passion for antiquity

Between the thirteenth and sixteenth centuries, a passion for antiquity profoundly shaped Italian cultural production. It first emerged clearly in the Veneto and Tuscany, in the works of Lovato dei Lovati (1240–1309) and Geri d'Arezzo (b. mid thirteenth century), as a reaction against a rising pre-professional approach to education that stressed functional competence in Latin rather than the study of ancient authors. From there it spread among teachers, notaries, artists, and other educated people to become what later historians called the humanist movement. Jacob Burckhardt (1818–97), the founder of modern Renaissance studies, described humanism primarily as a movement to *reproduce* antiquity. Fourteenth- and fifteenth-century humanists accepted as ideals for their own time cultural standards that they found in the works of ancient Roman (and later Greek) authors. They sought, Burckhardt wrote, to know what the ancients knew, to write as the ancients wrote, to think and even to feel as the ancients thought and felt.

Burckhardt's definition endured in part because his successors sympathized with the movement they studied. Renaissance scholars often took for granted the desirability of recovering the classical past, the capacity of humanistic methods (historical study, textual criticism, and literary imitation) accurately to recover it, and the relevance of that recovered past to subsequent ages. Since the 1960s, however, historians have challenged these premises. Many now see

Italian humanists not as like-minded colleagues but as distant, shadowy figures whose writings betray specific historical conditions and transitory preoccupations. Italian humanists, these historians argue, were aware of the complexities of emulating antiquity and were often more interested in making the past relevant for their contemporaries, in an artful but wrenching transposition, than they were in strictly accurate reconstruction. From this perspective, the importance of Renaissance humanism lies less in its faithful reproduction of the ancient world than in its commitment to making an elusive past speak to their present through techniques of reading and writing.

Humanism emerged in the thirteenth century in the novel political environment of the Italian city–states, or communes, whose notions of collective public authority and pursuit of the 'common good' encouraged the development of a distinctively civic culture. These urban, secular communes confronted issues that neither the chivalric culture of feudalism nor the scholastic culture of northern universities could address. Furthermore, because communes contested traditional notions of sovereignty, their members sought new understandings of the ancient past that could justify this novel political configuration. Texts, artifacts, and inscriptions from republican Rome, an era that Italians saw as their particular heritage, seemed to speak to the needs of these developing communal societies. Yet the ancient literary, philosophical, and artistic works to which Italians were now drawn clearly had emerged in a world that, despite some similarities, differed markedly from their own and required effort to understand. This capacity to see both meaningful affinities and stark differences, combined with the desire to emulate ancient cultural standards, sets Italian Renaissance humanism apart from earlier classical revivals.

Emergence of humanism: Padua and Florence

Humanists made ancient ideas about politics, ethics, the family, and the human person accessible to their contemporaries. Yet because antiquity—a term that embraced Greek and Roman history from

Homer to Augustine, from the eighth-century BCE to the fifth century CE—could be interpreted from many perspectives, humanism took different forms in different contexts. Particularly revealing is the contrast between two of humanism's first practitioners, Albertino Mussato (1261–1329) of Padua and Brunetto Latini (c.1210–94) of Florence, both notaries and both intimately involved in the politics of their cities. Padua and Florence were among the most important seedbeds for humanism, and Mussato and Latini alike were powerfully drawn to ancient literature. Yet the differences are striking. Mussato primarily wrote plays and histories in Latin, whereas Latini compiled an encyclopedia in French and translated Latin political and rhetorical treatises into Tuscan. Mussato preferred and imitated the philosopher and moralist Seneca, Latini the orator Cicero. These different interests reflect in part the contexts in which they worked.

Mussato's Padua witnessed a long struggle between its popular commune and an elite composed of aristocratic landed families. Having survived, in the mid thirteenth century, the rule of the despot Ezzelino da Romano, an ally of Emperor Frederick II, the commune of Padua remained vulnerable to similar threats from other families, one of which, the Carrara, eventually succeeded in supplanting communal institutions and establishing a *signoria*. Mussato, with his fellow citizens, recognized this danger. He turned to the classical past, particularly to Seneca, for themes and examples that could inspire Paduans to defend their liberties. Seneca's plays focused on struggles within and between powerful families, on political tyranny and the gullibility of most men in the face of power, and on the fragility of human institutions. Mussato's play *Ecerinis* self-consciously echoes Seneca's writings as it recounts Ezzelino's despotic rule.

Latini's Florence was moving in a different direction, away from exclusive control by elite families to government by a more diverse, fluid group composed of landholders, merchants, and guildsmen. In this more open environment, where policy issues were publicly debated and persuasive speech could be politically efficacious, classical ideas and rhetorical techniques seemed relevant not just to scholars who could read Latin but to all those who participated in civic life. As chancellor and author of public letters for the first popular government in Florence, Latini immersed himself in classical rhetoric. He translated into Tuscan Cicero's writings on the proper conduct of a republican citizen, and in his encyclopedic

Tresor he explicated Roman ideas about justice, virtue, and the common good.

These differences between Mussato and Latini suggest how variable the appropriation of ancient Rome could be, even within the common framework of a defence of communal liberties and the duties of citizens. As the movement to emulate antiquity spread, humanists in different parts of Italy continued to view the past from different perspectives, partly because their employers demanded it, and partly because the varied contexts in which they worked led them to emphasize different dimensions of the classical heritage.

Francesco Petrarca

While city–states like Florence and Padua provided the initial context for the development of humanism, the movement's first acknowledged leader, Francesco Petrarca (1304–74), lived unattached to any political community, and the relationship of his humanism to politics was always ambivalent. Petrarca was a gifted poet as well as a talented scholar. The son of an exiled Florentine, he grew up near Avignon, then home to the papal curia. He studied law and took minor orders, but from an early age he dedicated himself chiefly to Latin literature. Although this passion for ancient culture was not unprecedented, Petrarca surpassed his predecessors both in the range of practices through which he engaged the past and in his commitment to persuading others to follow his lead. He searched ecclesiastical and private libraries for copies of ancient texts, some unread for centuries. He even reassembled part of Livy's *History of Rome* from portions he found in separate manuscripts. One of his most significant discoveries came in 1345, when he located a copy of Cicero's letters to his friend Atticus, in which the Roman statesman frankly describes his political ambitions and the manipulative strategies he used to fulfil them. Disturbed by the political machinations of a man known as a great moral philosopher, yet deeply moved by the intimacy these private letters expressed, Petrarca in turn wrote two letters to Cicero, questioning his political judgement yet acknowledging his extraordinary eloquence. Petrarca even claimed Cicero as a model for his own correspondence.

As he sought out and corrected ancient texts, Petrarca revived classical genres, particularly the personal letter and the dialogue, which he used to cultivate a community of men who shared his passion for antiquity. Most significantly, Petrarca insisted on the ethical value of classical studies, in part by invoking the tradition that it was the poets and orators who civilized humankind and sustained social bonds. By arguing for a connection between 'eloquence', which he took to mean clarity and persuasive force as learned from ancient authors, and 'virtue', defined as the capacity to lead a fully human life, he gave humanism a compelling rationale that transformed it into a movement. As he searched for manuscripts, edited texts, and emulated ancient literary styles and genres, Petrarca developed a novel approach to the past that was simultaneously personal and historical. On the one hand, he recognized how different his world—his culture, his religion, his Latin—was from that of the ancients. On the other hand, he wrote to the ancients as if they were alive and cited their words and works as immediately relevant to his contemporaries. He longed, in short, for the kind of familiarity that temporal distance normally precludes. His complex relationship to the ancient past further distinguished Petrarca's humanism from that of his predecessors.

In 1341, Petrarca was crowned Poet Laureate in Rome, and his eloquence soon became a sought-after weapon. In 1343, he travelled to Naples for Pope Clement VI, and throughout his life he undertook numerous other missions on behalf of popes, kings, and rulers of cities. The same knowledge of the past that attracted powerful patrons inspired Petrarca's own political dreams: the restoration to Rome of the papal court from Avignon, where it had resided since 1309; and peace and unity in Italy. These two abiding desires find frequent expression in his writings. One of his best-known poems, quoted by Machiavelli at the end of *The Prince*, laments the wounds of war afflicting 'My Italy' and ends with an agonized plea for peace. The dream of a peaceful Italy led Petrarca to support the movement of the notary, student of Roman antiquities, and charismatic popular leader Cola di Rienzo (1313–54), who in 1347 established a revolutionary government in Rome and took for himself the ancient title of Tribune. Cola's enthusiastic study of the Roman past led him to the ancient inscription (the *lex de imperio*) that located the origins of imperial power in the rights of the Roman people, which he invoked to reclaim for Rome its past rights of sovereignty. Petrarca urged him on, exhorting the Roman people to reassume their destiny as guardians of liberty and peace and comparing Cola to the great heroes of antiquity. 'Romulus founded the city', Petrarca wrote to Cola, 'Brutus . . . gave it liberty; Camillus restored both. What difference then, most illustrious man, exists between these and you?'[1] Petrarca never gave up this elusive dream, even as he turned to more limited tasks. One of his last works, a letter to Francesco da Carrara (1325–93), describes both the attributes of any good ruler and the specific qualities required of the Carrara as lords of Padua.

Petrarca's passion for antiquity shaped all his writings. His collected works—letters, dialogues, treatises, polemics, pastoral poems, sonnets, an epic on the great Roman general Scipio Africanus, biographies, collections of ancient exempla and stories, critical editions— fill many volumes, and virtually every text engages the classical Roman past. By the time he died, his powerful authorial style and his fervent insistence on the ethical value of classical culture had convinced many of his contemporaries to follow his example.

Humanism in Florence

Petrarca's novel approach to the past found an early and receptive audience in Florence, where his admirers included Giovanni Boccaccio (1313–75) and Luigi Marsili (1342–94), an Augustinian friar who held informal meetings at his monastery to cultivate a group of men interested in ancient Latin literature. Such gatherings helped to sustain enthusiasm for classical studies and educational reform. As the movement spread, they became a central feature of humanistic culture in Rome, Naples, Milan, and other cities.

From the late Trecento through at least the mid Quattrocento, Florence was the centre of humanistic activity in Italy. Several factors contributed to this. Unlike Padua and Bologna, Florence did not have a strong university or scholastic tradition and thus lacked the group of professionals most likely to counter humanistic ideas. Second, the literate and wealthy Florentine elite began hiring humanist teachers

---

[1] *Petrarch: The Revolution of Cola di Rienzo*, eds. M. Cosenza and R. Musto (New York, 1986), p. 26.

for their children. Third, while political power remained in the hands of a small segment of the population, Florence was a republic and its elite, born not of a hereditary aristocracy but of commerce, banking, and a long tradition of participation in communal government, was a fluid, diverse class for which humanist literary activity, and particularly the celebration of Florence's position as heir to republican Rome, served to forge a common, compelling ideology in defence of their collective authority.

This close relationship between humanism and Florentine politics developed with particular force after 1375, when one of Marsili's friends, Coluccio Salutati (1331–1406) became chancellor of the republic and thus the prestigious author of the government's public correspondence. In this position, Salutati used his influence to garner support for humanistic studies. He was instrumental, for example, in bringing Manuel Chrysoloras to Florence to teach Greek. Furthermore, as chancellor he spoke for the government, and his knowledge of the Latin literary tradition and of ancient Roman history shaped the justifications he formulated for Florentine policy. When, for example, in 1375–8 Florence fought a war over territorial issues against its traditional ally the papacy, Salutati could not rely on inherited Guelf arguments that united the Church with Florence as upholders of communal independence against the emperor. He emphasized instead Florence's origins as a colony of the Roman republic and thus its mission as defender of republican liberty in the face of a tyrannical, territorially aggressive papal monarchy. In making these arguments, Salutati implicitly acknowledged Florence's communal heritage as he also revived a Roman political vocabulary that invoked civic responsibility, republican liberty, and government by consent along with the right to territorial expansion in the name of protecting the liberties of surrounding cities. Over the next few decades, these terms and the political vision they sustained provided a new unifying ideology for the Florentine elite to which even those formally excluded from political power could subscribe. Thus beginning with Salutati, humanistic activity and Florentine civic life were uniquely intertwined, and negotiations with the past defined as well as justified Florentine identity.

In addition to his duties as chancellor, Salutati replaced Marsili as informal leader within a widening circle of humanists that included the future chancellors Leonardo Bruni (1370–1444) and Poggio

Bracciolini (1380–1459) and the manuscript collector Niccolò Niccoli (1364–1437), whose books became the core of the first public library in the city. Together these men and the growing number of humanists in other parts of Italy edited and translated classical texts; they imitated classical styles and genres; and they argued that Latin grammar, ancient history, and reading ancient authors from Plato to the church fathers provided a better moral education than did scholastic dialectic and philosophy. At the same time, they grappled with the implications of taking aspects of the past as a cultural model, and they competed with each other for jobs and fame and patrons.

Bruni's *Dialogues* reveal the complex intellectual milieu in which humanists worked.[2] Most likely written in 1406–8, the *Dialogues* purport to record two conversations that took place in Florence among Salutati, Bruni, Niccoli, and the lesser-known humanists Roberto Rossi and Piero Sermini (who served as chancellor of Florence from 1406 to 1410). A preface precedes the two conversations in which Bruni dedicates the *Dialogues* to his friend Pier Paolo Vergerio (1368–1444), a humanist from Istria and Venice and the author of an influential humanist educational tract, *De ingenuis moribus*. There Bruni says he wrote the *Dialogues* both to acknowledge the possibilities for the revival of the 'liberal arts and of all human culture' in the uniquely equipped city of Florence (possibilities to which the recorded conversations attest) and to allow Vergerio, though absent, to benefit from such learned discourse.

Salutati opens the first conversation by urging his younger friends to practise 'disputation', or face-to-face debate about the literary and ethical questions central to humanistic study. Disputation ensured that important topics were investigated fully and allowed participants to develop oratorical skills as they demonstrated their knowledge of ancient literature, history, and ethics. Niccoli, the main speaker throughout the *Dialogues*, concedes that disputation is important, but, with so much ancient learning lost and replaced by scholastic nonsense, he doubts that disputation firmly grounded in knowledge is even possible. Salutati replies that while many books from antiquity have indeed been lost, learning and disputation can still flourish, and he cites as examples the three most illustrious figures of the Trecento,

---

[2] *The Humanism of Leonardo Bruni*, trans. G. Griffiths, J. Hankins, and D. Thompson (Binghamton, N.Y., 1987), pp. 63–84.

Dante, Petrarca, and Boccaccio. These men, Niccoli retorts, were not learned: Dante did not know Latin well, misinterpreted Virgil, and condemned Caesar's assassin Brutus to hell instead of praising him as a defender of republican liberty; Petrarca's supposed epic masterpiece *Africa* is practically unreadable; and Boccaccio was clearly inferior to these two. Salutati reiterates his position but defers any defence to another time. The next day, when Niccoli agrees to rebut his own words, he argues that Dante, Petrarca, and Boccaccio indeed deserve praise: Dante was a great poet who departed from accurate historical representation to use the figures of Caesar and Brutus as symbols, respectively, of just rule and criminal sedition. Petrarca excelled equally in prose and poetry, and his writings abound with learned 'exhortations to virtue, censures of vice, and many things which he wrote about cherishing friendship, about loving one's country, about the ordering of states, about disdaining fortune, about the correction of character'. Boccaccio's writings display learning, eloquence, humour, and charm. Given the deteriorated state of literary culture and the limited opportunity for achievement when they lived, Niccoli concluded, these men deserve admiration.

Bruni's *Dialogues* depict the kind of private literary circle in which humanism first flourished while also expressing, in their celebration of Florence as the city best able to sustain a literary revival, the imbrication of humanistic activity and civic life that characterized the movement there in the Quattrocento. Equally importantly, this text, which revives the classical dialogue and imitates the structure of the first two books of Cicero's *De oratore*, illustrates practices central to the humanist movement. Furthermore, Bruni's text alludes both to many classical texts and to works by Salutati, Vergerio, and even Bruni himself, thereby contributing to the creation of a literary tradition linking ancient authors to the humanists who emulated them. At the same time, Niccoli's attack on scholastic Aristotelianism, never refuted, undermines what was then a formidable alternative approach to reading classical texts. Finally, Niccoli's ambiguous attitude towards Dante, Petrarca, and Boccaccio reveals a fundamental anxiety about the viability of recovering and emulating an ancient, alien culture. From this perspective, Bruni's *Dialogues* acknowledge a paradox that inheres in the humanist project: the more one studies the distant past, the more one recognizes its otherness and thus its inimitability in the present. This paradox haunts the best humanist writing.

Bruni's *Dialogues* suggest how he and other humanists pressed for a new kind of literary culture that was founded on familiarity with Roman and to a lesser extent Greek literature and fashioned a cultural tradition linking ancient with modern authors to serve the needs of a republican city–state that saw itself as heir to Rome. Bruni's other works show how this new cultural vision shaped the articulation of Florentine political identity. His orations use ancient rhetorical techniques to describe Florence as heir to and guardian of ancient political traditions, with a government 'designed for the liberty and equality of all citizens' and the defence of free cities from territorial aggressors. While modern scholars dispute Bruni's representation of political realities, as did his Milanese contemporaries, this image of Florence as defender of liberty remained central to Quattrocento political discourse and established Bruni's fame as a man of letters. His translations of ancient Greek authors into classical Latin respected the style, rhetorical force, and unique attributes of each language, and his translations of Aristotle, then the central university author, into a specifically classical Latin idiom challenged long dominant interpretations of the philosopher's writings and traditional approaches to studying philosophy.

Bruni was even better known for his histories, which included a biography of Cicero (1415), a history of the first Punic war (1419), and, most importantly, his massive *History of the Florentine People* (1415–44). While this work is rightly celebrated as a milestone in the emergence of critical historiography, Bruni's sensitivity to language, his experience as a translator, and his familiarity with the methods of ancient historians (Thucydides, Plutarch, and Livy, for example) allowed him to recognize both the critical and the rhetorical dimensions of writing history. He was not neutral. He used his Latin literary skills and the sources available to him to argue that the meaning of Florence's history lay in its mission to defend the liberty it had inherited from republican Rome. The work reflects Bruni's critical acumen, his rhetorical talent, and his desire to promote his adopted city, which rewarded his service by exempting him and his heirs from taxation. Bruni's attention to thematic consistency, to sources, and to literary style influenced authors who wrote in other genres, as in Matteo Palmieri's chronicle *De temporibus*, or about non-classical subjects, as in Benedetto Accolti's (1415–64) history of the Crusades. Indeed Bruni's work represents an important moment in the development of modern historiography not only for its careful use of sources but also and more importantly for his awareness of authorial voice and of the interpretive dimension of recovering the past.

Bruni and his fellow humanists proved able advocates. More and more patricians accepted the argument that a grounding in classical languages and literature offered the best preparation for the life of a citizen. Gradually humanism became the dominant culture in the city. Even after 1434, when the Medici assumed unofficial control of Florence's government, their support for writers, artists, book collectors, and architects sustained the symbiotic relationship between humanism and civic life, although during these decades different aspects of the classical past, particularly Platonic philosophy, became increasingly prominent. The ideals of Florentine humanism attracted many talented private citizens who found in them an attractive alternative to traditional Christian condemnations of worldliness. In his vernacular *On Civic Life* (*c*.1434), the merchant Matteo Palmieri (1406–75) outlines the duties of citizens and echoes the ancient authors to praise childrearing and the accumulation of wealth as useful to the city. The architect and polymath Leon Battista Alberti (1404–72), the illegitimate son of an exiled Florentine family and a precocious humanist who had already served as a papal secretary, arrived in the city of his ancestors in the entourage of Pope Eugenius IV in 1434. Inspired by the growing fame of Florence's cultural achievements and by the splendour of what he saw, Alberti wrote a treatise (*On Painting*) that used principles from classical rhetoric to redefine painting as a learned, creative art that, like speech or writing, seeks to evoke specific feelings. His vernacular dialogues *On the Family* aimed to make the wisdom of ancient authors—their ideas about running a household, managing time, friendship, and education—available to a wider audience.

Varieties of humanism: Naples, Venice, Milan, and Rome

During the fifteenth century, humanism became the dominant intellectual force not only in Florence but throughout much of Italy. As it spread, it attracted the support of courtly as well as republican elites and rulers. Its proponents invoked the classical past in different political contexts and their negotiations with antiquity attested simultaneously to their scholarly interests and to the needs and interests of their patrons.

In Naples, humanism depended primarily on royal patronage, first under Robert of Anjou (r. 1309–43), a friend of Petrarca's, and attained its greatest influence under the Aragonese monarchy of Alfonso I (1442–58) and his successors. Robert supported the translations of Greek texts into Latin, employing the Calabrian monk Barlaam (c.1290–1348), Petrarca's Greek teacher, and Leonzio Pilato (d. 1367), later hired by Florence. Alfonso was an extraordinarily generous patron. He supported numerous humanists at his court, amassed a great library for their use, and introduced classical studies at the university level. Particularly influential was his nurturing of humanist writing about the recent past and the creation of the position of royal historiographer. Bartolomeo Facio (1405–57) bested Lorenzo Valla to win this post. His *De rebus gestis Alphonsi I commentarii* (1455) took Caesar's commentaries as a model to construct a narrative of Italian history from 1420 to 1455 organized around the deeds of a single man. Combining classical Latin style, historical narrative, and royal propaganda, this genre clearly could serve any prince's political ends, and other rulers soon sought out humanists who could write similar histories organized around themselves, their families, or their cities.

Under Alfonso, Naples played host to some of the most renowned humanists of the age, including Flavio Biondo (1394–1471), Panormita (1394–1471), and Giovanni Pontano (1422–1503). Their writings express typically humanist ideas: the centrality of Latin and Greek, the exemplarity of the classical past, the need for critical editions of ancient texts, and the relationship between eloquence and virtue. Yet the specific themes they used the past to address—how to be a good prince, the value of dynastic forms of government, the political role of the aristocracy, how to behave at court—reflected the interests of their primary patron. Humanism in Naples often spoke for, to, or about the king.

Until 1448 Alfonso's court included Lorenzo Valla (1407–57), a remarkable scholar whose humanist work comprised textual criticism, history, philosophy, biblical scholarship, and translation.

Previously Valla had taught in Pavia (1429–33) and later became papal secretary and a professor in Rome. Famous now for his colourful debunking of a putatively fourth-century imperial document allocating vast powers to the papacy, he also wrote *Elegancies of the Latin Language* (1444), an influential analysis of Latin style that aimed to re-establish ancient and, according to Valla, purer standards of usage. For Valla the study of language grounded other disciplines, and correct usage was a central civic as well as an intellectual obligation. His work demonstrates the implications—for philosophy, biblical exegesis, and history as well as for oratory—of making philology foundational.

Venetian humanism was influenced by its relations with the Greek East, the Aristotelian tradition sustained by the nearby university of Padua, and by the republic's hereditary ruling nobility. The ties to Constantinople entailed regular intellectual contact long before the fall of the Byzantine capital to the Ottomans in 1453 drove many Greek scholars to Italy. When Manuel Chrysoloras, a Byzantine diplomat and scholar, first arrived in Italy, he stopped in Venice before accepting, in 1397, Salutati's invitation to teach Greek in Florence, where his students included Bruni, Vergerio, and Guarino Guarini of Verona (1374–1460). Guarino later taught Greek and humanist Latin to future Venetian patricians, many of whom translated Greek texts whose descriptions of ideal citizens and political leaders appealed to the city's patricians. In part because of the proximity of the university of Padua and the founding in the early Quattrocento of the school of Rialto, devoted to philosophy, Venetian humanism remained comparatively unenthusiastic about strictly oratorical texts but very receptive to scholastic Aristotelianism. Lauro Quirini (c.1420–75), who studied at Padua, challenged Poggio Bracciolini's individualistic notion of virtue with a defence of inherited nobility based on Aristotle. The patrician humanist Ermolao Barbaro the Younger (1454–93), who had studied Greek with the émigré scholar Theodore Gaza (1400–76), lectured on Aristotle in his Venetian home. After 1490, the printer Aldo Manuzio (c.1450–1515) made Venice a centre for Greek philology and the dissemination of Greek texts.

Humanism first emerged in Venice among the city's notaries and secretaries, but after 1400 the political elite, educated by humanist teachers like Guarino, Vittorino da Feltre (1378–1446), Gasparino Barzizza (1360–1431), and George of Trebizond (c.1395–1484), increasingly charted its direction, using classical learning to defend the republic's policies and aristocratic values. Humanist patricians, for example Bernardo Giustiniani (1408–89), served as ambassadors and wrote letters, orations, and histories to celebrate Venice's benevolent intentions. They similarly used their learning to justify the structure of Venetian society. In his treatise *On Wifely Duties* (*c.*1415) Francesco Barbaro (1390–1454) defined aristocratic heritage, preserved through carefully planned marriages, as a social good and a central component of both virtue and the capacity to govern. Lauro Quirini's *On the Republic* (*c.*1450) appropriated Aristotle's political ideas to argue for aristocratic rule. Ermolao Barbaro the Elder's (1410–71) *Orations against the Poets* warned of the harm done to right order and civic virtue by precisely the ancient poetry that other humanists loved. The founding of the school of San Marco in 1446 institutionalized the connection between humanism and the ruling elite. After 1468, under the leadership of Giorgio Merula (*c.*1430–94), the school increasingly focused on philology, later providing well-trained scholars for Manuzio's printing business.

Milanese humanism depended on the patronage of the Visconti and Sforza dukes. They hired humanists as bureaucrats and created university positions for them both because literary activity increased their prestige and celebrated their leadership, and because humanists could write persuasively in elegant Latin and thus made effective spokesmen. As elsewhere, context shaped literary production. When Giangaleazzo Visconti sought to subject much of Tuscany to his rule, his humanist secretary Antonio Loschi (1368–1441) used his knowledge of ancient history and Ciceronian rhetoric to justify the conquest, arguing that Florence had deprived its subject cities of their liberty and that only territorial consolidation under one ruler could produce lasting peace. Pier Candido Decembrio (1392–1477) wrote a biography of Filippo Maria Visconti to which, during a brief period of republican rule following Filippo Maria's death, he appended a celebration of political freedom.

The capacity of humanist literary training to serve specific political interests emerges with stark clarity in Milan during the rule of Francesco Sforza, the mercenary commander who seized power in 1450 after crushing the 'Ambrosian republic'. Although Sforza had married a daughter of the last Visconti duke, he had no legal claim to the title. Furthermore, Alfonso of Naples and Frederick III, the Holy

Roman Emperor, also claimed Milan, and Venice occupied much of the Milanese territorial dominion. In the face of these external threats and rival claims, Sforza, a soldier, foreigner, and commoner, needed to make a clear, persuasive case for his right to rule. The humanists who worked for him wrote orations and crafted historical narratives that celebrated his career and justified his seizure of power. Francesco Filelfo (1398–1481) wrote a poem in imitation of Homer's *Iliad* commemorating Sforza's career. These writings imitated classical genres and style not simply for the sake of emulation but also to harness their persuasive force. They demonstrate how the needs of Milanese rulers shaped the approach of their humanists to the ancient past.

As the historic home of classical culture, Rome fired the imaginations of humanists from Petrarca on, but it only became a centre of humanist activity when the popes who met the challenge of conciliarism saw in humanism a powerful ally. By supporting an intellectual movement that increasingly defined the terms of political and cultural discourse and set the criteria for artistic achievement, the papacy enhanced its prestige. The papacy employed humanists as writers, secretaries, copyists, and archivists. Eugenius IV (1431–47) brought several important humanists, including Flavio Biondo to Rome. Nicholas V (1447–55) hired Lorenzo Valla and amassed an important library. Pius II (1458–64), born Aeneas Sylvius Piccolomini (1405–64), was himself an accomplished humanist author, poet, and imperial secretary when he began his ecclesiastical career. His *Commentaries*, a third-person account, part memoir, part history, of his pontificate describe key events (including his own election and the threat of the Ottoman Turks) in compelling Latin prose. Under Pius Rome became an important humanist centre.

Rome differed in significant ways from other Italian cities. First, its civic institutions paled in comparison to the ecclesiastical hierarchy, organized around the papal curia and the households of powerful cardinals. Some humanists in Rome took orders, and a few became high-ranking clerics. For such men, ancient Rome and papal Rome fused, such that classical culture and Christianity appeared compatible and even mutually sustaining. The humanist Lapo da Castiglionchio (1405–38) even argued that as a cultural centre the curia rivalled ancient Athens and Rome. For Valla, Christianity, whose language was Latin, ensured the ongoing vitality of the Roman empire's cultural legacy. 'Wherever the Roman language rules', wrote Valla, 'there is the Roman Empire.' Giannozzo Manetti (1396–1459) saw in Nicholas V the epitome of a union of Christian faith and classical studies. This peculiarly Roman perspective suggests how here, as elsewhere, humanists addressed the interests of their employers. In his portrait of the ideal cleric, Paolo Cortesi (1465–1510) presented humanistic study as essential to Christian ethics. Roman humanists used Ciceronian Latin, the purest language, to express the truths of Christianity, the universal religion, and they positioned Rome, the historical and ideological centre of both, as the cultural as well as the spiritual capital of the world.

Humanist communities

Petrarca had argued that studying Cicero, Virgil, and other classical authors—closely reading their works, learning to write in their styles, reconstructing their personalities—would help his contemporaries to lead ethical lives as Christians and citizens. As his followers pursued this agenda, they concentrated on recovering and correcting ancient texts and on making classical Latin grammar, literature, and oratory a focus of education and cultural activity. Niccolò Niccoli used his private wealth and contacts abroad to search ecclesiastical libraries for manuscripts containing previously ignored ancient texts. He and his friend Poggio Bracciolini, another avid collector, located lost works of, among others, Tacitus, Cicero, and Lucretius. Such finds generated enormous excitement. Indeed, humanists described them as resurrections. 'To Tertullian and many others who had been dispatched by fate, you have given life', Francesco Barbaro wrote to Poggio in 1417. 'You have resuscitated so many illustrious and very wise men who were forever dead.'[3] Perhaps Poggio's most important discovery came in 1416, when in a library in Switzerland he found a complete manuscript of the ancient rhetorician Quintilian's *Institutes of Oratory*, which became for many humanists the authority on Latin

---

[3] Francesco Barbaro, *Epistolario*, ed. C. Griggio (2 vols., Florence, 1991, 1999), vol. ii, pp. 20, 72–3. English translation (modified) of the letter from P. W. G. Gordan, *Two Renaissance Book Hunters: The Letters of Poggius Bracciolini and Nicolaus de Niccolis* (New York, 1974), pp. 196–203.

rhetoric and style and provided a conception of the orator as good citizen that supported humanism's ethical claims.

While Poggio, Niccoli, and others searched for manuscripts, humanist teachers, most notably Guarino da Verona, established schools that emphasized the close reading and later imitation of ancient authors. Although basic grammatical instruction changed little, Guarino and others produced new study aids outlining classical usage and style to supplement medieval grammar books. Most importantly, they argued, as had Petrarca, for the moral efficacy of classical studies, successfully persuading a generation of Italian elites that their children, destined for careers as merchants, businessmen, or public servants, needed a classical education to thrive. Such claims may have exaggerated the effects of humanistic education—no course of study can guarantee moral improvement—but they were persuasive. Indeed the ethical ideals of Renaissance humanists shaped school and university curricula in the West into the twentieth century.

No matter where they worked, humanists relied on informal networks through which they could borrow books, exchange ideas, and challenge each other's expertise. Such ties generated disputes and rivalries, but the desire to emulate antiquity was based on shared assumptions about human nature, time, and historical change. All humanist activity, from manuscript hunting to teaching Ciceronian oratory to writing histories, assumed that the chronological gap separating moderns from ancients was bridgeable, that the people of Quattrocento Italy had enough in common with the ancients to make reading their works rewarding. From this premise, humanist writings collectively imagined a distinctive intellectual community that not only transcended local differences but also included the ancients themselves. Its most famous depiction occurs in a letter from Niccolò Machiavelli (1469–1527) to Francesco Vettori that describes Machiavelli's daily 'conversations' with the ancients during which, as he writes, 'I am not ashamed to speak with them and to ask them the reason of their actions; and they, out of their humanity, answer me; and for four hours of time I feel no boredom, I forget every trouble, I do not fear poverty, death does not terrify me; I completely transfer myself into them.'[4]

[4] Translated in J. M. Najemy, *Between Friends: Discourses of Power and Desire in the Machiavelli–Vettori Letters of 1513–1515* (Princeton, 1993), p. 234.

The kind of community poetically described by Machiavelli used reading and writing to bridge temporal and geographical distance. It revolved around authorial voice, not physical presence. As a result, humanist discourse imagines as essential only the intellect—that which can be known through writing that endures—and the transient body as incidental: we can know Cicero intimately through his letters, speeches, and treatises even though we have never met him face to face. Indeed we know him better than those who met him in the flesh but did not know his writings. From this perspective, the text, understood as the exact words written by an author, itself functions as a kind of body that humanist labour can rejuvenate or restore. The humanist and poet Angelo Poliziano (1454–94) compared the mangled text of Cicero's *On the Nature of the Gods* to the mythical Hippolytus, whose body was torn to pieces by horses before being restored by the god Aesculapius. Poliziano the philologist does for Cicero what in the myth Aesculapius did for Hippolytus.[5] In this image Cicero's text is his body, and humanist labour undoes the violence of dismemberment and the ravages of time, just as, through reading and writing in humanist communities, authors from all times transcend the physical and overcome death.

Humanist practice: annotation, translation, citation

Every humanist text reflected the context in which it was produced. However, Quattrocento humanists, most of whom roamed the Italian peninsula from Naples to Milan, cannot be strictly categorized according to these local differences. Nor is Italian Renaissance humanism best understood only in terms of the different forms it took in different times and places. Humanism was also a set of textual practices that generated distinctive relations between past and present. The most studied of these practices is literary imitation. Humanists emulated classical genres, especially the personal letter, dialogue, oration, and various forms of historical narrative. They

---

[5] T. M. Greene, *The Light in Troy: Imitation and Discovery in Renaissance Poetry* (New Haven, 1982), p. 169.

also sought out, edited, and developed ways of teaching classical texts. Other equally important humanist textual practices include annotation, translation, and citation.

Humanists wrote in their books. Their annotations summarized or divided the text, highlighted important points, corrected corrupt passages, and noted imitable locutions. More importantly, humanists used annotations to define out of classical writings topics on which ancients and moderns could be made to speak to each other and to their Renaissance readers. In his copy of Quintilian's *Institutes of Oratory*, Lorenzo Valla filled the margins with extended quotations from other authors, including Cicero, Seneca, Pliny, Juvenal, Lactantius, and Jerome. These annotations create mutual interests and exchanges among temporally distant authors with very different convictions. By identifying such common interests (friendship, grief, old age, mortality) among ancients and between ancients and moderns, Valla and other humanists implicitly defined what about the human condition could, given a common language, transcend time. They made the past usable.

Many humanists, among them Bruni and Valla, made Greek texts accessible in Latin. Translation did not mean substituting the word for a thing in one language for the word for that thing in another. Instead, it meant bringing a text into the particularly rich linguistic system of classical Latin. The arbiter in the process of translation was not things in the world or philosophical truth or indeed anything external to writing but rather classical grammar and usage. When translating Greek philosophical terms, Bruni used the language of Cicero and Seneca, Latin authors who had written about, referred to, or imitated Aristotle. When he translated *The Peloponnesian War*, Valla imitated Sallust, who had written in Latin about Roman history but had used Thucydides as a model. Both sought to retain the mode of expression of the author being translated and to respect Latin as a potentially stable common language while showing less concern for the historicity or integrity of the original text. In this sense, their work invites comparison with Machiavelli's *Discourses on Livy*, in which Machiavelli aims to make useful across time and language the timeless insight of an ancient author and the exemplary deeds about which he wrote.

Humanists who cited long-dead authors thought their words carried weight for Renaissance readers primarily because they assumed that ancients and moderns possessed common human attributes. This assumption allowed humanist authors to describe their own thoughts, feelings, and experiences using words from ancient texts and to offer passages from ancient authors as consolation or advice to the living. They likewise assume a common human condition when they cite passages from ancient authors as general truths, for example about the nature of friendship or virtue. Examples like these that presume common topics of discussion account for most humanist citation.

Citation can also forge relationships between present and past by identifying a common, stable language. That is, humanist writers could structure their own arguments using definitions of terms or concepts found in or developed from ancient writings. In his dialogue *De avaritia*, Poggio Bracciolini takes an etymologically based definition of *avarus* as 'greedy for bronze' and explains how the introduction of other forms of wealth had broadened the meaning of *avaritia* to 'a kind of hunger to accumulate riches'.[6] This definition applies from the time when Romans esteemed only bronze to the Quattrocento, when people sought many forms of wealth. Humanists also forged a common literary language by using figures of speech found in classical authors to describe something other than what they originally described. Such a practice allowed writers to reuse stylistically or rhetorically powerful images without subordinating their own authorial voices to those of the ancients. Thus in one of his letters, Salutati claims that words from Virgil's *Eclogues* about three threads wound around an altar can describe the Christian Trinity.[7] In this way certain images or clusters of words, dissociated from their original signification, became available to other writers for appropriation, such that each individual author could fashion his own particular voice.

Although strategies of identification—between then and now, between themselves and classical authors—most often governed the approaches humanists took to the past, their citations sometimes highlight their distance from the ancients. This happens when the

[6] Poggio Bracciolini, *De avaritia*, in *Opera omnia* (Turin, 1964), vol. i, pp. 6–7; trans. B. G. Kohl and E. B. Welles in B. G. Kohl and R. G. Witt (eds.), *The Earthly Republic: Italian Humanists on Government and Society*, (Philadelphia, 1978), pp. 250–1.

[7] Coluccio Salutati, *Epistolario di Coluccio Salutati*, ed. F. Novati, (4 vols., Rome, 1891–1911), vol. i, p. 303.

original context of a particular passage intrudes on its reuse, so as to mark rather than efface the temporal difference between ancient and Renaissance texts. In such instances, citation dramatizes not continuity but change or even rupture across time. Francesco Petrarca's famous letter to Dionigi da Borgo San Sepolcro about his climb up Mont Ventoux uses citation not to identify with but to explore the differences between himself and the ancient authors he admires.[8] These differences emerge most clearly towards the end of the letter, in Petrarca's quotations from Augustine's *Confessions*. After a long climb, many delays, and much reflection on the similarity between the physical climb up the mountain and the spiritual ascent to the blessed life, Petrarca's narrator arrives at the summit and looks around. As he admires the view, he opens his copy of Augustine's *Confessions* and reads the first passage that meets his eyes: 'And men go to wonder at the heights of mountains and the immense waves of the seas and the broad flow of rivers and the expanse of the ocean and the revolutions of the stars, and they abandon themselves.'[9]

This scene of reading at the top of Mont Ventoux recalls Augustine's conversion, recounted in the *Confessions*. Suffering acutely because he cannot commit single-mindedly to Christianity, Augustine reads the first words that strike his eyes from St Paul's letters. The reading of the passage is both the culmination and resolution of the conflict within him: all his hesitations and doubts immediately evaporate, and hope floods his heart.[10] By identifying with the text, Augustine clarifies his own experience. But Petrarca's reading of Augustine serves a dramatic function completely at odds with that served by Augustine's reading of Paul. He reacts to the passage from Augustine by saying, 'I confess, I was stunned.'[11] The words from Book X of the *Confessions*, in which natural wonders are said to distract the mind from its focus on the self's relationship to God, undermine Petrarca's attempts throughout the letter to relate his physical climb to spiritual ascent. Now, as he stands on the summit, expecting that his

---

[8] Francesco Petrarca, *Le familiari*, ed. V. Rossi, (4 vols., Florence, 1933–42), vol. i, pp. 153–61. Subsequent references are to the section numbers of the letter. There is an English translation by H. Nachod in E. Cassirer, P. O. Kristeller, and J. H. Randall, Jr. (eds.), *The Renaissance Philosophy of Man*, (Chicago, 1948), pp. 36–46.

[9] Petrarca, *Familiari*, iv.1.27; Augustine, *Confessions*, x.8, 15.

[10] Augustine, *Confessions*, viii.12.

[11] Petrarca, *Familiari*, iv.1.28.

experience, like Augustine's before him, will be clarified and validated by a text, the passage he reads undermines the connection between ancient source and Renaissance writer.

Whereas much humanist writing takes for granted the efficacy of some form of identification as a strategy for negotiating between past and present, the Mont Ventoux letter questions the possibility of resuscitating the ancients, of making their words speak to contemporary experience. The letter thus offers a critique of the very strategies of identification that enabled Petrarca to write it. At such moments, when perceptions of concrete experience or of the material world undermine the fantasy of a transhistorical community, Italian humanist writing creates, through simultaneous connection and differentiation, its most distinctive relations with the past. This capacity to acknowledge both sameness and difference in another culture represents a powerful ethical legacy. If we seek evidence for the contemporary relevance of Italian Renaissance humanism, this is where we should look.

3

Religion and the Church

David S. Peterson

Religion and the Renaissance

The Renaissance was long relegated to a spiritual ghetto between the Middle Ages and the Reformation. It provided a denouement of waning devotion to a stained-glass vision of the medieval 'age of faith' and the backdrop of ecclesiastical corruption against which Protestant and Tridentine reforms were enacted. The revival of classical studies invited the charge that the Renaissance was essentially pagan or, at best, moving toward modern secularism. Jacob Burckhardt celebrated the dissolution of a medieval veil of 'faith, illusion, and childish prepossession' that freed its noblest spirits to approach the world objectively and to cultivate their subjective individuality; but he excoriated the 'decaying Church' for driving most Italians to unbelief, superstition, and paganism, by which the Swiss Protestant meant not classical culture but priestly sacraments and the veneration of saints and relics.[1] Catholic historians like Ludwig Pastor sifted artists and humanists of the 'pagan Renaissance' from those who served the 'true Renaissance' of the popes. Many preferred to locate the period's vital forces elsewhere entirely (in civic life, statecraft, classical studies, or science) rather than in a Church awaiting reform or lay religious sentiments apparently in decline.

---

[1] Jacob Burckhardt, *The Civilization of the Renaissance in Italy* (first published 1860), trans. S. G. C. Middlemore (2 vols., New York, 1958) vol. i, p. 143, vol. ii, p. 444.

The Church's failings were real enough. Renaissance popes became obsessed with creating a temporal state in central Italy that drew them ever deeper into secular politics, thereby diminishing their spiritual credibility. Prelates trafficked in bishoprics and abbeys as a source of enrichment rather than spiritual obligation. The ability of an increasingly bureaucratic and legalistic Church to respond to, let alone direct, the religious lives of laymen was compromised. Laudable efforts at reform foundered without institutional support. Storytellers like Giovanni Boccaccio and humanists like Poggio Bracciolini pilloried the foibles of lazy monks and licentious nuns, ignorant priests and greedy friars.

But criticism of the Church signalled rising lay religious expectations, not declining faith. Renaissance Italians invested the preponderance of their massive artistic production in churches, religious objects, and devotional texts. Ecclesiastical building projects financed by laymen mixed piety, civic pride, and social ambition, and dwarfed earlier medieval structures. Architects from Brunelleschi to Bramante embraced classical motifs to dignify these sacred spaces while artists like Donatello and Mantegna filled them with religious objects and images that were not just decorative but meaningful to a laity steeped in religious literature. Images embodying sacred power sanctified (and legitimized) temporal as well as ecclesiastical institutions.

As the ecclesiastical hierarchy faltered, lay people invested their lives with a greater share of the sacred. Italians articulated a series of distinctive cultural practices that reflected recent commercial development, urbanization, advancing literacy, and novel political structures, producing a new, Italianate form of lay Christianity. The mendicant (begging) orders promoted ideals of penance, charity, peace, and the common good. Increasingly inward and mystical devotional forms accompanied the creation of religious brotherhoods and charitable organizations that channelled religious conviction into practical public action. Myriad cults devoted to a new generation of lay saints, female and male, fused private religious ecstasy with social concerns. A burgeoning vernacular literature unveiled Christianity's rich literary patrimony and levelled the cultural field between clergy and laity. Humanists rejected theological speculation and insisted on the relevance of classical models to a Christianity of ethical and social commitment. Developing new critical approaches for analysing sacred texts, they made Christ a model of human dignity. Princes and civic governments increasingly regulated religious life and ecclesiastical institutions in their territories, and drew on religion to help legitimize their power. As they sanctified their lives and communities Renaissance Italians did for Christianity what they did for politics, shifting the emphasis from theory to practice. Sacred and secular no longer corresponded neatly to distinct clerical and lay orders, but required redefinition.

The Church in Italy

Italy was home to the papacy, yet precisely here the papal vision of Christian uniformity ran smack into a world of exceptional political diversity and precocious cultural experimentation. At no point before the imperial Sack of Rome (1527) was the contradiction between the popes' pretensions as monarchic heads of the Church and their interests as rulers of a temporal state in central Italy more glaringly highlighted than under Boniface VIII (1294–1303). Defending clerical freedom from French taxation and royal courts, in 1302 Boniface unabashedly synthesized papal ideology in the bull *Unam Sanctam*, asserting the 'fullness of power' that popes inherited from Christ's commission of the keys of heaven to St Peter, which elevated the spiritual power above the temporal and made it 'altogether necessary to salvation for every human creature to be subject to the Roman Pontiff'.[2] But just the year before, Boniface had dispatched the French prince Charles of Valois to reinforce pro-papal Black Guelfs in Florence and to reconquer Aragonese Sicily. The pope's humiliating seizure by Roman barons and French agents at Anagni in 1303 thus garnered him little sympathy and signalled a decline of papal power north of the Alps that would continue through the popes' residence at Avignon (1309–77), the papal schism (1378–1417), and beyond. But it also reinforced the popes' determination to secure a state in central Italy, making *Unam Sanctam* a compass of papal ideology throughout the Renaissance. Political thinkers from Marsilius of Padua to Machiavelli denounced papal politicking as the 'singular cause' of

---

[2] B. Tierney (ed.), *The Crisis of Church and State, 1050–1300* (Englewood Cliffs, N.J., 1964), pp. 188–9.

Italy's intranquillity and urged that the Church be stripped of its wealth and power. Dante blamed the evils of the world on 'the Church of Rome (which) confounds two powers in itself'.[3] But proximity, and the conviction that morality and politics were necessarily intertwined, continued to draw church and state intimately into each other's affairs.

Italy was saturated with bishoprics: 263 on the peninsula, 10 in Sicily, and 18 in Sardinia (compared to 131 in France and 67 in the British Isles).[4] Their large number made them ubiquitous; their small size exposed them to lay influence and political pressure. Southern dioceses were especially poor and their occupants correspondingly rapacious. Northern bishops had become comfortable urban rentiers who delegated much of the work of ordaining clergy, touring their dioceses, and administering schools and courts to vicars, cathedral canons, and lay notaries. They claimed the right not only to supervise clerical morality (celibacy, sobriety) and ecclesiastical property, but also to judge in matters of lay morality (consanguinity, legitimation) and even in sensitive (and lucrative) economic issues like last testaments and usury. They faced communes and *signori* increasingly concerned to limit clerical prerogatives and to regulate (and appropriate) features of their communities' religious life such as the cults of patron saints like Ambrose of Milan, John the Baptist in Florence, and the Virgin in Siena. Working at the intersection of church and state, local and Roman interests, bishops were among the Church's most politicized officers—and yet its best hope for reform.

Parishes remained important liturgical and social centres, especially in the countryside where they were grouped into baptismal parishes (*pievi*) served by colleges of priests. Churches were preferred sites for social display, youthful flirtation, and business agreements. Crucifixes and tabernacles dedicated to the Virgin protected country roads and bridges, city gates and thoroughfares, and relics were widely diffused. The sacrament of ordination distinguished priests from lay people, but most owed their benefices to parishioners or families with patronage rights. The education of wealthier urban clergy was a prerogative more of class than rank; those in the

---

[3] *Purgatorio* (xvi.127–8), trans. A. Mandelbaum (Berkeley, 1982), p. 151.

[4] D. Hay, *The Church in Italy in the Fifteenth Century* (Cambridge, 1977), pp. 9–20, 110–22, data on p. 10.

countryside learned by apprenticeship and tilled the fields alongside their parishioners. Performing the eucharistic miracle elevated priests above the laity in spiritual rank, but hearing confessions brought them intimately into their daily lives. Rites varied, and Byzantine influence was still pronounced in the Veneto and the South. Saints' days dominated the calendar, church bells rang out the canonical hours, and shorter periods were measured in the time it took to recite an Ave Maria or the Credo.

Ancient Benedictine abbeys defined city centres and punctuated the landscape, while Basilian monasteries still flourished in Sicily, southern Italy, and the Veneto. Many venerable Benedictine houses, including Montecassino itself, already reduced to repositories for the nobility's offspring, suffered further from the ravages of plague and papal exploitation. But Benedictine monastic and eremitic ideals remained popular. Houses of hermit-like Camaldoli monks stretched over the Apennines, and the reformed congregation of Vallombrosa ran from Tuscany up to Lombardy. Over the fourteenth century new congregations of Silvestrians, Celestines, and Olivetans fanned out from Tuscany and north-central Italy, followed by the Venetian congregation of Santa Giustina of Padua in the fifteenth. To eighty original Cistercian houses were added dozens of opulent charterhouses (*Certosa*) whose Carthusian hermits were especially favoured by the aristocracy.

Mendicant orders of friars appeared in the thirteenth century, and their preaching was so popular that cities erected massive new basilicas fronted by large piazze to accompany crowds that attended cycles of sermons during Advent and Lent. Preachers like the Dominican Antoninus of Florence (1389–1459) reminded their listeners that 'greater fruit follows from the word of God preached than from the Body of Christ consumed'.[5] The Franciscan appeal to penance, charity, and peace struck a resonant chord among Italians reeling from rapid commercialization, increasing social mobility, and consequent political strife, inspiring the foundation in Italy of 572 houses (half those of Europe). The Dominicans established friaries and schools in 108 cities centred in the university town of Bologna. Propagating the Thomistic synthesis of Christian revelation and Aristotelian

---

[5] P. Howard, *Beyond the Written Word: Preaching and Theology in the Florence of Archbishop Antoninus, 1427–1459* (Florence, 1995), p. 99.

rationalism, preachers like Giordano da Rivalto (Pisa, 1260–1311) emphasized that governments must serve the common good, not rulers. Two hundred houses of Augustinian friars centred in Lecceto (near Siena) combined the eremitic life with preaching and mendicancy, and as many houses of Humiliati spread out from Milan. Smaller groups of Servites and Carmelites combined Christocentric piety with special devotion to the Virgin.[6]

But success also bred tensions. The Franciscans generated a dissident minority of 'Spirituals' who worried that their order's prosperity and papal privileges constituted a betrayal of Francis's ideal of apostolic poverty. Some proclaimed Francis the heaven-sent leader of an order of spiritual men appointed to usher in a new age of the Holy Spirit. They preached the end of the corrupt Church and denounced Boniface VIII (and his successors) as Antichrist. Pope John XXII's (1316–34) condemnation of these radical views (in *Cum inter nonnullos*, 1323) reduced the Spirituals to heretical *fraticelli* (little brothers) pursued by inquisitors through the hills of Tuscany, Umbria, the Marches of Ancona, and southern Italy. But poverty remained a litmus test of spiritual rigour, and in 1368 an 'Observant' branch of Franciscans was launched to accommodate stricter members. The Augustinian friars followed suit in 1386, the Dominicans in 1390, and the other mendicant orders split into Observant and Conventual wings in the fifteenth century.

Italy without the popes

For much of this period the papacy was absent from Italy entirely. Certainly the removal of the curia to Avignon, 'impious Babylon . . . dwelling of sorrow, mother of errors,' as Petrarch dubbed it (*Canzoniere*, 114), reflected French influence in the aftermath of Anagni. But the popes' return was mainly prevented by Roman aristocrats and Ghibelline *signori*: John XXII and most of his successors spent over half of papal revenues (managed by Italian bankers) on

---

[6] C. M. de La Roncière, 'L'Eglise en Italie,' in J.-M. Mayeur *et al.* (eds.), *Histoire du Christianisme des origines à nos jours. VI: Un temps d'épreuves (1274–1449)* (Paris, 1990), pp. 720–55, 747–50.

foreign mercenaries who kept Italy in almost constant war fighting to regain the papal state. Nor, despite the laments of penitents like Venturino of Bergamo and the indignation of Catherine of Siena, were they much missed. Clement VI's 1350 jubilee, held *in absentia*, drew throngs: the relics of St Peter, wherever his successor, sanctified Rome.

Papal centralization continued apace from Avignon. John XXII claimed sweeping rights to appoint bishops (provision) and abbots (commendation) regardless of local elections. Overruling local potentates might facilitate reform, but it also allowed popes to collect common service and annate taxes on each appointment, encouraging them to turn over benefices rapidly. The poorest dioceses often went to mendicants, those in central Italy to Frenchmen. Elsewhere, popes negotiated appointments with Italy's temporal powers based largely on the degree of collaboration they enjoyed with their Guelf allies in Tuscany and Naples and the level of hostilities with their Ghibelline and Aragonese adversaries in the north and Sicily. Less than a third of episcopal appointees were local, usually scions of families with curial ties who did little to check encroachments on ecclesiastical rights and property by communes and *signori*.[7]

The Black Death moved across Europe from 1347 onwards, devastating clergy and laity alike. Numerous rural parishes were abandoned, and monastic populations dropped precipitously. Discipline collapsed and recruitment became difficult, particularly for nunneries, as every able young woman was pressed into reproductive matrimony. Yet, perversely, the plague improved ecclesiastics' finances by generating a flood of testamentary benefactions. Laymen now targeted their gifts to carefully chosen religious institutions and increasingly endowed private chapels and commemorative masses so that, as the notary Lapo Mazzei told the Pratese merchant Francesco Datini, 'you will not lose your investment with God, nor exhaust your fame among men'.[8]

Plague reinforced penitential and charitable strains of lay devotion that were already emerging. Increasing numbers joined the 'third orders' of laymen affiliated with the mendicants and took vows to live in continence, moderation, and non-violence. Others joined

---

[7] G. De Sandre Gasparini *et al.* (eds.), *Vescovi e diocesi in Italia dal XIV alla metà del XVI secolo* (2 vols., Rome, 1990).

[8] Ser Lapo Mazzei, *Lettere di un notaro a un mercante*, ed. C. Guasti (2 vols., Florence, 1880), vol. i, p. 211.

confraternities, religious fellowships attached to parishes or mendicant churches. Marian companies of *laudesi* sang hymns (*laude*) to the Virgin and by the fifteenth century helped stage elaborate religious plays (*sacre rappresentazioni*) in churches or religious processions. Flagellant groups pursued more rigorous penitential discipline, although ritualized whipping was gradually supplemented by prayer, masses, and preaching. Laymen, humanists, and sometimes women preached alongside friars at confraternal gatherings. Many confraternities were devoted to works of mercy, maintaining hospices for the indigent, distributing alms to the poor, caring for orphans and widows, rescuing women from prostitution, dowering the poor for marriage, and consoling condemned prisoners. Masaccio captured the ethos in his frescos of Peter's charitable acts in Florence's Brancacci Chapel (*c.*1425).

The Church's literary patrimony was opened up in a mass of vernacular translations that offered lay people greater control of their religious lives. Complete editions of the Bible (in Latin or Italian) were costly and rare even among parish clergy. But vernacular editions of the Psalms, Gospels, and Paul's Epistles circulated widely, as did writings by the Church fathers and medieval spiritual writers. Bernard of Clairvaux's *Meditations* on Christ's Passion and Mary's grief enabled laity to appreciate religious art, as Antoninus of Florence advised, 'with the eyes of the mind more than those of the body'.[9] An anonymous Tuscan translation of the *Little Flowers of St Francis* brought laymen into the debate on Franciscan poverty. At Pisa the Dominican Domenico Cavalca (1266–1342) and his assistants produced translations 'for simple and unlearned men' (clerical and lay) of *The Lives of the Fathers, The Summary of Virtues and Vices,* and other spiritual classics. Cavalca's *Mirror of the Cross* became a favourite meditation on Christ's loving sacrifice; his colleague Jacopo Passavanti's (less popular) *Mirror of True Penance* (1354) portrayed Christ as a stern judge of sin and Mary as a merciful intercessor. Bartolomeo da San Concordio's (1262–1347) *Pisanella* ('Little Pisan') circulated widely as a guide to confession (arranged alphabetically for easy reference). The Augustinian friar Simone Fidati of Cascia (d. 1348) emphasized that there could be no justification without faith. Girolamo of Siena's (d. 1420) *Aid for the Simple* argued instead

---

[9] Antoninus of Florence, *Opera a ben vivere,* ed. F. Palermo (Florence, 1858), p. 149.

that there could be no mystical ascent without works in the world, and his concise little chapters on 'The Seven Sacraments' and 'How to Act in Church' provided a handy primer on doctrine, ritual, and prayer. In Florence, the Dominican Giovanni Dominici (*c.*1356–1419) recommended in his *Rule for the Governance of the Family* that parents keep profane literature (e.g. Ovid) away from their children and adorn their homes with religious images.

Texts circulated in digests and anthologies of 'Flowers' that lay men and women of all classes transcribed into their chapbooks (*zibaldoni*). Merchants kept their accounts 'in the name of God and profit' and compiled religious maxims. Paolo of Certaldo cheerfully summarized the doctrine of collaborative grace: 'God says "help yourself, and I will help you in turn." '[10] Those wishing (or unable) to make a good old-fashioned pilgrimage to the Holy Land (or to Rome, Assisi, Loreto, or Compostela) might turn to the accounts of Marino Sanudo the Elder (d. 1343) or Leonardo Frescobaldi (*c.* 1384). Some literate laymen grew impatient with older cults of relics and objects: Franco Sacchetti composed an *Exposition of the Gospels* and insisted that God 'desires our heart and our mind; he is not interested in our wax images nor in such conceits or vanities'.[11]

Saints' lives were immensely popular. Powerful patrons and intercessors who protected their friends (and cities), saints were increasingly role models as well. Jacopo da Voragine's (1228/30–98) *Golden Legend* provided a helpful baseline of medieval lives. The Renaissance contributed a burst of new saints: 127 of 190 cults that emerged in Europe between 1300 and 1500 were Italian.[12] Alongside earlier martyrs and prelates now came laymen, many of humble origins, and women. Their cults spread even though most were not officially recognized by the papacy until centuries later. Renaissance hagiographers dwelt at length on their protagonists' psychological development—from youthful rebellion to mid-life discontents, stale marriages and unfulfilling careers—as they struggled to reconcile intense spiritual anxieties with the realities of daily living. Giovanni Colombini (1304–67) was a wealthy merchant who rose to the summit of Sienese

[10] Paolo da Certaldo, *Libro di buoni costumi*, ed. A. Schiaffini (Florence, 1945), p. 147.

[11] *Il Trecentonovelle* (CIX), in Franco Sacchetti, *Opere*, ed. A. Borlenghi (Milan, 1957), p. 347.

[12] D. Weinstein and R. Bell, *Saints and Society: The Two Worlds of Western Christendom 1000–1700* (Chicago, 1982), p. 167, Table 6.

politics. But reading the 'Life of St Mary of Egypt' precipitated a crisis: he attended mass more frequently, vowed continence in marriage, began to bring home lepers, separated from his wife, and after much wandering founded a new religious order, the Gesuati, devoted to proclaiming the name of Jesus.

As it became laicized, Italian Christianity was feminized as well. Religion offered a vital form of expression to women whose worldly options were narrowly circumscribed. The humbly born and controversial Catherine of Siena (1347–80) avoided marriage and monastic enclosure by becoming a Dominican tertiary after a vision in which Christ accepted her as his bride. Living almost entirely on the Eucharist, she ministered to lepers, mortified herself by drinking the puss of cancer victims, and was rewarded with an ecstatic vision of nursing on Christ's redemptive blood directly from the breast-like wound in his side. Catherine emphasized that suffering was not redemptive per se but as an expression of desire to conform to God's will. This required not escape but charitable engagement with society, 'for every virtue ... and vice is put into action by means of your neighbors'.[13] She exhorted Pope Gregory XI (1370–8) to 'be a courageous man for me' by reforming the Church,[14] and inspired her confessor Raymond of Capua (1330–99) to found the Observant Dominicans and Bernardino of Siena (1380–1444) to propagate the Franciscan Observance.

Within this practical concern to balance the inner approach to God with charitable social action, the humanist Francesco Petrarca (1304–74) established the relevance of the pagan classics to Christian moral life. Responding to scholastic philosophers who derided him as 'a good man without learning', he ridiculed the pretensions of theologians 'whose time is spent in learning to know God instead of loving Him'. Setting moral philosophy above speculative theology, and embracing Augustine's anthropology of the will over the scholastics' Aristotelian faith in reason, Petrarch insisted that 'it is better to will the good than to know the truth'. Scholastic syllogisms might teach virtue, but their technical language could never inspire it. 'He who looks for that will find it in our Latin writers, especially Cicero

[13] Catherine of Siena, *The Dialogue*, trans. S. Noffke (New York, 1980), p. 33.
[14] Catherine of Siena, *Letters*, trans. S. Noffke (2 vols., Tempe, Ariz., 2000), vol. ii, p. 61.

and Seneca.'[15] The 'studies of humanity' (*studia humanitatis*) were a rejection not of religion but of theological speculation in favour of faith-based Christian moral engagement to which the classics could make a hortatory contribution. Petrarch inspired a generation of Florentine humanists to seek out additional classical and patristic texts. Ambrogio Traversari (1386–1439) studied the Greek as well as Latin fathers. Chancellor Coluccio Salutati (1331–1406) resolved the tension Petrarch had felt between the active and the contemplative life by articulating a vision of the *vita activa* as Christian citizenship. Though his defence of the classics drew a sharp rebuke from the volatile Giovanni Dominici (*The Glowworm*, 1405), within half a century the Church itself embraced humanism.

Papal schism and civic control of religion

Gregory XI returned the papacy to Rome in 1377. But his territorial ambitions had alarmed neighbouring Florence, hitherto the papacy's staunchest Guelf ally and financier. In 1375 the Florentines fomented a series of uprisings throughout the papal state in the name of 'Italian liberty'. So long as Florence's 'War of the Eight Saints' was against papal armies, even clergy applauded it: 'Christ sent them [priests] to preach: but I see nothing in the Gospel that says he sent them to rule', declared the Augustinian Luigi Marsili (1342–94). Gregory's interdict prohibited Florentines from viewing the elevation of the host: 'But we see it in our hearts,' declared a defiant chronicler, 'and God well knows we are neither Saracens nor pagans.' But Florence's radical decision to expropriate local clerical property to finance the war transformed the public mood. Flagellants took to the streets, and 'it seemed indeed that they wanted to defeat and humiliate the pope, and that they wanted to be obedient to the Church'. Consciences were tested, and in 1378 Florence erupted in political division and sued for peace.[16]

---

[15] Francesco Petrarca, 'On his own ignorance', trans. H. Nachod, in E. Cassirer *et al.* (eds.), *The Renaissance Philosophy of Man* (Chicago, 1948), pp. 62, 103, 105.

[16] D. S. Peterson, 'The War of the Eight Saints in Florentine memory and oblivion', in W. J. Connell (ed.), *Society and Individual in Renaissance Florence* (Berkeley, 2002), pp. 173–214 (190, 196, 200).

Gregory died immediately afterwards. The College of Cardinals split the Church in 1378 by first electing one pope, Urban VI (1378–89), and then, when he appeared determined to reform the curia, selecting another, the Frenchman Clement VII (1378–94), who returned his papacy to Avignon. Italian support was remarkably soft for the 'Roman' line of popes. Savoy, Naples, Sicily, and numerous cities in the papal state all supported Avignon at one time or another. Milan was officially neutral and Florence 'Roman', though it managed to maintain bankers and cardinals at both curias. The Florentine Gino Capponi expressed the view of many Italian statesmen that 'a divided Church benefits our freedom and our liberty'.[17] The Council of Pisa (1409) sought to end the schism, but produced instead a third line of popes. However John XXIII (1410–15) of the Pisan obedience was persuaded to convoke the Council of Constance (1414–18) by a promise of imperial support to subdue the papal state. The council declared its superiority to the papal office, removed the rival popes, and ended the schism by electing the Roman Oddone Colonna as Pope Martin V (1417–31).

Deciding which obedience to support was an important measure of the leadership Italian rulers had come to exercise in the religious life of their communities. During the schism Milan, Venice, and Florence expanded their territories and tightened their control of local ecclesiastical institutions. The Visconti of Milan created an agency (the *Economato*) to screen candidates for benefices before forwarding acceptable names to the papacy. Venice's Senate took votes on all candidates for prelacies in the territory before submitting their names to Rome. Florence carefully monitored the traffic in benefices, and its Merchant Court (*Mercanzia*) assumed jurisdiction of usury cases. All three states passed legislation to halt the flow of property from lay testators to tax-exempt ecclesiastics and regularized measures against criminous clerks throughout their territories.[18]

Rulers also sought to promote religious life in their communities

---

[17] G. Folena (ed.), ' "Ricordi" politici e familiari di Gino di Neri Capponi', in *Miscellanea di studi offerta a Armando Balduino e Bianca Bianchi* (Padua, 1962), pp. 29–39 (36).

[18] G. Chittolini, 'Stati regionali e istituzioni ecclesiastiche nell'Italia centrosettentrionale del Quattrocento', in G. Chittolini and G. Miccoli (eds.), *Storia d'Italia. Annali IX: La Chiesa e il potere politico dal Medioevo all'età contemporanea* (Turin, 1986), pp. 149–93.

and to embrace safe, legitimizing forms of public devotion. They kept a sharp eye on confraternities, whose meetings might be occasions for sedition but which also provided an important release of social tension. Likewise, they limited the size and forms of marriage and funeral ceremonies. They favoured popular churches and monasteries with subventions and tax relief and were especially active in coordinating the operations of charitable institutions. 'It is no less beneficial for the republic to make useful regulations concerning . . . spiritual matters than it is to legislate concerning temporal affairs,' declared Florence's councils.[19] Festivals of patron saints were a lay counterpart to ecclesiastical Corpus Christi processions, sanctifying cities (and their leaders), providing opportunities to extract ritual acts of homage from subject territories, to honour new saints, and to venerate old ones, thus creating virtual civic pantheons.

Governments increasingly superseded Church authorities in regulating public morality. Gambling, prostitution, and ostentatious women's dress were traditional objects of pious scorn and lucrative sources of fines. Demographic and religious concerns moved many cities to legislate norms of sexual and reproductive behaviour and to create commissions to prosecute male homosexuality, to dower women for marriage, and to protect the chastity of nuns. Cities competed to host renowned preachers like Bernardino of Siena, John of Capistrano (1386–1456), and James of the Marches (1393–1476) who exhorted their audiences against sodomy, vanity, and factionalism, and urged them to make peace (among themselves, with their rulers, and with the Church). By the end of the schism leadership in shaping Italian religious life had clearly passed from the Church to Italy's temporal governments.

A flawed recovery

The prelates who elected Martin V at the Council of Constance aimed not simply to end the schism but to carry out a broader reform of the Church 'in head and members'. The council limited the size of the curia, restricted papal rights of taxation and provision to

---

[19] Florence, Archivio di Stato, *Provvisioni, registri*, 71, fol. 242v (17 February 1383).

benefices, and proclaimed (in *Haec Sancta*, 1415) an alternate vision of Church government that vested sovereignty not in the papacy but in 'the community of the faithful' represented by the council. *Frequens* (1417) required that popes convoke regular supervisory councils. Constance had an immediate impact on clergy like Florence's, who established a local council to oversee their archbishop. To gain political support in their struggle against conciliarism, Martin and his successor Eugenius IV (1431–47) ceded much of the papacy's practical power of taxation and provision to temporal rulers north of the Alps in a series of concordats, and spent the next three decades re-establishing the papal monarchy and its power base in central Italy.

Returning to Rome Martin was taunted by children in Florence for his political weakness and penury. He made due with half the revenue of his Avignon predecessors by efficiently exploiting the papal state. But Eugenius was forced to flee to Florence and faced in the Council of Basel (1431–49) a determined effort, supported by Milan and Savoy, to implement conciliar principles. His Florentine hosts (including Cosimo de' Medici) financed the rival Council of Ferrara–Florence (1438–9) which briefly reunited the Latin and Greek churches and acknowledged the pope as head of the universal Church. Nicholas V (1447–55) renewed Martin's northern concordats and negotiated new ones with Milan, Savoy, Venice, and Genoa (1450–3). The Peace of Lodi (1454) included the papal state as one of Italy's five major powers (with Naples, Florence, Venice, and Milan), and in 1460 Pius II (1458–64) officially condemned the doctrine of conciliar superiority over popes (*Execrabilis*).

While combating conciliarism, popes embraced alternative models of monastic and episcopal reform. Martin and Eugenius supported the Observant movement among the mendicants and approved the reforms of the Venetian Lodovico Barbo (*c*.1382–1443), who organized the Benedictine Congregation of Santa Giustina of Padua to combat the evils of commendation to abbeys. Relations between reformed and older houses were often testy, and the new mendicant Observants and monastic congregations developed as parallel branches of their orders. They practiced stricter standards of poverty, asceticism, and enclosure, and encouraged greater interior devotion among their members through systematic private prayer. Their spread was facilitated by lay political and financial support; consequently, they were often regarded as extensions of regional power structures. The dukes of Milan resisted admitting the Venetian-influenced Congregation of Santa Giustina to their territories. Because Milan so dominated the Lombard Congregation of the Observant Dominicans, Savonarola made the creation of a separate Tuscan congregation central to his plan to reform Florence.

Barbo completed his career as bishop of Treviso, initiating a notable series of reforming bishops, most drawn from the reformed religious orders, that included Ermolao Barbaro (c. 1410–71) at Verona, Niccolò Albergati (c. 1375–1443) at Bologna, and Antoninus (Antonino Pierozzi, 1389–1459) at Florence. Maintaining residence in their dioceses and leading chaste, sober, and exemplary lives, they convoked synods and established schools for clergy, disciplined fractious cathedral chapters, curbed monastic licence, toured their dioceses (often consolidating moribund parishes), and made their courts readily available to the laity. Likewise, they intervened more directly in the religious lives of laymen, supervising charities, reviewing the statutes of confraternities and organizing new ones for youth, curbing the ostentation of civic religious rituals, and reasserting ecclesiastical supervision of sexual (and other) sins. Promoting the Church's leadership of religious life helped restore its legitimacy. Antoninus became so renowned for his confessional manuals and moral tracts that the biographer Vespasiano da Bisticci claimed that, had he been elected pope (he received several votes in 1447), 'he would assuredly have reformed the Church'.[20]

Instead, with the popes re-established in their central Italian state by mid century, Italy's ruling elites in turn reclaimed the papacy. Thereafter, with the exceptions of the two Spanish Borgia popes, Calixtus III (1455–8) and Alexander VI (1492–1503), and Hadrian VI of Utrecht (1522–3), all the Renaissance popes were Italian: the Romans Martin V and Paul III (Alessandro Farnese, 1534–49); the Venetians Gregory XII (Angelo Correr, 1406–15), Eugenius IV (Gabriele Condulmer), and Paul II (Pietro Barbo, 1464–71); Nicholas V (Tommaso Parentucelli, 1447–55) of Sarzana and Innocent VIII (Giovanni Battista Cibo, 1484–1492) of Genoa; the Sienese Pius II and Pius III (1503), both Piccolomini; the Florentines Leo X (Giovanni de' Medici, 1513–21) and Clement VII (Giulio de' Medici, 1523–34) and the Della

---

[20] Vespasiano da Bisticci, *Renaissance Princes, Popes and Prelates*, trans. W. George and E. Waters (New York, 1963), p. 163.

Rovere of Savona, Sixtus IV (1471–84) and Julius II (1503–13). All exploited the papacy to promote their families' political and economic interests. The horror provoked by the cardinalates and bishoprics that Sixtus IV showered on his licentious and bloodthirsty Riario nephews (six bishoprics to Pietro) was exceeded only (perhaps) by Alexander VI's favours to his son Cesare Borgia, Captain General of the papal armies.

The Roman curia became a marketplace for trafficking in benefices, and scarcely a letter was written or a document sealed without a hefty fee (or favour). Though almost every pope appointed a reform commission, their recommendations were just as often shelved—largely because they unfailingly took aim at the curia itself. To finance his ambitious building projects and wars, Sixtus IV doubled the number of venal offices to 625 and coordinated their sale with that of indulgences. Under Leo X the number of offices for sale exceeded 2,000. Cardinals were especially well placed to dispense patronage. Their Roman palaces became courts in their own right. By 1500 their number had expanded from the limit of twenty-four set by Constance to thirty-five. To dilute their power Leo X added thirty-one cardinals at a stroke in 1517, the year Luther posted his ninety-five theses.

Princes realized that with benefices being traded in Rome they might better control their local churches through agents at the curia. Francesco Gonzaga, raised to the cardinalate at age seventeen in 1461, explained to his father Marquis Ludovico in 1466 that by also accepting the bishopric of Mantua and administering it *in absentia* he could assure that other Mantuan benefices 'will never go to foreigners ... (and) I will obtain other graces and immunities ... which a mere bishop could not'.[21] Lorenzo de' Medici got his thirteen-year-old son Giovanni (the future Leo X) made a cardinal by Innocent VIII in 1489, advising the boy: 'You are now to reside at Rome, that sink of all iniquity ... [But it will not] be difficult for you to favor your family and your native place ... You should be the link to bind this city [Florence] closer to the Church, and our family with the city.'[22] By the early sixteenth century the curial, territorial, and princely elites of Italy had become mutually supporting and interdependent.

[21] D. S. Chambers, 'A defense of non-residence in the later fifteenth century: Cardinal Francesco Gonzaga and the Mantuan clergy', *Journal of Ecclesiastical History*, 36 (1985), pp. 605–33 (609).

[22] W. Roscoe, *Life of Lorenzo de' Medici* (London, 1851), p. 287.

Nicholas V, impressed by a decade spent in Medicean Florence, initiated the papal policy of patronizing Renaissance art and letters, convinced that 'a popular faith, sustained only on doctrines, will never be anything but feeble and vacillating. But if the authority of the Holy See were visibly displayed in majestic buildings . . . all the world would accept and revere it.'[23] Building accelerated under Sixtus IV and acquired a sharper ideological focus: Perugino's *Christ Giving the Keys to St Peter* (1481) in the Sistine Chapel pointed directly to the foundation of all papal claims to power, and parallel fresco cycles of the lives of Christ and Moses connected Petrine power to that of the Old Testament lawgiver. As liberator of the Israelites, Moses was even more significant to the warrior pope Julius II, who was delighted that Michelangelo included a figure of Moses in his planned tomb. To the Petrine and Mosaic motifs, Julius added an imperial theme. Styling himself JULIUS CAESAR PONT[IFEX] II, he wore the beard of a Roman emperor for his portrait by Raphael, and was unashamed to don silver armour to celebrate his triumph over Bologna in 1506. That year he laid the foundation stone for Bramante's new Basilica of St Peter, itself redolent with imperial architectural motifs. Having become Italian princes, popes portrayed themselves as successors of the emperors as well as of Peter.

Like his successor Pius II, Nicholas V was a humanist who collected Greek and Latin manuscripts for the Vatican Library that Sixtus IV opened in 1475. The Church allied with humanism, tolerating even Lorenzo Valla (1407–57) who applied new philological techniques to expose the (eighth century) Donation of Constantine as a forgery (1440) and to demonstrate the errors in the official Latin translation of Scripture (the Vulgate) by comparing it to the Greek original. His *Annotations on the New Testament* (c.1455) greatly influenced Erasmus. Giannozzo Manetti (1396–1459) added Hebrew to Greek studies. His *On the Dignity and Excellence of Man* reversed the traditional appreciation of God's condescension to mankind by emphasizing that Christ, as God, embodied the divine potential of humanity. Piero della Francesca conveyed this optimism in his *Resurrection* in Borgo Sansepolcro (c.1458). In Florence, Marsilio Ficino (1433–99) drew on Platonism to locate humankind exactly at the midpoint of a hierarchy

---

[23] L. Partridge and R. Starn, *A Renaissance Likeness: Art and Culture in Raphael's Julius II* (Berkeley, 1980), p. 38.

of being from base matter to godly spirit. Giovanni Pico della Mirandola (1463–94) wove together Christian, classical, cabalistic, Hermetic, and other traditions (including magic and the occult) in a syncretistic vision of knowledge. Because God had created humanity entirely free of the natural order, it was possible, like Jacob climbing the ladder, to ascend through the study of philosophy and theology until, in 'the bosom of the Father who is above the ladder, we shall be made perfect'.[24] Pico drew a warning from Pope Innocent VIII for overstepping the doctrine of Original Sin. But his vision of a harmony of truth (*pax philosophica*) was enthusiastically embraced by Pomponio Leto, Paolo Cortesi, and other Roman humanists.

Awaiting the deluge

By the late fifteenth century Italian Christianity exhibited some remarkable strains. The literature of private devotion expanded while public religious spectacles grew increasingly lavish. The Rosary encouraged veneration of the Virgin, Carnival the release from conventional social inhibitions. Though many religious practices emphasized formula and routine, prophecies of dramatic religious change intensified. While popes listened to refined humanist sermons in the Sistine Chapel and built monuments to impress the masses, printing dramatically accelerated the circulation of middlebrow devotional literature among the laity.

Niccolò Malermi's translation of the Bible appeared in 1471; a cheaper pocket edition came out in 1475. Thomas à Kempis's hugely popular *Imitation of Christ* circulated alongside spiritual treatises by Jean Gerson and Lodovico Barbo. Antoninus followed Domenico Cavalca as one of the most trusted writers of the age: by the mid sixteenth century his confessor's manual counted sixteen editions, and the guide he wrote for laymen forty. Little eight-page primers on confession appeared (with handy lists of sins) that may have made confession more formulaic but assured that in their negotiations clergy and laity were 'on the same page'. Works for and by women,

---

[24] Giovanni Pico della Mirandola, 'Oration on the dignity of man', trans. E. L. Forbes, in Cassirer *et al.* (eds.), *Renaissance Philosophy of Man,* p. 230.

like Caterina Vigri of Bologna's (1413–63) *Seven Spiritual Arms* and Camilla Battista Varano's (1458–1524) *The Mental Suffering of Christ*, were increasingly prominent. Ambitious preachers rushed their sermons into print: Savonarola's *Compendium of Revelations* went through five editions in its first year (1495).

Traditional prophecies of an Angelic Pope who would reform the Church, or of an Emperor of Peace or a Second Charlemagne, who would pacify Europe and liberate the Holy Land, acquired new life. Bearded hermits appeared in piazze wearing sackcloth or hides and calling for reform of the church and renewal of society and announcing the imminent apocalyptic end of a decrepit age. Princes patronized 'living saints' like Columba of Rieti and Osanna Andreasi of Mantua who combined asceticism with prophetic powers. After the French invasion of 1494 images of the Flood and the Last Judgement proliferated, as did public fascination with monstrous births. Luca Signorelli frescoed his *Preaching of the Antichrist* in Orvieto Cathedral (1499–1504). Leonardo da Vinci filled notebooks with sketches of the deluge, and Machiavelli compared Fortune to a river bursting her dykes. Michelangelo frescoed the Sistine Ceiling from the Creation to the Flood in 1508–12 and added the Last Judgement in 1536–41.

Christians grew more suspicious of outsiders. Under Sixtus IV concern about sorcery and witchcraft increased. Franciscan preachers like James of the Marches and Bernardino da Feltre (1439–94) organized *monti di pietà*, public pawnbroking and lending banks offering Christians low-interest loans meant to break the power of Jewish moneylenders. Eighty-eight were established in Italy from 1458 to 1515. Humanists denounced the errors of their Hebrew teachers. In 1475 Jews in Trent were accused of ritualistically murdering a young Christian boy who was then venerated as a martyr. Similar incidents occurred in Treviso (1480) and Vicenza (1486).

During Advent 1492, the Observant Dominican preacher Girolamo Savonarola (1452–98), brought to Florence from Ferrara by Lorenzo de' Medici and quickly befriended by Ficino and other Florentine literati, had a vision 'of a black cross above the Babylon that is Rome, upon which was written *Ira Domini* (Wrath of God)'.[25] The arrival of

[25] Girolamo Savonarola, 'On the renovation of the Church', in J. C. Olin (ed. and trans.), *The Catholic Reformation, Savonarola to Ignatius Loyola: Reform in the Church, 1495–1540* (New York, 1992), p. 9.

a 'sword of God' in the figure of Charles VIII of France and the flight
of Piero de' Medici catapulted Savonarola into the role of mediator
between the king and Florence, God and the city. Convinced
that good government and true religion were interdependent, 'the
Christian and the civic life combined', Savonarola set out to restore
Florence as a 'New Jerusalem' by reforming the Church and renewing
Florence's republican heritage. A government directed to the common good, 'with special concern for religion', would be especially
pleasing to God. And 'if religion and morality improve, government
is bound to be perfected'. The reform of religion 'is not so much a
matter of having more ceremonies as of . . . fostering good, holy, and
learned clergy'.[26] Savonarola and his followers were moral conserva-
tives whose greatest innovation was using the printing press to
denounce the Church's corruption. They held bonfires of vanities,
called for the expulsion of Jews and prostitutes, passed legislation
against sodomy, blasphemy, and obscene art, and deployed youth
brigades to keep their elders under surveillance. Condemned by
Alexander VI and burned by a Florentine government that turned
against him in 1498, Savonarola's ashes were scattered over the Arno
River lest he be venerated as a saint.

Still, the hierarchy ignored calls for reform. Despite urgent
recommendations at the Fifth Lateran Council (1512–17) from the
Venetian reformers Paolo Giustiniani and Pietro Quirini that Leo X
require bishops to reside in their dioceses, reform the religious orders,
and curb the extravagance of the curia itself, the council did little
more than limit benefices to four per person (excepting cardinals),
confirm the separation of Observant and Conventual Franciscans,
and reissue *Unam Sanctam*. A decade after Luther's challenge, the
Sack of Rome by Emperor Charles V's Spanish and German Lutheran
troops shocked cardinals like Gian Matteo Giberti of Verona into
returning to their dioceses to work for reform. The Venetian aristocrat Gasparo Contarini (1483–1542) helped draw up another series of
recommendations for reforming the papal curia that were promptly
published in 1537—by Martin Luther! Despite numerous local and ad
hoc efforts at reform, including the creation of a charitable

[26] Girolamo Savonarola, 'Treatise on the constitution and government of the city of
Florence', in R. N. Watkins (ed. and trans.), *Humanism and Liberty* (Columbia, S.C.,
1978), pp. 233, 247, 257.

confraternity, the Oratory of Divine Love, inspired by Caterina Fieschi of Genoa (1447–97) and a branch for clerks regular, the Theatines, by Giovanni Pietro Carafa and Gaetano da Thiene in 1524, it was only after Paul III determined to counter the challenge of Protestantism by approving the Jesuit Order (1540), reorganizing the Inquisition (1542), and convoking the Council of Trent (1545–63) that these groups acquired significant institutional momentum.

As remarkable as the papacy's dilatory response to Lutheranism was the ambivalence of the Italian laity. Few peoples of Europe had suffered more from papal pretensions and clerical negligence. 'We Italians owe this first debt to the Church and to the priests,' declared Machiavelli: 'we have become irreligious and wicked; but we owe them an even greater debt still . . . that the Church has kept, and still keeps, this land of ours divided.'[27] Italians greeted Lutheran ideas with keen interest. The Benedictine Benedetto Fontanini of Mantua's *Benefit of Christ's Death for Christians* (1543), an amalgam of Lutheran, Calvinist, and evangelical ideas, was an instant best-seller. Mendicant preachers laced their sermons with subtle allusions to Luther's doctrine of salvation by faith alone. Groups of artisans, nobles, and intellectuals sprang up in nearly every city, meeting in shops, confraternities, and academies to discuss reformed ideas. In Naples Juan de Valdés (c.1509–41) headed a circle of evangelicals drawn from the courtly and intellectual elite of Italy. At Urbino Cardinal Ercole Gonzaga's sister, Duchess Eleonora, held philo-Protestant discussions and meetings. 'Articles, sects, heresies, faiths, and religions have so multiplied,' observed Bernardino Ochino, 'that everyone wishes to treat faith after his own manner.'[28]

Yet nowhere do committed Protestants appear to have numbered more than a few percent of the population or to have coalesced into groups prepared to challenge the Church directly. The task of the Roman Inquisition in Italy was not to stamp out a broad Protestant movement but to sweep up the remnants of one that never really materialized. Italy's foremost Protestant leaders, Bernardino Ochino and Pietro Martire Vermigli, promptly fled to Geneva. The strategy of Nicodemism, or dissimulation, adopted by those who stayed behind

---

[27] Niccolò Machiavelli, *The Discourses* (i. 12), in P. Bondanella and M. Musa (trans.) *The Portable Machiavelli* (New York, 1979), p. 212.

[28] J. Martin, *Venice's Hidden Enemies* (Berkeley, 1993), pp. 9–10.

was an embrace (to Calvin's exasperation) of permanent minority status.

Love (or, before 1542, even fear) of the hierarchy was the least of Italians' reasons for remaining Catholic. Francesco Guicciardini, papal governor of Modena, was a consummate insider:

I don't know anyone who dislikes the ambition, the avarice and the sensuality of priests more than I do ... Nevertheless, the position I have enjoyed with several popes has forced me to love their greatness for my own self-interest. If it weren't for this consideration, I would have loved Martin Luther as much as I love myself—not to be released from the laws taught by the Christian religion as it is normally interpreted and understood, but to see this band of ruffians reduced within their correct bounds.[29]

Like many of Italy's ruling elite, Guicciardini had interests that were too closely tied to the Church to make breaking with Rome attractive. Nor, though he yearned for the castigation of the hierarchy, did he find Lutheran theology itself alluring.

Italy's temporal rulers had little to gain by embracing Lutheran reform. Through their bureaucracies and Roman connections they already had effective control of ecclesiastical institutions in their territories. Patrician families filled cathedral chapters with their sons and nunneries with their daughters. 'Anyone who is noble and rich,' Cardinal Gonzaga reminded his father the marquis in 1478, 'if he has two sons puts one into the Church.'[30] Lutheran doctrines annulling the power of priests, the value of the sacraments, and the efficacy of votive masses would have voided the massive investments in chapels and parochial patronage rights they had made over the preceding two centuries.

Intellectuals were divided. Reformers like Contarini and the evangelicals were drawn to Lutheranism because it seemed to extend traditions emphasizing the primacy of faith that had been a feature of Italian piety since the fourteenth century. Not until the failure of the Regensburg Colloquy (1541) did they fully appreciate and reject the anti-sacerdotal consequences of that theology. Savonarola's successors, on the other hand, were attracted precisely by Luther's scoldings of popes and clergy. But when they recognized that the underlying

---

[29] Francesco Guicciardini, Maxim 28, in A. Brown (trans.), *Guicciardini: Dialogue on the Government of Florence* (Cambridge, 1994), p. 171.
[30] Chambers, 'A defense of non-residence', p. 619.

theology of *sola fide* conceded no redemptive value to (charitable) works, they were appalled and quickly re-embraced traditional soteriology.

Most Italians wanted Church reform, few a new theology. Over the preceding two centuries they had elaborated a panoply of saints, texts, civic rituals, and devotions into a distinctively Italianate form of Renaissance Christianity. Most preferred to keep their own religious practices rather than adopt 'German' theology. Love of the Virgin and saints, more than respect for the hierarchy, kept them in the Catholic fold. And when it finally roused itself to action, the papacy appropriated as much as it repressed of the lay Christianity that had grown up in the Renaissance—its art, devotions, and particularly its emphasis on the interrelationship between individual penance and charitable social action—ultimately moulding Renaissance Christianity into modern Roman Catholicism.

Family and marriage: a socio-legal perspective

Julius Kirshner

Old and new perspectives

Standing out among the works on family history in the Italian Renaissance is Nino Tamassia's *The Italian Family in the Fifteenth and Sixteenth Centuries*, published in 1910. According to Tamassia, agnatic lineages (unilineal descent groups tracing their origins from a commonly regarded male ancestor on the father's side) of the late Middle Ages began to dissolve in the Renaissance into intimate modern families anchored by a married couple and their unmarried children. His thesis was shared by other scholars of the late nineteenth century, who, like Tamassia, were inspired by Jacob Burckhardt's identification of Renaissance Italy with the beginnings of modernity. Their association of the cult of the individual with the emergence of strong regional states hostile to powerful, violence-prone lineages and their client networks served as an intuitively plausible explanation for the demise of lineage-centred families.

An historian of law, Tamassia first outlined the distinctive contributions of Germanic customs and Roman civil law and canon law to the regulations governing the legal capacities of women and the marriage and inheritance regimes stretching from the Alps to Sicily. Emphasizing the links between wealth and lineage solidarity, he placed the management and preservation of patrimonies across generations at the heart of social relations in the late Middle Ages. The almost universal exclusion of daughters with dowries from paternal inheritance (*exclusio propter dotem*) was underscored as the primary means for preserving lineage solidarity, by transmitting the greater part of family estates to male descendants and paternal kinsmen. Tamassia was aware that reliance on legal sources, which typically centre on regulations and dispute resolution, would give a distorted picture of family matters and marriage. More positively, he relished the prescriptive advice and moralizing presented in a remarkable set of works, including the vernacular sermons of San Bernardino of Siena (1380–1444), *On the Education of Children* of the Dominican preacher Giovanni Dominici (1356–1419), the dialogue *On the Family* by the Florentine humanist Leon Battista Alberti (1404–72), *On Wifely Duties* of the Venetian patrician humanist Francesco Barbaro (1390–1454), and the acerbic stories (*novelle*) of Franco Sacchetti (*c.*1333–1400) and Matteo Bandello (1485–1561). He orchestrated non-legal as well as legal sources to illustrate the aspirations, fears, and practices of families persevering in a period of social and political turmoil. Above all, he lavished attention on Florence, the birthplace of the Renaissance, and on its allegedly bourgeois families, who were admired as bearers of nascent modernity.

Since the 1960s, a flood of historical, quantitative, anthropological, and gender-driven research drawing on Italy's archival riches has revolutionized our understanding of family life in the Renaissance. The story that the Renaissance brought about a dissolution of lineages into intimate conjugal nuclear families is now considered a romantic myth. In Italy, families living under the same roof—from ancient Rome, through the Middle Ages and the Renaissance, to the early twenty-first century—were overwhelmingly nuclear households of a husband and wife with or without immature children. Family (*familia/famiglia*) meant different things. The narrow meaning referred to the conjugal household, including servants and slaves. Families expanded and then shrank as they coursed through the life cycle. We find married sons remaining in their father's household; brothers first sharing, then dividing the estate of their deceased father; a widow residing with her children; and a childless widow returning to her natal family. Since daughters and illegitimate children were ordinarily omitted from family genealogies, it is an error to equate kinship with the totality of blood relations. It is also erroneous to limit the concept of family to households. The broader meaning of *familia* encompassed loosely knit lineages—agnatic kinsmen living in their own households but sharing a common surname. The fortunes and internal coherence of lineages were subject to demographic, economic, and political trends. A classic example is the Medici, down-and-out in the mid fourteenth century, but virtual rulers of Florence in the fifteenth, and hereditary dukes and grand dukes in the early modern period. Lineages that had coalesced in the Middle Ages into confederations like the *alberghi* of Genoa were thriving political entities in the fifteenth and early sixteenth centuries.

Intralineage hostilities caution us not to assume political loyalties solely on the basis of a family name. Family solidarity was also perishable. New political realities eroded lineage power, as happened in the Piedmont cities of Asti, Chieri, and Turin when Savoy emerged as a regional state in the late fifteenth century. Records of family-rending disputes over property and the spoils of power would suggest that lineage solidarity is just another myth. Yet, a vast array of archival records documenting gifts, marriages, fiduciary and guardianship arrangements, powers of attorney, inheritance, and funeral and burial practices attest to the mutual ties binding lineage members. Family memoirs, genealogies, and coats of arms also testify to a self-conscious fixation with agnatic kinship. Politics and society in north and central Italy between 1350 and 1550 were increasingly dominated by aristocratic lineage-based oligarchies linked through marriage—hardly the stuff of bourgeois modernity.

Legal framework

A monolithic legal system, let alone a discrete and internally coherent body of family law, did not exist in the Renaissance. Urban and rural communities, small and large, generated their own autonomous customs, statutes, and legislation. Some 500 printed volumes of such Italian municipal statutes housed in the Library of Congress in Washington, D.C. affirm the dynamism of municipal lawmaking. When municipal laws proved inadequate, appeal was made to the *ius commune* or common law, which, strictly speaking, referred to the

Corpus iuris civilis, promulgated in 528–34 by the Roman Emperor Justinian, together with companion glosses and commentaries. The *ius commune* long remained a source of law in north and central Italy, save in Venice, and in parts of southern Italy, Sicily, and Sardinia. Canon law was the law of the Church, but it was also treated as *ius commune*, owing to its authority and universality and to the fact that in our period jurists studied both Roman civil law and canon law. By the fifteenth century, the authority of Lombard law (the laws promulgated by the Lombard kings who ruled Italy from the sixth to the eight centuries) had greatly diminished in the presence of the *ius commune*. Yet Lombard law's preference for male agnates decisively moulded local inheritance laws throughout Italy. The notable differences among these bodies of law gave opportunistic leeway to litigants, administrators, and jurists, but one must not overlook converging assumptions and rules owing to centuries of reciprocal borrowings.

Current socio-legal research rejects the naive assumption that law establishes paper boundaries easily circumvented or irrelevant to social practices. It focuses instead on law as a proactive discourse that simultaneously constructs and erases identities, encourages altruism and self-interest, generates consent and resistance, and universalizes and naturalizes contingent social practices and cultural values. The frictions between law and social practice were mediated by university-trained jurists, such as Bartolus of Sassoferrato (1313/14–57) and Baldus de Ubaldis of Perugia (1327–1400), who produced tracts, commentaries, and, especially, thousands of legal opinions (*consilia*) on every aspect of family life.[1] By 1550, convenient access to collections of *consilia* was possible through printed editions. Local notaries also provided legal advice and representation. In addition to carrying out the legal affairs of individuals, businesses, and groups, notaries drafted a wide variety of legally enforceable contracts and agreements for all social classes. Between 1505 and 1553 the notary Benedetto Castiglioni of Milan prepared over 11,000 documents, a sizeable percentage of them pertaining to family matters. The boilerplate language of legal documents and their systematic recording in notarial registers furnished a structure of authentication, predictability,

---

[1] M. Ascheri, I. Baumgärtner, and J. Kirshner (eds.), *Legal Consulting in the Civil Law Tradition* (Berkeley, 1999).

and social memory that crucially facilitated the affairs of families, businesses, and public institutions.

Patria potestas

Within the *ius commune*'s repertoire of family-shaping institutions none was more consequential in Renaissance Italy than *patria potestas*: the indivisible, inalienable, and perpetual power exercised by the household's head or *paterfamilias* over his children and direct legitimate descendants traced through the male line—chiefly his sons and their children. The *paterfamilias* was the eldest living male agnate and therefore legally independent. Daughters were subject to paternal power, but not the married daughters' children, who were in the power of their own *paterfamilias*. Children of a legitimate marriage assumed their father's legal and civic status, whereas children born out of wedlock (estimated to account for fewer than 5 percent of all births in our period) assumed their mother's. *Patria potestas* could be acquired by legitimation of illegitimates through a grant of the Holy Roman Emperor, or a municipal council. Such legitimations, however, were relatively infrequent. Rarer still was legitimation by the subsequent marriage of the father to the mother. In theory, *patria potestas* over a person not in another's power could be acquired through adoption. Much in evidence in ancient Rome, adoption was a strategy for preserving the name and property of childless families, rather than a means for providing a loving home for orphans. But, owing to a pervasive attachment to legitimate blood relations, adoption was extremely rare in the Renaissance.

The proprietary capacities of children under *patria potestas* were restricted. A contract between a child in power and a third party was invalid unless the *paterfamilias* had given his consent. Children in power were strictly prohibited from making last wills, although with paternal consent they could make donations in anticipation of death. The *paterfamilias* was vested with the right to administer any gifts or legacies children received from their mothers, relatives, or other persons. Whatever profits a son earned from such cash and goods through his own labours belonged to him. But a *paterfamilias* was entitled to half of the profits when they derived from cash or goods that he himself provided. A son's eligibility for public office did not require paternal consent, for the *ius commune* and municipal statutes treated fathers and office-holding sons in power equally as citizens. In contrast to canon law, marriage under Roman civil law did not release children from paternal power. Married sons and, in principle, married daughters, remained in the father's power as long as he lived or until they were legally emancipated. Upon her husband's predecease, the married daughter was again unreservedly subject to her father's power.

Patria potestas was extinguished with the death of the *paterfamilias*, a fact reflected in one's very name. 'Lucas quondam Marci' (Luca, son of the deceased Marco) signalled to the world that Luca was legally independent, and, if not a minor (under twenty-five years of age in the *ius commune*, under eighteen in the statutes of Cremona, Naples, and Florence), fully responsible for his own contractual obligations and acts. Much less often children were released from *patria potestas* by an act of legal emancipation recorded in a notarial document. Emancipation had little to do with children's liberation. Rather, fathers emancipated their children when it served their own strategic interests—for example, because they wanted to retire, shield property from creditors by transferring it to their children, or conversely enable them to transfer property to him before they entered a religious order. Fathers similarly deployed emancipation to reduce their own liabilities for obligations and debts incurred by unemancipated children. Children joining religious orders were also released from *patria potestas*, and it was the order, not the father, which administered whatever movable properties and rents the entrants had or would later acquire through gifts and bequests.

Emancipation did not extinguish the affective bonds between the *paterfamilias* and his legally independent children, nor did it occasion disinheritance. The *paterfamilias* was duty-bound under natural law to educate and support all his legitimate minor children, duties that a wealth of evidence suggests fathers performed with genuine care and affection. When the *paterfamilias* died, both his emancipated and unemancipated children were assured at least a minimum share of the paternal estate, called *legitima*. While emancipated children no longer shared liability for paternal debts, they were expected to revere their fathers, comply with their demands, and provide parents in need with food, clothing, shelter, and medical care. Although illegitimate children did not legally belong to the father's *familia*, they were entitled under the *ius commune* to his support. Many illegitimates were reared in the paternal household and upon the father's death received modest legacies and dowries. Many others were committed to foundling hospitals, like the Florentine Ospedale degli Innocenti designed by Brunelleschi, famous for both its refined beauty and appalling rates of neonatal mortality.

The full rigour of *patria potestas* had been mitigated in the late Middle Ages. First, commercial expediency enabled unemancipated sons to enjoy meaningful de facto autonomy. The ability of sons to operate freely was essential when fathers and sons, although co-residents in the same household and members of the same business firm, were operating in different localities and transactions had to be executed quickly. In Florence, unemancipated sons matriculated in merchant and artisan guilds were able to engage in business and credit transactions for themselves and their fathers without express paternal authorization. By the same token, creditors could rely on the legal presumption that such sons were acting with tacit paternal knowledge and consent, unless a father had expressly renounced liability for the sons' obligations and debts. Second, a majority of the men contracting first marriages in our period, on average between the ages of twenty-five and thirty, had already been released from *patria potestas* upon their fathers' predecease.

Still, it would be misconceived, at least for the many regions in Italy where the *ius commune* was in force, to infer from these mitigating circumstances that *patria potestas* was of marginal consequence for real-world families. As part of a never-ending cycle, legitimate sons who had been subject to paternal power not only became legally independent, and heirs, upon the death of the *paterfamilias*; they themselves also assumed the status of *paterfamilias* with its distinctive masculine powers. The wife of a travelling merchant or a widowed mother necessarily took on greater responsibilities for the children's rearing, but they were absolutely denied the capacity to wield paternal power. Lacking *patria potestas*, they could not adopt, legitimate, or emancipate children, share the husband's authority over their children, appoint guardians for them (though widows were appointed as legal guardians of their children and grandchildren), alienate family property, transmit to legitimate children their own civic status, or act as legal representatives for family members involved in civil litigation. At bottom, *patria potestas* persisted unquestioned as the structural mainstay of family solidarity until the late seventeenth and eighteenth centuries, when reformers led by Cesare Beccaria charged that a father's *potestas* over his adult children, including hypothetically sexagenarians, was irrational and contrary to republican liberty.

Demographic framework

Renaissance Italy was highly urbanized, with about one-third of the population living in cities. After 1450 the population, devastated by the recurring lethal plague that had first entered Italy via Sicily in 1347, increased measurably. The population of Florence, numbering more than 100,000 before 1348 and plummeting to less than 40,000 in the first half of the fifteenth century, rose to 60,000 by 1552. The pre-plague population of Venice, estimated at 110,000, plunged to 85,000 by 1422 and then increased to 150,000 by 1548. Verona experienced similar growth, from 20,000 in 1409 to 46,000 by 1545. Even more dramatic was the recovery in Sicily, whose population, particularly in the cities of Palermo, Siracusa, and Messina, nearly doubled in the second half of the fifteenth century. Population growth has been attributed to declining plague-related mortality and increased immigration. Immigrants came from nearby rural districts but also from other towns and even beyond the Alps in search of economic opportunities. Population increases were unevenly distributed. The majority of the lovely but economically feeble hill towns dotting Lazio, the Marche, Umbria, and Tuscany failed to recover fully. Siena's population declined from 45,000–50,000 around 1300 to less than 10,000 in 1552. In the same period, Gubbio's declined from 17,000–20,0000 to about 6,500.

Households were relatively small. A pioneering investigation of the Catasto—the fiscal survey of Florence and its Tuscan dominion covering 260,000 persons spread across 60,000 households—reveals that average household size in the city was 3.8 in 1427.[2] It also reveals a

---

[2] D. Herlihy and C. Klapisch-Zuber, *Tuscans and Their Families: A Study of the Florentine Catasto of 1427* (New Haven, 1985).

positive correlation between wealth and larger households crammed with young children. The increase of Florence's population after 1450 mirrored the gain of average household size, which reached 5.8 in 1552, while in Verona it increased from 3.7 persons in 1425 to 5.9 in 1502. Nuclear family units—consisting of a husband and wife with or without children, or a widow or widower with children—represented 60 percent of the households in Florence in 1427; 65 percent in Parma in 1545; 74 percent in Verona in 1545; and 63 percent in Milan in 1576. Multi-nuclear households, consisting of married brothers, are more noticeable in rural areas than in cities. But 20 percent of Florentine households in 1427 consisted of only one person, a grim figure capturing the carnage wrought by early fifteenth-century plagues.

Marriage norms

Robust debate is a hallmark of modern Renaissance scholarship, but there is a consensus on the centrality of legally recognized marriages in the creation of new families, the conferring of legal status and social rank, and the transmission of property. Marriage was raised to the status of a full-fledged sacrament at the Council of Florence in 1438, but its sacramental character had been recognized for centuries. San Bernardino of Siena and St Antonino of Florence (1389–1459) taught that through the sacrament of marriage spouses were voluntarily united into one perpetual and monogamous flesh. Marriage was distinguished from concubinage—the long-term cohabitation of non-married couples—by the intention of the partners, without reservation, to treat each other as husband and wife. The formalization of this reciprocal intention was expressed in a mutual exchange of consent embodied in a contract of marriage. In theory, the free and mutual exchange of spousal consent in the present tense (*verba de presenti*) before witnesses sufficed to make a valid marriage, subsequently perfected by sexual relations. Mutual promises to marry in the future (*verba de futuro*) followed by sexual relations likewise constituted a valid marriage. The Church admonished that ecclesiastical supervision of the nuptial rite served to promote the sacramental nature of marriage and prevent secret unions, bigamy, forced consent, violation of the impediment of consanguinity, and the marriage of individuals who had not reached lawful age (twelve for brides, fourteen for grooms). In actuality, marriages in the presence of a priest were more likely to occur in England, France, and other regions beyond the Alps than in central Italy, where marriage vows were ordinarily solemnized by a notary. Only after the Council of Trent in 1563 did church marriages in the presence of a priest and two witnesses, preceded by the publication of banns, begin to take hold in Italy.

Roman civil law and municipal statutes prohibited children in power from marrying against the *paterfamilias*'s wishes. Children who married without parental approval could be, and were, punished with disinheritance. Although under canon law a couple was in principle free to marry without parental approval, marriages lacking the consent, or at least knowledge, of senior family members were stigmatized by canonists as well as civilian jurists as contrary to sound morals. In the upper classes, romantic attachments, premarital sexual relations, individual choice of a mate—preconditions of present-day marriages in the West—were taboo. The Lombard custom of transferring the father's protective custody over his obedient daughter to the husband continued to inform statutory regulations. Statutes everywhere fined brides under a certain age (e.g. eighteen at Padua, twenty at Arezzo, twenty-five at Perugia) who married without paternal approval. A daughter could disobey her *paterfamilias*, in principle, if he attempted to force her to marry an unworthy man when a worthy one was available. In reality, a prospective upper-class bride, on average in her mid to late teens, played no part in arranging her own marriage. Choice of a spouse was subordinated to the interests of one's immediate family and relatives. With the death of the father, older brothers, sometimes acting with paternal uncles, assumed the duty to marry off female siblings. We also find widows and senior female kin performing the fathers' role in arranging marriages.

Making marriage

Marriage among elite families in Renaissance Italy was a multi-stage affair taking place over several months, and often longer when alliances, family honour, and large dowries were at stake. Detailed records of marriage negotiations, weddings, and dowries in Florence are provided by family memoirs (*ricordi, ricordanze*) compiled by the heads of families. More than 300 of these books have survived, constituting a unique source for the domestic and business affairs of the Florentine elite. Matchmaking called for patience, timely information, plain luck, and marriage brokers to assist in finding suitable mates. An ideal bride was not consanguinally related to the prospective groom and was reputed to be morally fit, healthy, respectful, attractive, and young. It is conceivable that the preference for brides in their teens, who would enjoy on average more years of fertility, was motivated by the desire to replenish families devastated by high rates of mortality. For certain, bridegrooms were motivated by the desire for unspoiled young girls, as well as for submissive creatures who would be easily integrated into their households. The sexuality of winsome teenage girls provoked both delight and fear. The female protagonists in Boccaccio's *Decameron* and in the salty stories of Giovanni Sercambi (1348–1424) begin conjugal or amorous relations between the ages of thirteen and fifteen. Renaissance portraits of females are almost exclusively of nubile adolescent girls from socially prominent families. Fathers, in turn, anxious about the budding sexuality of teenage daughters and about preserving the family's honour, sought to marry them off quickly. Some noble Venetian fathers specified in their wills that their daughters be given in marriage between the ages of fourteen and sixteen.

The bride's family, including her kinsmen, had to be socially and politically compatible with the bridegroom's. Intermarriage among families of roughly equal status was the norm.[3] Members of high-status lineages had the greatest success in finding appropriate mates. An even higher rate of endogamous marriages was practised among Venice's patrician families. Misalliances, social climbing, and fortune-hunters certainly existed, as in Venice where patrician men in straitened circumstances sought non-patrician women with large dowries. Meanwhile, the prospective bride's representatives focused on the probity, health, family status, and resources of the prospective groom and his family. On average husbands were seven to ten years older than their brides in southern European towns; in Florence the gap

[3] A. Molho, *Marriage Alliance in Late Medieval Florence* (Cambridge, Mass., 1994).

reached a phenomenal twelve years. The late marriage of upper-class husbands was largely due to lengthy periods of apprenticeship and the obligation of brothers to delay marriage until their sisters married. In rural areas where cultivation required the labour of complete families, the average age of first-time husbands was twenty-five years. In northern and north-west Europe, the percentage of teenage brides was low, with both women and men marrying in their mid twenties.

In Tuscany, a handshake or kiss between the representatives of the families customarily sealed a marriage agreement. Soon after, the agreement would be solemnized by a notary in a contract of betrothal, which committed the prospective bride and groom to marry in the future and provided terms and guarantees regarding the amount and delivery of the dowry. The prospective bride's consent was almost always given by proxy, and if she failed to raise an objection it was legally presumed that she had voluntarily ratified the arrangement. Soon after the betrothal, the couple exchanged marriage vows in the present tense and the bride received a ring from the bridegroom, acts witnessed and recorded in a marriage contract. Next came the wedding festivities culminating in the consummation of the marriage, which, in late fifteenth-century Florence, most often occurred in the house of the bride. Finally, the husband publicly led and introduced the bride to his household, usually on a Sunday, so that as many people as possible could witness the transfer of the bride. This rite took on an added significance in northern Italy and the rest of Europe, where notaries were not customarily engaged to record nuptial rites. Under the *ius commune*, the public transfer of the wife to the husband's household—never the reverse—established a legal presumption that a present-consent marriage had been consummated.

Dowries

A dowry that reflected the worth and honour of the couple's respective families was indispensable. The dowry was the wife's principal material contribution to the new conjugal household. Under both the *ius commune* and statutory law, a daughter was entitled to receive an honourable dowry in conformity with the resources and social rank of her father. When a father failed to perform this duty, brothers, mothers, and other kin became responsible for funding the dowry. A husband—or, if he remained subject to paternal power, his father— had the exclusive right of possessing and disposing of a dowry (which consisted of cash, immovables, personal items, and credits, such as shares in the public debts of Florence, Genoa, and Venice) whose valuation had been established at the beginning of the marriage. By law, the husband and his father were obligated to treat the dowry with care and diligence, and were expected to place dowry capital in secure investments and apply profits in support of the conjugal household. Payment of the dowry usually coincided with the public transfer of the bride and the consummation of marriage. Legally, a husband who had not received full payment of the dowry could refuse to cohabit with his wife. The threat of this shame-inflicting remedy, though exercised only sporadically among elite families, put unspoken pressure on the bride's family to display good faith in paying dowries on schedule.

Satisfying the dowry demands of potential grooms was daunting. Even wealthy families did not have copious cash reserves to pay large dowries completely and immediately, and endowing several daughters required forethought. Wealthy families sought to limit exorbitant dowry expenditures by consigning one or more daughters to a religious order—a less costly, though honourable, option that was increasingly taken from the early sixteenth century onwards. Most importantly, the size of the dowry served as a sign of family rank. Ever larger dowries and extravagant weddings became imperative for maintaining family status and forging alliances with equally worthy families. Because the mounting expenses of marriage were perceived as a wasteful diversion of capital from productive business enterprises, and therefore as undermining the social order, governments everywhere imposed limits on lavish nuptial expenses—but with negligible success. The Florentine widow Alessandra Macinghi Strozzi complained that 'the world is in a sorry state, and never has so much expense been loaded on the backs of women as now. No dowry is so big that when the girl goes out she doesn't have the whole of it on her back, between silks and jewels.'[4] In 1425, Florence launched a dowry fund (*Monte delle doti*) with the dual purpose of raising funds for its

---

[4] Alessandra Macinghi Strozzi, *Lettere di una gentildonna fiorentina*, ed. C. Guasti (Florence, 1877), pp. 548–9; trans. in E. Cochrane and J. Kirshner (eds.), *The Renaissance* (Chicago, 1986), p. 116.

war against Milan and making dowries affordable for middling and upper-echelon families. Under an initial model investment plan (which was repeatedly modified), fathers were invited, on behalf of their daughters, to invest 100 florins which would mature to 250 florins after 7½ years and 500 florins after 15 years. These amounts were paid to the daughter's husband only after he furnished proof of having consummated the marriage. The dowry fund, which attracted thousands of investors and became a central institution of Florentine public finance, remained in operation into the second half of the sixteenth century.

The belief that dowries were essential for preserving women's honour was dramatized by the popular legend of St Nicholas of Myra, whose gift of dowries rescued three impoverished sisters from a life of prostitution. Depicted by Ambrogio Lorenzetti of Siena, Agnolo Gaddi of Florence, and Gentile da Fabriano, the legend inspired Renaissance testators to direct bequests to nubile girls without dowries and to married women who lacked sufficient dowries and were thus in limbo waiting to be introduced into their husbands' households. In his will of 1429, Pietro Miani, bishop of Vicenza, left funds for the dowries of sixty poor servant girls who had reached the age of fourteen, stipulating that payment was conditional on the brides having joined their husbands' households. Confraternities like Santissima Annunziata in Rome, founded in 1460, were established with the exclusive mission of providing assistance to unmarried girls from poor families. Non-governmental marriage funds were established in Bologna, Todi, and Naples and in the dioceses of the Abruzzi and Molise to provide poor girls with articles of clothing and modest dowries. As a final resort, poor adolescent girls, mostly foundlings, were placed with families to work as domestic servants for a number of years, after which they would receive dowries. These girls were vulnerable to sexual abuse from their surrogate fathers and the high risk of not receiving the promised dowry.

Living marriage

The founding truth of marriage, derived from a conflation of Paul to the Ephesians 5:23, and Matthew 19:5–6, was that the husband is the head of the wife with whom he has joined as one flesh. This view of marriage was fortified by the *ius commune*, which held that the wife owes her husband eager obedience and deference, must reside where he chooses, and must work for his benefit. Regardless of her age, the wife was treated in both the *ius commune* and municipal law as a minor not fully capable of conducting her own affairs and therefore requiring paternalistic protection. Still, the *ius commune* granted the wife a significant measure of liberty to administer and dispose of the wages, rents, and profits she received outside the domestic household and which legally belonged to her. This liberty also extended to non-dotal goods and properties that she possessed before, or acquired during, marriage. Non-dotal goods were essential in enabling wives to perform the soul-saving duty of almsgiving.

Opposed to the *ius commune*, though aligned with Lombard law, municipal statutes in every region of Italy denied the wife liberty to enter into contracts, dispose of her own earnings, alienate property, make a last will, or select a place of burial without obtaining her husband's authorization. Legal transactions and contracts of Florentine wives were in theory valid only if authorized by a legal guardian. In practice, these restrictive statutes were neither easily monitored nor enforceable in advance; it is not surprising, therefore, to find that married women, without authorization from their husbands, made retail purchases on credit, borrowed from pawnbrokers, alienated and leased properties, gave gifts, and made last wills. Since wives working as artisans, moneylenders, victuallers, and midwives could not feasibly obtain approval for every legal transaction, jurists concocted the convenient legal fiction that they were understood to have acted with their husbands' tacit authorization.

More than half of socially mixed marriages in mid fourteenth-century Venice lasted longer than ten years, and more than one-quarter longer than twenty, with noble marriages lasting appreciably longer than commoner marriages.[5] Almost half the marriages among elite Florentine families lasted at least twenty years.[6] Given the elevated rates of mortality, owing to plague and dangers attending childbirth, this finding is remarkable, but not surprisingly it reflects

---

[5] L. Guzzetti, 'Dowries in fourteenth-century Venice', *Renaissance Studies*, 16 (2002), pp. 430–73.

[6] C. Klapisch-Zuber, 'La Fécondité des Florentines (XIVᵉ–XVIᵉ siècles)', *Annales de démographie historique*, (1988), pp. 41–57.

the advantages of high status. These perdurable Florentine marriages were also extremely fertile. The employment of wet-nurses made frequent pregnancies possible: the median interval between births was about eighteen months. Similarly, by the early sixteenth century, Veneto women were giving birth to more children at shorter intervals over longer periods, thus contributing to the region's demographic upsurge.

Ideally, the 'good wife' was sexually faithful, deferential, and her husband's trustworthy agent. As head of the household, the 'good husband' affectionately cared for his wife, provided for the educational and material needs of his children, and responsibly managed his business and properties. Flanking the ideals of mutual support and trust, however, was a tenacious double standard. Proverbial wisdom held that, for maintaining the husband's mastery, both 'good and bad women need to be thrashed (*buona femmina e mala femmina vuol bastone*)'.[7] More typically, husbands were encouraged to wield the sweet violence of moderate force against disobedient wives, while wives with overbearing husbands were encouraged to exercise forbearance. Some husbands engaged in casual extramarital affairs with relative impunity, while adulterous wives, whose reputed lust made a mockery of the husband's *potestas*, were penalized with loss of dowry and marital support. If a husband committed himself to a relationship with another woman that created the appearance of bigamy, a jilted wife had legal recourse. Complete divorce, dissolving the marriage bond and permitting the spouses to remarry, was not recognized. Nor was annulment an option, for it applied only to marriages that were invalid from the beginning. But the wife could petition a church court to compel her husband to leave his lover, or to grant a judicial separation and restitution of her dowry. Church and secular authorities prosecuted husbands who, by cohabiting with a lover in flagrant adultery, caused public scandal.

In the marital disputes adjudicated before the bishop's court in Lucca around 1400 all the plaintiffs were men, some of whose wives had deserted them for other men — including several priests.[8] On pain

---

[7] Franco Sacchetti, *Il Trecentonovelle*, ed. E. Faccioli (Turin, 1970), novella lxxxvi, p. 233.

[8] C. Meek, 'Women, the Church and the law: matrimonial litigation in Lucca under Bishop Nicolao Guinigi (1394–1435)', in M. O'Dowd and S. Wichert (eds.), *Chattel, Servant or Citizen: Women's Status in Church, State and Society* (Belfast, 1995), pp. 82–90.

of excommunication, deserting wives were ordered by the bishop's court to return to their husbands. Since an estranged wife's passionately felt desire to escape from a poisonous marriage was insufficient grounds for a court-ordered separation, a wife typically pleaded in her defence that the husband's cruelty and beatings caused her to desert. But she had to prove with unimpeachable witness testimony that she had been battered by her husband before a suspicious and reluctant court would grant a separation. In cases where wives acquiesced to reconciliation, the chastened husbands promised to stop abusing them. When unplacated wives refused to return after having been admonished to do so by the court, they could be excommunicated and their husbands granted a separation. The inability or unwillingness of improvident husbands to provide support was another commonly alleged reason driving wives to abandon the marital household. In Florence, Venice, and elsewhere we find out-of-court settlements in which husbands separated from their wives retained the dowry but agreed to pay annual support equal on average to 8 to 10 percent of the dowry's value. These wives were more fortunate than the 'white widows' with children whose husbands had moved away, never to be heard from again, and under the law were considered dead.

Termination of marriage

A distinctive characteristic of marriages in the Renaissance is the high percentage of older husbands who predeceased their wives. In anticipation of death, husbands prepared wills arranging for the satisfaction of outstanding obligations, charitable bequests, and the orderly distribution of their estates among family members. Will-making in the Renaissance was a normal activity among all classes, save the propertyless. Intestacy, or dying without a will by choice or negligence, occurred with some as yet undetermined frequency. A husband's will first provided for the required restitution of the wife's dowry and her non-dotal properties. Husband–testators often tried to avoid actual restitution of the dowry, which placed a heavy financial burden on their heirs, usually their sons; they also tried to discourage their wives from remarrying, which would reduce their sons' claims to the maternal dowry. Instead of restitution, they promised that as long as the wife neither demanded her dowry nor remarried, and remained in the husband's household, she would receive basic support for the rest of her life. The same conditions applied to the marital bed with its silk coverings and expensive gifts of clothing, rings, belts, and necklaces, which husbands customarily left to surviving wives. Husband–testators routinely appointed their wives among the guardians of minor children on condition that they not remarry. For older widows, whose remarriage prospects were limited, residing in the husband's household was an attractive option, since they would have immediate and decent support while avoiding the messy conflicts and delays attending the restitution of dowries.

Remarriage of widows was also fairly common, and typically arranged in the upper classes by kinsmen intent on forging new social and political alliances. Canon law recognized a widow's right to remarry someone of her own choosing or to remain unmarried, and both the *ius commune* and municipal statutes protected a widow's right to reclaim her dowry. While most widowers quickly remarried, among widows those under thirty were the most likely candidates for remarriage. Widows brought their new husbands the restored dowry, but they almost always left their children behind with the deceased husbands' kinsmen. Widows unable or unwilling to live with their husband's kinsmen or without means of support frequently returned to their natal families. With no family to which to return, poor, kinless widows might find shelter in a municipal hospital, asylum, or religious community.

Inheritance

Under the *ius commune*, inheritance was partible, meaning that all legitimate children, regardless of age, sex, and capacity, inherited the paternal estate in equal shares. Yet in accordance with local statutes fathers generally named sons, without their sisters, as coequal heirs. Statutes excluding dowered daughters from inheritance were characteristic of this period and defended by the jurists on the grounds that the 'immortality' of the family, both symbolically (name, coat of arms, reputation) and materially (direct male descendants, patrimony), did not depend on daughters, who by reason of marriage became members of another family, but primarily on sons and secondarily on distant agnatic kin. A father should love his sons more than himself, according to the jurists, because, even after death, he continues to live through them. Since approximately 20 percent of married couples produced only female children (while another 20 percent would not have a surviving child of either sex), daughters and female kin became heirs of last resort. But as a rule they were excluded from inheriting family dwellings and real estate, which were reserved for the husband's male agnatic kin.

The policy of excluding daughters with dowries from inheritance has led several scholars to view the dowry negatively, as the functional equivalent of legal disinheritance. Adding insult to injury, not only did sons inherit more than their dowered sisters, they also looked forward to collecting a dowry when they themselves married. But others contend that sons did not in reality inherit a disproportionate share of the paternal estate, first, because dowries represented sizeable intergenerational transfers of wealth, sometimes exceeding the inheritance received by the daughter's brothers, and second, because sons—who regularly took up the father's occupation and continued to reside in his household even after they married—willingly contributed, by their own labours, to the paternal estate that they expected to inherit.[9] If sons' contributions to paternal inheritances are included, a rough parity seems to have existed between dowered daughters and son–heirs, reflecting in economic terms an efficient outcome. Whether the dowry functioned as a premortem inheritance providing women with an adequate safety net or as disinheritance continues to be debated. What can be said is that, unlike sons, daughters, even with enviable dowries, occupied an anomalous legal space. Technically speaking, they were neither legally disinherited nor legally heirs.

Only a minority of married women made last wills, which is understandable in light of the limited legal capacity they had to dispose of their property. Venice was an exception. Venetian married women were free from the constraints and legal infantilization that

---

[9] M. Botticini, 'A loveless economy? Intergenerational altruism and the marriage market in a Tuscan town, 1415–1436', *Journal of Economic History*, 59 (1999), pp. 104–21; M. Botticini and A. Siow, 'Why dowries?', *American Economic Review*, 93 (2003), pp. 1385–98.

inhibited women's contractual and testamentary capacity throughout the rest of Italy. Venice also sought to prevent spousal coercion by prohibiting husbands from being present when wives made their last wills. Wherever they lived, both married women and widows tended to name their children and blood relatives as heirs. Statutes reserved to widowers, in the absence of surviving children, and as compensation for their marital expenses, a portion of the dowry ranging from one quarter in Spoleto, one third in San Remo, one half in Lucca and Pisa, to the whole dowry in Florence, Milan, and Modena. Widowers with minor children kept control of their wives' dowries, although they eventually inherited only a portion if the wives had vested ownership in the children. Married women testators in Ragusa (Dalmatia), Siracusa, Trieste, Genoa, Amalfi, Naples, and Sorrento were free, in varying degrees and subject to the claims of their children, to dispose of the dowry and other goods at their discretion.

Conclusion

The promotion and preservation of agnatic kinship, the practice of endogamous marriages among elite families, and the exclusion of dowered daughters from paternal inheritance constitute the principal socio-legal motifs of elite families in the Renaissance. Far from representing innovations, these motifs had originated in the twelfth and thirteenth centuries and point to long-term continuities. Agnatic kinship was further bolstered in early modern Italy, with widespread recourse to practices that would radically transform family structures and marriage patterns: primogeniture and enforced renunciation of inheritance rights by daughters (both prohibited by Roman law); enforced celibacy of younger sons and a greater percentage of daughters; and perpetual trusts limiting the inheritance of family property to the owner's lineal descendants, all of which became highly visible after 1550. Other critical changes were introduced by the Council of Trent, which gave the Church unprecedented formal authority over marriage and family matters.

Families in the Renaissance should command our attention for their dominating presence in public as well as private life, not for their place in the putative unfolding of modernity. However one defines modernity, what is striking is the range of differences between the constitutive features of families in the Renaissance (*patria potestas* and agnatic kinship, arranged and indissoluble marriages, dowries, marital sex as the only legitimate means of procreation, and high birth rates with relatively limited life expectancies) and practices in present-day Western Europe (individual self-determination, extra-marital cohabitation with a high percentage of children born to unwed parents, free-choice marriages, sex as pleasurable recreation and entitled self-fulfillment, divorce by mutual consent, and low birth rates with longevity). The pre-modern Renaissance world of relatively self-reliant agnatic lineages and strong families sometimes rivalling the power of weak governments stands in telling contrast to today's world of hyperindividualism and fragile families whose welfare is dependent on service-delivering nation states.

Bodies, disease, and society

Diane Owen Hughes

Bodies as social texts

The body served as a powerful metaphor for society, one that defies a search for social margins. The concept of social marginality is based upon a textual image: a printed page surrounded by a margin, the contents of which are strictly subordinated to the text itself. It is the kind of page invented by humanists, who in purifying ancient texts also disciplined the page by eliminating or reducing the extensive marginalia that often threatened to invade the texts of medieval manuscripts. But the redrawn boundaries of the humanist text page did not provide a social model. In the Renaissance, it was the body rather than the text that gave shape to society: the well-run republic, claimed the Florentine humanist Matteo Palmieri, was like 'a healthy, powerful, and well disposed body'. At a more cosmic level, the human body was recognized as a source for understanding God's creation of which it was deemed a microcosm. Each body was thus a reductive representation of a universe that could be read through its signs. This concept, ancient in origin and well developed in the Middle Ages, attained new mathematical precision through the study of Vitruvius's treatise on architecture, which presented the pro-portional symmetry of the human body as a model for architectural, and by extension social, design. On the theory that each member had an exact mathematical correspondence with the whole, Renaissance man could indeed be a measure of a Christian cosmos perfectly designed by God.

If the ideal cities of the Renaissance reflect an attempt to create in stone the perfect geometric forms from which Plato had believed the cosmos was constructed, their planners often posited a relation between the urban fabric and the human body. For both Filarete and Leonardo, man was the measure of architectural design. Filarete designed his ideal city, Sforzinda, named in honour of the duke of Milan, as a star within a cosmic circle, but felt he had to accommodate in his buildings all the voids, entrances, and hollow places that the body required for its maintenance. Leonardo envisioned the city anatomically with the roads as arteries, its domes as skulls, and the buildings of its governing class as the brain. The microcosmic/ macrocosmic analogy permitted, perhaps even encouraged, social construction based on hierarchic concepts. In the great Tower of Vice and Virtue that Filarete designed to dominate Sforzinda, one ascended from the base, which would house prostitutes and ruffians and cater to the pleasures of the flesh, through the realm of virtue and the intellect (in ways that resemble a neo-Platonic ascent from sensual to intellectual love and understanding) to the astronomical observatory at its summit.

But the body metaphor did not encourage the construction of social margins. Palmieri might contrast 'the parts of the body destined for honorable functions' and others 'in whose appearance and functions there is ugliness and baseness ... located in a more remote region',[1] but, like Filarete, he deemed them all necessary to its existence. They might be hidden but could not be separated. And the mendicants had long impressed on Italian society that the legitimation of its commercial economy depended on the poor. Brunelleschi's Hospital of the Innocents in Florence, a flagship of the new Renaissance architectural style, testifies to this symbiotic relationship. Francesco Datini, the merchant who funded the hospital, hoped that by establishing an institution to save the children of the poor, he might squeeze through the eye of the spiritual needle and find a way to salvation. His friend and spiritual advisor, the notary Lapo Mazzei, told him that, while churches and paintings were certainly worthy as forms of charity, for every time Christ said anything about them he mentioned the poor a hundred times. Charity to the poor offered to the men whose wealth fuelled the

---

[1] Matteo Palmieri, *Vita civile*, ed. G. Belloni (Florence, 1982), pp. 133, 82.

cultural revolution of the Renaissance a means of saving their souls.

Such an understanding quickly became embedded in social design as secular governments made the needs of the poor and needy visible in stone. Hospitals, long a focus of urban charity, assumed a central place within the urban landscape. Filarete described the great hospital he designed for Francesco Sforza in the centre of Milan as a house dedicated to Christ's poor. The Spedale Grande was intended to bring Lombardy up to the standards of Tuscany, where Florence's Hospital of Santa Maria Nuova was celebrated by humanists as 'the first hospital among Christians'. Yet the large investment in hospitals by fifteenth-century governments throughout the peninsula was also an attempt to deal with disease, a frightening spectre that seemed to threaten not only individual health but also social and political stability.

Plague and syphilis

The Renaissance was a golden age of disease, bracketed at both ends by epidemics for which doctors were hard pressed to find an ancient source. After its first appearance in 1347–8 when a third or more of the population succumbed, plague, 'neither heard of nor described in books before', as the learned medical observer Gentile da Foligno claimed before a college of his peers, remained an enduring threat to Italy's public health and posed a continuing challenge to physicians and governments throughout the period. Syphilis, which first struck Italy almost a century and a half later in 1494, though less demographically devastating, created both medical and cultural lesions within society. By this time more classically trained doctors were reluctant to label it new, since, as they reasoned, neither God's creation nor man's nature had changed in ways that might engender new forms of disease. But a learned medical debate on its nature and origins held at the court of Ferrara in 1497 did not convince a local chronicler, who described Alfonso d'Este's malady, which was undoubtedly syphilis and may have inspired the debate, as 'extraordinary and unknown to physicians'. A decade later a study by the Genoese physician Jacopo Cattaneo acknowledged that it was 'never before seen in any century, and [was] unknown throughout the whole world'. The mysterious character and terrifying spread of both plague and syphilis persuaded the medical community to look beyond ancient medicine's concern with the diseased body and to consider the nature of disease itself, that is, to move beyond restoring humoral imbalance within individuals and to seek external causes in the hope that diseases themselves might be eradicated. A widely shared religious belief that these diseases were punishments inflicted by God on a sinful people provoked efforts to identify the reasons for his wrath. Throughout the fifteenth century, the mendicant friars who traversed the Italian peninsula associated contemporary pestilence with the apocalyptic plagues that were to precede the Second Coming, while at the same time offering remedies for moral reform that might postpone it. In this spirit, Ercole d'Este issued in 1496 a programme of social purification to protect Ferrara from the pestilences that God had rained down upon the land. After syphilis appeared in the city, his court physician Coradino Gilino described it too as an instrument of divine intervention, 'which has now spread not only through Italy but across almost the whole of Christendom'.[2]

Beyond their mysterious aetiology, both diseases shared another quality: they were contagious. If sent by God, they were spread by man. If ordinary observers saw the plague's infection spreading by sight and touch, as well as through clothes and other belongings, the medical community, in accordance with textual authority, often felt compelled to attribute the contagion to miasma, a polluted condition of the air through which disease was disseminated. The two views merged to produce civic action in the form of quarantine. As early as the first onslaught of plague, the council of Pistoia imposed travel restrictions to and from other infected regions, barred used clothing from entering the city, kept citizens from contact with the homes and families of the ill, and replaced biers with closed caskets to prevent the stench of the dead from poisoning the air. As plague became endemic by the fifteenth century, quarantine and sanitary regulations (along with commissions to enforce them) were established in most of Italy's major cities.

Although less immediately deadly, syphilis too inspired a horror of

---

[2] J. Arrizabalaga, J. Henderson, and R. French, *The Great Pox: The French Disease in Renaissance Europe* (New Haven, 1997), pp. 56–87.

contagion, as Gilino, remarking its wildfire spread through Italy, immediately recognized. Alert observers also noticed the venereal nature of its transmission, but that did not annul a more general sense of its contagious powers. Canons of the cathedral of Florence, in an attempt to fend off the disease, began in 1504 to isolate the vessels and vestments they used to serve their communicants from those employed in their own devotions. Girolamo Fracastoro, the Veronese physician who gave syphilis its name, recognized that it was chiefly through sexual intercourse that the disease spread. What particularly distinguished syphilis from the plague, however, was its chronic wasting quality. Although cures were proposed, tried, and even celebrated, syphilitics lived all of their natural lives with a disease that ate away their flesh. In this sense the 'new disease' resembled the very old disease of leprosy, the victims of which had been traditionally tracked down, marked, and confined. Florentine statutes of the fourteenth century still required that lepers be identified and expelled from the city and its suburbs. In the leper hospitals that received them on the outskirts of cities, their bodies might be cared for, but they died a civil death.

In the fifteenth century, plague victims and syphilitics were not marked with the demeaning bell, clapper, and yellow cross that had been imposed on lepers in the twelfth century by an ecclesiastical council. Treating the contagious became an exemplary act of urban charity. A Venetian Easter ritual brought members of the patriciate to its hospital for incurables in 1524 to wash the feet of syphilitics. A public means of demonstrating their humility, this was also a way of advertising an institution recently created through the cooperative efforts of lay charity and the public health board, or Sanità. The Company of Divine Love, a charitable fraternity inspired by the mystical piety of Caterina Fieschi and established in her native Genoa in 1497 when syphilis appeared there, spread throughout Italy a concern for incurables whom the established hospitals often rejected. In tending the urban poor, members of the Company tended the body of the wounded Christ, which was also the body social. The influence of fraternal bodies like the Company of Divine Love helped to increase the presence of hospitals in the Italian urban landscape. The services they rendered were recognized as exceptional even by Martin Luther when he visited Italy in 1511: 'The hospitals are built like palaces; the best food and drink are given to everyone; the nurses are diligent, the doctors learned, the beds and clothes clean, the beds painted.'[3]

Fear of contagion helped to persuade governments to foster and underwrite the medical charity of their citizens. In supporting the foundation of a hospital for incurables in Rome, Pope Leo X noted the 'offence to the sight and sense of smell' they created. In Venice the Sanità, remarking that their 'stench may breed infection and disease, to the universal damage and destruction of this our city', required those suffering from syphilis or other incurable diseases to be confined within the new hospital. Quarantine was also increasingly demanded of plague victims as public health boards began intervening aggressively to track and contain its outbreaks. In the particularly vigilant city of Milan, the Sforza dukes refined and extended the sanitary regulations of their Visconti predecessors, mapping the progress of plague through examination of victims and their contacts. Everywhere in Italy special plague hospitals were designed to house the contaminated. Venice's *lazzaretto* became operational as early as 1424; Milan's came into use in 1488; and, after decades of planning and indecision, Florence's finally opened its doors in 1494. By the sixteenth century, *lazzaretti* were everywhere understood to be places of quarantine to which many would be sent, from which some might return, but in which many would die. Quarantine decisions lay with health boards that had the right of house examinations and medical triage, sending the infected to the general hospital, into house quarantine, or to the pesthouse. In Florence, during a ferocious outbreak of plague in 1523, when beds in the *lazzaretti* were insufficient to accommodate the afflicted, huts were set up along the city walls to house 'suspects' before they could enter and infect the city.

These notoriously contagious diseases had always been seen as foreign and alien. The plague, as its earliest chroniclers noticed, was a disease that came out of the East and had been transmitted to Italy through the agency of the Mongols. A number of equally alien sources were posited for syphilis, including the invading French army of Charles VIII (hence the name *mal francese*, the French disease), natives of the New World who were said to have infected the Spaniards (a theory popularized by Guicciardini in his *History of Italy*), and Jews who had been driven out of Spain into Italian exile.

---

[3] G. Cosmacini, *Storia della medicina e della sanità in Italia* (Rome, 1994), p. 188.

But wherever it had come from and in spite of the number of eminent men who suffered and died from it, syphilis was quickly categorized as a disease of the poor, who also came in this period to bear the stigma of plague. While pious Christians might use this association to strengthen their commitment to public health as a form of charity, governmental elites instead found reason to strengthen quarantine practices, which also became a means of preventing disorder within cities.

Was a diseased body displeasing to God? Christians who focused their devotions on the broken body of the crucified Christ or directed their prayers to saints whose bodies bore marks of holy afflictions would not have thought so, for their physical sacrifice provided a basis for the salvation of the Christian community. It was this understanding that empowered the Dominican tertiary Domenica Narducci del Paradiso to petition God 'to gather all of the Florentine plague into her body and then to accept all of her blood, to be poured from her veins, offering all that she had in an exchange' in order to spare the city during a brutal plague of 1527 that took as many as 500 victims a day.[4] To that suffering, redemptive flesh, Renaissance artists counterposed aestheticized bodies that also housed cosmic meaning. Galenic principles of humoral balance lent medical force to this analogy since the four bodily humours were held to be intimately related to the four universal elements and in sympathy with planetary movement. The perfectly formed, not the broken, body of Christ became a symbol of this godly harmony, as both physicians and artists began to offer and represent it as an example of perfect humoral balance.

This set of beliefs encouraged learned doctors to find a cause of disease in planetary disharmony and to treat individual victims by trying to expel the agent that was putrefying the humours in order to restore their natural balance. Evicting victims from the city was thus a way of removing the bestial corruption in order to balance the city's humours and restore those 'clean and beautiful districts, inhabited by rich and noble citizens' that plague, according to one account in 1527, had made 'fetid and savage and filled with the poor whose rash

---

[4] G. Calvi, *Histories of a Plague Year*, trans. D. Biocca and B. T. Ragan, Jr (Berkeley, 1989), p. 209.

indiscipline and fearful cries' frightened off the citizenry.[5] The exclusion of the dangerously ill from the city throughout the sixteenth century struck hardest at the urban poor, whose exposed and diseased bodies seemed to threaten the physical health and social order that both Galenic medicine and repressive regimes sought to maintain. Yet the afflicted bodies of the poor and diseased retained some potency. In addition to the draconian sanitation measures they issued to combat the plague of 1630, the Medici grand dukes decided to allow ritual space for the canonization investigation of Domenica del Paradiso. Her body, offered up over a century earlier as a plague sacrifice, was now judged whole and uncorrupted, a pledge of the future purification of the city.

Jews, prostitutes, and the body social

As the human body was subject to disease, so was the social body vulnerable to invasion by agents of corruption: an analogy strengthened by the Church, which had long associated diseases of the body with those of the spirit, physical with moral infection. Thus it sought to mark lepers, heretics, and Jews with infamous signs as a quarantine device to protect a Christian society from their contagion. Medieval Italian governments had occasionally gone further by altogether banning such undesirables. The *podestà* of some Italian communes were required by oath of office to keep Jews and heretics from inhabiting the territories they governed. The laws of numerous towns likewise kept prostitutes from plying their trade within the walls, and, if admitted, they were often assigned a costume or mark that visually associated them with lepers (bells and gloves) and Jews (yellow veils). Public rituals of humiliation further linked Jews and prostitutes.

Infamous signs might be seen as evidence of the marginality of those who wore them. But even an age that contemplated exclusion and expulsion recognized their organic function within Christian society. Their vital place in the body social is laid out in an anonymous

---

[5] J. Henderson, 'Epidemics in Renaissance Florence: medical theory and government response', in N. Bulst and R. Delort (eds.), *Maladies et société (XIIᵉ–XVIIIᵉ siècles)* (Paris, 1989), p. 186.

letter sent in 1566 to Pope Pius V, who wanted to free the Holy City from the stain of sin by banning prostitutes, just as his predecessor Pius IV had isolated it from the threat of Jews by placing them under the 'quarantine' of the ghetto. These unhealthy elements are necessary, its author argued, as a way of strengthening the constitution of the body social. Without them and their sins, 'it would not have been necessary for His Divine Majesty to come [to earth] for our salvation . . . , as your Holiness knows, you who, in imitation of the Lord, have tolerated in the world Jews, adulterers, and prostitutes; some as witnesses to His sacred law, others so that there may be wicked people in the world for the exaltation of the righteous and other sinners for the conversion of the righteous.' The pope's beneficence might also bring the body into better balance, 'and in this way you will win over with your tolerance many Jewish souls, as you have already done, and you will convert them by choice and not by violence, not to speak of many evil women, guiding their lives toward a better end'.[6] Jews and prostitutes were as intrinsic to the Christian body social as were the vices housed in Filarete's great tower to the urban fabric of his imaginary Sforzinda.

It was also they who could offer society the most visible signs of its restoration and regeneration as a moral entity. The defaming marks assigned them had two purposes. One was to alert members of society to the danger they posed to its moral health. The long campaign of the Church, and especially the mendicant friars, to attach signs to the Jews was based on this clear principle. As Bernardino of Siena instructed the Florentines in 1425, such quarantine was necessary because 'the evil person is very powerful and will make you evil even as you think to make him good . . . Do not converse with any sodomite [or] heretic lest he contaminate you; similarly do not converse with any Jew since the *Decretals* prohibit it.'[7] It was also the premise of the Florentine court that investigated a married woman accused of 'public adultery' in 1400. When the testimony of neighbours persuaded the judge that she entered 'the houses of many men . . . who did many illicit and indecent things with her, touching and fondling her with their hands, as is done by public prostitutes', he

[6] E. Rodocanachi, *Le Saint Siège et les juifs: Le ghetto à Rome* (Paris, 1891), pp. 316–17.

[7] Bernardino da Siena, *Le prediche volgari: Quaresimale fiorentino del 1425*, ed. C. Cannarozzi (3 vols., Florence, 1940), vol. ii, pp. 15–17.

declared her a prostitute and assigned her the gloves, bells, and high-heeled slippers that would protect the community from a corruption that might otherwise insidiously pervade it. Palmieri believed this had happened in his own day when 'fashions once worn in our city by public prostitutes for their indecent and shameless purposes were adopted by the flower of noble womanhood', who thereby threatened the city's honour.[8] If intended to shame and to isolate, the signs also allowed the society to mark its recovery as they were removed when prostitutes turned to honourable lives and Jews accepted Christian baptism. Both events were anticipated in the sermons they were often forced to attend and in the charitable institutions built to aid in their moral recovery. The need for spiritual transformation and the possibility of achieving it, beliefs that lay at the heart of Christian doctrine, could thus be visually displayed by society's basest members. Prostitutes, who personified the loss of honour, could through their reformation bestow it on the city. Jews, who personified the absence of belief, could though their conversion demonstrate God's grace.

The Jewish population of Renaissance Italy was deeply enmeshed in Christian society for a still more profound reason: because Christ had been born a Jew and his Father was God to both religions. Tribute was paid to that special role of the Jews during pageants staged in 1454 for the annual celebration of Florence's patron saint, John the Baptist. They presented the cycle of Biblical history, from Creation and Fall to Resurrection, Ascension, and Last Judgement, each stage of which was represented in the central square by members of a confraternity, except for one. Moses was portrayed 'on horseback with a sizeable cavalcade of the leaders of the people of Israel' from the Florentine Jewish community.[9] The pageant forcefully acknowledged their unbroken line of descent from those biblical Hebrews on whom God had bestowed his Law. If they stubbornly refused to embrace the New Testament message that the pageants displayed, Florence's patron saint, who had baptized the Jew Jesus, held out the hope of their conversion. This was an Augustinian view of the place of Jews within Christian society to which the Church generally adhered. Trapped in the Law and unable to accept the Spirit, Jews nevertheless had to be

[8] G. Brucker (ed.), *The Society of Renaissance Florence* (New York, 1971), pp. 192–5; Palmieri, *Vita civile*, p. 92.

[9] Matteo Palmieri, *Liber de temporibus*, ed. G. Scaramella (Città di Castello, 1906), pp. 172–3.

protected by the Church as God's chosen people, whose part in the unfolding of Christian history was centrally important. The Apocalypse, which would finally unite the Old Jerusalem with the New, would be ushered in by the conversion of the Jews.

Jews and prostitutes were also uniquely able to provide effective remedies for social diseases whose treatment challenged Christian ethical norms. These diseases struck at urban economic and reproductive capacity, concerns brought together in Florence in 1433 during a deliberation over sumptuary control. In authorizing a new code to restrain 'the barbarous and irrepressible bestiality of women', the city's governors associated the expensive and luxurious dress of Florentine women with their failure to replenish the city with children in accordance with God's command to 'increase and multiply and replenish the earth'.[10] Such expenses so depleted family revenues that men, they claimed, were shunning marriage, thus threatening the reproduction of society. The creation in these same years of the *Monte delle doti*, a government investment fund that served both to guarantee dowries and to underwrite state debt, also attests to the ways in which sexual reproduction and economic stability were connected in the minds of Florence's governing class. Prostitutes and Jews both provided solutions to this crisis of shortage.

The decline in the birth rate to which the Florentine legislators alluded was attributed by mendicant preachers to the sin of sodomy, which threatened the 'disappearance of the race'. Bernardino of Siena agreed with local wisdom that Italy was the mother of sodomy, and Tuscany her favoured offspring. The region's dramatic demographic decline in the first decades of the fifteenth century he blamed not on plague but on a failure of conception. 'Tuscany', he claimed, 'has the fewest people of any country in the world on account of this vice', which kept eligible men from the marriage market. For once 'youths have been enticed by this pestiferous vice, they are hardly ever cured, and scarcely or belatedly, if at all, do they allow themselves to be united in matrimony. If by chance they take a wife, they either abuse her or they do not love her. For this reason they do not procreate children.'[11] In Florence, where a special magistracy was created in 1432

---

[10] Brucker, *Society*, pp. 180–1.
[11] Bernardino of Siena, *Opera omnia* (9 vols., Florence, 1950–65), vol. ii, p. 83.

to expose and punish sodomites, well over 1,000 men were convicted and fined over the next seventy years. In fifteenth-century Venice over 400 were accused and most of them convicted. The lesser evil of prostitution was thought to provide a way of keeping men from the corruption of the greater evil of sodomy before they entered holy matrimony. If this is why Bernardino, who met a sinner at every corner, refrained from castigating prostitutes, it may also help to explain the protection, even encouragement, of their trade by governments. In Florence, as the clergy launched a written campaign against homosexuality in 1415, the government authorized the construction of communal brothels whose pleasures were celebrated by the humanist Panormita in the *Hermaphroditus*, a poem dedicated to Cosimo de' Medici. Since this world of carnal pleasure consisted of mainly foreign women, Florence's governors could still preserve the honour that rested on its ability to protect the chastity of the city's own women. Prostitutes were thus uniquely positioned to keep the city's men open to eventual marriage and the city to demographic reproduction.

Renaissance states also turned in this moment of crisis to remedies that Jews were able to provide. Christian prohibition of usury, uncompromisingly defined by Bernardino as everything that bears interest on capital, made pawnbroking morally suspect, even though it was a service required by the poor. When Christians risked their souls to engage in the enterprise, they did so for stunningly high rates of interest. Jews offered a way out of this moral quagmire by providing a service that Christians shunned. Loan banking fostered a Jewish presence throughout the peninsula as community after community offered contracts of settlement (called *condotte*) to Jews, who were permitted to open banks offering loans at fixed rates of interest. Given rights of citizenship and exempted from defaming signs, they were allowed to live where they chose, establish places of worship, keep their religious holidays, and build libraries of Hebrew books. Economic need encouraged even the hostile republican governments of Venice and Florence to succumb to the allure of Jewish banking services. When in 1406 Florence denied Jews the right to engage in usury anywhere within its territory, its subject towns and cities, whose poorer inhabitants had become heavily dependent on Jewish loans, quickly and successfully petitioned for exemption from the ban. In 1437, Florence, now under Medici control, also established a *condotta* with Jewish moneylenders. The requirement that they open three banks in the city that would extend loans of 40,000 florins by their third year of operation suggests both the needs of the city and the extent of their capital. By the end of the century, Jewish banks had inserted themselves deeply into the economic structure of Florentine society.

Their socially healing powers offered both Jews and prostitutes entry into Renaissance culture. Talented prostitutes might escape the brothel to convert themselves into courtesans, women who controlled their own sexual commerce and found their clientele among rich and cultivated men. Rome, where a growing papal bureaucracy was forbidden marriage, and Venice, where ruling families preserved their wealth by restricting marriage to one or two sons, were renowned for their many 'honourable courtesans' (*cortegiane oneste*). Whereas Panormita celebrated the denizens of Florence's brothels for their physical beauty and sexual activities, later descriptions of courtesans in Rome and Venice emphasize the cultural attainments valued in Renaissance society: a knowledge of literature, musical abilities, and conversational skill. These were perhaps exaggerated. In his *Dialogues* Pietro Aretino mocks the culture of courtesans as superficial: the young courtesan Pippa is instructed to 'sing as best you can a little ditty you learned as a joke, strum the monochord, whack the lute, be seen reading *Orlando furioso*, Petrarch, and Boccaccio's novellas, which should always be on your desk'.[12] But at least Pippa had a desk. Numerous courtesans succeeded in entering literary and humanist circles, and a few became celebrated poets. Through portraits, artists like Raphael and Titian turned the courtesan into a Renaissance icon, not the chaste and unattainable Petrarchan lady, but rather an elusive, almost teasing figure, whose body might be available but whose spirit was her own. Although it was probably not Veronica Franco's poetic abilities that drew a future king of France to her bed during his stay in Venice in 1574, she encouraged him to remember her by sending him not only her portrait but also her poems. Venetian legislators saw such self-creative potential as an unacceptable attraction to other women and thus sought to demean all prostitutes by forbidding them the rich costume of the noble and

---

[12] Pietro Aretino, *Ragionamento-dialogo*, ed. P. Procaccioli (Milan, 1998), pp. 371–2.

honourable, whose social identity was determined by their place within the patriarchal structure.

Jews also rose to new cultural prominence within Renaissance Italy. The growth of Jewish communities in northern and central Italy, swollen by exodus from France and Spain as well as by migration from Germany, Rome, and the South, made Christian cultural inter-action with Jews both more dynamic and more frequent than in previous periods. Many were medical doctors whose skilled services were highly valued in the papal and secular courts. Others were scholars, whose knowledge of Hebraic religious and philosophical texts was sought out by Christian humanists. In Florence Hebrew joined Greek and Latin as one of a trinity of ancient languages neces-sary to the *studia humanitatis*. Giannozzo Manetti found several teachers of the language in Florence, one a banker who brought with him a Hebrew library. Giovanni Pico della Mirandola gathered a school of Jewish scholars who aided him in his search for religious syncretism. On a continent where Jews were being expelled and the Talmud burned as heretical, Italy stood apart: privately and in *Yeshivot*, study of the Talmud, published by an Italian press in 1484, flourished.

Jews in turn absorbed and deployed knowledge gained within the Christian world. Abraham Farissol, an immigrant from Avignon who worked as a scribe for powerful bankers in Mantua before settling in Ferrara in 1471, was able to satisfy an interest in Renaissance geog-raphy in Medici and Este court circles. There he found the maps, texts (including a copy of Ptolemy's *Geography*), and travel accounts that formed the basis in 1525 for his *Iggeret Orhot Olam* [Letter on the Customs of the World], the first geographical study by a Jew to include the new discoveries in Africa, Asia, and America. Judah Messer Leon, who attained doctorates in both philosophy and medi-cine, was so influenced by humanist study of the rhetorical arts that he composed in Hebrew a compendium of classical sources to facili-tate their reception within the Jewish community, whose leadership he believed it would serve. The successful synthesis of scholasticism with neo-Platonism, and of Jewish with pagan sources, achieved in the *Dialoghi d'amore* of Judah ben Isaac Abravanel (known as Leone Ebreo) evinces a deep understanding of the texts and language of Italian humanism. The attempt of this Spanish émigré to engage Judaism in a search for divine illumination shared by all men and nations not only challenged Jewish exclusivity but also attracted a broad Christian readership. The danger that some Jews sensed in such intellectual exchange gives evidence of its powerful attraction. Farissol condemned Italian Jews who converted to Christianity, and Pico clearly intended his synthesis as a means of converting Jews. But their 'conversions' sometimes reveal remarkably original ideas generated by the exchange. One convert from Pico's circle used cabalistic sources to prove the existence of the Trinity and developed a novel theory of salvation based on movement from the inanimate to the fleshly to the spiritual that could be fully experienced, he believed, only with the religious and esoteric understanding to which Christian cabalists (like himself) had access.

Social contagion

The visibility of Jews and prostitutes in Italy did not depend on their numbers. Both groups formed small minorities of the population: no more than a hundredth of the urban population at the time of the first formal enclosures of Jews on the peninsula, beginning with the Venetian Ghetto in 1516. And while moralists claimed that prostitutes numbered in the thousands or tens of thousands, sixteenth-century census figures considerably reduce those estimates. Anxiety about the presence of both groups nevertheless generated vigorous public discourse and encouraged ambitious social engineering projects that left durable imprints, including the word ghetto itself, which derives from the foundry area in Venice where Jews were first confined. Although both groups were from time to time driven to the spatial margins of society through ghetto or brothel enclosure, neither Jews nor prostitutes can be regarded as marginal in a modern sociological sense of the term.

It is not sociology but rather pathology that provides a key to the uncanny union forced on Jews and prostitutes by social critics and reformers. The language applied to both groups was shaped by medical and hygienic discourse. When Brescia decided to expel its Jewish population in 1494, it justified the act in terms of public health: 'While the Christian Church may tolerate the Jews, it has in no way decreed that they have to be tolerated in Brescia; they should be treated as public prostitutes, who because of their filth are tolerated [only] while they live in a brothel. In like manner should those Jews live their stinking life in some stinking place, separate from Christians.' In terms of a medical science that had an imprecise awareness of contagion, their filth would have been understood to create *miasma*, putrid air through which disease was believed to be communicated. Both sets of bodies were also thought more prone to harbour disease. The genital nature of prostitutes' work made their bodies subject to inspection for syphilitic lesions by sixteenth-century health authorities. In the case of Jews, one observer trying to determine the origin of syphilis found its source in leprosy (since both diseases manifested themselves in the genitals) to which he claimed Jews were prone by nature. Since pigs were also carriers of leprosy, abstention from pork only underscored Jewish vulnerability to the disease. He concluded that syphilis must have been introduced into Italy by Iberian Jews recently expelled from Spain, just as the leprous Hebrews, according to an old tradition, had been exiled from Egypt. By such twisted pathogenetic logic even one Jew or prostitute posed a threat: one diseased body might metastasize to consume the whole Christian organism.

A final link in the process of thought that bound Jews to prostitutes was supplied by a long theological tradition that privileged the spirit over the flesh and made chastity an important Christian practice. Prostitutes were part of the parade of sexualized female bodies that had tempted Christian ascetics since the time of the early Desert Fathers. The carnal knowledge they offered made them handmaidens of Eve, who had plunged the world into a sin so deep that only the sacrifice of God himself had been sufficient to redeem it. By rejecting Christ's offer of spiritual redemption, the Jew was held to be trapped in the body just as the Jewish religion was distinguished by rituals: from circumcision and the *mikveh* (the purifying bath required of menstruating women) to the preparation of foods. Christians who sought to mark and segregate Jews were not unaware that they were, in a sense, turning the Jews' own restrictions against them. In first placing a sign on the Jews in 1215, Pope Innocent III noted that he was enforcing the Law of Moses, which required the Hebrews to wear a distinctive costume. Two centuries later Bernardino da Siena called for their segregation and warned: 'When you drink and eat with Jews, you commit a cardinal sin . . . , for just as they are forbidden to eat with us, so we must not eat with them.'[13] Their bodies became signs for the damning carnality of the Old Law when it was not infused with the spirituality of the New.

The usury that financed the Jews' entrance into Christian society also focused Christian eyes ever more fearfully on bodily relations between Christian and Jew, sometimes in clinical terms. Bernardino denounced the 'concentration of money and wealth' into 'fewer and fewer hands and purses' and compared it to 'when the natural warmth of the body abandons the extremities and concentrates only in the heart and the internal organs' and makes death imminent. Such concentration of wealth is 'even more dangerous', he added, when 'concentrated and gathered into the hands of the Jews. For in that case, the natural warmth of the city—for that is what its wealth represents—is not flowing back to the heart to give it assistance but instead rushes to an abscess in a deadly hemorrhage, since all Jews, especially those who are moneylenders, are the chief enemies of all Christians.'[14] To weaken the power of Jewish moneylenders (and to aid the poor), the Observant Franciscans invented the *monti di pietà*, public charity loan banks where interest was to be minimal. The rise of these *monti* in the later fifteenth century eroded the position of Jews, not because they ever effectively replaced Jewish moneylending, but because the mendicant rhetoric that created them placed the Jew and his usury so firmly outside the moral boundaries of Christian society. Informed of the successful campaign to establish *monti* in Tuscany, for example, a humanist was reminded of Cato the Elder's comparison of usury with murder: 'Asked what it is to lend at interest, he [Cato] responds, "What is it to kill a man?" ' If even a pagan saw the nature of the crime, he reasoned, even more should Christians condemn it. Was this an echo of popular accusations that Jews were stained with the blood of Christ?

The height of the *monti* campaign coincided with the first serious accusation of blood libel in Renaissance Italy in Trent, a town that stood at the crossroads between German and Italian culture. At Passover in 1475, a group of Jews was tried, condemned, and executed for ritually killing a young Christian boy in a mockery of the Passion

---

[13] Bernardino of Siena, *Opera omnia*, ed. Johannes de la Haye (Venice, 1745), vol. iii, p. 333b.

[14] F. Mormando, *The Preacher's Demons* (Chicago, 1999), p. 189.

and a blasphemy of the Christian God. Within months over a hundred miracles were attributed to the young 'martyr', Simon of Trent. Celebrated in Latin verse by humanists, emotionally preached in Franciscan Lenten sermons, and graphically illustrated in a rash of printed books and on the walls of churches, the cult quickly travelled the length of Italy as further accusations of ritual murder followed in its wake. The Venetian Senate immediately tried to stem such religious enthusiasm by forbidding preaching against the Jews, but the cult prospered in Venetian territory. Accusations lodged in Treviso in 1480 brought three Jews, 'lamenting and ululating', to a gruesome death by fire in the Venetian capital where they confessed under torture. In Lombardy, numerous accusations of blood libel may have provided a way for communities unhappy with the rule of the Sforza to express their anger over *condotte* with Jews and to demand their expulsion. This was the case in Ferrara, where blood libel accusations in 1481 supported popular opposition to the Este court's bankers, two of whom had recently been killed by the resentful populace. But in Florence in 1488 the government acted quickly to expel the anti-Jewish preacher Bernardino da Feltre and prevent violence against Jews by an angry crowd of boys.

Each child of whose ritual murder Jews were accused was at once the tortured body of the crucified Christ and, by metonymy, the body of Christendom that was being drained by alien Jews. Often formulated crudely in popular verse, this was also forcibly expressed in a polished Latin account of the alleged murder of Simon of Trent penned by the examining physician and quickly published by numerous Italian and German presses. He exhorted the 'magnificent rectors and most eminent citizens' of his home town of Brescia to read his *Hystoria* of the martyrdom as a sign from Christ, 'in order that our Catholic faith, if somewhat weak, may be configured as a tower of strength, and that the ancient infestation of the Jews may be exterminated from the Christian sphere and their living memory disappear completely from the earth'.[15]

In 1555 Pope Paul IV established the Roman ghetto. Although the name derived from the Venetian Ghetto, the purpose was different. The Ghetto in Venice was associated with commercial compounds

---

[15] F. Ghetta O.F.M., 'Fra Bernardino da Feltre e gli ebrei di Trento nel 1475', *Civis*, suppl. 2 (1986), p. 134.

that housed and kept separate from the Venetian populace foreign merchants such as Germans and Turks. In Rome, a city that housed an ancient and abundant Jewish population, the pesthouse provided the model. As a papal bull made clear, the city's Jews were to be confined so that they might be cured of the disease of Judaism and 'make all haste to arrive at the true light of the Catholic faith'.[16] To this end, they were forced to accept the medicine of conversionist sermons. Within a century, Italy was filled with ghettos, most built on the papal model. A distinction had now been made between ancient Hebrews and contemporary Jews. The former were chosen by a God who spoke directly to them; the latter were shackled by a Law first given by Moses and then excessively elaborated by the rabbis. Manetti, the humanist Hebrew student, maintained that God's chosen people had initially magnified the soul over the body, which was merely a kind of dress. Deepening a distinction of his own day that described post-biblical Hebrews as Jews, he reserved the first name for those who lived before Moses transmitted the entrapping Law to his people. Christians claim descent not from Jews but from the aboriginal Hebrews. Christian Hebraism consequently remains the ancient Hebraism of the spirit that comes from the mouth of God. Thus were Jews deprived of their claim to stand as the heirs of an unbroken classical Hebrew culture.

Humanist study of the Hebrew language and its sacred texts, often guided in its initial stages by Jewish scholars, deprived Jews of their earlier linguistic authority. Manetti intended his translation of biblical texts as a tool in the ongoing polemic against the Jews. He participated in the great translation project initiated by Pope Nicholas V that spawned a vibrant collaboration in Rome between Christian and Jewish scholars into the sixteenth century. The rise of Christian Hebraists, however, eliminated the need for guidance from Jews, who came now to be defined not by the sacred books common to both religions but by rabbinic texts, and especially the Talmud, which was publicly burned in Rome on Rosh Hashana in 1553, two years before the creation of the ghetto.

Like diseased and contagious members of society isolated and treated in the pesthouse until clear signs of recovery let them be

---

[16] K. R. Stow, *Catholic Thought and Papal Jewry Policy, 1555–1593* (New York, 1977), pp. 291–8.

moved to a hospital, the Jews of the ghetto were plied with sermons designed to cure them of their blindness and promote their conversion, after which they entered *case dei catechumeni*, institutions that supported them until, sufficiently strong in the faith, they could be integrated into Christian society. *Case delle convertite* provided a similar service for reformed prostitutes. If the apostle Paul served as a model for Jews, Mary Magdalene did likewise for prostitutes. The aristocrat and poet Vittoria Colonna, patron of a halfway house in Rome for reforming prostitutes, requested that Titian paint her the most pitiful Magdalene of which he was capable to highlight not only the Magdalene's repentance but also her sin. It was a sin that became associated in the sixteenth century with the outward marks of contagion. A poetic *Lament of the Ferrarese Courtesan* describes her perilous descent as she loses her beauty and status not only through ageing but also from the ravages of disease. Her pearls transformed into the boils of syphilis, she undergoes the ritual disgrace of display as she is transported through the city in a cart and to permanent enclosure in a hospital for incurables. A papal physician had associated the eradication of syphilis with the containment of prostitutes as early as 1497 when he recommended that the authorities round up and quarantine prostitutes in an attempt to extirpate what he regarded as a contagious and incurable disease. But it was only in the sixteenth century that his advice began to be heeded. In Venice the incurable hospital quickly came to serve as the site for a new centre devoted to the rehabilitation of prostitutes, now identified with a range of transients who threatened to infect the city. After expelling thousands of beggars suspected as carriers of plague, in 1539 Venice's Council of Ten banished all prostitutes who had not lived in the city for more than two years. Similar expulsions occurred in many cities, including the Rome of Pius V. The fascinating, if illusory, power of the courtesan to transport a man had changed into the real and devastating power to destroy him.

The containment and expulsion of both Jews and prostitutes in sixteenth-century Italy must, of course, be placed in the context of a new morality set in motion by the Protestant Reformation and the Catholic response to it, events that traditionally mark the end of the Renaissance. As Protestantism advanced through the Catholic world, it can be argued, Judaism could more easily be perceived to be eroding it from within. As Protestants criticized clerical celibacy and the lack of clerical chastity, the Roman courtesan became a symbol of papal laxity that made the Church more vulnerable to attack. As Catholicism was condemned for replacing the word and the spirit with material structures and rituals, perhaps the Church felt a need to divorce itself from the carnality of both Jews and prostitutes. The model of society as a perfectly proportioned and humorally balanced body which had to be purged of the poisons of disease encouraged, in an age marked by two mysterious, contagious, and often incurable diseases, the development of ideas of medical isolation that would have far-reaching social consequences. Throughout the Renaissance both Jews and prostitutes had been bound into the body social to which they were deemed to contribute vital services. As that perception faded in the sixteenth century, they became more vulnerable to new policies of marginalization.

The economy: work and wealth

Franco Franceschi

Prosperity or hard times?

Economic historians have recently shown little interest in the concept of the Renaissance. The most important debates on economic themes have been primarily concerned with issues like 'proto-industrialization', the role of Italy and its most economically dynamic cities in the creation of a European 'world economy', and the formation of economic regions. Even more striking is the fact that few recent studies have taken up the question of the possible connections between economic and cultural developments that lay at the heart of Robert Lopez's provocative claim that economic recession gave rise to the cultural flowering of Renaissance Italy. Nor has there been much interest in the connections between economic developments and state structures, or in the material and economic foundations of the 'Renaissance State', which still remain largely unstudied.

In the 1950s and 1960s the situation was quite different. At that time scholars investigating the Renaissance economy included, in addition to Lopez, Michael Postan and Harry Miskimin, Gino Luzzatto and Carlo Maria Cipolla, Jean-François Bergier and Michel Mollat, Frederic Lane and Raymond de Roover. And Armando Sapori and Federigo Melis engaged in feisty exchanges on the figure of the Renaissance merchant–entrepreneur. With the passing of many of these leading post-war historians, the debates lost much of their impetus. This, however, was a gradual process, and indeed down to the 1970s the Renaissance as a transitional phase between 'feudalism' and 'capitalism' continued to arouse keen interest. The debates over the patterns of economic development in the centuries between the Middle Ages and the modern period retained their vitality, not least because of Ruggiero Romano's compelling analysis of the causes of Italy's alleged economic decline between the fourteenth and the seventeenth centuries and the increasing attention given to the 'crisis of the fourteenth century'.

This last issue still generates some interest among scholars, but it has been largely dissociated from the idea of a single, distinctive 'Renaissance economy' characterized by unifying features. Indeed, the whole question has now been reformulated, and recent research, focusing on particular areas, has tended to replace the idea of a generalized crisis involving the whole of Europe and all the main sectors of the economy with images of a crisis differentiated by region, sectors, and time periods. The new approach seems particularly well suited to Italy, a land of marked regional differences. Moreover, apart from the fragmentation of the 'general crisis' into numerous 'sub-crises', the very nature and effects of these crises are now understood from a quite different perspective. Many historians now see the larger picture of Italy's economic history in these centuries as a temporary, albeit significant, contraction of economic activity caused primarily by population decline and followed by a period of adjustment during which a number of positive developments took root that made possible a new expansion of production and trade from the mid fifteenth century as population began to expand again in Italy and throughout Europe. This trend, it is claimed, was not seriously affected by the material and financial losses, the negative effects on production and trade, or the dispersion of labour that resulted from the 'wars of Italy' (1494–1530). The very term 'crisis' has in fact been losing ground among scholars to notions of 'reconversion' and 'transformation'. In short, although the older 'catastrophic' interpretations have not completely disappeared, at least from a strictly economic point of view it is now widely believed that, once the most acute phase of economic difficulties beginning in the middle of the fourteenth century had been overcome, the period was, if anything, more notable for its elements of innovation and positive development than for the stagnation in production on which post-war historians had dwelt.

The least controversial issue regards demographic changes. A recent revision of traditional estimates suggests that in 1300 Italy's pre-modern population peaked at about 12,500,000 (17.9 per cent of Europe's total population excluding Russia). Fifty years later, after the catastrophe of the Black Death, the population had fallen to 9,000,000 and the decline continued in the following half-century to 7,300,000 in 1400. It was not until the middle of the fifteenth century that the trend was reversed, with an increase to 9,000,000 by 1500. But there were also signs that Italy's demographic dynamism had weakened in comparison with other countries, since even this recovery left its share of the European population at only 13.4 per cent. The recovery strengthened in the following decades: in 1550 the number of Italians reached 11,500,000 and in 1600 stood at 13,500,000, finally exceeding the level of three centuries earlier. This upward trend did not affect every part of Italy in the same way, and the relationships among the peninsula's regions, cities, and 'urban systems' emerged profoundly changed with respect to the early four-teenth century. The population recovery involved the cities more than the countryside, thus demonstrating that cities continued to be the main centres of economic and social development.

Yet no matter how crucial population change was in societies in which the production and exchange of goods had to contend with limited technological development, it was never the only factor shap-ing economic life. Demographic decline did not automatically mean economic decline, nor did population growth guarantee an increase in wealth. The most fundamental question is the evolution of the relationship between the number of people and the available resources. It is now widely believed that around 1300, while popula-tion growth was still strong, there were already signs that the econ-omy was struggling. Declines in productivity and in the volume of agricultural production were already causing subsistence crises and commercial difficulties. What followed was of course far more trau-matic. If the first part of the fourteenth century was probably a period of stagnation, the tormented decades between the Black Death of 1348 and the 1380s marked the transition to an openly downward phase of the cycle. The mortality caused by the epidemics sent pro-duction plummeting both in the cities and the countryside. This is reflected in the persistence of high prices for agricultural products until around 1370. But, as Paolo Malanima has argued, the situation changed in the final quarter of the century: 'the epidemics destroyed human beings but not land and capital, and for the survivors the period cannot be defined as a time of crisis'. In theory at least, 'a greater quantity of goods was available to each person than before, even if the amount of land under cultivation had contracted and many villages had been abandoned'.[1]

More 'optimistic' scholars are convinced that wages as well as land ownership increased among much of the peasant population, while the prices of agricultural products fell (after 1370) because of the fall in demand. According to Malanima, 'Considering that there was an increase in per capita income, this period could be defined as one of growth rather than crisis.'[2] Re-evaluating what had long been minority views (like those advanced since the 1950s by Cipolla), some historians maintain that the greater economic opportunity created by the population decline benefitted the lower and middle classes of urban and rural areas, who were now able to consume better-quality food and to purchase affordable textile products (see, for example, the studies of Stephan Epstein and Bruno Dini). It also benefitted the lay and ecclesiastical elites, whose appetite for luxury goods now gave a decisive stimulus to the production of works of art (as Richard Goldthwaite has argued). Interpretations that portray the crisis as a 'beneficial fever' pay more attention to economic and demographic than social factors and argue for a long-term increase in per capita incomes and their redistribution. But these claims are not consistently confirmed by the sources: an important point to which we will return.

Three cases of 'reconversion'

Despite these differing interpretations, there is no doubt that Renaissance Italy witnessed significant changes in the geography of economic activities and in the types of goods produced and sold. At the beginning of the fourteenth century the two driving sectors of the urban economy were international trade and the export-oriented

---

[1] P. Malanima, *Economia preindustriale. Mille anni, dal IX al XVIII secolo* (Milan, 1995), p. 203.

[2] Ibid.

cloth industry. The latter included chiefly the manufacture of medium- to high-quality woollen cloths (mostly in Milan, Como, Brescia, Monza, Verona, Florence, and Prato) and cotton cloths (in Milan, Cremona, elsewhere in the Po Valley, in Bologna and Genoa). However only in the economic system that centred on Milan was manufacturing preponderant, whereas in Venice, Genoa, Pisa, and numerous other inland towns (Asti, Pavia, Cremona, Piacenza, Lucca, Siena, San Gimignano, and, to a large extent, Florence itself) trading and banking dominated.

Two and a half centuries later, Genoa and Venice, with their great fleets of ships, carracks, boats, 'market' galleys, and medium-tonnage craft, continued to dominate international maritime trade and the distribution of a vast range of products, from raw materials such as wool, silk, leather, timber, alum, and dyes, to foodstuffs like wheat, wine, and olive oil, to textiles and exotic items including sugar and pepper. Moreover, these old maritime republics, where the manufacturing sector had long been subordinated to mercantile priorities, were now also important industrial centres. Alongside traditional and 'sectorial' activities such as shipbuilding and soap and rope manufacturing, a strong textile manufacturing industry had now also developed, especially in the area of export-oriented, high-cost luxury silk cloth. In Genoa in the first half of the sixteenth century the silk industry employed about 25,000 people and their numbers grew to 35,000–38,000 in the 1570s. In Venice the number of silk looms, estimated at 400 in 1430, grew to 1,000 in 1493 and 2,400 in 1554; the number of people working in the industry was 25,000 in 1529 and more than 30,000 in 1561.

These successes, though, were not the result of an uninterrupted period of growth but of the ability of these two economies to transform and 'retool' in response to market trends and broader political and economic changes. For example, after decades of prosperity following victory over the Pisans in 1284, the fortunes of Genoa's maritime trade see-sawed until, beginning in the 1370s, the volume of its trade with the Black Sea as well as with England, Flanders, and Spain fell far more sharply than did its own population or that of Europe. But the partial decline of Genoa at the end of the fourteenth century was compensated by the expansion of Venetian activity. The competition between the two cities for hegemony in the area between the Black Sea and Egypt was not restricted to trade but involved long and exhausting military conflicts that culminated in the War of Chioggia (1378–81) in which Genoa suffered a military and diplomatic defeat. For Venice, despite the Turkish conquest of Constantinople (1453) and the loss of its colonies in the Black Sea and the Aegean (1474 and 1479), the fifteenth century was on the whole one of commercial growth. Venetian merchants continued to play an important role in the spice trade even after the Portuguese rounded the Cape of Good Hope (1498) and opened the sea route to the East. In the fifteenth century the Genoese began to make up lost ground: although they were now second to the Venetians in the Levant, where they nonetheless still held the important base of Chios, they strengthened their penetration of the western Mediterranean, especially of north Africa (Tunis, Tripoli, Oran, and Tlemcen) and the Iberian peninsula (Gibraltar, Málaga, Seville, Valencia, Granada, and Cadiz). The rise of the Spanish monarchy and the creation of its colonial empire also provided new opportunities for Genoese businessmen. In the sixteenth century they became ever more dominant in international banking and finance and by mid century the annual interest on Genoese loans to the Spanish crown was worth 600 kilos of gold.

The development of the Florentine economy has provoked endless debate among historians, and it too offers an example of the constant effort to adapt manufacturing and trade to economic trends and changing patterns of domestic and foreign demand for goods and services. The economic expansion that had lasted for three centuries came to an end in the 1340s, with a succession of food shortages, bankruptcies of major trading companies (Bardi, Peruzzi, Acciaiuoli), the collapse of communal finances, and finally the tragedy of the Black Death. The short-term result was a sharp reduction in the total volume of manufacturing output, trade, and banking that led to the contraction of the average size of businesses and the disappearance of many great commercial companies.

But if the scale of Florentine mercantile–entrepreneurial activity declined, new sectors and trends also emerged. Until the early fourteenth century, Florentine businessmen had been able to exploit the opportunities offered by the final phase of the prolonged European 'economic boom' and had established themselves as bankers and middlemen in the circulation of goods from all over the world. One example is their role in the export of Flemish woollen cloths and the sale of English wool in Flanders. In the second half of the fourteenth century the Florentines continued to be active in these fields, but they now also created a stable system for the export of cloths produced in Florence, especially prime-quality woollen cloths made from the finest English wool. Partly because of the contemporary crisis in the Flemish textile industry, Florentine luxury cloths made headway in the lucrative international market in quality textiles. But this period of success proved to be short-lived. First came the upheaval of the Ciompi uprising (1378) and then at the beginning of the fifteenth century the city's population again declined. The situation was aggravated by the growing difficulty of obtaining supplies of English wool and by keener competition from new textile manufacturing centres in England, Flanders, Catalonia, and Languedoc. These factors led to a drastic reduction in the volume of Florentine production, which fell from approximately 20,000 bolts in 1381 to little more than 10,000 around 1430.

Here too the difficulties were overcome by a gradual process of conversion to new products and by the opening up of new sources of supply and new outlets. Using raw materials from Spain and from Italy itself (Abruzzo), Florentine entrepreneurs now began to produce a medium-quality, medium-priced cloth that became hugely successful in the Ottoman Empire and especially in Turkey. In 1489 this type of cloth already accounted for three-quarters of overall production, which rose again to 17,000 bolts per annum and was later to climb to 20–23,000 bolts in 1530 and 33,000 in 1572. An equally creative response that developed at the nadir of the depression in the wool industry was the growth in the manufacture of silk cloth. The value of the products of the Florentine silk works, estimated at around 230,000 florins in 1437, rose to 300,000 florins in 1462 and 400,000 by the 1530s.

As is evident from even these few examples, the mercantile, financial, and entrepreneurial elites of the Italian cities were able to adapt their strategies successfully to changes in domestic and external markets. These changes included the expansion and growing sophistication of the banking system, in which international currency transfers were becoming increasingly important; the intensification of long-distance trade in a vast range of low-grade products, made possible by the revolution in the costs of maritime transport; and the parallel expansion in the demand for luxury goods, especially for silk cloths and for works of art. By restructuring and strengthening the manufacturing sector, by enhancing the already impressive mercantile-banking network, and by taking advantage of their own traditional expertise in economic and business management techniques (well evidenced by the emergence of more flexible and articulated types of trading companies on the model of the Medici Bank), the Italian entrepreneurial elites succeeded in maintaining a leading role on the international scene. Favourably situated in the Mediterranean, which was still the centre of European economy and culture, in 1570 Italy was second only to Flanders and the Low Countries for its level of urbanization. It enjoyed the highest average per capita income and boasted a balance of trade that was decidedly favourable compared with that of the leading European states.

The origins of 'proto-industry' and the formation of 'economic regions'

A common feature in the economic history of the three cities just considered (but the observation also applies to Milan, the other pillar of what Fernand Braudel called the 'developed quadrilateral') was the growing importance of silk cloth manufacturing. The rise of this industry presents particular characteristics. It played a central part in the economy of Lucca, whose silk cloths achieved high levels of quality as early as the thirteenth century. Before the Black Death the industry also existed on a lesser scale in Venice, Bologna, and Genoa, and by the end of the fourteenth century in Florence as well. But it was only in the 1430s and 1440s that the industry entered a phase of more marked expansion, becoming stronger in places where it was already established and extending to new locations. By the end of the century, Milan, Ferrara, Modena, Siena, Perugia, Naples, Catanzaro, and Messina were also producing silk cloth, and in the course of the sixteenth century silk manufacturing extended to a whole series of smaller places in Piedmont and the Trentino, to larger cities in the Po Valley, to Pisa, Rome, Catania, and Palermo. These developments have often been seen as compensating for the decline of other textile industries, but woollen manufactures, which had been struggling virtually everywhere in the hundred years following the population crisis of the mid fourteenth century, later on showed signs of considerable dynamism, especially in Lombardy and the Veneto. Even more significant is the fact that the Renaissance witnessed the development in many smaller towns and villages of cloth making (wool, linen, cotton, fustian) intended for regional and supra-regional markets. The phenomenon appears particularly marked in north and central Italy but was not unknown in the South. Contrary to a long-held view, these 'semi-urban' manufactures not only exhibited organizational structures similar to those of urban industries, they also enjoyed greater success where a strong tradition of guild-based urban industry already existed because they were able to benefit from accumulated know-how and from the business networks typical of densely urbanized areas.

The importance of textiles in Renaissance Italy should not cause us to overlook the vitality of other industries. There is abundant evidence of the high standards achieved in mining and metalworking, in particular the mining of iron on Elba, which was then processed in Pistoia and Voltri (Genoa), and in the Trentino, in Friuli, in the province of Brescia, in the Val Camonica and the Val Trompia. Mining was closely linked to the manufacture of armour and weapons, including firearms, in Milan and Brescia. Other industries include marble quarrying at Carrara and the mining of alum at Tolfa (Civitavecchia), which was used in fixing wool dyes and in glass making. Another important sector was papermaking, which occurred in numerous places in northern and central Italy, particularly Verona and Genoa, but also in smaller centres such as Fabriano, Colle Valdelsa, and Pescia. Among the growth industries was the newcomer, printing. Venice's European leadership in this field should not be allowed to obscure the fact that by 1480 print shops already existed in 45 other Italian cities. Shipbuilding was a stronghold of the Venetian economy, but was also becoming more important in Genoa and Naples. The building trade expanded in the second half of the fifteenth and in the sixteenth century thanks to the new wave of town planning in the 'capital cites' and also in provincial centres like Vicenza, Bergamo, Cremona, Pavia, Brescia, and towns in the papal states. Finally, another huge and important sector sustained by rapidly expanding demand from both inside and outside Italy was the production of a massive array of artwork: frescoes, altarpieces, panel paintings, large sculptures, pottery in precious metals, glazed maiolica and terracotta, inlaid, carved and painted furniture, tabernacles, devotional images, embroidery, boxes, masks, and even playing cards. The production of some specialized items (maiolica is a notable example) was typically based outside the major manufacturing cities.

The rise of manufacturing in the smaller towns and rural areas did not result in a revival of the exclusivism that had characterized the communal period, because it developed at a time when the Italian peninsula was being reshaped both geopolitically and economically. Venice, Milan, and Florence were becoming centres of regional economies: consequently, the territories over which the big cities of northern and central Italy now exercised political hegemony became more closely integrated and were organized on the basis of the industrial specialization of their various sub-regions. Even Genoa, whose dominion extended only along the coastal strip east and west of the city, was able to relocate many processing industries in its territory while reserving for itself commercial and administrative management and the more profitable areas of production. Similar developments took place, albeit more slowly, in central Italy and in the South. The reconstitution of the papal state turned Rome into a capital which, in the course of the sixteenth century, was able to incorporate the entire region into a single fiscal and economic system. Naples, at the centre of the 'Aragonese common market', dominated the southern kingdom. Debate about the nature of the southern economy has recently been reopened, with some supporting the older view that emphasizes its essentially subordinate character in comparison with the economic activities of merchants and bankers from northern and central Italy. In this view, the South's economy depended largely on the exchange of agricultural products and raw materials and not on the exchange of money, industrial goods, and commercial services. But others have argued that the capital resources provided by outside operators stimulated local productive potential, one example being the take-off of textile manufacturing in Naples.

Proponents of this 'regionalist' interpretation, however, acknowledge that such developments were neither homogeneous nor painless. Stephan Epstein, for example, who has written a comparative study of Lombardy, Sicily, and Tuscany, stresses that these economies exhibited quite notable developmental differences. He attributes this to the diversity of their political and institutional contexts (the nature and role of the state, the distribution of authority between the state and the cities, between the city and the countryside, and among the cities themselves), and to the differing capacity of individuals and groups to control the system of exchange and hold down transaction costs. He thus contrasts the dynamism of Lombardy, and to a certain extent also of Sicily, with the 'relative economic stagnation or decline' of Tuscany in the fifteenth and sixteenth centuries.[3]

Whether or not one agrees with these conclusions, there were clearly many different ways in which economic regions came to be formed. Lombardy under the Sforzas, and then under Spanish rule, constituted a great industrial area in which the wealth of Milan's manufacturing industries did not impede the economic growth of the subject communities and where competition stimulated a realignment of the division of labour between 'city' and 'countryside'. But this happened in the framework of a territorial state characterized by widespread autonomies, privileges, and immunities, rather than one of centralization, administrative standardization, or the economic domination of the capital and its economic elite. In Medicean Tuscany, by contrast, Florence's domination of its territory assumed a more direct form through an institutional reorganization that separated the ancient *contadi* from the towns by which they had hitherto been governed, and incorporated them into new districts under the control of Florentine rectors. At the same time the population imbalance between Florence and the larger cities in its dominion was exacerbated, and their economic subordination to Florence was tightened. In these subject towns, the manufacturing activities that survived and even flourished in the fifteenth and sixteenth centuries were those that did not compete with Florentine industries: cotton cloth manufacturing in Arezzo, metalworking and weapons in Pistoia, papermaking in Colle Valdelsa and Pescia, terracotta in Volterra, and linen goods in Cortona.

The organization of work

In Italy's cities the range of modes of production in the non-agricultural sector was so rich and varied that the approaches traditionally used by historians often appear inadequate. Scholarly debate

---

[3] S. R. Epstein, 'Town and country: economy and institutions in late medieval Italy,' *Economic History Review*, ser. ii, 46 (1993), pp. 453–77 (473).

actually begins with what should be the simplest question of all: how to define the most common form of urban labour in the Italian Renaissance cities—artisan work. Some argue that the distinctive feature of artisan status lay in the ownership of the means of production, others say that it was the possession of specific skills, and still others claim that it was the small size of their enterprises. These differences are by no means marginal and the implications even less so. If priority is given to the ownership of raw materials, this would mean devaluing the role of all those artisans who worked within structures defined by a merchant–entrepreneur who owned the means of production, as occurred in the textile industries. By contrast, giving priority to artisans' skills and technical knowledge entails emphasizing the specific nature of such skills in comparison with those of other kinds of workers—skills that were no less present when artisans were unable to set up their own shops and worked as wage-labourers under other, independent, craftsmen. This seemingly paradoxical situation occurred with some frequency. These 'wage-earning masters', as they have been called, were distinct from simple wage-earners and enjoyed special prerogatives. In the workshops of Florentine goldsmiths of the early sixteenth century, for example, they worked at a *tavolello*, as we learn from Benvenuto Cellini: that is, unlike other subordinate workers, they had their own workbench, complete with chairs and tools, and were even able to accept independent commissions.

A second type of work organization was needed when the technical complexity required by the work exceeded the capability of a single artisan's shop and called for the collaboration of various specialists. This type of organization was adopted extensively in the textile industries (especially woollen cloth manufacturing) and also in metalworking. In such a system each of the workers employed in the long chain of operations leading up to the finished product was a 'stage' worker, while the entrepreneur (often also a merchant) coordinated the entire process. This system has been variously described as 'large-scale craftsmanship', 'putting-out', 'decentralized' or 'disseminated' manufacturing. Here too multiple definitions reflect differing interpretations, particularly regarding the importance of 'disseminated manufacturing' as a 'transitional' form toward the concentration of production, with implications about relative degrees of 'modernity'.

Beside craftsmanship and the 'putting-out' system a third type of work organization was 'centralized manufacturing', in which wage-earners worked in one place, under the direction of an overseer, using tools that often, but not always, belonged to the merchant–entrepreneur. In the countryside it was prevalent primarily in mining and glassmaking, while in cities it occurred mainly in large construction sites, naval arsenals, print shops, and tanneries. It was also adopted in certain subdivisions of industries long characterized by the decentralization of operations, like textiles and metalworking. For example, the preparation (beating, cleaning, and combing) of raw wool was concentrated in the merchant–entrepreneur's workshop in Florence, elsewhere in Tuscany, Milan, Venice, and Verona. In Lombard cities cotton beating and weaving took place frequently in the shops of the *fustagnari* (fustian makers). In Bologna the spinning and the throwing of silk were carried out in highly mechanized silkworks that assembled scores of workers. As for metalworking, one type of highly centralized production was typical of gold beaters who supplied the silk industry with precious thread: in Florence they worked in the workshops of merchant–entrepreneurs, and in Venice in middle-sized artisan firms. In Milan centralized manufacturing was prevalent in certain large enterprises involved in armour making.

Even from these brief summaries it is clear that the main forms of organization of urban work can only with difficulty be neatly separated and assigned to specific sectors. In this sense a further confirmation comes from the building industry, where we find 'artisans without a workshop': in fact the individual master mason who, with one or more assistants, independently carried out small-scale construction jobs, was at other times part of a more extensive and complex structure on the construction sites of churches, *palazzi*, and fortifications. These often imposing sites witnessed the convergence, at different times and with different working patterns, of squads of workers with all manner of different skills: diggers, foundation layers, plasterers, painters, roofers, sawyers, stonemasons, and carpenters. All worked under the coordination of foremen and master builders with whom they negotiated separate terms of employment and by whom they were assigned their tasks.

In quantitative terms the industrial sector of urban economies was characterized less by centralized manufacturing, which, according to perhaps risky estimates, accounted for perhaps 10–15 percent of total industrial production, than by the prevalence of decentralized manufacturing in its various forms and by equally widespread and varied forms of artisan labour. Despite considerable differences in work organization, economic enterprises in the Italian cities had one very significant feature in common: a high level of integration and interconnection among different activities. Textiles, building construction, and shipbuilding, the making of weapons and armour, the processing of skins and leather, papermaking and book production had in common the fact that the final product was the result of collaboration among numerous specialists and the synthesis of various kinds of skills and knowledge.

This was also true of many categories of what have been called 'pure' artisans, as, for example, in the case of artworks, whose range and importance within Renaissance consumption have already been underscored. The best-studied example of this remains the Florentine one. When Lorenzo Ghiberti proudly wrote in his autobiographical *Commentarii* that he had been involved in almost all the most important works carried out in Florence in his time, he was reflecting this collaborative dimension of Renaissance art. The same was true of painters like Neri di Bicci whose workshop entered into contractual agreements with related businesses: with woodworkers who provided a regular supply of products and panels of all sizes to paint; with goldbeaters who supplied precious metal foils for the backgrounds of paintings and for highlighting particular elements of their compositions; and with apothecaries and illuminators on whom they depended for the necessary chemicals. There is evidence of the same phenomenon from other Tuscan cities and from Bologna and Milan. In Milan, for example, artists decorated manuscripts, supplied drawings to engravers, and produced maps under the supervision of expert cartographers. For some art historians, the picture that has emerged of the real nature of workshop production has been very surprising. Collaboration with partners or subcontractors is at odds with the emphasis on the individual character of the artwork and threatens to undermine the idea of its uniqueness, the basic presupposition for defining it as a 'work of art'. But for economic and social historians, it confirms the difficulty of pinning down any single definition of the 'pure' artisan even where we should most expect to find him. This picture of the urban economy challenges the idealized image of the 'cellular' nature of the workshop and the uniqueness of its products, emphasizing instead the vast network of relationships, often strongly hierarchical but also at times rather more between equals, through which raw materials, work, and money circulated.

The 'real economy' and the guild system

This was an open and flexible system, regularly able to extend the chain of cooperation, subcontracts, and hirings, and characteristic of all social and occupational groups. It is significant, for example, that we find conspicuous differences even among the Florentine Ciompi, traditionally considered the lowest category of hired labourers in the wool industry, differences that resulted from the restructuring of production at the end of the fourteenth century and at the beginning of the fifteenth. In much of the work performed directly under the wool entrepreneur we often find, in addition to, or instead of, the individual worker, partnerships of two or more members that at times became formal companies. A wage-labourer might also employ one or more workers through regular labour or apprenticeship contracts, thus becoming the head of a small team on the model of work gangs in the building industry and obtaining in his own name the contract for a particular job.

A similar picture is evident in the organization of silk winding in Venice. This was carried out exclusively by a female workforce, composed of small groups within which the division and hierarchy of labour were based partly on seniority and experience. The older *maestre* concentrated on organization and coordination with the spinners who provided the semi-finished product. Adult women at their physical peak did the main work and also trained the younger women and girls who normally transported materials between their workplace and the spinning and throwing workshops. Female winders with a good reputation or with particular initiative were able to get themselves assigned far more silk than they and their group were able to process; they passed it on to other women and probably made some money from their role as middlewomen.

Situations such as these indicate that we also need to revise our ideas about the nature and role of guilds. Emphasis on the institutional rigidity and conservatism of these professional trade associations implies that there was little interaction between the dynamics of economic life and the guilds. But the central position of guilds in Italian society and their capacity to survive for centuries challenge the idea that the 'real economy' and guilds were not closely interdependent. This is why debate on the artisan guilds is currently undergoing radical re-evaluation, with growing recognition that, in addition to their primary function of training skilled workers through the system of apprenticeships, they often played a forceful role in the adoption of new technologies and were capable of responding to changes in patterns of production and commerce. We are therefore dealing with institutions that were far from being unable to adapt.

From the thirteenth century onwards, in response to the growing division of urban labour and the spread of more complex organizational systems of work (like 'disseminated manufacturing'), new guilds were being created whose profile was quite unlike the associations of equal masters practising the same trade. Some guilds now grouped together many different kinds of artisans on a theoretically equal basis, although they engaged in constant struggles for leadership. Such was the Florentine guild of Por Santa Maria, which brought together cloth retailers, merchants and manufacturers of fabrics, doublet-makers, goldsmiths, armourers, stocking-makers, used cloth merchants, embroiderers, and others. A different model was that of the wool and silk guilds of many cities that produced for the export market, in which a relatively restricted group of textile entrepreneurs held full rights and controlled all the workers involved in cloth manufacturing. Artisans were normally enrolled in separate categories, *membri minori* with limited rights, while wage-earners had no right of participation in the guilds that controlled them. Alternatively, as in Verona, separate guilds might exist for the different categories of artisans, all under the control of the association of merchant–entrepreneurs. In the cotton industry, the customary model came from Venice, Verona, and Milan, where the guild included both masters and certain categories of workers hired by them, who nonetheless enjoyed equal rights. Guilds thus adapted to economic and social change by subjecting wage-earners, originally excluded from the hierarchy composed exclusively of masters and apprentices, to guild discipline by enrolling them among their subordinate members (*sottoposti*). Furthermore, faced with the expansion of paid labour, which by the turn of the thirteenth century involved both the industrial sectors and artisan workshops where the presence of one or two hired workers became normal, guilds in Venice, Genoa, Piacenza, Bologna, and Florence went so far as to modify the apprenticeship contract itself to permit apprentices to be paid. This continued, albeit with local variants, until the economic situation called for other measures. Such changes took place at a time when it was becoming increasingly difficult to guarantee promotion from the status of apprentice to that of master. Guilds responded to this situation not only by encouraging the practice of shorter, paid employment, but also with a wide range of measures that tended to reduce the number of apprentices and to give preference to the sons and close relatives of masters. It is quite misleading, therefore, to contrast the presumed hidebound traditionalism of the guilds with the flexibility of the 'real economy'. In Florence and Venice, changes in labour relations had the approval and sanction of the relevant guilds. It is indeed because of guild records that we know of these changes.

The distribution of wealth and its imbalances

Throughout the Renaissance, cities in the more highly populated and urbanized centre and north of Italy continued to be multifunctional centres with strong manufacturing and commercial sectors. Estimates for the second half of the sixteenth century indicate that 15–20 percent of the urban population drew its livelihood from the manufacturing of high-quality woollen cloth. The percentage more than doubles (c.30–50 percent) if we include those engaged in all the textile industries. Another 20–30 percent were in building construction and the lesser crafts. The situation was quite different in the South, where export-oriented production was far less important and artisan labour, small retail businesses, and services predominated. These differences yielded different types of income: the prevalence of manufacturing activities in the north and the centre, especially those oriented towards the export market, resulted in a predominance of profits and salaries from the industrial–commercial sector of the economy over those from the agrarian and artisan sectors.

The prevalent opinion nowadays is that, after the demographic upheavals of the fourteenth century, disposable wealth grew considerably, thanks to the continuing favourable balance of trade and the economic expansion that affected both the agricultural and industrial sectors. Furthermore, since, it is argued, the population did not regain its peak of 1300 until after 1550, per capita wealth increased even more. Even if we accept the validity of this hypothesis, however, it must be remembered that a high level of wealth does not of itself guarantee the overall prosperity of the population. The critical factor is how wealth is distributed. For example, the major holders of wealth were the inhabitants of central and northern Italian cities, but the imbalance between city and countryside, or even between the centre–north and the South, was probably considerably less than the inequalities within each city. Some examples: in Turin in 1349, 3.8 percent of those enrolled in the fiscal assessment owned 31 percent of the land, while 57 percent owned only 10 percent. In Sulmona in 1376, 7.7 percent of wealthier taxpayers owned 55.8 percent of the wealth, the lower 65 percent owned 13.2 percent, while just under 10 percent owned nothing. In Florence in 1427, slightly more than 1 percent of the households owned more than 25 percent of the city's wealth (and about one-sixth of the wealth of the entire territorial state), while the poorest 60 percent held a mere 5 percent. One-seventh of Florentine households had no property of any sort. In Tivoli in 1467, the richest 10 percent owned 41.7 percent of the wealth and the poorest 60 percent owned 21.5 percent. In Perugia in 1493, the 2.7 percent richest households owned 28.8 percent of assessed wealth, whereas 53 percent were recorded as owning nothing. And in Bologna in 1502, less than 1 percent of landowners owned more than a quarter of the land as against the poorest 54 percent who owned a mere 4.5 percent. Clearly, there was a stark contrast between the large majority with limited economic means and a privileged minority that varied in size from city to city and owned much or most of the wealth.

One might object that this evidence is fragmentary and drawn mainly from tax surveys more concerned with the ownership of real estate than with overall wealth. Another problem is that such data give us 'snapshots' but do not permit us to evaluate the mechanisms of change over time. Convincing hypotheses about broader developments require a consideration of other kinds of evidence. Richard Goldthwaite, for example, has compared tax assessments with private records and notarial acts from Venice, Genoa, Verona, Florence, and Rome. He concludes that during the sixteenth century 'the rich get richer' and that in the following century 'the level great fortunes reached [. . .] was extraordinarily high even by the standards of private wealth in those countries in northern Europe undergoing the greatest economic expansion'.[4] Among the reasons for this were: the growing use of primogeniture among families of the upper classes (in place of the traditional practice of partible inheritance), the tendency of governments to lighten the tax burden on the wealthier as military expenditures declined and financial markets encouraged government borrowing, and the opportunities for profit that opened up as a result of the new phase of expansion and trade. But the same trends worked to the detriment of the larger population.

After the Black Death, the collapse in demand reduced prices and kept them low until the mid fifteenth century. Nominal wages increased sharply because of the lack of manpower and remained high for over a century. In rural areas this reduced the incomes of landowners and raised the living standards and the bargaining power in agricultural contracts of labourers and cultivators of leased land. In cities employers had to concede substantial increases to wage-labourers, as for example in the case of textile workers and domestic servants. The combination of high wages and falling prices for staple foodstuffs gave poorer consumers greater purchasing power than they had had before the plague, which allowed them to improve their diet and clothing and at times to purchase property. Therefore the hundred years following the onset of the great fourteenth-century epidemics were generally favourable to those deriving their income principally from paid employment.

The picture began to change wherever landowners and merchant–entrepreneurs, with the support of governments, succeeded in instituting measures aimed at tipping the balance of contractual relations back in their own favour (for example, by establishing maximum wages). Mostly, however, it was the population recovery after about 1460 that negatively affected workers. Prices (especially of wheat) went up, while real wages stagnated or declined. Large landowners benefited from higher returns on the sale of their products, but

---

[4] R. A. Goldthwaite, *Wealth and the Demand for Art in Italy 1300–1600* (Baltimore, 1993), pp. 54, 60.

smallholders who relied on their land for essential consumption needs were forced in years of poor harvests to buy what they needed at higher prices. The fall in real wages also hurt agricultural day-labourers, particularly numerous in southern Italy, while greater stringency in agricultural contracts weakened the position of share-croppers in the central and northern regions. By the second half of the fifteenth century the expansion and, in some areas, the modernization of agriculture were accompanied by reductions of the property of smallholders and an increased level of indebtedness of all cultivators. Their living standards worsened and conflicts with land-owners intensified. In the cities, too, the other face of economic expansion seems to have been the fall in real wages, the greater concentration of wealth, and the deepening of the gulf between social classes. Scholars have documented in particular the increasing poverty that characterized urban centres such as Rome and Naples where demographic growth was very intense during the sixteenth century. But income had been diminishing in smaller cities like Padua and Perugia in the previous century.

If this was really the long-term evolution of living standards, it is difficult to challenge the view that the decades following the 1348 plague represented, at least comparatively, a golden age for wage-earners. But why then did the largest number of urban uprisings occur precisely in the second half of the fourteenth century: in Lucca (1369), Siena and Perugia (1371), Florence (1378), Genoa (1383 and 1399), and Verona (1390)? The apparent contradiction disappears if we reject explanations simply in terms of economic conditions. Rather than protests against food prices, wages, or taxes, the uprisings are better understood as the result of a new phase in the long struggle among factions and classes for political control, a phase dominated by the economic and political demands of workers and by aspirations to improved status on the part of the *popolo minuto* that had been excluded from the guilds and denied political rights. These demands and aspirations gathered greater force wherever the development of large-scale cloth manufacturing, with its distinctive system of organizing production, had put a markedly conflictual stamp on social relations. The Perugia insurgency, the revolt by the Compagnia del Bruco in Siena, and the Ciompi uprising in Florence all took place in cities with large concentrations of workers who owned no tools and were dependent for their subsistence on wages paid by the manufacturing owners who dictated working hours and conditions and used the authority of the guilds to buttress the subordination of the workforce.

It is possible that the economic and social effects of the high levels of mortality helped to create a climate that favoured rebellions, but not for the reasons usually invoked. If anything, the greater bargaining power of the artisans and salaried workers as well as the consciousness of their greater strength gave them courage to conceive of more radical actions. It is no accident that, by contrast, a century and a half later, when the same social and occupational groups were confronted by worsening living conditions, they remained largely passive. A limited exception is the Straccioni uprising in Lucca in 1532. By the sixteenth century, the bargaining position of workers was weakened by their own increased numbers. Moreover their militancy was dampened by new and more flexible forms of manufacturing organization introduced by the merchant–entrepreneurs, while the chances of successful protest were reduced by the emergence of more powerful states.

The popolo

Andrea Zorzi

In the thirteenth century political regimes were established in many Italian communes in which the 'popolo' participated for the first time. Until then power had been the prerogative of nobles and the knightly aristocracy, but the advent of the popolo would affect the political development of Italy for a long time and make it distinctive. What was the popolo? Broadly speaking, it consisted of the middle ranks of urban society and of families that were not as old as the aristocratic lineages. It is more difficult to mark them off from those lower on the social ladder. 'Popolo' should not be given the modern connotations of the 'people'. It did not include groups at the bottom, or on the margins, such as unskilled workers, hired labourers, peasants, or the poor. The base of the popolo consisted of self-employed artisans organized in occupational guilds, skilled workers, masters and foremen, small traders and entrepreneurs, small property owners, notaries, teachers, and doctors. But the political leadership was usually taken by merchants, some of whom engaged in long-distance trade and banking, others in regional and local commerce. In short, the popolo was a heterogeneous group drawn from different social and occupational classes with varying levels of wealth and culture and sometimes divergent interests. Its two key components were the merchants and the artisans, and the shifting relations between them determined the political fate of popular movements and governments.

'Popular' governments were not democratic in the modern sense. Like the regimes that preceded and followed them, they represented sectional interests. Participation in such governments never extended to the entire city population and was generally limited to a minority. Eligibility requirements for councils and magistracies included stipulated periods of residence in the city (from five to thirty years), membership in a guild, payment of taxes over a given period (up to twenty-five years), and minimum age levels (from twenty-five to forty for different offices). The evolution of the popolo over the long term reveals certain underlying social trends. On the one hand, families engaged in commerce and banking, or with large investments in land, regularly rose to prominence and adopted the lifestyles and political tendencies of the older elites of knights, titled nobles, and quasi-noble families. Guild artisans and shopkeepers struggled to maintain their influence against the merchants and bankers on one side and the workers excluded from guilds on the other. The former sought to contain the guild communities, while the latter challenged the exclusivity of guild federations by demanding to become part of them.

The engine behind the popolo was the demographic and economic expansion of the Italian cities from the twelfth to the mid fourteenth century, which produced the rapid rise of new families and the movements that resulted in popular governments. The crisis of the fourteenth century caused acute conflicts in the highly developed manufacturing cities and gave rise to loud political demands on the part of workers. Not by coincidence, the fourteenth century also saw the last significant experiments in popular government. The economic recession that began in the middle of the century and continued into the second half of the fifteenth century lay behind the political retreat of the popolo. Social mobility slowed, and, as ruling groups turned to oligarchic political solutions and rule by *signori*, the popolo lost vitality. The occasional republican revivals of the fifteenth and early sixteenth centuries occurred in a context dominated by *signorie* and urban patriciates.

Popular associations and governments

Before they created governments, popular movements emerged and followed certain consistent patterns from the end of the twelfth century. The critical factor was the rise in economic power and status, through trade and manufacturing, of individuals and families hitherto excluded from politics by the aristocracies that dominated the early communes. It was mainly through collective associations that these new social groups became politically active. First were the merchants' associations, of which the earliest were in Piacenza (1154), Milan (1159), and Florence (1182). Then came a proliferation of guilds in virtually every city between the end of the twelfth and the beginning of the thirteenth century. Guilds ceased to be limited to merchants and bankers, as cloth manufacturers, notaries and jurists, doctors, furriers, blacksmiths, bakers, butchers, masterbuilders, shoemakers, and dozens of other categories of shopkeepers, artisans, and providers of services all formed separate guilds whose executive consuls, legislative councils, and written statutes made them in effect miniature republics.

New forms of urban territorial organization also emerged. Neighbourhood associations organized collective responsibilities, including maintaining rosters for guard duty at the gates and walls, enrolment of citizens in the communal army, the preservation of public order, tax assessments, assemblies for the election of representatives to communal councils, and devotional and ceremonial practices. In such contexts individuals and families, including streams of immigrants from the countryside during the great *inurbamento* of the thirteenth century, had their first political experience in promoting initiatives, addressing assemblies, holding offices, and learning leadership skills they would later apply in communal politics. District associations also formed armed companies for defence of the popolo in the conflicts that plagued neighbourhoods living in the shadow of the towers and fortress-like palaces of aristocratic lineages. Popular armed companies were already active in Cremona and Lucca at the end of the twelfth century, and by 1208 in Siena. In some cities their number was very high: twenty in Florence and twenty-four in Bologna and Modena.

Popular movements could thus originate either in these territorial organizations or from the guilds or sometimes from both jointly. Their earliest demands were for the more equitable assessment of taxes and limits on the privileges and abuses of the nobility. In Milan, the Credenza di Sant'Ambrogio, an association of artisans and small traders that took the name of the city's patron saint, successfully demanded participation in the management of communal finances. In Florence in 1224 the communal council admitted for the first time twenty 'popular' members from each sixth of the city and appointed a commission of inquiry into the commune's fiscal administration. Hand in hand with these protests, the popolo demanded direct participation in communal offices. By 1197 in Lucca, for example, the priors of the twelve popular district associations were among the advisers to the *podestà*. In Cremona (1210), Vicenza (1215), and Siena (1222), the popolo obtained a third of all communal positions. In Milan (1212), Piacenza (1221), and Siena (1233) offices were shared equally between the popolo and the nobles. These political victories were sometimes obtained by peaceful means, but more frequently by mobilizing the armed neighbourhood militias and sometimes the guilds as well. City chronicles frequently refer to the conflicts between *populares* and *nobiles* as between infantrymen (*pedites*) and cavalry (*milites*).

The period of popular participation in government was followed in the middle decades of the thirteenth century by the establishment of governments directly controlled by the popolo. This happened first in Bologna in 1228–31 when the popolo instituted a board of elders (*anziani*) as the highest executive magistracy of the commune. The old ruling group was excluded from power, and offices were shared equally between the guilds and the territorial militias. In the 1250s leadership was assumed by the guild of judges and notaries, which was especially powerful in a city where, in both the university and the commune, legal experts had been accumulating considerable experience in the management of public affairs. Relations among the different social components and institutions of the popolo varied. In some cities, like Asti, guilds did not develop at all and the popolo took control through territorial organizations. The guild component was also weak in Pistoia, where organization centred on the neighbourhoods. Open conflict broke out within the Milanese popolo, setting the merchant and banking families against the artisans of the Credenza di Sant'Ambrogio. In Perugia, on the other hand, the popolo gained power through the guilds (under the leadership of merchants), which in 1260 dissolved and absorbed the neighbourhood associations.

In cities where the popolo took power, the old aristocracy was sometimes completely marginalized, as in Padua where popular 'elders' were established before 1236, in Modena (1250), and in Perugia (1255). But forms of shared government were more common, for example in Pistoia (1237), Florence (1250), and Parma (1253). Popular institutions usually existed side by side with older communal institutions, giving rise to a dual political system indicated by expressions like *commune et populus*. Particularly in the Tuscan and Umbrian communes, the older legislative councils were generally flanked by a new 'council of the popolo' in which citizens of more modest status had a voice for the first time. The popular commune's principal governing body was the committee of elders or priors, which became widespread particularly from the 1250s and usually had eight to twelve members representing the territorial and guild associations. The popolo also created the office of the *capitano del popolo*, a judicial and military official whose role was in many ways analogous to that of the *podestà*, and who was appointed from the same pool of itinerant functionaries. The *capitano* represented and coordinated all the popular components, especially the armed companies. The appearance of *capitani* (in Parma in 1244, in Piacenza, Florence, and Lucca in 1250, in Orvieto in 1251, and in many other cities) consolidated popular governments.

Even when they operated within a dualistic constitution, popular governments claimed to represent the entire commune and promoted policies that diverged markedly from those of the preceding aristocratic regimes. Tax exemptions formerly enjoyed by the nobility and ecclesiastical entities were abolished. New fiscal systems included direct taxes based on evaluations of the wealth and property of all citizens. The wealthy were obliged to furnish the cavalry of the communal army, either by serving personally or through cash contributions. In the judicial sphere, popular governments protected their own by carefully scrutinizing the workings of the *podestà*'s court and frequently supplanting its jurisdiction. Criminal law underwent a marked expansion, with the spread of investigative prosecution. The popolo also promoted town planning and great construction projects, including city walls, public *palazzi*, cathedrals, but also new streets, paving of existing streets, and sewerage systems. In economic policy, popular governments strove to guarantee the supply of foodstuffs, the organization of markets, and the protection of commerce. Expanded government initiatives caused an increase in the number of boards and offices and a growth in the daily documentation of public business. Each office was assigned a notary who recorded its activities, and the resulting proliferation of public records required improved methods of preserving documents. Loose papers and rolls were replaced by bound registers in which laws, council deliberations and votes, judicial, fiscal, and military administration were carefully recorded—the original nuclei of the archives in which historians now conduct research. These innovations of popular government have sometimes been identified as forerunners of 'the State'. But it would be more exact to say that such measures gave new vigour to attempts at making city government function better. While this aimed above all at securing the interests of the popolo, it was accompanied by an explicitly ideological appeal to the principles and values of the common good and the *res publica*.

Magnates and *popolani*

Many popular communes adopted prescriptive or proscriptive measures that targeted those they designated as 'magnates', families officially identified by the presence of members with titles of knighthood or by their reputation for lawlessness and violence. These criteria, especially the latter, were flexible enough to encompass the older noble families and the newly rich who emulated their lifestyle. Anti-magnate laws generally decreed the complete or partial exclusion of magnates from executive offices, severe penalties, special judicial procedures, and collective family responsibility for crimes, the obligation to post monetary sureties to be forfeited if they committed acts of violence against non-magnates, and various restrictions in times of unrest on movement and assembly. These laws sought to discipline the behaviour of the more violent and remove political adversaries and enemies from power. In Bologna in 1282, the popolo designated ninety-two magnates from forty families. In Modena in 1306, eighty individuals were declared 'unworthy to be part of the popolo'. Anti-magnate measures weakened the old ruling groups by splitting them into magnates and non-magnates, but they neither targeted the whole of the old elites nor totally excluded from public life even those designated as magnates. Many continued to play a leading role in the armies, in diplomatic and consultative functions, and in some cases successfully negotiated their readmission to executive offices.

Florence and Bologna promulgated the most complete sets of

anti-magnate legislation, and Florence penalized the greatest number with magnate status: 147 families (seventy-two in the city, the rest in the countryside) and 1,500 individuals were obliged to provide 'guarantees' by posting surety for good behaviour. The term 'magnate' first appears in Florentine documents in the 1280s when the popolo found its greatest strength in the guilds. In 1282 the movement created the 'priorate of the guilds' which soon became the chief executive magistracy of communal government. The first anti-magnate measures were passed in the 1280s and incorporated into the *Ordinances of Justice* of 1293, which excluded magnates from communal and guild offices and subjected them to specific penalties and restrictions. The *Ordinances* were reinforced by the reconstitution of the territorial armed companies and the creation of the Standard-Bearer of Justice and later the Executor of the Ordinances of Justice, both responsible for enforcing them and punishing transgressors. In Bologna, laws severely punishing acts of violence perpetrated by magnates were issued in 1271–2. The popolo, led by the notary Rolandino Passeggeri, stripped the nobles of power and in 1282–4 targeted them with special ordinances, termed 'sacred' and 'most sacred'. In 1292 the ordinances were renewed and the list of persons outlawed and exiled was updated. Many magnates subsequently negotiated their reinstatement to the ranks of the popolo.

Anti-magnate legislation was not universal. In Milan, Verona, Piacenza, and Mantua, attacks against the older ruling groups did not take the form of proscribing political enemies as magnates. In fact, there was no anti-magnate legislation at all in these places, which relied instead on judicial methods of exclusion to outlaw opponents. In other cities, where the merchant component of the popolo was solidly ensconced in government, the replacement of the older ruling group was achieved with less conflict. In Siena, for example, the regime of the Nine from 1287 to 1355 was an alliance between aristocratic and popular families with similar economic interests. Although it formally excluded magnates, this was hardly a popular government. In fact, it was distinctly oligarchic: only sixty families (from a population of 50,000) made up the ruling group. This regime commissioned the allegorical paintings by Ambrogio Lorenzetti in the Palazzo Pubblico in the 1330s, which celebrated 'good government' and the *concordia civium* by contrast with the 'misrule' of tyrants. In Genoa, a mercantile–financial oligarchy also came to power in the late thirteenth century when older aristocratic families and newer families of popular origin reached an agreement in 1290 to share offices equally. In Venice in 1297 the Great Council was enlarged to a membership of 1,000 to include 'new men' and non-noble families. The resulting leadership, united by powerful economic and mercantile interests, excluded both old noble families and the lesser families of the popolo. In virtually all these cities the common element was the growing gap in interests and orientation between the merchant families that gravitated towards the old ruling group and the artisans who were progressively excluded from the new oligarchies. This split sometimes yielded short-lived governments by the *popolo minuto*. Perugia experienced the most radical phase of its communal history in 1303–9 with the creation of a government whose social base consisted of artisans, shopkeepers, and labourers. The most famous example, as we shall see, comes from late-fourteenth-century Florence.

The popolo in Florence, Siena, Rome, and Genoa

The most important cities in which republican government survived beyond the early fourteenth century were Genoa, Bologna, Venice, Lucca, Florence, Siena, Perugia, and Rome. With the exception of Venice, where oligarchy was already solidly established, it was in these cities that some form of popular constitution also survived and where the fourteenth century's most significant instances of popular government occurred. In Cremona, Brescia, Parma, Modena, and Orvieto, popular governments lasted for a shorter time and alternated with *signorie*. Elsewhere *signorie* were now the dominant form of government.

Florence has often been taken as paradigmatic of the evolution of communal institutions. However, despite the incontestable longevity of its republican constitution (the priorate lasted until 1532), the Florentine experience was actually more of an exception than the rule. Two trends, only apparently contradictory, mark Florence's development: the rise of new social groups through the second half of the fourteenth century as a result of economic opportunities and social mobility, and the formation of a composite oligarchy that was both mercantile and 'post-magnate' into a patriciate that by about 1400 marginalized the artisans and guilds. This process has recently been described as a 'dialogue of power' between the guild community and the elite. The former looked to the equality and autonomy of the guilds to legitimize the republican constitution, while the latter aimed at achieving a politics of consensus through the control of elections. After the popular achievements of the late thirteenth century, the mercantile elite dominated the political scene until the 1330s, but the guild community took the upper hand in the crisis years of 1343–8, reissuing the *Ordinances of Justice* and establishing electoral procedures that opened the priorate to many new families of modest social rank. Over half of the 265 priors of these years came from 136 families never previously represented in the office. The guilds returned to power once more in 1378–82 and again promoted a wave of new men into government, in part by giving political representation to two new guilds of textile workers and artisans.

In 1343, the popular government faced a huge public debt inherited from the preceding regime's war policy. It first tried to pay it off and then, in 1345, realizing that full amortization was impossible, it funded the debt, cancelling the repayment of principal and transforming credits into interest-bearing shares yielding a modest 5 percent. The great bankers, who had lent the commune large sums expecting both the return of principal and higher interest, lost a fortune. Shares were negotiable, and when their market value fell, speculators from the popolo's mercantile and financial wing bought them up at discounted prices while still collecting interest on the nominal value. The guild government of 1378–82 initiated even more radical fiscal reforms. It instituted a direct tax to reduce the government borrowing preferred by the elite, and, as a basis for allocating the new tax, it implemented the *estimo*, a systematic appraisal of every household's wealth, including land, investments, and shares of (and interest from) the public debt. These measures were vigorously opposed by the wealthier strata and created a rift between the merchant and artisan components of the popolo. The government then reformed the debt. In the intervening generation the merchant oligarchy had increased interest on voluntary investment to 10 and 15 percent. Interest was paid with the receipts of indirect consumption taxes (*gabelle*), which resulted in a de facto transfer of wealth from the bulk of the population to wealthy shareholders in the debt. Thus, in 1380, the popular government reduced interest once again to 5 percent, a measure that provoked deep resentment within the merchant elite and led to the abolition of the *estimo* in 1381. Shortly thereafter, the popular government broke apart as the oligarchy returned to power, dissolved the workers' guilds, and restored the management of the debt to policies that benefitted the wealthy. The merchant component of the old popolo severed its ties to the artisans, who were irreversibly excluded from power over the next few decades. The outcome was an arrangement that combined broad political participation by merchants with a concentration of real power in the hands of a narrow leadership elite.

In Siena the fall of the oligarchic government of the Nine in 1355 marked the start of three decades of more or less broad popular governments. Power was in the hands of an unstable alliance of artisans and magnates until 1368 when an uprising installed a new government in which members of the *popolo minuto* prevailed and families that had controlled earlier regimes were admitted to the council as a minority group. A telling official document from 1368 decreed that the 'the popolo should be united and one body' but then instructed that henceforth the *popolo minuto* was to be the 'popolo of the greater number', those from the regime of 1355–68 the 'popolo of the middle number', and the Nine the 'popolo of the smaller number'. This was the last Sienese government with a broad turnover of power. Between 1369 and 1385, fully 80 percent of major officeholders held high office just once. The regime fell because of military reversals, and in 1385 the merchant families of the old Nine regained control. A Florentine chronicler described it as 'the new government of the *grassi*, that is, the return to power of the Nine'. Thus Siena too moved toward more closed forms of power under an oligarchy of powerful families.

Even Rome, which until recently historians considered a politically weak commune dominated by the lawlessness of the great noble families, or 'barons', experienced notable periods of popular government. The first, in 1252–8, instituted a *capitano* and a board of 'good men' representing the city districts and adopted a series of anti-baronial measures. Subsequent elections of captains, compilations of statutes, and the creation of representative councils suggest the vitality of the Roman popolo. In the second half of the fourteenth century a coalition of the minor urban nobility and popular forces led by merchants succeeded in overcoming the barons and produced a series of popular governments between 1347 and 1398. The first and best known (thanks to the vivid account given by an anonymous chronicler and to Petrarch's enthusiastic reaction) was the 'tribunate' of Cola di Rienzo. Cola was a notary from a lower-class family, and a learned and enthusiastic admirer of antiquity. In 1347, with the support of merchants, agrarian entrepreneurs, jurists, and the *popolo minuto*, he implemented a programme to rein in the barons, making skilful use of pageantry and the iconography and rhetoric of peace and justice. After his fall, the popular government was strengthened in 1358–9 by the creation of the seven 'reformers' or 'governors'. The commune's highest magistrate, the Senator of Rome, could no longer be a Roman baron and had to be an outsider. A militia for defence against the barons was created with the name of the 'glorious company of crossbowmen and shieldsmen', whose leaders shared in political power. In 1363 a new redaction of statutes was promulgated with extensive anti-magnate legislation. Roman popular governments lasted until 1398 when Pope Boniface IX took advantage of the suppression of a conspiracy against himself to abolish the autonomy of the commune and re-establish papal sovereignty.

In Genoa, the fourteenth century saw the successful establishment of a 'popular' government controlled by merchants, but with the broad participation of artisans as well. In 1339 Simone Boccanegra, a wealthy merchant whose ancestor had been *capitano del popolo* for a ten-year term at the time of the first popular government in 1257, was elected doge for life. The office of doge, copied from Venice, replaced the *capitano* and was flanked by a committee of fifteen elders chosen from the popolo. Nobles were excluded from important positions, including the dogeship, which became however the prerogative of a small number of leading merchant families (Adorno, Campofregoso, de Murta, Montaldo). This new arrangement was actively supported by the artisans, to whom the statutes issued by doge Gabriele Adorno in 1363 guaranteed half the positions reserved for the popolo. In 1399 the artisans even succeeded in electing four 'priors of the guilds' who briefly governed the commune. But the reinstatement of the nobles was already under way. Between 1396 and 1413, they regained fully half the seats on the board of elders and other offices. The half of the posts reserved to the *popolani* were now split between the merchants (to whom the dogeship continued to be reserved) and the artisans.

The *popolo minuto*

In some cities the strength and vigour of republican government enabled the *popolo minuto* of workers to engage in protests and open revolt. In Lucca in 1369, in Siena in 1371, in Perugia throughout the early 1370s, and in Florence in 1378 textile workers previously subject to the guilds of the merchant–entrepreneurs demanded radical reforms: the right to form their own guilds, redistribution of the fiscal burden, and participation in political and economic decision-making. In Perugia workers rebelled against the government of the wealthy popolo to protest the rise in bread prices and the grist tax and to call for political reforms. In Siena workers (in an association known as the Bruco) rose against the guild leaders and stormed the town hall. They reorganized the government and took the majority of seats on the executive committee. But they proved powerless against the fierce repression unleashed only two weeks later by the magnate Salimbeni family with the support of the merchants and the other guilds. The regime of the Florentine insurgents lasted five and a half weeks in the summer of 1378. At first the revolution was led by skilled workers (dyers, carders, and trimmers) who created their own guilds, gained access to the priorate, and demanded a series of reforms, including the reduction or abolition of consumption taxes on salt, bread, and flour, the cessation of interest payments on the debt and its amortization over a period of twelve years, a moratorium on forced loans, and the institution of an *estimo* (which was implemented, as already noted, by the guild government that succeeded this workers' regime). At the end of August the unskilled and more radical workers, the Ciompi, attempted to seize power by themselves and required the governing priors to swear an oath to their representatives, the 'Eight Saints of the People of God'. Here too repression came instantly, and it united the whole of the rest of Florentine society, from wealthy merchants to artisans. The Ciompi were defeated, but the guild community remained in power for another three and a half years and enacted much of the programme presented by the insurgents in the summer of 1378.

The workers' revolts of the 1370s did not give rise to lasting rearrangements of power. They marked instead the culmination and end of the movements of the popolo, the last assertion on the political stage of new social groups seeking a share in government. The revolts actually precipitated the consolidation of oligarchic regimes, the stricter definition of office-holding elites, and the rigidification of social and political relationships. The guild-led governments in Florence (1378–82), Siena (1368–85), Genoa (1399–1400), and Bologna, where in 1411 artisans and workers 'without breeches' (*senza brache*) gained control of the government for some months, were the final stages of the social expansion of the popolo.

Reaction against the popolo

Elsewhere the political role of the guilds had already been marginalized. Wherever *signorie* were established, the guilds came under tight control. In Ferrara, for example, where the communal phase was short-lived and a 'popular' movement never developed, the Este actually abolished the guilds in 1287 and later revived them in purely ceremonial form. In Visconti Milan, guilds were restricted to exclusively economic activities and were dominated by the wealthier merchants. They could be abolished at any sign of political unrest, as happened in 1326 when a Della Torre conspiracy was suspected. Although the Pepoli *signoria* in Bologna had been established with the support of the popolo in 1337–9, Taddeo Pepoli turned the guilds into purely professional organizations, limited their jurisdiction, took control over their budgets and the election of officers, and reserved to himself the right to convene their assemblies. In Verona too, by the end of the thirteenth century, Alberto Della Scala prohibited the council of guild leaders from meeting without his permission. In other cities, hierarchies of greater and lesser guilds were established, and the lower guilds were formally subordinated to the merchant guilds.

The pre-eminence of families engaged in trade, banking, and manufacturing (many also with considerable investment in land) grew more marked. The fortunes of the two pillars of the popolo, the merchants and the artisans, began to diverge. Moving upwards were the rich merchants and bankers who possessed large landed holdings, commercial investments, and retinues of clients, and who lavishly flaunted their wealth with their splendid and luxurious lifestyles. The gap in outlook and values separating the artisans from the bankers and wealthy merchants became unbridgeable. Virtually everywhere hierarchical divisions hardened by the end of the fourteenth century. In their internal governance as well, guilds were controlled by elites from within or without.

As they lost political functions, guilds turned towards charitable activities. Reflecting the rise of new religious sentiments and a widely felt need for more direct forms of Christian social commitment, lay fraternities emerged alongside guilds, dedicated to performing works of charity, not only for members, but for anyone in need because of sickness, accident, debt, or indigence. The best known are the Venetian 'Scuole', devotional and charitable associations that operated alongside the guilds. From the second half of the fourteenth century, increasing numbers of hospitals, mutual assistance funds, and benevolent associations were founded, mainly by wealthy merchants, among them the *Misericordia* founded in Milan in 1368 and the foundling hospital of the Innocenti in Florence, established by a bequest from the wealthy merchant from Prato, Francesco di Marco Datini, and administered by the guild of Por Santa Maria.

In the late fourteenth and fifteenth centuries, popular institutions were stripped of the social and organizational dynamism that had earlier made them active, and at times leading, players on the political scene. This decline is also evident in the city militias and armed companies that had protected civic order by mobilizing the men of the popolo against magnate violence. Maintenance of public order had done much to legitimate popular governments, but this nexus was broken as oligarchic regimes and *signorie* struck directly at the militias. In Siena, after the uprising of the Bruco, the government stripped the captains of the districts and the leaders of the guild militias of their insignia and banners and created a new armed force to guard the city that was no longer linked to the popolo. In Lucca, after their rise to power in 1392, the Guinigi *signori* immediately created a guard of 200 trusted men ready to intervene in defence of the new regime in the event of sedition. The dissolution of the armed companies and the creation of militias no longer based on social and territorial representation severed the link between armed social movements and their political representation that had been a decisive element in the rise of the popolo. A similar process had begun even earlier in the communal armies. The citizen–soldiers of the thirteenth century were gradually replaced by mercenaries, and the artisans, shopkeepers, bankers, merchants, doctors, and notaries who made up the popolo lost their military functions and traditions. The gradual disengagement of the popolo from the practice of arms coincided with the policy of oligarchies and *signorie* to disarm their populations. The employment of mercenaries sundered the relationship between the political community and its military forces—a rupture perceptively analysed by Machiavelli as a chief cause of Italian military weakness a century later. Even his own plan for a Florentine militia, though inspired by the Roman model of citizen–soldiers imbued with the values and interests of the state, drew its recruits from the *contado*, and not the city, because of upper-class objections to arming the city's working classes.

Popular ideology and culture

When the popolo asserted itself in the thirteenth century, it lacked a political tradition. Until then political theory had been concerned with the universal powers of empire and papacy and the nature of monarchy. Popular movements took shape in an intellectual framework in which they had no place. The beginnings of popular ideology can be seen in anti-magnate legislation. The Bolognese legislation used the biblical metaphors of the 'ravenous wolves' and the 'gentle lambs' to suggest the possibility of coexistence between popolani and magnates, provided that magnates post surety for good behaviour. The Florentine *Ordinances* drew upon the Roman law definition of justice as the 'constant and unfailing disposition to secure to each his own right' to assert why the *Ordinances* were 'deservedly called "of justice" '. Echoing the Roman law maxim, 'that which touches all must be approved by all', they affirmed the principle of consent in the guild federation, which was declared to be 'most perfect' because it 'consists of all its parts and is approved by the judgement of them all'.

Painted images were another expression of popular ideology. In the paintings that Cola di Rienzo chose for the façades of the Capitol in Rome in 1347, the misrule of the barons was represented allegorically by lions, wolves, and bears, their advisers and followers by dogs, pigs, and roebucks, and corrupt judges and officials by rams, dragons, and foxes.

In treatises, sermons, and chronicles, notaries, preachers, political theorists, and jurists elaborated a panoply of civic values and virtues exalting republican government as founded on the rotation of offices, written laws and statutes, and ideals of peace and the common good. In a section on the government of cities in his encyclopaedic *Tresor* (1260s), the Florentine notary and proto-humanist Brunetto Latini identified impartiality, justice, and adherence to law by both rulers and citizens as the preconditions for a virtuous and peaceful community. In the early fourteenth century, the Florentine Dominican preacher Remigio de' Girolami wrote tracts on justice and the common good in which he condemned factionalism and invoked the primacy of the community over the individual as the foundation of civic life. The greatest theorist of popular government was the Paduan Marsilio dei Mainardini (Marsilius of Padua), whose *Defensor pacis*, completed in 1324, argued that legitimate government required the consent of the citizens and the supremacy of laws over rulers. Only through the legislative sovereignty of the *universitas*, or corporation, of the citizens, or their representatives, was consent (and thus peace) possible. The jurist Bartolus of Sassoferrato, in treatises written in the 1350s, developed the concept of the city as a sovereign unto itself.

At the heart of the popolo was a notarial culture that provided the movement with a political education in law and Roman history. Notaries played important roles in the early popolo and helped define its ideology. Brunetto Latini, chancellor of the first Florentine popular government of 1250–60 (and perhaps Dante's teacher), popularized Roman history and civic culture by translating Cicero. In Bologna, Rolandino Passeggeri was chancellor of the commune, taught at the city's renowned university, and authored a treatise on the notarial art that was imbued with the ideals of a participatory civic culture grounded in speech. Cola di Rienzo's professional training as a notary imbued him, through Roman law, with the dream of reviving the glory of ancient Rome. Chroniclers likewise contributed

to the popolo's cultural formation and memory. The Florentine merchant Dino Compagni (d. 1324), a leading figure in the guild movement that created the priorate and promulgated the *Ordinances of
Justice*, wrote an eyewitness history of the rise and fall of the popolo
between 1280 and 1312. He proudly recounts his role in its early
successes and angrily denounces those who failed to defend the
popolo against the onslaught of upper-class factionalism. Although
the level of Compagni's literary education (evident in his numerous
allusions to classical sources) probably exceeded that of most popular
leaders, his culture nonetheless reflects the popolo's turn to Roman
history, oratory, and civic ideals for its inspiration. This can be seen in
Latini and Compagni in Florence, in the political theorist Bartolomeo
Fiadoni (called Ptolemy) of Lucca, and in the Paduan poet and historian Albertino Mussato, to name only the best-known figures. But the
literary culture of the popolo went deeper still. In Florence the chronicle of the 'Squittinatore' (so called because he participated in the
electoral scrutiny of 1378) narrates the dramatic events of the Ciompi
revolt from a vantage point of deep personal commitment to the
values and aims guiding the *popolo minuto*. Even after the popolo lost
its political strength, individuals from artisan backgrounds continued
to write about politics. Florentine authors of memoirs, or *ricordanze*,
blending personal and family matters with political chronicle, include
the wineseller Bartolomeo del Corazza, the coppersmith Bartolomeo
Masi, and the apothecary Luca Landucci. Artisans from Bologna and
its region who wrote political chronicles include the mason Gaspare
Nadi and the stationers Pietro and Floriano Villola, father and son,
who for decades kept a chronicle of the city's affairs that could be
freely consulted in their shop. Its public availability allowed it to play
an important role in shaping the future memory of citizens. Other
such chronicles from the fifteenth century include those by
the Bolognese barber Giacomo di Marco, the painter–decorators
Giovanni di maestro Pedrino and Leone Cobelli from Forlì, and the
barber Andrea Bernardi, called Novacula, also from Forlì.

Thus, side by side with the more learned culture of notaries was an
authentically artisan culture that reflected the growth of mass literacy
(including writing skills) that reached high levels in many parts of
Italy. This also gave rise to the keeping of account books and business
records, and to the production of handbooks on the techniques of
many trades (cloth-dyeing, silk and wool production, and, not least,

painting) that paralleled the pragmatic business culture of merchants. Each social and professional component of the popolo developed its own form of written expression that contributed to a broader understanding of the common good and pride in the civic community.

Late revivals

The ideal of a broader participatory polity survived to find expression in Machiavelli and re-emerged in sporadic and belated republican experiments of the fifteenth and early sixteenth centuries. The Ambrosian Republic instituted in Milan after Filippo Maria Visconti died heirless in 1447 appealed to the Milanese 'community of liberty'. Initially supported by the nobles, rich merchants, and jurists who had constituted the governing group and financial support of the Visconti, the new republic began as an oligarchic experiment led by twenty-four 'captains and defenders of the liberties of the commune' assisted by a small 'council of liberty'. The latter selected the members of the Council of 900, which met simply to approve the proposals of the captains. The government sought to maintain the network of dominion offices of the Visconti period and thus to preserve Milan's role as the capital of a territorial state. But rebellions by the subject cities, the ever more pressing financial demands generated by war, and disagreements over the distribution of taxes quickly shattered the republic's unity. As tensions mounted, the republic was increasingly dominated by radical artisans and notaries and lost the support of the nobles. Gripped by a food shortage, the government was finally overthrown in February 1450 following a riot skilfully manoeuvred by nobles who opened the gates of the city to Francesco Sforza. The Ambrosian Republic reveals the persistence of republican sentiments well into the fifteenth century, even under a *signoria*, but also the difficulty of maintaining cohesion among the forces that gave it life because of the widening gulf between the elite and the artisans. The alienation was reflected in the evolution of political language. In Florence in 1459, the Medici regime changed the 'priorate of the guilds' (an echo of its popular origins) to the 'priorate of liberty', underscoring the widespread patrician prejudice against the 'vile mechanical trades'. The watchwords of guild ideology (peace, the common good, fraternity, and justice) gave way to a more adaptable and amorphous 'liberty'.

Many of the surviving republics of the Renaissance alternated between oligarchy and periodic calls for a broadening of participatory government. The principal battleground was access to offices and the composition of the ruling elites. The marginalization and exclusion from offices of guild representatives went hand in hand with the emergence of systems of co-option, control over electoral procedures, and the growing recourse to plenipotentiary commissions (*balìe*) that were created alongside the executive boards and often came to replace them. Restricting or broadening participation became the central issue of political life. In Genoa in 1506 an anti-noble revolt initially led to a new division of public offices, which were no longer shared equally between nobles and the popolo, but were now divided into thirds among the 'orders' of nobles, merchants, and artisans. Under pressure from the *popolo minuto*, the revolt even led to the creation of 'tribunes of the plebs' and to the election in 1507 of the silk-dyer Paolo da Novi as doge, the only artisan doge in the city's history. After only a few weeks the intervention of the French army put an end to this last political insurrection in Genoa of a genuinely popular nature. In Lucca in 1532 the revolt of the so-called 'ragamuffins' (Straccioni) erupted when the silk-spinners rose up against limits imposed on the production of silk cloth because of a recession. There were many similarities with the uprising of the Florentine Ciompi, especially in the call for constitutional reforms that would guarantee a more secure defence of workers' economic and political rights. Members of prominent families were targets of violence, and the ensuing military and judicial repression was decisive and harsh.

In Florence, the struggle between proponents of a narrow government of patricians and the tenacious supporters of broader participation was drawn out through a long series of revolutions and constitutional changes. In 1494 the post-Medicean republic dominated by Savonarola instituted the huge Great Council that re-established republican sovereignty. Admission to the council was open to all citizens who had an ancestor eligible for high office in the preceding three generations, and periodic new admissions of citizens without such qualification were also allowed. The result was a roll of

3,500 men eligible for the council. The popolo supported the council, but the elite proponents of narrow government boycotted it and demanded changes. In 1502, a compromise was reached with the election of a lifetime Standard-Bearer of Justice, Piero Soderini. The revived republic lasted until 1512, when Spanish arms caused its demise and reinstated the Medici.

When the Medici were again driven out in 1527, one more attempt was made to revive a genuinely republican government. Here too its form was contested between an oligarchic vision and popular pressure for broader government. The Great Council and the militia were restored. The moderate patrician Niccolò Capponi was elected Standard-Bearer and tried to mediate between popular and oligarchic demands. But he was soon forced to yield to more radical leaders from the popolo, who revived the old anti-aristocratic ideology and implemented a direct attack on privilege and wealth. The radicalized last republic went to war to prevent the return of the Medici and created a large army of city residents in preparation for the inevitable siege. Orations and sermons inspired the troops with a mix of patriotic republican and religious ideals. The republic undertook an impressive program of fortifications, and Michelangelo took charge of fortifying the section of wall south of the river by building bastions and moats and broadening the guard circuit in order to create better defensive positions for the artillery. But all was in vain: after resisting the siege by papal and imperial armies for eleven months, the republic was starved into submission and surrendered in August 1530. Executions, deportations, and confiscations inexorably ensued, and the Florentine elites, frightened by the radicalism of this last revival of the popolo, promptly agreed to the Medicean principate desired by emperor Charles V.

In the final years of the 1520s, Tuscany was the only part of Italy in which as many as three republics survived, in contrast to the constellation of principalities that, excepting Venice and Genoa, dominated the other regions. That they survived so long is testimony to the deep-rooted political tradition of participatory government and civic liberty nourished and protected by the popolo. The establishment of princely rule in Florence and Siena in the middle of the sixteenth century marked the end of the popolo's political involvement, not only in these two cities, but in Renaissance Italy as a whole.

The power of the elites: family, patronage, and the state

Dale Kent

Authority and attitudes: continuity and change

Most states of Renaissance Italy were governed de facto, if not de jure, by a small group of elite families in whose hands power, usually associated with wealth, was concentrated. From 1300, the golden age of the independent communes, to 1550, when great territorial states like Florentine Tuscany and Milanese Lombardy were ruled under the aegis of the Spanish Empire, through changes of regime and constitution, despite recurrent plagues after 1348 and invasions beginning in 1494, the elites endured.

This was true of both republics and the principates (*signorie*) that were once misleadingly regarded as despotisms or tyrannies on the assumption that the rule of their lords was absolute. In fact by the fourteenth century the kings of the Angevin, Aragonese, and Spanish dynasties who successively ruled Naples, and *signori*, such as the Este of Ferrara or the dukes of Milan (in the fourteenth and early fifteenth century the Visconti, and after 1450 the Sforza), could no longer rely on force alone to secure and administer the territories they had inherited or conquered. They needed the support of powerful local families with a tradition of exercising authority and of serving as counsellors or governing magistrates. In republican city–states like Venice and Florence, where government was entrusted to large and rapidly rotating groups of officials chosen either by election or by lot, a continuity of expertise essential to vital operations, among them wars, finance, and foreign policy, was achieved through the counsel of 'wise and experienced' men who, as the Florentine government put it, had 'something to lose or to gain of the state'.

From the ranks of these elites of power and prestige came most princes and leaders of republics. Although their actions and policies were partly shaped by the interests and protests of less prestigious citizens, particularly during the popular revolts of the fourteenth century, and especially in republics committed to a civic ideal of broad participation in politics, it was the elites who dominated political life. They were effectively the creators of the Renaissance state, long, if perhaps inappropriately, regarded as the precursor of the modern state, and described as 'a work of art' by Jacob Burckhardt,[1] whose 1860 study defined the modern idea of the Renaissance. More recently, a distaste for privilege and exclusivism has inclined scholars to focus more on the experience of the general populace governed, and often oppressed and exploited, by the elites. Nevertheless, since the elites were the chief record-keepers of their societies, most of the surviving evidence for this period relates to them and to the images they projected of themselves, not only in political actions and reflections like those of Machiavelli and Guicciardini, but also, in view of the elites' preponderance among patrons of the arts and letters, in the creation of the brilliant visual and literary culture that gave the Renaissance its name.

Seen in its own terms, rather than praised for its incipient modernity or blamed for its social injustices, Renaissance Italy was a culture in which authority—of God, the scripture, law, or a revered classical literature, whose writers were known as 'the authorities'—was generally respected. That God had ordained a hierarchy of authority over the terrestrial world was a commonplace, and government was usually considered the prerogative of those of greatest

---

[1] Jacob Burckhardt, *The Civilization of the Renaissance in Italy* (first published 1860), trans. S. G. C. Middlemore (2 vols., New York, 1958).

experience and wealth, especially since office-holding demanded a degree of leisure not available to all. These prevailing assumptions led to a sense of entitlement among the elites, a conviction that the right to rule was part of their patrimony, to be preserved and defended at all costs, and passed down to their heirs. In a society where government was perceived not as distant and abstract, but rather immediate and personal, the elites were those who had a share—'a piece'—of the state.

The social attitudes, economic values, and political objectives of the elites, and their strategies for gaining and maintaining power, were fundamentally similar in spite of the constitutional differences between republics and principalities, and the heterogeneous nature, in terms of social origins and sources of wealth, of the elites of most states. Elites were composites, evolved over centuries, of merchants enriched by trade and commerce in the urban communes, and feudal lords and landholders of the territories that surrounded and nourished the towns. The distinctive culture of Renaissance Italy was forged in urban centres resembling the *polis* or the *urbs* of the Greek and Roman world, which Renaissance states adopted as their model. But since city and countryside were interdependent, the commercial elites of Florence, Milan, and eventually even Venice usually had extensive rural property. The leaders of the great Genoese clans (*alberghi*) and the barons of Naples combined commerce, public office, and property in the city with fiefs, lordships, and castles in the hinterland. *Signori* like the Gonzaga of Mantua, the Manfredi of Faenza, and the Montefeltro of Urbino, whose power was based on feudal lordship and military conquest of territories, made cities the centres of their states.

Between 1300 and 1550 there were some changes in the style and behaviour of the Italian elites. In 1300, in most states frequent conflicts of values and authority among various economic interest groups, family alliances, and factions continued to lead, as in the medieval world, to violence and vendetta. By 1550, most elites were trying harder, in the face of domestic challenges and foreign threats, to settle their internal differences in the interests of survival; elites promoted ideas of concord and consensus even where factions endured. They sought to exercise their influence and maintain power by participation in the administration of sophisticated bureaucracies, which operated increasingly through the rule of law, rather than by force or intimidation. They competed to create a more civilized image through their cultural patronage, and lived in palaces that were more often opulent expressions of their owners' cultivated tastes than defensive structures.

Despite continuing elements of dynamism within the elites, and a degree of social mobility generally much greater than elsewhere in Europe, the overall trend across this period was towards an increasing concentration of power in the hands of ever smaller groups, as elites everywhere eroded the power of guilds and popular institutions. Within the framework of changing circumstances, and a cycle of renewal in which new families replaced older ones that declined or died out, there was a remarkable degree of continuity. Of the leading families of Dante's time, dozens endured to dominate Italy in the age of Machiavelli. In Florence these included the Medici, Capponi, Guicciardini, Salviati, and Strozzi; in Venice the Dolfin, Corner, Bembo, and Contarini; in Genoa, the Doria, Fieschi, Grimaldi, and Spinola; in Rome the Colonna and Orsini. The fortunes of these lineages might wax and wane; the Medici were expelled three times from Florence before they became its dukes in 1532, and the Bentivoglio, Baglioni, and Guinigi, lords respectively of Bologna, Perugia, and Lucca for much of the fifteenth century, were toppled from the heights of power by its end. But their families retained their prominence in the ranks of the established elites from which they had arisen. However, in speaking of 'the elites', it is important to avoid envisioning too literally a class with fixed interests and purposes, and a consistent will to act. Nor should the elites of the Renaissance be expected to have learned from an imaginary collective experience to behave more as we, from a distance of 500 years, might have wanted them to.

Defining the elites: size, wealth, office-holding, prestige

Modern scholars use the term 'elite' somewhat loosely to refer to those who enjoyed privilege and exercised power in Renaissance Italy, in place of more precise contemporary terms which had distinct meanings in different societies; this makes it difficult to compare the size and nature of elites across the peninsula. Renaissance social and political commentators claimed to know who ran their states, referring to them as 'nobles' or 'gentlemen' (terms derived from the feudal world), the 'patricians' (in imitation of the legal ruling class of ancient Rome), or more pragmatically, the *ottimati* (the best ones) or the *uomini da bene* (men of substance). In states where members of the elites held titles, among them lords, counts, and barons, they were easier to distinguish. But especially in republics, even contemporaries had difficulty in pinning down the truly elite at any particular point in time, and when it came to making crucial decisions about favourable marriage and political alliances, great effort was invested to identify them.

Wealth and access to public office, through which power was exercised, were obviously essential attributes of elites. But social prestige and reputation derived from a pedigree of old wealth and a tradition of influence were also important, and much harder to measure. Fine distinctions are more apparent in the better-documented republics of Florence and Venice. Detailed tax declarations make it easy to track wealth and its sources. The intense preoccupation of citizens with holding offices that conferred honour (they were often called 'honours') and sometimes profit, and which were, as Lorenzo de' Medici once observed, essential to the defence of wealth because public finance and taxation were primary issues of state policy, produced extensive documentation of electoral processes and office-holders. Florentines copied lists of the priors who were the city's chief magistrates after 1282, in order to have a record of the date on which their families first occupied that office; this became a significant measure of social age. In Venice, where the noble class was defined as those who had sat on the Great Council before 1297, families were required to prove their noble status. However, the question remains as to whether every family with a modicum of wealth, members eligible to public office, and some family tradition, should be described as 'elite'.

An elite of wealth is easily identified. Perhaps the most startling revelation of scholarship in recent decades concerns the extreme inequity in the distribution of wealth in this society, as revealed in the tax records of Florence and Venice, and their dependencies, among them Pisa, Arezzo, Vicenza, and Padua. In Florence, of a population of about 40,000 in 1427, the richest 100 households, 1 per cent of the total number, owned more than a quarter of the city's wealth; this was more than the poorest 87 per cent of households, and one-sixth of the total wealth of the Florentine dominions in Tuscany.[2] In Venice in 1379, out of a population of around 84,000, just over 2,000 individuals had assets sufficient to be taxed with loans to the republic; the richest fifteen families within this group (less than 10 percent) commanded 50 percent of its total wealth.

However, contemporaries who referred to the *ottimati*, or *nobili*, usually translated as the elite, were often speaking primarily not of wealth, but of those who ruled the state. In Florence in 1433, 2,084 individuals (only 327 of them minor guildsmen or artisans) from 307 families constituted the official governing class, a much larger one than in most Renaissance societies, since it comprised roughly one in five adult males. The number of politically qualified individuals increased gradually over the fifteenth century until 1494, when the Medici family were expelled, a truer republic restored, and the pool of those eligible to hold high office, and now indeed to attend meetings of a Great Council and vote on taxes and elections, swelled notably, if briefly, to more than 3,000 (in fact about the same proportion as in 1433 of the general population, which had increased to 50,000–60,000). The official ruling class of Venice, whose population was roughly twice that of Florence in the later thirteenth and fourteenth centuries, included in this period 244 families, though not all at the same time. This group was certainly much smaller than in Florence; throughout the Renaissance, male nobles and their families are estimated at less than 5 percent of the Venetian population.[3]

But how many of these men actually exercised effective power? Even in republics in which office-holding was held almost sacred, there were more direct routes to influencing political action, particularly through the operation of patronage dispensed either directly by a lord, as in Padua under the Carrara or Orvieto under the Monaldeschi, or through the favours of more powerful fellow citizens. As Gino Capponi, a leading statesman of Florence, declared in

[2] D. Herlihy and C. Klapisch-Zuber, *Tuscans and their Families: A Study of the Florentine Catasto of 1427* (New Haven, 1985), p. 100.

[3] D. Kent, 'The Florentine *"reggimento"* in the fifteenth century', *Renaissance Quarterly*, 28 (1975), pp. 575–638; S. Chojnacki, 'In search of the Venetian patriciate: families and factions in the fourteenth century', in J. R. Hale (ed.), *Renaissance Venice* (London, 1973), pp. 47–90.

1420: 'Offices are in the hands of more men than ever before, and the state in fewer.' In 1531 a member of the Sienese elite, Claudio Tolomei, citing the examples of the ancient city–states of Greece and Rome as well as of contemporary Venice and Lucca, observed that 'in every republic, however broadly-based (*larga*), in every state, however popular, seldom are there more than fifty citizens who rise to the rank of command at any one time'. The inner circle which the fifteenth-century priors of Florence drew upon for regular consultation as 'those to whom the government of the republic pertains' numbered around seventy. The 'inner oligarchy' of Venice in this period is estimated at about forty families. Moreover, not only was the innermost circle or elite of even a large republic relatively small; public affairs were often settled in private. As another Florentine observer of the early fifteenth century remarked, the city in his time 'was governed more from the dinner-table and the study than from the [Priors'] Palace'.[4]

Most members of the innermost circles of power were notably wealthy. But there was a surprisingly limited correlation between wealth and office-holding only a little lower down the social scale. Of the wealthiest 600 heads of Florentine households in 1427, only 165 were enrolled in 1433 as eligible to hold major office. So about two-thirds of the city's wealthiest householders were outside its ruling group. The match is only slightly closer if measured in terms of lineages. A similar mismatch is apparent in Padua, Verona, and Vicenza. In Venice in the late fourteenth century, although both office-holding and wealth were heavily concentrated in the hands of roughly one-quarter of the families who were members of the Great Council, rather less than one-half of this group at any time possessed all the indices of power and affluence. Neither wealth, often quickly acquired and as quickly lost, especially in commercial ventures, nor offices, whose incumbents might or might not be those who actually ruled the state, are entirely reliable measures of elite status.

The complexity of identifying a republican elite is vividly illustrated by a description of 1484 from Piero Guicciardini, father of the historian Francesco, of the five gradations within the Florentine

---

[4] 'Ricordi di Gino di Neri Capponi', ed. G. Folena, in *Miscellanea di studi offerta a A. Balduino e B. Bianchi* (Padua, 1962), p. 29; Tolomei, cit. S. Bertelli, *Il potere oligarchico nello stato-città medievale* (Florence, 1978), p. 1; Giovanni Cavalcanti, *Istorie fiorentine*, ed. G. di Pino (Milan, 1944), p. 20.

ruling class of those eligible for major office. He considers the relationship of members of this group to the *reggimento*, or current regime, and to the acknowledged social elite.[5] To the highest echelon belonged the 'men of the great families' (*uomini di famiglie*) like the Bardi and Rossi, ancient magnate houses whose members had renounced their feudal traditions to gain eligibility to a guild-based government,[6] but most of whom by 1484 had only 'a little of the *reggimento* or none at all'. The most favoured in qualifying for office were 'those in the middle', newer families like the Serristori, but next to them were families from the second stratum, those 'nearest to the extremely noble'. Among these 'ancient houses of the *popolo*' who 'have a share in the *reggimento*' were the Corsini, Soderini, and Albizzi; others of the same social prestige, like the Peruzzi, Strozzi, and Ricci, who had fallen afoul of the Medici, were 'kept back' by their more powerful social peers, the 'men of substance' (*uomini da bene*), the 'great (*grandi*) of the state'. The lower echelons of the ruling class were occupied by minor guildsmen and artisans who by definition could not be considered socially elite, and those 'who have just gained the Priorate', and were therefore of insufficient political antiquity. Nevertheless, observed Guicciardini, in time 'they will move up and be ennobled by means of their role in the state'. By contrast, in cities like Lucca and Verona the distinction between the urban patriciate and the nobility persisted; families of mercantile and professional origin were never admitted into the upper ranks of a nobility reserved for the oldest families of feudal and military origins. The Vicentine patriciate, on the other hand, although ill-defined and conspicuously lacking in continuity, by 1500 had simply declared themselves by law to be noble.

The continuing possibility of mobility, stimulating rivalry between Florentine families and factions, has been adduced to explain a perceived contrast between the two apparently most comparable states, Florence and Venice. Florence is seen as essentially factious (a major theme of both Dante's *Divine Comedy* and Machiavelli's *Florentine Histories*), despite broad areas of consensus; Venice as essentially

[5] N. Rubinstein, *The Government of Florence under the Medici (1434–1494)*, 2nd edn (Oxford, 1997), pp. 363–72.

[6] C. Klapisch-Zuber, 'Honneur de noble, renommée de puissant: la définition des magnats italiens (1280–1400),' *Médiévales*, 24 (1993), pp. 81–100.

stable, despite pockets of conflict (as noted by its chief chronicler, Sanudo). Recently, closer investigation of these cities' elites has modified this contrast. A fundamental continuity is discernable in Florence, where twenty or thirty families were among the leaders of the republic for most of the period from 1282 to 1532, and remained prominent in the bureaucracy of the ducal state. In Venice it appears that, although the ranks of the patriciate were closed by law in 1297, there were constant adjustments to its definition, with new procedures in the early fifteenth century to establish credentials, and the replacement of members up to and beyond 1506, when the names of the patriciate were inscribed in a 'Golden Book'. The same was true of Vicenza and Verona. By comparison, in Genoa the patriciate was not officially closed until 1528, when to the mainly noble group of recognized clans a few popular *alberghi* were added. In Milan, Archbishop Ottone Visconti instituted the *Matricula nobilium* to register nobles as early as 1277, but later dukes considerably altered the composition of this group; a 1471 list of feudatories in the Sforza state contains some 115 names.

It is difficult to generalize about the Italian states. In the fourteenth century the most prominent numbered more than thirty, each with its unique history and configuration of power. However, the elites of states ruled by *signori*, or wherever ownership of land was the primary source of wealth, were usually smaller, and often more stable, except for relatively rare instances of radical changes made by a prince. Mantua seems to have been the only state in which the elite was defined essentially in terms of each family's relationship with its Gonzaga lords, but the role of the ruler in creating and maintaining the elites of all princely states was crucial.

Some elites were particularly tenacious and flexible, defending their power with a range of resources and strategies. The noble houses of the city of Naples, under Angevin and, after 1442, Aragonese rule were able to reinforce their position independently of their lord through the acquisition of titles, fiefs, and marriages to the kingdom's baronial houses (numbering fifty-six in the mid fifteenth century), whose vast landholdings gave them such wealth and authority over men that at times they successfully opposed their interests even to those of the king. From the mid thirteenth to the mid fourteenth century some fifteen great feudal families of the Roman hinterland dominated city politics. Of these the Colonna, Orsini, and Caetani were also *condottieri* (military captains) who with the aid of their private armies resisted the attempts of the papacy to control them, and instead powerfully influenced papal elections with their support or opposition.

Lucca's elite was mainly of mercantile origins, but a small oligarchy of perhaps twenty-five wealthy families, presiding over large composite clans of families bound together by ties of neighbourhood, business, and marriage perpetuated their power with a stranglehold on the major offices of the state. They supported, overturned, and outlasted a dizzying succession of different regimes. Between the *signorie* of Castruccio Castracani (1320–8) and Paolo Guinigi (1400–30) there was a period of Pisan rule (1342–69) and a republican interlude (1370–1400); the republic restored after the fall of Guinigi lasted another 350 years. Guinigi and Castracani (a *condottiere* from the mercantile family of the Antelminelli) rose above the rest of the elite by exploiting its feuds and rewarding supporters with the privileges pertaining to a *signore*. However, after these lords lost power, their families and also those of their opponents, including the Cenami, Buonvisi, and Ghivizzano, remained among the leaders of the Lucchese elite.

The church was ultimate overlord of a large group of territories including those around Rome and the regions of Emilia, the Marche, and the Romagna; among the papal states' more important cities, which often functioned as largely autonomous states, were Ferrara, Bologna, Rimini, Urbino, and Perugia. The territories of the feudal or military *signori* who ruled them might encompass several cities. The Este dominion centred on Ferrara, but at one time included Modena and Reggio, and the Malatesta, lords of Rimini, also acquired Pesaro and Fano. However, most held their titles of authority from the pope, and superimposed their rule on urban communes and elites that predated and often outlasted them.

The Este, who ruled Ferrara from 1240 to 1597 with papal patronage, owed their durability partly to the support of the local nobility whom they cultivated by granting fiefs in return for fealty. Although Este patronage and court service became the main sources of social advancement, an elite largely defined by lifestyle, behaviour, and reputation, not all of whom held their fiefs from the ruling family, were central figures in the political and social life of the Ferrarese state. The Malatesta lordship, dating from 1295, was eventually overturned in 1498 by Pope Alexander VI and his *condottiere* son, Cesare Borgia, with the support of the aristocracy of Rimini. They had been offended, as Caterina Sforza observed, 'in their property, their honour, and their persons',[7] by being denied expected employment in the armies and administration of their lord, who favoured his foreign clients.

The collapse of the Sforza dynasty under Lodovico in 1499 is attributed to his failure to integrate vassals of the large territorial state of Lombardy, assembled by a combination of conquest and inheritance, into a political system administered from the major urban centre of Milan. The city's elite was a mixture of rich merchants, urban professionals, office-holders in city, state, and church, and wealthy feudatories whose rights antedated the authority of the Visconti and Sforza dukes and who maintained virtually private armies within the city walls. This disparate group was united only by a common fear of popular unrest, and by the efforts of successive rulers to make their courts representative of the wide range of particular interests within the existing elite. At Christmas 1474 alone, Duke Galeazzo Maria created 100 new courtiers. His successor Lodovico also created many new nobles whose power depended upon their personal ties to him, rather than their participation in city government. Consequently, the close identification between private patrician and public interests notable in Venice and Florence was absent among the Milanese elite. At the same time, Lodovico was unable to control the behaviour of powerful vassals like the feuding Rossi and Pallavicini families who terrorized Piacenza.

Issues of inclusion and exclusion: popolo and magnates

It is clear that social and political elites never entirely coincided and that only a very fine line separated those considered elite by virtue of tradition and reputation from those just below them on the social scale, especially in the republican city–states. Periodic challenges to

---

[7] P. J. Jones, 'The end of Malatesta rule in Rimini', in E. F. Jacob (ed.), *Italian Renaissance Studies* (London, 1960), p. 248.

the elites from the popolo, predominantly a mixture of lesser traders, notaries, and artisans, have often been interpreted in classic Marxist terms. However, the urban patriciate was not a distinct class in this sense, because its relationship to the means of production was no different than that of other less eminent citizens who might in fact possess more wealth and hold more offices than some members of an elite broadly defined by these very attributes. This was true of Florence and particularly of Venice, where the exclusion of most new families from the patriciate of Great Council members was offset by the recognition of a less prestigious, but still privileged class of *cittadini originari* (original citizens). While not an elite in social terms, as a group to whom particular offices, occupations, and responsibilities were reserved they could participate as much in government and civic life as many members of the designated noble class. Even after the closure of the patriciate, some *cittadini* with long-standing ties to its members were co-opted into its ranks in order to maintain the numbers necessary to fill essential offices. Similarly the Medici, needing to re-form a government in Florence after their recall in 1512, compiled lists of likely supporters that added to the 'principal citizens' some 'faithful citizens of popular origins', 'citizens who should be rewarded', and 'friends among the well-born'.[8]

The really well-born—the oldest families—were often magnates. This originally feudal class remained prominent, often predominant, in the elites of *signorie* of feudal or military origins. In most city–state republics, however, towards the end of the thirteenth century (in Florence, for example, in 1293) those designated as magnates were declared a juridical class, excluded from major office on the grounds that their warrior lifestyle conflicted with urban and commercial values, and that the loyalty many magnates commanded from bands of retainers attached to their lands threatened the peace. By the mid fourteenth century, anti-magnate laws had become an instrument to punish political enemies, whatever their origins or lifestyle; at the same time, a swelling stream of magnates was renouncing name and lineage to rejoin the political class as *popolani*. In Perugia, by the mid sixteenth century a few powerful clans controlled both wealth and offices; a high proportion of these had once been magnates. Some

---

[8] M. Bullard, *Filippo Strozzi and the Medici: Favor and Finance in Sixteenth-Century Florence and Rome* (Cambridge, 1980), p. 33.

magnates preferred to exercise the influence that wealth and prestige brought in their train through personal patronage and their ties with kinsmen who had become *popolani*, like the Tornaquinci of Florence and their *popolano* offshoot, the Tornabuoni. Throughout our period Pistoia was dominated by about twenty of its wealthiest families, most of them established before 1300. Some were of merchant origin, but many were magnates who were free of the discipline of commercial commitments and obligations, and who, despite their exclusion from office, monopolized property and power through factions based on blood and friendship. The elite was divided from the thirteenth to the fifteenth century by the feud between Panciatichi and Cancellieri. Its violence was untamed by Florence's acquisition of the city in 1351; instead many Florentines, among them the Capponi and the Medici, were caught up in just the sort of conflict that had inspired Florence's anti-magnate laws.

From 1287 to 1355 Siena was ruled by the regime of the Nine, an oligarchy of rich merchant industrialists and bankers from some sixty families, many of whom, like the Montanini and Petroni, were noble descendants of the original citizens of the commune. All owned extensive rural properties and had intimate social and business ties with the major magnate families (among them the Salimbeni, Tolomei, and Piccolomini), who possessed by far the largest share of land in both town and surrounding countryside (*contado*). These magnates also enjoyed a larger share in making and executing government policy than their Florentine counterparts. While excluding them from its ranks, the ruling group of Siena attempted to neutralize the threat posed by violence-prone magnate houses strengthened by armed retainers and reinforced by family connections that extended beyond the confines of Tuscany, and to utilize their connections, authority, and fighting skills, by allowing them to serve on important councils and financial commissions. As ambassadors and military commanders, magnates a played major role in the subjection and integration of the Sienese *contado*. In 1355, both excluded social groups, the magnates and the lesser popolo, combined to overturn Siena's governing elite with the cry of 'Death to the Nine!' Over the next fifty years a series of ever more popular revolutions resulted in an extraordinary expansion of the office-holding class to embrace almost half of the city's population. However, Siena's real rulers remained the families of greatest age and social distinction.

Personal bonds: the cement of elites and the basis of patronage

The element of private interest in the public sphere, resulting from the dominant role in most polities of a restricted and self-interested elite of those with a stake in the state, was both mandated and maintained by a network of personal bonds which obliged families to the defence and promotion of kin, relatives by marriage, neighbours, and friends. *Parenti, vicini,* and *amici* were the triad of associates to whom an individual and his lineage owed allegiance and assistance in all their endeavours. Since even the strongest Renaissance governments were unable to guarantee the protection of rights, privileges, or even security, men cultivated and relied upon networks of personal support that had precedents and roots in both classical and feudal societies, whose traditions shaped the social and political structures and ideals of Renaissance Italy. Among the elites, preoccupied with family genealogies and associations, these ties tended to be more enduring, and acquired added significance as the means by which wealth and authority could be translated effectively into political solidarities, and hence into political action.

A man's first loyalty and recourse were to his kin. The constitution and laws of most states presumed that family units would act in concert, thus offering the most reliable basis for the support of regimes, or alternatively the most serious threat to their continuance. The power of elite *consorterie* had been a major obstacle to the establishment of public authority; the agnatic lineages that replaced them were no longer cohesive military or even economic units, but they maintained a powerful sense of solidarity. Tracing descent through the male line alone, the members of lineages proclaimed their ties to the past through their attachment to family names and coats of arms, and preserved in family records the memory of their collective achievements in warfare, business, or politics. They expressed their distinctive identity by building family palaces and villas, and in the patronage of family chapels and churches. Kinship was not, however, a static force. There was conflict not only between families competing for honour and influence, but within lineages; between households often very disparate in social and economic status and concerns; or between individuals who took opposing sides in the sharply factional politics of this period. Wills and legal actions attest to the dynamic quality of the family, a complex realm of interaction in which fundamental elite values could be expressed and realized, but where disharmony and even dysfunction might sometimes prevail.

Marriage alliances were vital to elite families, not only as a means of ensuring survival, especially in a period where the chief challenge to the elites was probably a demographic one; they also offered an opportunity for the blood-group to acquire whatever it lacked, whether wealth or prestige or an abundance of relatives to assist it. Legal historians have recently heightened our awareness of the myriad ways in which relations within and between families might be mediated by property, especially through inheritance and dowries. Calculations concerning the comparative advantages of possible unions were lengthy and complex. For a prospective husband, marriage with a bride from a well-to-do family, obliged by considerations of honour to provide a substantial dowry, could rescue failing fortunes or position him to extend his entrepreneurial options; her family might hope to offset its expenses with an improvement in social status. Either party to the contract might see it as an occasion to bind political allies more closely and permanently.

These considerations affected members of the elites of most societies, although the consequences of marriage alliances could vary with political circumstances. Often marriages reinforced already solid blocks of associations, but in large republics like Florence and Venice marriages might further tangle a complex web of conflicting obligations. A marriage involving the head of a ruling dynasty might change the course of politics and the destiny of all the other families of the ruling elite. Francesco Sforza's marriage to Bianca, daughter of Filippo Maria Visconti, shortly before Visconti's death in 1447, helped to make Sforza the chief contender to succeed Visconti as duke of Milan. Marriages linking the elites of the *signorie* created over the fifteenth century an increasing sense of a peninsula-wide courtly aristocracy most famously dramatized in Baldassare Castiglione's *Courtier*. The setting of his dialogues was the Montefeltro court of Urbino, but speakers came from all over Italy, including Naples. Although the Venetian and Florentine elites seldom married outside their own cities, Lorenzo de' Medici's wife Clarice was a member of the Roman Orsini, who had long been associates of the Medici family in banking and diplomatic activities.

Aristotelian views of the nature of the ideal society, which influenced the early Italian communes and were reinforced by humanist teaching in the fifteenth century, accorded to personal bonds relating and circumscribing individuals an organic part in the evolution of the state. Dante's influential *Convivio* built upon a passage from Aristotle's *Politics* describing the natural need to extend the biological union of husband and wife to embrace successively the wider family, the neighbourhood, and ultimately the *polis*, the city or polity, since as 'the Philosopher says . . . man is naturally a sociable animal' (*Convivio* iv.4). In most city–states neighbourhoods (parishes, *gonfaloni, sesti, contrade*) fulfilled vital community functions. Initially they furnished the citizen militia; later they were responsible for the maintenance of law and order. In Venice, local groups provided much of the pageantry of civic ritual that defined the city's sense of self; in Florence, parishes were the bases of religious confraternities that performed the sacred plays central to the community's devotional life. In Milan, the influential families of particular neighbourhoods obliged the Sforza dukes to consider their interests in the development of hospitals and churches; in Siena, *contrada* solidarities both united and separated groups of elite families well into the modern period.

Inevitably, then, leading families of the urban elites, with the notable exception of Venice, saw neighbourhoods as the most natural arenas for the extension of their spheres of influence. This was particularly so in Florence, where the *gonfalone* or ward was the basis of the crucial assessment of taxes and of eligibility for office. The Medici began their rise to power by moving from their ancestral inner-city district, where most citizens had long been entwined in networks of patronage dominated by great old families, to a newer ward outside the ancient city walls, where many of their neighbours were from newer and less socially eminent families, with whom they could establish fresh ties of patronage. In Genoa, aristocratic families expressed most clearly the ancient association between territory and blood. When, in the late thirteenth and fourteenth centuries, factional strife, declining economic opportunity, and demographic crisis threatened the stability of many great lineages, they created new artificial clans called *alberghi*, into which neighbours, including prosperous merchants, notaries, and occasionally even rich artisans, were formally integrated. The *alberghi* carved out physical enclaves centred on commonly held towers, family shops, and a private family church or chapel; they have been described as 'the final proof in Genoa of the strength of the lineage as the aristocratic social ideal'.[9]

Authority and power in public matters often derived from leadership of an eminent lineage, augmented by various personal bonds analogous to those of kinship, among them godparentage, membership of confraternities, and 'instrumental' friendships with business or political associates who became honorary kin, described in correspondence as 'honoured as a father', 'beloved as a brother', 'dear to me as a son'. The entailed exchange of favours and obligation to mutual assistance, particularly in ameliorating taxes and obtaining offices, blurred the line between the affairs of the family and the affairs of state. Alberti likened the family to a small city, and described Florence in the fifteenth century as a republic of many families who almost resembled one great family.

The personal patronage extended by eminent men to others less wealthy and powerful became the chief means of mediating between private and public worlds; a great patron's associates in turn projected his power and identity beyond household and lineage into the larger sphere of the city and its government. The patriarchal state, modelled on the lineage, was exalted and even sanctified by its resemblance to the heavenly order, with God the father at its apex. Cosimo de' Medici, the extraordinarily wealthy banker who was Florence's leading citizen between 1434 and his death in 1464, was *paterfamilias* of a large Florentine lineage of some twenty-seven households in 1427. He extended his patriarchal protection to a multitude of friends and supporters, and after his death was honoured by his city's government as its *pater patriae*. While historians have judged patronage contrary to modern ideals of objectively just government, and Renaissance citizens also recognized that the fulfillment of obligations to bestow personal favours might on occasion interfere with justice and conflict with the common good, the acknowledgement of such obligations was a natural consequence of honouring the most sacred loyalties to family and to the divine order as manifested on earth. In the patron's role as intercessor for his clients, his

---

[9] D. O. Hughes, 'Domestic ideals and social behavior: evidence from medieval Genoa', in C. E. Rosenberg (ed.), *The Family in History* (Philadelphia, 1975), p. 124.

raccomandati, men saw a parallel with the intercession of the Virgin and other saints on behalf of sinners facing judgement in the next world; saints were described as *avvocati*, and their devotees as *raccomandati* at the heavenly court. As Giovanni Tornabuoni wrote to his nephew and patron Lorenzo de' Medici: 'I have God in Heaven, and your Magnificence here on earth.' Another client referred to his benefactor as 'Father, Son and Holy Ghost'.[10]

Patronage, politics, and the state

The reliance of Renaissance elites on government through patronage has been seen as inhibiting the rise of the modern, centralized, bureaucratic, rational state, traditionally considered one of the significant developments of this period. But in fact the gift of public offices, regarded as fiscal relief or reward for personal allegiance, was an essential support of the governing elites of both republics and *signorie*, and a persistent element in the evolution of the new 'refeudalized' territorial states of the later fifteenth and sixteenth centuries. As Giorgio Chittolini pointed out in an imaginative re-evaluation of the public, the private, and the state: 'Structures of aggregation, both horizontal and vertical, such as clans, kin groups, courtly circles, factions, and parties', which form part of systems of patronage and clientage, 'are private in that they are not always formalized like public institutions', but they are in fact 'vital and robust nuclei of the political organization of society' whose essential influence in 'shaping political strategies' needs to be recognized. Institutional history cannot be separated from politics in this wider context; 'private' and 'public' elements are in constant interplay in the operation of the state.[11] Renaissance citizens thought of the latter in terms of 'authority',

---

[10] M. Bullard, 'Heroes and their workshops: Medici patronage and the problem of shared agency', *Journal of Medieval and Renaissance Studies*, 24 (1994), p. 187; F. W. Kent, 'Patron–client networks in Renaissance Florence and the emergence of Lorenzo as "maestro della bottega" ', in B. Toscani (ed.), *Lorenzo de' Medici: New Perspectives* (New York, 1994), p. 286.

[11] G. Chittolini, 'The "private," the "public," the state', in J. Kirshner (ed.), *The Origins of the State in Italy, 1300–1600* (Chicago, 1995), pp. 40–1.

an attribute not so much of institutions, as of the persons who administered them.

Did elites then govern entirely in their own interests? They were heavily committed to self-defence, but this necessitated accommodating and embracing alternative concerns. For example, while the Florentine patriciate reacted with fear and loathing to the popular challenge of the Ciompi revolt of 1378, a desire to placate popular sensibilities may have contributed to the continuing fidelity of an increasingly fixed fifteenth-century elite to the basic structure of the guild-based constitution of 1282, and to communal ideals of the common good it enshrined. The Venetian patriciate was not, in accordance with the 'myth' it strenuously promulgated to shore up its own authority, preternaturally patriotic or wise, but its members were capable of serious sacrifices in the interest of the republic. So was the Florentine elite, who in 1427 adopted the Catasto, a more equitable system of taxation, even though it was against the interests of the rich. Leading fifteenth-century statesmen, among them the Albizzi and the Medici, admitted governing in the interests of their friends and supporters, but they were also deeply devoted to the honour and advancement of their city. When, in Lorenzo de' Medici's latter years, the 'principal citizens' were perceived by both patricians and *popolani* as exploiting the state they governed, the stage was set for the overthrow of the regime; this was accomplished in 1494, two years after Lorenzo's death, when the French invaded Florence.

Renaissance patricians' perceptions of themselves as guardians of their communities were increasingly emphasized in civic rituals that expressed their aspirations and values and represented their authority. The fusion of secular and spiritual in public celebrations reinforced the power of the ruling elites with the suggestion that their governance both effected and was underwritten by the will of God. By the fifteenth century, the widespread employment of classical symbolism, evoking the admired rulers of antiquity and inviting a comparison with Renaissance elites, invoked yet another authority in the process of their legitimation.

Governments and governance

John M. Najemy

Renaissance Italy contained an array of governments. The South was a nominally unified kingdom, but sometimes functioned as a loose federation of noble baronies. In the centre, the papal state was a composite of cities and territories mostly governed by local lords and communes. Though popes made extravagant claims to universal temporal and spiritual authority, they could not even contain the Roman nobility. The centre and north (Venice excepted) were officially part of the Holy Roman Empire, but by 1200 nearly every city was an independent commune. After 1300 republican government survived in Venice, Florence, Siena, Lucca, Perugia, and intermittently in Bologna and Genoa. But many communes were supplanted by lordships, or *signorie*, which first emerged as unofficial regimes of factional leaders and later gained legitimacy as hereditary dynasties: the Este in Ferrara, Visconti in Milan, Della Scala in Verona, Gonzaga in Mantua, Carrara in Padua, Montefeltro in Urbino, and a host of lesser ruling families, especially in the Romagna. By the fifteenth century most cities were absorbed into the territorial dominions of the emerging regional powers: Milan, Venice, Florence, and the papal state.

In 1300 most Italians were subject to a confusing variety of overlapping and conflicting governmental authorities. At the local level guilds regulated professional or economic activities and sometimes functioned as vehicles of political representation. Family-based factions often controlled neighbourhoods and even entire cities. Rural nobles exercised semi-feudal jurisdiction in their territories.

Urban communes legislated, exercised civil and criminal jurisdiction, collected taxes, and required military service. In theory, the empire authorized all jurisdictions, licensed notaries, and exercised supreme overlordship. And the Church claimed jurisdiction not only over clergy but also over the moral and economic affairs of laypersons. From this bewildering range of 'governments' the communes and *signorie* had gradually emerged as the centres of real power, absorbing the functions of guilds, constraining noble factions, limiting interference from the papacy and pushing aside the last vestiges of imperial power. The particular form of government in each city depended on relations between the elites (merchant bankers and/or landed nobility) and the popolo, the middle classes of guildsmen, notaries, local merchants, and artisans whose popular governments regularly challenged elite power. Many communes alternated between popular and oligarchic republican governments, and the struggle between them was usually in the background of the rise of the *signori.*

Republics

Older idealizations of the communes as incubators of democracy and equality gave way decades ago to a debunking of the 'myth of the commune'. Many historians now regard the independent communes as unstable because of their tumultuous social inequalities: dominance by elites and the political marginalization of the labouring classes. Critics of the 'myth' claim that the *signorie* at least provided stable government and social peace. While no doubt an important corrective, in some hands this revision has obscured the achievements of communal governments. As Machiavelli argued in the *Discourses*, the absence of social conflict does not ensure good government; competition between classes can in fact safeguard liberty.

A basic principle of communal government was the separation of legislative and executive functions, the former entrusted to councils ranging in size from dozens to hundreds of members, the latter to smaller committees of consuls, elders, or priors elected for short terms with powers strictly defined by the legislative councils. Executive committees oversaw the day-to-day business of administration, finance, military affairs, and diplomacy. Executive committees normally had the exclusive right to initiate legislation (Genoa, where the councils also did so, was a notable exception), but proposals became law only when approved by the larger councils. Unlike medieval monarchies, in which law derived either from immemorial custom or the will of the prince, the Italian communes created statutory law through representative citizen councils.

But nowhere did participation extend to the entire population. Women, clergy, and the working classes (except in revolutionary situations) were excluded. The body of citizens eligible to hold office depended on complex electoral systems sometimes involving representatives of guilds and neighbourhoods, and sometimes large appointed voting councils. In Florence the governing committee of the priorate was instituted by the popular movement in 1282, but only in 1328–9 were stable procedures for selecting its members devised. Every few years, several thousand citizens were nominated and voted on, one by one, in a 'scrutiny' by a large ad hoc council. The names of successful nominees were placed in pouches from which they were drawn by lot. Short terms and prohibitions against immediate re-election ensured that the office-holding class was large and socially diverse. By 1400 nominations reached 6,000, and those approved eventually exceeded 2,000. Not all eligibles actually held office, but between 1282 and 1400 members of more than 1,350 families shared (albeit very unequally) nearly 5,700 available positions. After the 1380s, however, complex controls allowed the emergence of a narrow leadership elite, and in 1434 the new Medici regime began handpicking office-holders. Separate committees administered Florence's revenues, treasury, funded public debt, communal property, construction projects, and much else. At any time hundreds of citizens, and over a generation several thousand, held offices, more still if guild officials are counted. Such numbers meant that the political class always included representatives of both the popolo and the elite families. A high rate of social mobility, especially in the fourteenth century, meant the regular inclusion of new families. For more than a century, elite and popolo competed within these institutions for control over government, until the elite established an oligarchy around 1400.

Venice, alone among the republics, circumscribed a closed and ultimately hereditary 'nobility' whose members constituted the Great Council and had the exclusive right to hold major executive offices.

But the class of nobles was large and kept increasing, despite the formal 'closing' of the Council that occurred in stages beginning in 1297. During the fourteenth century it consisted of approximately 1,000 members (from 100–150 families), and over 2,000 in the fifteenth. Beneath the nobles were the so-called 'citizens', eligible only for administrative positions. Another unusual feature of Venetian government was the doge, elected for life as the nominal head of government and assisted by a six-member ducal council. Although their constitutional powers had been limited long before 1300, forceful doges with substantial followings could still exercise considerable influence. Between Venice's Great Council and its quasi-princely head of state, real power rested with two bodies: the Senate, consisting of some 300 members, and its inner steering committee, or *collegio*; and the Council of Ten, which handled crimes against the state. Other influential offices included the appeals court of the Forty, the Communal Attorneys with jurisdiction over the conduct of officeholders, and the Procurators of Saint Mark, who controlled the republic's finances and administered church property, wills, and guardianships of minors. Other committees administered justice, supervised the guilds and the church, handled public finance, and, not least, Venice's fleets and far-flung maritime empire. Already by 1300 Venice's government included at least 500 posts, and over the next two centuries citizen committees multiplied, as they did in Florence, as governmental functions expanded. Venice acquired a reputation for stability that made it an object of admiration and emulation. The Genoese began electing doges in 1339, and after banishing the Medici Florence instituted a Great Council (1494) and a doge-like lifetime chief executive (1502).

Not since antiquity had cities claimed the right to institute their own governments and make law for themselves without authorization from a superior sovereign power. Medieval political thought assumed that jurisdiction had to be delegated by imperial or royal authority, and even in Italy some contemporaries rejected the legitimacy of the communes. In his *Monarchia* (*c*.1314) Dante argued that all legitimate secular authority derived exclusively from the Holy Roman Emperor. But other theorists reflected on the similarity of the communes to the ancient city–states whose theoretical foundations they absorbed from Aristotle's *Politics* and the defenders of the Roman republic, Livy, Sallust, and Cicero. The communes seemed living examples of ancient ideas about the state as a product of the 'coming together' that Cicero, like Aristotle, saw as a 'social instinct natural to man', and about citizenship as active participation under law and dedication to the common welfare. Early theorists who defended the legitimacy and sovereignty of the communes with this prestigious arsenal of authorities included the Florentine Dominican Remigio de' Girolami (d. 1319); Bartolomeo (called Tolomeo, or Ptolemy) of Lucca (d. 1327); the influential jurist Bartolus of Sassoferrato (d. 1357); his successor, the jurist Baldus de Ubaldis (d. 1400); and, above all, Marsilius of Padua (d. 1343), whose *Defender of Peace* (1324) located sovereignty in the 'people, or the legal corporation [*universitas*] of the citizens', to which he attributed exclusive authority to make law and enforce obedience. The executive, or 'ruling part' of the state, whether a civic magistracy or a single person, must always be subject to laws approved by the people or their representatives. According to Marsilius, consent and election are the fundamental criteria of legitimate governments. Marsilius defended the communes against both ecclesiastical interference (the Church, he said, should be restricted to its pastoral and sacramental functions) and the *signori*. Agreeing with Aristotle that 'the state is a community of free men', he declared that 'every citizen must be free and not undergo another's despotism, that is, slavish dominion' (1.12.6).

Marsilius's citizen was a speaking participant in his city's government and political life. Proposals had to be put before the council so that 'if any citizen thinks that something should be added, subtracted, changed or completely rejected, he can say so' (1.13.8). Communal governments, needing the councils' approval of their policies, especially tax bills, had to listen to at least some of their citizens. Because Florentine councils, which often rejected tax bills, voted but did not debate, the executive priorate regularly convoked *pratiche* of leading citizens to hear their views. In other republics, debates took place in the legislative assemblies: in Venice's Great Council and Senate, and in Genoa in ad hoc councils in which speakers had a remarkable degree of freedom to propose measures and express their views before voting. The sheer amount of political speech that occurred in republics, even oligarchic ones, sharply distinguished them from *signorie*.

Signorie

If the intellectual defence of the communes seemed secure by the first half of the fourteenth century (when, ironically, many of them were yielding to signorial regimes) defending the legitimacy of the *signori* was more difficult, at least in the early stages when they lacked titles. Although a guest in exile of the lord of Verona, Dante complained that 'the cities of Italy are all full of tyrants' (*Purgatorio* vi.124–5). Bartolus began his treatise *On the Tyrant* by underscoring the 'treachery of tyranny swelling its might'. He was willing, 'with God's help', to take up the 'chilling and horrifying subject of the perverse nature of tyranny', so that 'all may be able to rid themselves utterly of . . . [this] horrendous evil, namely, the slavery of tyrannical rule' and its 'stern and unbridled governance' and 'rejoice together in the sweetness of . . . liberty'.[1] When in the 1350s Petrarch went to live in Milan, he was criticized for cosying up to the Visconti 'tyrants'. His self-defence was a sign of the growing acceptance of the *signori*: his hosts were not tyrants, he replied to a critic, but 'leaders of their homeland'.[2] In the 1370s he penned a long letter on good rulership to another *signore* whose hospitality he accepted, Francesco Carrara of Padua, lauding him as a model ruler who governed his subjects as a loving father raises his children.

Modern historians have tempered the harsh judgements that once damned the *signori* as tyrants (without necessarily seeing them as benevolent fathers), and it is no longer fashionable to call them despots. At first *signori* were leaders of factions victorious in the endemic fighting within elites. In Milan the Visconti led a faction of the feudal nobility in a struggle over many decades against the rival Della Torre faction. In Ferrara the Este *signoria* emerged from a long fight with the Torelli family, and in Mantua the Bonacolsi and Gonzaga contended for supremacy. *Signorie* took hold more permanently as a defensive reaction of threatened elite and feudal classes that coalesced behind a single family to meet the challenge of the popolo. With elite support,

---

[1] Bartolus, *On the Tyrant*, trans. J. Kirshner, in E. Cochrane and J. Kirshner (eds.), *The Renaissance* (Chicago, 1986), pp. 9–10.

[2] *Petrarch: An Anthology*, ed. D. Thompson (New York, 1971), p. 143.

signori took power by controlling key judicial and military offices and persuading (or intimidating) the councils to approve their election, then re-election, and finally succession within their families. Ottone Visconti, Milan's *signore* and archbishop in the late thirteenth century, had his nephew Matteo appointed as Captain of the People; Matteo later got the council to designate him as 'rector' of the city. In 1349 his son Giovanni, another archbishop, persuaded the General Council of the commune to declare him 'true and legitimate lord by birth' of Milan and to accept his descendants' right of hereditary succession.

But *signori* needed legal bases for their authority that were not dependent on the tenuous and revocable approval of communal councils. Thus many sought designation as vicars, or bearers of the legal authority, of the empire or the papacy. Vicariates were in theory revocable, temporary, and without right of succession, but they at least freed the *signori* from dependence on the communes and were an important step toward legitimacy. Matteo Visconti secured an imperial vicariate as early as 1294 and had it renewed in 1311 when Emperor Henry VII, after failing to install his own vicars, resigned himself to awarding vicariates (for cash payments) to many *signori* in northern Italy, including Cangrande della Scala of Verona, Passerino Bonacolsi of Mantua, and Ghiberto da Correggio of Parma. Emperors could dissolve vicariates, as Ludwig of Bavaria did with the Visconti in the 1320s. But as imperial power gradually faded and disappeared from Italy after the 1330s, the vicariates remained as legal foundations of legitimacy no longer linked to communal sanction.

A bolder step toward legitimation was the claim to 'plenitude of power', the authority, heretofore limited to popes and emperors, to override statutory and Roman law. As early as the 1320s, Verona's Cangrande affirmed his right to settle disputes 'from the fullness of our power', as did Azzone Visconti in the 1330s. With 'plenitude of power' *signori* asserted the right to issue edicts valid throughout their territories. In 1396 Giangaleazzo Visconti secured from the emperor the acknowledgment that as duke he was entitled 'to manage, discharge and administer in the duchy . . . that which . . . the emperors had the power to manage, discharge and administer, even from plenitude of power'.[3] The last stage in the legitimation of the *signorie* was the

---

[3] J. Black, 'The Visconti and *plenitudo potestatis*', forthcoming. My thanks to the author for kind permission to cite her paper.

acquisition of more exalted titles. The ducal title that Giangaleazzo bought from the emperor in 1395 was irrevocable and heritable; it made him and his successors dukes not merely of Milan but of all the cities and territories they ruled. Gianfrancesco Gonzaga became marquis of Mantua in 1433. Borso d'Este acquired two ducal titles, one over Modena from the emperor in 1452, and another over Ferrara from the pope in 1471. Federico da Montefeltro, hitherto count of Urbino, was made duke by pope Sixtus IV in 1474.

With each step toward legitimacy, *signori* could increasingly afford to ignore or eliminate the councils, committees, and representative institutions of the communes. The old legislative councils continued to exist, but shorn of their former authority. Where once they had the power to legislate and tax, they soon found themselves handling matters of purely administrative scope or merely confirming the *signore's* powers and ratifying his decisions. Typical was the co-existence in Rimini of the Malatesta *signoria* and the communal councils, the largest of which granted the family its *plenitudo potestatis* in 1334 but was otherwise confined to routine matters. The Visconti reorganized Milan's government in 1364 and left the General Council in place; but it was convened with ever decreasing frequency, and never to decide government policy. The dukes appointed committees called the Office of Provisions to manage local affairs in Milan and other cities.

Signorial government almost everywhere rested with small, handpicked groups of advisers consisting of nobles and jurists. Councillors served at the pleasure of the lord without any system of representation, fixed number, or formal terms of office. In the early stages of a small *signoria* like Padua, councillors were for a long time indistinguishable from household officials. But by 1400 the council assumed formal existence as an advisory rather than an administrative body. In the larger and more complex state of Milan, the duke's council was separated from the household much sooner. In 1385 Giangaleazzo divided his council into two bodies: the Secret (or privy) Council, which he kept with him (mostly at Pavia) to handle foreign policy, war, diplomacy, and finances (the latter through a separate branch) and which also functioned as the court of highest appeal; and the Council of Justice, placed in Milan to deal with more routine administration. In the seventeen years of his rule (1385–1402), some sixty persons served as members of Giangaleazzo's privy council, many fewer at any one time. Filippo Maria, whose reign was twice as long (1412–47), relied on only forty councillors over thirty-five years, perhaps ten at any one time. Under Francesco Sforza, the council numbered between ten and fifteen. With (or without) their privy council, the dukes of Milan, like other *signori*, made law by decree, revised the statutes of subject cities, adjudicated petitions, commuted sentences, and imposed taxes.

In Angevin Naples central government emerged from the royal court, where nobles holding a variety of posts constituted an informal council of advisers. Under the Aragonese after 1442, the council exercised a combination of advisory, administrative, and judicial functions. Many noble councillors were reduced to purely ceremonial functions, as Alfonso selected his real advisers and ministers according to the needs of the moment. The council oscillated between the smaller body of experts he preferred and larger groups including barons accustomed to prestigious positions under the weaker Angevins. But Alfonso never surrendered his prerogative of summoning the advisers he wanted, whenever he wanted them. In this respect royal government in Naples was similar to ducal government in Milan. A major difference between the kingdom and the *signorie* was the tradition in the former of 'parliaments', in origin periodic meetings of barons, ecclesiastical notables, and representatives of the demesne towns under the king's direct rule. Parliaments never had legislative powers and were convened at the king's pleasure. But grants to the crown of taxes or subsidies beyond ordinary revenues required their approval. The Angevins called parliaments less frequently and generally invited only the feudal barons, but after 1442 Alfonso revived them, included representatives of the cities, and regularly asked them to provide him with funds. The territorial barons also administered their own provincial governments and resisted royal intrusion whenever they could. The effectiveness of royal government depended on the crown's relations with landed nobles who aspired to create autonomous *signorie*.

Territorial states

The most important change in Italy's 'governmental map' after the mid fourteenth century was the incorporation of many formerly independent cities and *signorie* into territorial states. Although each city had governed its immediate hinterland (*contado*) from the earliest days of the communes, the formation of large territorial dominions occurred mostly after 1380. Visconti rule had extended to Bergamo and Brescia by the 1330s, but Giangaleazzo absorbed territories to the east as far as Padua and south to Bologna. When he died in 1402, his empire disintegrated and Venice quickly seized Verona, Vicenza, and Padua. Filippo Maria Visconti reconstituted a more durable territorial state closer to Milan that included Novara, Como, Pavia, Piacenza, Parma, and Cremona. By the 1370s, Florence had taken control of Prato, Pistoia, San Gimignano, and Volterra but subsequently extended its dominions to include Arezzo, Montepulciano, Pisa, Cortona, Livorno, and Sansepolcro. But nowhere were the newly acquired cities and territories integrated into the governments of either republics or *signorie*. Dominions were governed as subject territories, with no right of representation or participation in the councils of the dominant states, which controlled security, defence, criminal justice, and taxes, leaving routine administration to the localities through their old communal institutions. The failure to integrate subject cities resulted in weak ties between centre and periphery, while subjugation without representation generated considerable resentment.

Territorial states were administered by officials, variously called commissioners, *podestà*, vicars, captains, and in Naples provincial justiciars, appointed or elected by the *signori* or dominant cities. Although sent to enforce and represent the power of the ruling centre, they also mediated between the local populations and the capitals. In the Florentine dominions these officials developed patronage ties and formed clienteles that they sometimes protected from the fiscal demands of the Florentine government. The Medici, in particular Lorenzo (d. 1492), built a thick network of such ties and created complex triangular relationships among the subject populations, the Florentine government, and the Medici. Venice sent to each city in its dominion a *podestà* to administer justice and finances and a captain in charge of security and military matters. To prevent the patronage and clienteles that Florentine patricians built, Venice prohibited reappointment to the same city or appointment to localities where officials had property, relatives, or friends. Venice did not build a professional bureaucracy and allowed subject cities to keep their institutions, statutes, jurisdiction, and much autonomy in internal affairs.

The Visconti similarly allowed local autonomy to subject cities, but even more to the noble feudatories who were in effect lords in their own domains. The Sforza moved towards greater professionalization and hierarchy among dominion officials by instituting three distinct layers: roughly 200 *podestà* and captains sent to maintain order and exercise police functions and criminal jurisdiction in the separate localities; overseers in each of the ten major subdivisions of the dominion of different aspects of administration (military security, provisioning, tax collection, roads, and canals); and quasi-ministers with dominion-wide responsibility for the same areas of governance. But the dukes never secured the full cooperation of either the officials or the local populations in collecting taxes, enforcing unpopular decrees, and establishing the priority of ducal justice over the privileges and traditional autonomies of localities and feudatories.

In the territorial states of the Church the popes claimed overlordship in the so-called Patrimony of St Peter around Rome, in Umbria, the March of Ancona, and the Romagna north-east to Bologna and Ferrara. But papal control was always precarious. Like the emperors in the north, the papacy instituted vicariates, for similar purposes and with similarly counterproductive results. Although meant to limit the authority of the *signori* and turn them into officials of papal administration, vicariates actually consolidated signorial rule. After failed attempts to impose direct rule over Ferrara, John XXII gave the Este a vicariate in 1329. The Alidosi of Imola gained theirs in 1341 from Benedict XII. With the arrival in 1353 of the Spanish cardinal legate Egidio Albornoz, appointed by Innocent VI to undertake the task of forging a state from these disparately governed territories, one petty lord after another, especially in the recalcitrant cities of the Romagna, became papal vicars. Albornoz sought to subordinate the *signori* to papal authority and harness their power to broader administrative structures. He promulgated the *Constitutiones Egidianae* (1357), a code of law and administration defining the duties of provincial administrators and judges and standardizing criminal and civil jurisdiction. He divided the territories into provinces and instituted provincial parliaments to which the cities were to send representatives at the behest of provincial rectors who could also require military service. Albornoz's vision of centralized and representative government could have produced the best-governed region of Italy. But the popes lacked the power to implement the programme. Some communes turned it to their own advantage. In Orvieto, for example, submission to Albornoz was part of an agreement to strengthen communal institutions against noble factions. After he died in 1367, the vicariates that were intended to limit the power of *signori* consolidated their claims to jurisdiction and taxation.

During the schism (1378–1417), when competing popes had little time and few resources for territorial governance, the *signori* fortified their status as rulers of largely independent states. Fifteenth-century popes renewed efforts to control them, but with only sporadic successes. Even the Borgia pope Alexander VI and his famous son Cesare failed to make the latter's conquest of the Romagna in 1500–3 last beyond Alexander's death. More successful was Julius II, who led his own troops to retake Bologna and Perugia in 1506, and the Medici popes Leo X and Clement VII, who brought Urbino, Modena, Reggio, Parma, and the Romagna under more stable papal governance. But by this time the viability of all the territorial states depended on the policies of France and Spain, and many subject cities actually welcomed foreign intervention as an opportunity to liberate themselves.

Functions of government

What did governments in Renaissance Italy actually do? What difference did they make in the lives of citizens and subjects? Their basic task was to create and enforce a framework of law and institutions. Governments legislated: the republics in particular produced a continuous flow of laws through their councils, while *signori* made law by decree. Most governments enforced commercial law to punish fraud and prevent reprisals from foreign governments, oversaw bankruptcies to protect creditors, and regulated grain supplies and prices. They constructed roads, bridges, city walls, and secular and ecclesiastical buildings. They received and acted on petitions from citizens and institutions (guilds, churches, confraternities, and hospitals), and, increasingly in the fifteenth century, they regulated civic and religious rituals, philanthropy, and hospitals, enforced limits on conspicuous consumption, and policed sexual morality. But the indispensable and primary responsibilities of all governments were public order and control of violence; justice; military organization and war; taxation and public finance; and diplomacy.

Public order and justice

Governments assiduously prosecuted the ordinary criminality of theft, assault, and murder, limited the carrying of arms, and maintained police forces. In Venice police functions were supervised by citizen committees: the Five of Peace, with jurisdiction over unauthorized bearing of arms; and the Night Lords, who jailed thieves and sexual offenders. Elsewhere, except in the southern kingdom, police functions were entrusted to the staff of the *podestà*, a judicial official selected from another city. All states prohibited the carrying of weapons except for self-defence. Giangaleazzo Visconti decreed that merchants could carry swords and knives when travelling, whereas peasants were limited to their tools. Policy regarding public order was a function of class antagonisms. Popular governments in Florence, Bologna, Genoa, Padua, Perugia, Rome, and elsewhere considered unruly elite families the chief menace to peace and enacted tough laws to punish magnates who battled each other with private armies from fortress-like palaces and towers in their inner-city enclaves. But elite-dominated governments saw the labouring classes as the chief threat to social order. Fearful of working-class insurrection, such governments denied workers the right to organize in guilds or convene in large numbers and distributed grain to remove one obvious cause of lower-class unrest. Anxiety over the working classes became particularly acute in the late fourteenth century, when conflicts in the textile industry generated workers' revolts in several cities. Thereafter the issue of public order was dominated more by acute, if exaggerated, fear of the lower classes than by older perceptions of elite misbehaviour. In Florence in 1378, immediately after the Ciompi insurrection, even what was still a popular government created the magistracy of the Eight on Security with police functions directed mainly against the lower classes. The Eight could arrest, convict, and punish suspects without procedural protections for the rights of the accused. In Venice similar powers were assigned to the Council of Ten, created after several conspiracies and much social unrest. At first an emergency committee with policing powers, the Ten was made permanent in the 1330s and developed into a court that operated in secret with unfettered jurisdiction and no appeal, also not bound by Roman law protections for the accused.

Closely related to public order was the administration of justice. In Naples, justice was a royal prerogative. The kings appointed justiciars in each of the kingdom's eleven provinces, in theory with unrestricted criminal and appeals jurisdiction overriding the baronial courts. In practice they functioned more as intermediaries between provincial and royal courts. Alfonso abolished the Angevin courts, which had enjoyed some independence, appointed judges for criminal cases, and made his privy council the highest court. He boasted of having brought justice to a previously lawless kingdom. In most states (the main exceptions were Venice and Naples) justice was entrusted to the Roman law courts of the *podestà* and captains. They brought trained judges, who heard arguments, interrogated witnesses, and sometimes applied torture to extract confessions (whose validity had to be confirmed in court). Notaries meticulously recorded every detail of the proceedings. In the fourteenth century most cases were initiated by victims' accusations, but thereafter court-initiated prosecutions increased. Procedural norms required that the accused be summoned to appear and present a defence, and each side cross-examined the other's witnesses. This system was often slow, because it gave the accused considerable rights, and it sometimes failed to serve the interests of ruling classes, because, as foreigners, *podestà* and their judges were less susceptible to political pressure. Thus, as governments came more firmly under elite control, they intervened quite openly to influence court decisions and hear appeals. The Venetian patriciate had always preferred to keep the republic's judicial institutions in the hands of citizen committees like the State Attorneys who indicted suspects, the Council of Forty that conducted trials, and of course the Ten who could accuse and convict. In Florence the jurisdiction of the *podestà* and two other foreign rectors gradually eroded as judicial authority passed to citizen committees, like the Eight, that dispensed with traditional Roman law procedures and applied 'summary justice'.

In the *signorie* ruling lords everywhere claimed a more radical right, often delegated to their inner councils, to intervene in the judicial process to commute sentences and hear appeals. Where they held vicariates or ducal titles, *signori* could legally claim such rights from delegated *merum* (criminal) and *mixtum* (civil) *imperium* (jurisdiction). The Visconti and Sforza frequently transferred cases from the regular courts to the ducal councils, provoking a series of protests from Milan's judges that forced the Sforza to limit this practice. When the Sforza regime fell to the French in 1499, the Milanese requested the elimination of such interference and the right of citizens to appeal cases to the resurrected General Council of the commune. Subject towns, beginning with Pavia, wanted the autonomy of their traditional *podestà* and judges restored.

The most intriguing attempt to centralize the administration of justice occurred in Mantua and Ferrara. In the 1470s and 1480s Marquis Ludovico Gonzaga and Duke Ercole d'Este both experimented with a judicial commissioner with authority to override the statutes, bypass traditional procedures, render summary justice, and enforce a tougher policy on crime. It was to the same man, Beltramino Cusadri, whose fascinating career has recently come to light,[4] that these two rulers entrusted the task of creating a more standardized and rigorous system of justice. Cusadri had degrees in Roman and canon law and a reputation for stern enforcement and a willingness to stand up to entrenched privilege, especially the rural noble families accustomed to protecting clients through politically influenced local justice. Despite the enthusiastic support and protection Cusadri enjoyed from both rulers, in the end the powerful families accused him of tyranny and undermined his programme of reform. His story illustrates the difficulty of attempts to streamline justice and impose uniform codes in states, even fairly small *signorie*, that were still patchworks of locally administered territories with originally separate jurisdictions.

Armies and war

Renaissance governments similarly tried to bring military force under their exclusive control, but again with mixed results. Communal

[4] D. S. Chambers and T. Dean, *Clean Hands and Rough Justice: An Investigating Magistrate in Renaissance Italy* (Ann Arbor, 1997).

infantry had consisted of rotating portions of urban populations organized by neighbourhoods, together with village-based rural units, both called into action as needed and disbanded when campaigns ended. The cavalry came from wealthy families who could afford the expense of horses, armour, and knighthoods. In the 1260 battle of Montaperti against Ghibelline Siena, all but 200 of the Florentine army of over 16,000 were Florentine citizens or from the immediate *contado*. But as class antagonisms exploded over the next half century and made elites and popolo each reluctant to see the other armed, and both loath to arm workers and peasants, armies were no longer composed of citizens. Popular governments destroyed upper-class military power, and elite regimes disarmed the popolo. Governments increasingly turned to mercenaries, employing professional freelance military commanders (*condottieri*), which in theory made it possible to pay for military power only when needed. But as mercenary forces became larger and *condottieri* more independent, governments competed for the best commanders, who demanded payment in both peace and war and plundered undefended countrysides to make their demands effective. Demilitarized republics were especially vulnerable to marauding companies that wandered throughout Italy threatening, plundering, and extorting. Between 1342 and 1400 Siena's countryside was raided thirty-seven times by these stateless powers that forced the city to pay large sums to limit the destruction. In 1375 Florence paid the pope's chief mercenary and the greatest captain of the age, the Englishman John Hawkwood, the astonishing sum of 130,000 florins for an agreement *not* to attack Florentine territory. Hawkwood negotiated with the pope's enemy as a free agent; indeed he soon switched sides to fight for Florence and thereafter remained faithfully in the republic's service.

By the fifteenth century, the large states, particularly Venice, established more stable working arrangements with their *condottieri*, offering longer contracts, allowing them a role in military policy, showering them with gifts and tax exemptions, and even granting them citizenship. But mercenaries were never completely under the control of governments. Even Venice suffered occasional defections of its captains. In 1499 the Florentines accused their chief captain of deliberately stalling operations against Pisa and executed him. The Visconti, aware of the dangers of excessive reliance on mercenaries, recruited a small elite cavalry corps of 1400 knights from Lombard noble families linked to them by feudal ties. Angevin Naples had similarly relied on the feudal obligations of the barons to provide military service. But precarious baronial loyalty persuaded Alfonso to rely on recruits from the royal demesne and on mercenaries, led by some of the same captains who dominated the military scene elsewhere in Italy. So powerful were professional soldiers that they sometimes seized the governments that employed them. The best example is Francesco Sforza, who fought for the Visconti and betrayed the Ambrosian Republic to become Milan's duke in 1450. Some *signori* from the Gonzaga, Este, and Malatesta families, but most notably Federico da Montefeltro, combined rulership with professional soldiering.

Until 1375 wars in Italy were relatively brief. Beginning with the Florentine–papal war of 1375–8, however, Italy entered a seventy-five year period of longer, more costly, nearly non-stop warfare, including the Florentine–Milanese wars of 1390–1402 and 1423–40, with Venice joining Florence in the mid 1420s; Neapolitan invasions of the papal states and Tuscany in 1409–14 and again in the 1440s; and the war between Venice and Milan in the late 1440s and early 1450s for control of northern Italy, in which Cosimo de' Medici, now directing Florence's foreign policy, reversed the traditional antagonism towards Milan and joined his ally Sforza against Venice. These wars caused armies to become larger and more permanent. Venice went from 8,000 cavalry and 3,000 infantry in 1425 to 12,000 cavalry, 8,000 professional infantry, and a militia of 11,000 recruited from its territories in 1432. By 1452 Venice had 16,000 cavalry, Milan 18,000, and Florence 10,000. Galeazzo Maria Sforza reportedly had an army of 42,000 men, half of them a standing permanent force. Machiavelli decried the dependence on mercenaries as the fatal weakness of the Italian states (underscored through the irony of having a professional soldier, Fabrizio Colonna, laud citizen armies in the *Art of War*), but he underestimated the size and relative stability of these forces in the fifteenth century.

Taxation and public finance

The costs of war put enormous strain on the fiscal capacities of Renaissance governments. In the early fourteenth century most governments relied on gabelles (indirect sales taxes on a long list of items) to cover ordinary expenses. But prolonged wars drove expenditures far beyond ordinary revenues, and, because the republican upper classes generally rejected direct taxes, the expedient to which most republics had recourse was heavy borrowing from their own citizens. The Florentine elite abolished direct taxation in 1315; thereafter only emergency rulers or revolutionary governments tried it. Oligarchic governments always preferred to borrow money from the wealthy and repay it with interest from the receipts of regressive indirect taxes. Direct taxes they reserved for the subject towns and cities.

To borrow money governments regularly imposed mandatory loans on citizens, and public debts grew enormously: over 6 million florins in Venice and Florence by the mid fifteenth century and 3 million in Genoa. In all three cities accumulating indebtedness forced governments to forego repayment of principal, consolidate debts, and issue negotiable shares that earned interest funded by revenues from indirect taxes. Venice and Genoa did so before 1300, and Florence followed in 1345. Governments faced no more urgent task than finding the revenue to pay the promised interest. Defaulting on interest damaged the credit and confidence necessary to induce citizens to pay the sums assessed by their governments. When in 1380 the Florentine popular government reduced interest to only 5 percent (from the 10 and 15 percent promised by elite regimes), a chronicler remarked that it was the most important action by any Florentine government in a century.[5] Traditionally, neighbourhood committees had apportioned forced loans through assessments of household wealth, but in 1427, during a severe fiscal crisis, Florence instituted the Catasto, a remarkable system of self-assessment by every household in the city and the dominion. Fiscal necessity pushed governments to new levels of sophistication in budget planning and information gathering about families and their patrimonies that would have been unthinkable, and unnecessary, a century earlier. Even this was not enough, and Florence relied on the very wealthy for short-term emergency loans repaid with handsome interest. This resulted in dependence on the Medici, whose banking fortune enabled them to

---

[5] Marchionne di Coppo Stefani, *Cronaca fiorentina*, ed. N. Rodolico, in *Rerum Italicarum Scriptores*, new edn (Città di Castello, 1903–55) vol. xxx, pt. 1, pp. 384–5.

underwrite the government's needs and thus to climb to political power. Venice escaped this fate because of a willingness to accept direct taxes and overall higher revenues: by 1500 over one million ducats annually, twice what was needed for ordinary expenses.

Neither Naples nor the papal state relied on regular borrowing or assessments of household wealth. Sources of income in Naples traditionally included revenues from royal properties, customary feudal aids, sales taxes, sales of offices, and parliamentary grants of subsidies that assessed each town and barony a portion of the tax. Alfonso added an annual hearth tax of two ducats per household and a tax on transhumance. Except for sales taxes, this was all direct taxation, and regular annual revenues amounted to 830,000 ducats. The fiscal administration of the papal state reflected its fragmented character. It levied direct taxes on cities and towns and an annual subsidy on the sizeable communities of Jews. Traditional ecclesiastical revenues from throughout Europe were in sharp decline, as popes traded away the right to tax in return for the support of governments against the conciliar movement. Achieving more effective control over their Italian territories thus became a matter of fiscal necessity.

Milan's dukes ruled over the wealthiest region of Italy and relied successfully on indirect taxes and customs duties. They demanded monthly payments from the subject communes, which for most of the fourteenth century met these obligations from their own indirect revenues. But here too war created greater need and called for new measures. Under Giangaleazzo the ducal camera assumed direct administration of the finances of all subject cities. In 1388 the annual total of their payments came to 840,000 florins. Milan led the list, with 175,000 florins, followed by Brescia (63,000), Pavia (62,000), Novara (52,000), Como (51,000), and so on. A generation later, receipts fell to 650,000 florins, but, while other cities paid less, Milan was now assessed at 240,000 florins. Heavy taxes were clearly weakening the smaller cities. Giangaleazzo imitated the Venetian and Florentine systems of assessing household wealth by neighbourhood committees, but the attempt to attract voluntary loans failed. Forced loans were limited to the wealthiest subjects, who were also placed in charge of ducal finances. Neither the Visconti nor the Sforza accumulated large public debts.

The sheer number of governments, each with its own hefty military expenses, and the need of each to tax, and in some cases to borrow, at high levels to meet these expenses, had two deleterious long-term consequences. The first was the drain of so much wealth into unproductive military expenses: one reason perhaps why Italy lost its primacy as Europe's richest region by the seventeenth century. The second stemmed from the dependence on borrowing rather than direct taxation. Interest went to those wealthy enough to make loans and was funded by regressive indirect taxes whose burden fell most heavily on workers, artisans, and shopkeepers, thus exacerbating an already unequal distribution of wealth.

Diplomacy

The chancery was a central office of government, responsible for official correspondence and staffed by notaries trained in letter-writing and Roman law. Notable literary figures served as chancellors even before 1300 (Brunetto Latini in Florence and Pier della Vigna under Emperor Frederick II). In Florence the chancery was headed by distinguished humanists from Coluccio Salutati to Leonardo Bruni, Poggio Bracciolini, Benedetto Accolti, and Bartolomeo Scala. In Milan Pier Candido Decembrio was secretary to Filippo Maria Visconti, as was Antonio Beccadelli, il Panormita, under Alfonso in Naples. Official letters held a prestigious place in inter-state communications. Giangaleazzo Visconti was famously reported to have said that one letter of Salutati was worth a troop of cavalry. Formal letters in elegant humanist Latin were a form of public diplomacy.

By the fifteenth century most governments kept resident ambassadors, or 'orators', regularly posted to the major states of Italy and beyond. Generally recruited from the elite classes and accompanied by secretaries and humanists, some remained for years at their posts and became influential figures. The Sforza ambassadors to Florence gave significant support and advice to the Medici in political crises. Venice required its ambassadors to make detailed reports to the Senate about conditions in the states to which they were sent. Less visible than ambassadors, whose every move was accompanied by much ceremony, were envoys sent to deliver messages, conduct secret negotiations, and collect information. By 1500 they were numerous and essential to inter-state negotiations. The best known is Machiavelli, who sent regular dispatches to his government about every detail, change of mood, conversation, and any hint of the intentions of friends and enemies alike.

The new paternalism

After about 1400, Renaissance governments, especially the republics, regularly intervened in social and moral issues. Increasingly, they regulated luxury consumption and sexual behaviour; provided social assistance, philanthropy, care of abandoned children and elderly widows, and dowries for poor girls; took control of their local ecclesiastical establishments; and supervised the religious observances of the laity. Although the Church was also active in these areas, to a striking degree secular governments took the lead in defining and implementing norms of private morality, social welfare, and even religion with an impressive array of legislation and institutions.

Government role in religion was well established by 1300 as an aspect of the communes' efforts to affirm their legitimacy as sites of sacrality and Christian virtue. Cities likened themselves to the ideal Jerusalem of Christian imagination as loci, under divine protection, for the implementation of peace, justice, concord, and the common good. Savonarola's political ministry for reform in Florence in 1494–8 is but the best-known example. Governments assumed the responsibility to foster religious devotions, honour patron saints and guard their relics, organize religious processions especially in times of crisis, protect the local church and the honour of its nunneries, fund and supervise the construction of cathedrals, and imbue every aspect of their authority with the idea that good governance earned God's favour. Under these assumptions, but also because the church was a vast field of lucrative patronage, Renaissance governments heavily influenced the appointment of bishops, the assignment of benefices, and the transfer of monasteries.

Government social and philanthropic activities were largely modelled on those of the Franciscan and Dominican orders, which had taken the lead in founding hospitals for the poor, sick, and elderly. For most of the fourteenth century Milan's hospitals were still under ecclesiastical administration. But the government's role grew, as did a differentiation of services among institutions generically called 'hospitals'. In mid century Bernabò Visconti made donations and gifts of land to hospitals, and in 1399 Giangaleazzo attempted, unsuccessfully, to reform services along the lines of the centralized and government-regulated hospital system in Siena. He even appointed a commission to search for the mentally infirm and bring them into hospitals. The centralization of Milan's hospitals was finally achieved in the mid fifteenth century with reforms begun by the Ambrosian Republic and continued by Francesco Sforza, who built the great Ospedale Maggiore and made it the centre of a government-supervised network of hospitals that specialized in different kinds of care. Many of Florence's hospitals were founded by wealthy merchants and administered by the city's major guilds. Here too government intervened to regulate and protect them from ecclesiastical control and taxation and to supervise the specialization of services. The most famous of Florence's new hospitals was the Foundling Hospital, created from a bequest by the wealthy merchant from nearby Prato, Francesco Datini. It opened its doors in 1445 and became the refuge for thousands of abandoned children. The government approved the institution's tax-exempt status on the grounds that 'from such a praiseworthy enterprise, divine mercy might not unreasonably be hoped for, to the end of preserving the liberty of the people of Florence and . . . the benefactors of that hospital'.[6] In Genoa, a new hospital founded with private money in the 1420s, and later regulated by communally approved statutes, grew with government support until it acquired and consolidated thirty old hospitals. The government required mothers who entrusted children to the foundling hospital to reveal the identity of the fathers and compelled the latter to pay support costs. Fifteenth-century Venice had some forty hospitals. In 1467 the Senate decided to build a new one and secured a papal grant of plenary indulgence for all benefactors. But the Great Council and city health commissioners decreed that hospitals be kept firmly under government, rather than ecclesiastical or private, control.

The enforcement of morality also took on new dimensions from about 1400. While none of these concerns was new, heightened

---

[6] P. Gavitt, *Charity and Children in Renaissance Florence: The Ospedale degli Innocenti, 1410–1536* (Ann Arbor, 1990), p. 66.

urgency drove government action in several areas. Prostitutes were regulated, taxed, and protected in Florence (1403), Venice (1460), Genoa (1418 and 1459), and elsewhere. Governments restricted them to certain neighbourhoods or houses and forced them to wear specific items of clothing (or colours) by which they could easily be recognized and not confused with 'honourable' women. In Florence between 1440 and 1520 over 1000 fines were levied against both prostitutes and clients who abused them. In Florence and Lucca prostitution was deemed a necessary evil to lure unmarried men away from homosexual temptations. Fear of homosexual sodomy, if not the practice itself, grew in the fifteenth century. Preachers thundered against it and governments decreed new prohibitions and punishments. In Venice, the powerful Ten became increasingly involved in sodomy cases after 1400, and prosecutions increased dramatically. In mid century new legislation intensified police surveillance and required surgeons and doctors to report to the authorities physical evidence of sodomy. In Florence in 1432 the government created the Officials of the Night to enforce a new policy against sodomy that replaced harsh but rarely imposed penalties with fines. Citizens were invited to submit anonymous accusations, and the Officials investigated and decided whether to convict or acquit. Between 1432 and 1502, 15,000 accusations resulted in 3,000 convictions and fines; half a dozen men were executed, mostly for the rape of children. Lucca passed complex legislation against sodomy in 1458, as did many other cities. Governments thus took the lead in institutionalizing a culture of surveillance and social control that extended into citizens' sexual practices.

One of the oldest forms of government intervention in private life was the control of excessive ostentation and luxury in dress and ritual. Governments, more the republics than the *signorie*, passed hundreds of sumptuary laws, especially in the fifteenth century, regulating weddings, funerals, and, above all, women's dress, a concern that generated no fewer than 120 laws. The factors adduced to explain the motives behind this legislation include class antagonisms, patriarchal attitudes toward women, and the influence of mendicant preachers. But common to all sumptuary legislation was the assumption that governments had a responsibility to ensure the moral health of citizens. By 1500 this well-entrenched conviction set the stage for the more elaborate systems of social reform and discipline that accompanied the response of the Italian states and the Church to the Reformation. If not in their territorial governance, where upper-class privileges and local autonomies prevented the emergence of integrated states, perhaps in the growing intensity of their interventions in the social, moral, and religious well-being of their populations it can be said that Italian Renaissance governments were precursors of the modern state.

The South

David Abulafia

Is the South different?

The aim of this chapter is to examine the history of the Italian South in the context of the Italian peninsula as a whole. Reference to most standard histories of Renaissance Italy, whether concerned with culture, politics, economy, or society, reveals a chasm in the writing of Italian history: the South, which nowadays claims with some reason to have been neglected by modern politicians and industrialists, has also suffered neglect at the hands of historians. It was not always so. Jacob Burckhardt saw in Frederick II of Hohenstaufen, king of Sicily and Holy Roman Emperor, the precursor of the princes of Renaissance Italy who owed much in his methods of rule and cultural interests to the model of 'despotism' provided by formerly Islamic Sicily.

Historians today tend to see the Italian South as something essentially different in character from the north and centre of the peninsula. For it was a land ruled by kings of foreign origin—the Angevins of Naples originally arrived from France and the Aragonese of Sicily from Spain—although as the generations passed their links to the ancestral land became weaker. Some kings were absentees, like the fifteenth-century rulers of Sardinia and Sicily, who resided in Aragon–Catalonia. Absentee monarchs ruling through viceroys, as also in mainland southern Italy after 1503, suggest a colonial regime, whose main aim was the extraction of revenue in order to finance programmes of expansion further afield, in Africa or the Balkans. The essential contrast in the traditional approach becomes that between the lands of conquest and subjection, in the South, and the lands of freedom and individualism, in the north.

This argument might be pursued further, by falsely insisting that monarchy was something alien to the Italian peninsula in the late Middle Ages. Naples and Sicily appear as a pair of feudal kingdoms, states whose political development towards liberty failed to be maintained, while the north and centre created new, 'better', types of political community, in the form of the city–state. This Whiggish argument omits to mention that by the fifteenth century the free city–state was itself a rarity in the peninsula, despite the glittering successes of two independent republics, Florence and Venice. Indeed, the age of the *signori* saw the re-establishment of a form of dynastic monarchy in which power was often handed down from father to son; and many *signori* were similar to the southern monarchies in the reassertion by the *signore* of his feudal authority over the nobility. In addition, the rulers of the South acquired their own powerful political influence in the north; in the early fourteenth century, the Angevin Robert of Naples became overlord of Genoa (from 1318 to 1335) and of Prato, while his son Charles of Calabria took charge of the government of Florence in 1326–8; as late as the end of the fifteenth century there were enclaves in Tuscany over which the king of Naples exercised a form of dominion.

Despite neglect in most histories of Renaissance Italy of the internal history of southern Italy and Sicily, there has always had to be some room for south Italian kings in accounts of the politics of the peninsula. Frederick II (who was also Holy Roman Emperor, and thus king of northern Italy as well) campaigned in the centre and north, in the 1230s and 1240s, and is often presented as an autocrat seeking to destroy urban freedom. Strong commercial and diplomatic ties bound the Guelfs of Tuscany to the Angevin kings of Naples around 1282, especially in the aftermath of the great Vespers revolt in Palermo. Ladislas of Naples posed a threat to Tuscany at the start of the fifteenth century, as did the Aragonese kings of Naples thereafter (they even acquired bases on the Tuscan coast). And Naples stood at the centre of Italian politics in 1494–5: the French invasion of Italy in 1494 had as its target Naples and the installation of the French king on the Neapolitan throne. The subsequent Italian wars revolved to a significant degree around the duel for Naples, between several French and Spanish kings. Intimate alliances bound dukes of Milan, marquises of Mantua, dukes of Urbino, lords of Piombino, and other Italian *signori*, great and small, to Naples. Thus the politics and diplomacy of north and south were inextricably intertwined, so that the ties between Naples and Florence, around 1325, or between Naples and Milan, around 1460, had an essential role in maintaining the balance of power in the peninsula.

Were southern politics indeed so different in character from those of the north and centre? Central Italy was nominally under the authority of the pope, and therefore constituted another (though very distinctive) monarchy. Was the relationship between the popes and the great families of the papal state—the Orsini near Rome, the Malatesta far from Rome—very different from that between the kings of Naples and such great vassals as the princes of Taranto or the Sanseverino? Indeed, the great noble families of the papal state, particularly the Colonna and Orsini, did not see the boundary of the kingdom of Naples as in any way impermeable. They held extensive estates in southern Italy and exercised considerable influence there in the fourteenth and fifteenth centuries. (It should also be remembered that the kings of Naples held their crown from the pope and in this sense were the greatest of that constellation of papal vassals in central and southern Italy.) The great princes in the kingdom of Naples relished their autonomy and sought, in the often lengthy contests for the crown of Naples, a king who would guarantee that autonomy. We should guard against the view that these great princes were the proponents of local anarchy. Some, such as the princes of Taranto, had close links with the outside world (in this case, with the Malatesta of Rimini) and sought in a similar way to consolidate their lands, revenues, and jurisdiction. Their preference was for kingship that was far away, but effective when needed, for example in the face of the Turkish threat.

Political structures are only part of the argument. To understand the place of the South in the history of Renaissance Italy we also need to consider the adoption and adaptation of humanistic culture to the needs of royal and princely courts. The ideas about princely authority that the king of Naples derived from his reading of classical texts were generally applicable also in the north, where allies such as the Este dukes of Ferrara sought to consolidate their power with similar methods. In addition, the kingdom of Naples had an important role in the debate about the nature of papal political power, even before Alfonso the Magnanimous welcomed to his court the most acerbic critic of papal claims to territorial authority, the humanist Lorenzo

Valla. Territorial princes in the South exercised cultural patronage too, in ways not dissimilar to the north Italian *signori*, commissioning manuscripts and seeking to acquire a rounded classical education. In the late fifteenth century the prince of Altomonte had a particularly fine collection of Greek texts, but earlier still Boccaccio had turned to the Calabrian Greek Barlaam for instruction in the Greek language.

A further area where the South appears to have been disparaged is its economic history. Southern Italy was indeed less urbanized than the north, and its economic profile was dominated by the production of foodstuffs and raw materials, many of which were consumed or processed in the cities of northern Italy and the Catalan lands. Of course, one must not underestimate the extent to which these primary products were also staples of the north Italian economy at this period; but it was certainly the case that the merchants of northern Italy penetrated across vast distances and sold the industrial products of Tuscany and Lombardy both in the South and far from Italy, in a way that the south Italians and Sicilians could never match. Even after the shock of plague and depopulation in the late fourteenth century, Tuscany and Lombardy had 'powerhouse' economies, which was not the case in southern Italy and Sicily. Yet recent historiography insists that the South was economically more resilient than has been supposed. It was not necessarily locked in the dependent relationship with northern Italy that was to characterize its modern history, even though some elements of that dependency can already be identified, notably the greater financial power of visiting merchants from the north of Italy and from the Catalan lands. Intimate links tied the great finance houses of Florence to the courts and grain estates of southern Italy, from the time of the Bardi and Peruzzi (around 1300) to that of the Medici and Strozzi (in the late fifteenth century). In the sixteenth century, the Genoese achieved an unrivalled position dominating the finances and economy of Naples, while Venice still exercised powerful influence along the Adriatic shores of southern Italy. The natural resources, strategic position, and political alliances of the Italian South created such strong ties with northern Italy that—and this, surely, is the central point—it really does make sense to talk of the peninsula as 'Italy' in more than a geographical sense: there was a common economic, cultural and political history binding together northern and southern Italy, and involving Sicily as well, though Sardinia took part to a rather lesser extent.

The crisis of monarchic centralization

The thirteenth century saw a series of major changes in the political identity of the South. The kingdom of Sicily, which then also included southern Italy, had been founded by the Norman warlord Roger II in 1130, with the consent of his barons and the papacy. He operated a strong bureaucracy based in Sicily and lived off healthy revenues, while adopting aggressive policies towards his neighbours in the Byzantine Empire and North Africa. Under Roger's illustrious grandson Frederick II (d. 1250), the Sicilian kingdom became involved to a far greater degree than before in the politics of central and northern Italy, mainly because of Frederick's assumption of the crown of the Holy Roman Empire, with authority over Germany and northern Italy. Power struggles developed between the emperor and rebellious Lombard cities, increasingly supported by the papacy. But there is no real evidence that Frederick sought to impose on northern Italy the sort of centralized rule with which he was familiar in southern Italy and Sicily. His intervention crystallized the factional divide in northern Italy between the supporters of the Empire, known as Ghibellines, and the adherents of the papacy, the Guelfs. It did not create that divide, because factionalism was already endemic in the cities, and rival aristocratic clans tended to seek out protectors among the great powers in the hope of consolidating their hold on local power. After Frederick's death the papacy seized on the argument that the ruler of the kingdom of Sicily was a papal vassal in order to insert its own candidate on the Sicilian throne. The papal champion was Charles of Anjou, count of Provence, brother of the French king, who acquired the crown of Sicily in 1266, but who never ceased to be seen by the Sicilians as a foreigner. Strict government and heavy taxation, already in evidence under Frederick, generated resentment, especially in Sicily. Naples, rather than Palermo, became the effective capital under the Angevins, and the petty nobility, bureaucrats, and merchants of Sicily lost their traditional access to royal favours.

The revolt of the Sicilian Vespers against the Angevins in Palermo in March 1282 was the political equivalent of a volcanic eruption. It cast a cloud over the politics of the Mediterranean for twenty years, and its tremors could still be felt after 200 years. This was not quite the popular revolt of legend. Knights, businessmen, and lawyers rapidly took charge. Although the Sicilian rebels sought to expel their harsh French king, they saw the necessity for a new king, elected by a Sicilian parliament. One was ready to hand in Peter III, king of Aragon and count of Barcelona, the husband of the granddaughter of Frederick II. Amid endless betrayals, it is remarkable how quickly Peter consolidated his hold on the island of Sicily. But any hope of conquering the mainland, to which he also laid claim, was frustrated by the vigour of the Angevin armies under Charles I and II, and by the lack of severe unrest in continental southern Italy. Thus by the time Peter III and Charles I died in 1285, there were two kings 'of Sicily' in the South, one controlling the mainland, the other the island. The politics of the period were further complicated by strife within the royal house of Aragon, which led Peter's youngest son, Frederick, to seize independent control of the island; he was rewarded, once again by its parliament, with its crown, in the face of a papal interdict. The pope (and Frederick's elder brother the king of Aragon) dangled before him an exchange of Sicily with Sardinia or even Albania, but Frederick was not tempted to swap gold for silver or base metals. Thus an independent Aragonese dynasty came into being on the island, constantly under threat from irredentist neighbours in Naples who explored every opportunity to win back the island they had lost in the Vespers rebellion. Nevertheless, there were many structural similarities between the two Sicilian kingdoms, the result of a common heritage going back to Byzantium, and of common political developments, as the nobility gained ever greater influence, while the towns failed to match the freedoms gained by cities in northern Italy.

The years around 1300 saw significant changes in the ethnic and religious composition of the Sicilian kingdoms. In 1300 Charles II of Naples deported the entire Muslim population of Lucera, the descendants of Sicilian Muslim rebels settled in southern Italy by Frederick II. He also encouraged a brief but fierce attempt to force the Jews to convert to Christianity. In both Sicily and southern Italy, the once large Greek element in the population lost ground: a single Greek bishopric lingered thereafter at Rossano in Calabria. The two Sicilian kingdoms increasingly became Italian-speaking lands (with the famous exception of Malta), and these lands were now primarily Catholic in religion, though the Jewish communities recovered from persecution. Frederick III of Sicily was active in rebuilding the church and promoting religion after he made peace with the pope in 1302; he encouraged mendicant friars and acted as host to evangelical figures such as the Catalan publicists Arnau de Vilanova and Ramon Llull. The kings of Naples, too, despite their political ties to the papacy, showed sympathy for radical Franciscans; one heir to the throne, Louis of Toulouse, brother of King Robert, even renounced his claim in order to live a godly Franciscan life.

In the early and mid fourteenth century, the reconquest of Sicily became an obsession of the kings of Naples, as it is now convenient to call the Angevin rulers of mainland southern Italy. On their charters, they sported a grander title, 'king of Jerusalem and Sicily', later adding Hungary; but in none of these areas did they exercise authority. Still, the rulers of Naples had long indulged in an ambitious policy of expansion, whose costs had in part necessitated the high taxes that led to the Vespers revolt. They intervened in Albania and Tunisia, built marriage ties to Hungary, and asserted their political influence in northern Italy as protectors of various cities. As counts of Provence and Piedmont, they also had a major stake in the political affairs of north-western Italy; they worked hard to consolidate their authority around Asti, and this gave them additional leverage in Lombard affairs. But the loss of Sicily deprived these kings of the better part of their revenue, for the island was rich in exportable foodstuffs. To compensate for lost revenue from trade they increasingly had recourse to Tuscan bankers, who secured in return the right to carry vast amounts of Apulian grain out of southern Italy. Perhaps the high point of Neapolitan influence in Italy was reached under King Robert the Wise (r. 1309–43), an amateur theologian who bored his court with his endless sermons (he even imposed them on his subjects in Genoa) but was also an avid defender of royal prerogatives. As Samantha Kelly has recently observed, Robert's avid pursuit of a reputation for wisdom formed part of a wider programme for the enhancement of monarchy: 'wisdom was proclaimed as Robert's defining characteristic, the source of all his other virtues and the summation of his style of rule'.[1] He led the Guelf resistance in Italy to the German emperor, Henry VII of Luxembourg (d. 1313), and the

---

[1] S. Kelly, *The New Solomon: Robert of Naples (1309–1343) and Fourteenth-Century Kingship* (Leiden, 2003), p. 283.

intellectual defence of his kingdom's autonomy yielded notable results. His legal counsel, figures such as Andrea of Isernia, argued that, even though a papal vassal, the king exercised full authority within the borders of his kingdom, as 'emperor in his own kingdom'. These were important arguments against popes and emperors who claimed the right of intervention in the kingdom's affairs. Henry VII apparently assumed that his universal authority as notional successor to the Roman emperors entitled him to dethrone Robert, but his attempt to do so only succeeded in lodging Robert more firmly on his throne.

After Robert's death in 1343, however, the foreign connections of the house of Anjou began to haunt the rulers of Naples. Robert's granddaughter Joanna I (r. 1343–80), a rare queen regnant in late medieval Europe, made an unfortunate marriage to her boorish Hungarian cousin, which was cut short by her advisers when they tipped him out of the castle window in Naples. The consequence was two massive invasions of southern Italy, led by the dynamic Hungarian king Louis the Great. He unleashed devastating mercenary bands, whose raids compounded the economic difficulties engendered by the repeated cycles of bubonic plague in the region, pushing down the population and damaging agricultural production. Factional strife arose between barons supporting different branches of the house of Anjou, that of Durazzo and that of Taranto, from which Joanna chose her energetic second husband. Grants of land to favourites deprived the crown of much needed revenue at a time of growing economic crisis. A good example is the career of the ambitious Florentine Nicola Acciaiuoli, a member of a distinguished banking dynasty who flaunted the title 'count of Melfi' and became Grand Seneschal (in effect, prime minister) of the kingdom. But even Nicola's head was turned by the prospect of invading the island of Sicily; so more money was expended, and, despite initial successes, only a tiny foothold was secured on the island.

The difficulties of the mainland monarchs were not very different from those experienced by the rulers of island Sicily. Powerful baronial factions, some favourable to the return of the Angevin dynasty, others strongly opposed, were able to take advantage of a series of royal minorities and Angevin invasions to consolidate their own power. Frederick of Aragon formally agreed that after his death (in 1337) the island would be reintegrated into the Angevin state; but in fact he nominated his son as heir, thus making it clear that he supported the continuing independence of the island from both Naples and Aragon–Catalonia. The traditional view sees late-fourteenth-century Sicily as a land immersed in severe crisis. The Black Death had deprived Sicily of markets for its wheat because of falling demand for grain from a shrunken European population, and the island was preyed upon by leaders of the rival clans of Chiaramonte, Palizzi, and Ventimiglia. An alternative approach would see the power of these barons as a force for consolidation and integration, for why should the historian automatically side with the monarchy and assume that baronial power was inherently wicked? Images of Sicilian history from the days of the great nineteenth-century latifundia have perhaps been imposed on a rather different medieval reality. True, the island was split into three, and later four, sectors, often in conflict with one another as the factions known as 'Latins' and 'Catalans' struggled for ascendancy, and royal power was of little consequence. But it would be wrong to imagine that the barons mismanaged all their affairs. What they succeeded in creating was well-organized statelets, reminiscent of north Italian *signorie*, which they kicked into new life by patronizing fairs, fostering local trade, and managing their own estates with care. They took from the crown the right to mint coins and to judge capital crimes, but this did not necessarily undermine either justice or the economy, as Stephan Epstein has powerfully argued.[2] What it did achieve, however, was the demise of the centralized, bureaucratic monarchy that the Normans had founded.

In reality, the choice between a very positive and a very negative view of developments on the island is a false one. In the 1360s, Angevin raids, 'Latin'–'Catalan' rivalry and abandoned rural estates suggest serious crisis. But it was arguably a short-term one, and the arrival in 1392 of armies from Aragon–Catalonia, intent on bringing the island under direct rule from Spain, gradually put an end to internal squabbles and stabilized the political and economic life of the island. Catalan settlers began to arrive and were rewarded with lands, but the kings of Aragon rapidly became aware that they could not press this generosity too far without irritating the greater barons. Piece by piece, the Aragonese monarchy was able to recover

[2] S. R. Epstein, *An Island for Itself: Economic Development and Social Change in Late Medieval Sicily* (Cambridge, 1992).

traditional rights such as the control of higher criminal cases. Closer royal bonds with the towns counterbalanced baronial power as well, and the towns were never permitted the sort of autonomy that characterized the city–states of northern Italy, even as rivalries among the three major cities, Palermo, Messina, and Catania, remained intense. The fifteenth century, under absentee rulers such as Alfonso V of Aragon (r. 1416–58) and Ferdinand the Catholic (r. 1468–1516), appears to have been a somewhat somnolent but certainly not disastrous time for the island's inhabitants. The grain trade recovered as Alfonso, dreaming of a Catalan–Aragonese 'Common Market' in the western Mediterranean, encouraged his Catalan subjects to turn to Sicily for grain. The island's governors listened to the petitions of the Sicilian parliaments and corresponded regularly with their masters, the kings of Aragon in Spain or, after 1442, Naples.

The south Italian mainland also experienced crisis followed by a degree of recovery. In the factional struggles that saw Joanna I assassinated in 1382, followed to her grave not long after by her arch-rival Charles of Durazzo, the territorial power of the great nobles only increased and the monarchy appeared to become a cipher. Lalle Camponeschi, lord of L'Aquila, the major city of the Abruzzi, was able to function as a free agent in the late fourteenth century and is indistinguishable in conduct and authority from the *signori* in the papal states not far to the north. he worked hand in glove with the city councillors to promote the prosperity of the Abruzzese frontier region. L'Aquila minted its own coins, gave privileges to foreign merchants, and occasionally showed its teeth by refusing to support one or another claimant for Naples' throne. It is far from clear what real political issues divided the south Italian barons: the most potent one seems simply to have been who had the best claim to the throne, especially since both Joanna I and Joanna II (d. 1435) had no surviving heirs. Another issue of importance was the Great Schism in the papacy, which began in 1378 when a group of exasperated cardinals rejected the authority of an irascible and unpredictable Neapolitan who had been raised to the pontificate as Urban VI. Joanna turned against him, and Urban tried to unseat her. Amid the squalid royal murders, this meant that the Balzo Orsini, Sanseverino, and other barons were left to build princely power in the provinces. A rival Angevin dynasty, which had already acquired Provence, set itself up as claimant to the Neapolitan crown and disrupted southern Italy with a series of invasions that left the kingdom divided between the nobles and towns loyal to the house of Anjou–Durazzo and those that supported the branch of Anjou–Provence. The latter had to rely for its funds and political support on the greater barons, who seized the chance to enhance their privileges and obtain grants of royal estates. It is thus a curious question why anyone was so desperate to win a crown that seemed to be worth so little.

Spanish kings and French intruders

The house of Durazzo certainly attempted to restore royal authority. King Ladislas (d. 1414) retained the old Angevin enthusiasm for foreign adventures, attacking Florence and meddling in Sicilian affairs. In part this was necessitated by the attempts of his rivals from Provence to mobilize opposition both inside and outside the kingdom of Naples; and he evidently hoped that successes in wars fought abroad would bring him respect at home. Ladislas addressed the problem of baronial power in the *Regno*, turning on the supporters of his Provençal rivals. His surprise tactics included the mass arrest of the Marzano clan at a wedding feast. But this is not to suggest that noble power was broken: around 1399 the Balzo Orsini family laid their hands on the former royal principality of Taranto, in the heel of Italy, which they held until 1463 and became by far the most powerful principality within southern Italy.

The indecisive Joanna II nominated both the house of Anjou–Provence and Alfonso, king of Aragon, as her heir. Alfonso took seven years, following her death, to make good his claim, and his capture of Naples in 1442 still did not put an end to the insistent counter-claim of the romantic adventurer René, duke of Anjou–Provence. But the arrival of Alfonso from Catalonia did not make the kingdom of Naples into a mere appendage of the Spanish lands of the crown of Aragon. For one thing, Alfonso was already king of the islands of Sicily and of Sardinia, and his interest in southern Italy formed part of wider hegemonic ambitions in Italy, which may even have included aspirations to control of Milan. And, beyond Italy, he saw the kingdom of Naples as the launching pad for expeditions into the Balkans, where he set his sights on Hungary, Albania, Greece, and, ultimately,

Constantinople, which fell into the hands of the Turks in 1453, five years before he died. He resided in Naples and was content to leave the government of his Iberian kingdoms to his viceroys. He did not attempt to reunite the two Sicilian kingdoms, which, after all, had been separate entities for 160 years. But he did seek to weld together his kingdoms in Italy and Spain by promoting trade in cloth and grain between his territories, and his reign saw the implantation in Naples of a vigorous colony of Catalan merchants. Alfonso was also fascinated by Italian humanistic culture, styling himself as the successor to the Spanish Roman emperors, such as Trajan, whose reign had seen the maximum extent of the Roman Empire. He proposed to transform political conditions in his kingdom by fostering good relations with the barons; some of his former opponents received high office, for he rewarded loyalty even if it had been shown to his rival René. He raised funds through taxation of his subjects, permitting the great feudatories considerable autonomy in their lands so long as they acknowledged his needs, partly to achieve his grandiose objectives beyond southern Italy. If anything, therefore, Alfonso's policies enhanced the tendency towards the formation of baronial *signorie* in the provinces. Another major source of income was fees paid for the transhumance of sheep in Apulia, where vast flocks, whose numbers grew prodigiously at this time, migrated between summer and winter pastures. Alfonso's personal charm and lavish tastes won over many doubters, most significantly the dukes of Milan. Thus by the end of his life a Naples–Milan axis came into existence, in the hope of guaranteeing the 'peace of Italy'. Alfonso hesitantly adhered to the Italian League in 1455. However, he had more difficulty than he expected with the papacy, especially because the pope, Calixtus III Borgia, was a former civil servant of his who clearly wanted to demonstrate that he was now greater than his erstwhile master. The popes were, after all, technically overlords of the kingdom of Naples, and, while they were prepared to accept that he had won the kingdom and could not be dislodged, they noted with concern his insistence on appointing his illegitimate son Ferrante (Ferdinand) to succeed him in Naples, while his Spanish lands, along with Sicily and Sardinia, were destined for his brother John, king of Navarre. Alfonso saw Naples as his personal conquest, his to dispose of as he saw best.

Royal power in the kingdom of Naples rested on the three foundations of right by conquest, approval of Alfonso's claims (however reluctantly) by the papacy, and the fragile relationship between king and barons. Given the authority Alfonso wielded throughout the western Mediterranean, we can perhaps understand why his power in Naples was not seriously challenged once he captured the capital. For his son Ferrante (r. 1458–94), whose authority was confined to a single kingdom, and who still faced the challenge of the elderly René of Anjou, controlling the *Regno* was a more difficult and delicate matter. Ferrante's reign saw two baronial rebellions, met by the king's attempts to emancipate himself from dependence on the feudal nobility and to tie his fortunes to the towns. His policy rested in part on an imaginative economic policy that sought to promote trade and industry. He welcomed to Naples Jewish artisans expelled from Spain and Sicily in 1492. The considerable extension of the system of sheep transhumance, already in full expansion under Alfonso, also promised considerable revenues; but the pastures were severely damaged during the first baronial revolt and remained a fragile asset. He hoped that commercial treaties with kingdoms as far away as England might one day produce a viable income and thus sought to create a financial base sufficiently broad to free the monarchy from baronial grants of taxation. It is hard not to see in the opposition of the barons to Ferrante their hope of a collapse at the centre, with the prospect of a further increase in their regional power. Put simply, the barons identified the house of Anjou with weak central government, and that of Aragon with centralization. Ferrante's insistence on the crown's rights may be gauged from the fact that he revived the moribund University of Naples as a centre of legal study. Such issues came to the fore in the second baronial rebellion, of 1485, which appears to have been aimed not so much at the king, now fat and old, but at his son Alfonso, a skilled soldier but a less than tactful politician. The barons accused Alfonso of trying to consolidate the royal domain around Naples at the expense of noble interests, while he dreamed of making the city into a magnificent capital graced by fountains and boulevards. The Aragonese kings wanted to be seen as allies of the city elites rather than of the aristocracy. Such trust as they retained in the nobility after the first rebellion twenty years earlier now completely evaporated, and the king and his son systematically despoiled the possessions of the defeated rebels in 1486, taking delight in the expropriation of rich libraries as well as extensive estates.

Ferrante's close involvement in the politics of northern Italy was at first based on an intimate link with the Sforza of Milan, who held the duchy of Bari in southern Italy and who were linked by marriage to Ferrante's family. His policies culminated in conflicts with Medicean Florence in 1478–80 that came to an unexpected end when Lorenzo de' Medici sealed a tight alliance with Naples: in 1483 Lorenzo became titular Grand Chamberlain of Naples, and he and Ferrante worked closely together during the War of Ferrara (1482–4). But Ferrante was wrong if he assumed that the death of his long-time rival René and his heirs spelled the end of external challenges, for the Angevin claim passed to the royal house of France. Whereas King Louis XI had been content to combine official support for René with a lack of any interest in direct intervention, his son Charles VIII, influenced by chivalric dreams of the reconquest of Constantinople and Jerusalem, saw the recovery of Angevin rights over Naples as the essential first step. That the kingdom had a role to play in the battle against the Ottomans went without saying. The Turkish siege of Otranto in 1480–1 had proved that Ottoman designs went further than the Balkans. Southern Italy faced Albania, which had been lost to the Turks despite the formidable opposition of the warlord Scanderbeg, a close ally of Alfonso and Ferrante. The massive French army that invaded Italy in 1494 also had the temporary support of Lodovico il Moro, the de facto ruler and aspiring duke of Milan, who was prepared to sacrifice the long-standing links between Naples and Milan in order to bolster his position at home. In fact, the invasion descended into tragic farce; Ferrante's son Alfonso, now king of Naples, fled in the face of conquering French armies, which were however unable to establish a secure hold on the fractious kingdom. The retreating French were attacked in 1495 by an alliance of Italian states, including Milan. Yet the French invasion was certainly much more than a quick storm in the kingdom of Naples. Following the restoration of the Aragonese dynasty, the new king, Federigo, had to make handsome concessions to his subjects in order to win back their loyalty. The Venetians took over Monopoli and other ports on the Adriatic coast. Nor did Federigo enjoy the international support for which he may have hoped, once his relative the king of Aragon decided to raise his own banner independently in the South of Italy.

Ferdinand the Catholic, king of Aragon, plays a highly ambiguous role in the subsequent history of the Italian South. Machiavelli underscored his duplicity and hypocrisy, observing (in *Prince* xviii) that, although he preached nothing but peace and good faith, he was in fact the bitter enemy of both. Ferdinand saw himself as a new Alfonso the Magnanimous who would bring Naples back under the same rule as the other Aragonese dominions. The new French king, Louis XII, was pressing claims to both Milan and Naples. For a brief while Ferdinand and Louis were even able to agree on the division of the kingdom of Naples between Aragon and France, assigning the areas closer to Sicily to Ferdinand, already king of the island. In reality the brilliant Spanish general Gonzalo Fernández de Córdoba ('The Great Captain', as the Italians called him) was poised to seize the whole of southern Italy from Louis, achieving his objective by 1503, often in the face of apparently superior French armies. Naples rose to prominence in Ferdinand's plans after his wife Isabella, the Castilian queen, died in 1504 and he was denied royal power in Castile; peeved, he travelled to Naples to make real his rule over southern Italy. Having finally pieced together the western Mediterranean empire of his uncle Alfonso, he aspired to even greater successes against the Turks in the eastern Mediterranean.

Yet, unlike Alfonso, he could not stay in Naples permanently, for his Iberian concerns soon called him back to Spain. Thus he had to govern Naples from afar through viceroys whom he did not always find easy to control. This is plain from his differences with Gonzalo de Córdoba, possibly motivated as much by jealousy of the Great Captain's popularity and by fears that he would establish his own permanent power base in southern Italy (conceivably using Castilian support) as by any serious policy differences. Ferdinand understood the kingdom of Naples to be a personal prize, an inheritance from his uncle Alfonso who had unwisely conferred the kingdom on his illegitimate son Ferrante instead of on his legitimate successor, Ferdinand's father. He did not see it as an integral part of the lands of the crown of Aragon but as a disposable asset that he was even occasionally prepared to trade in complex marriage deals with the house of Habsburg. The kingdom was certainly not treated as a colonial appendage of the Spanish lands. Ferdinand and his viceroys took care to confirm the privileges granted by Alfonso and Ferrante (although they questioned the acts of subsequent rulers whose claim to the throne Ferdinand challenged). Ferdinand understood the need to restore the old order, to appear as a traditional south Italian monarch, even as an absentee ruler.

We can gain some idea of Ferdinand's obsessions by looking at one question that particularly troubled him. Ferrante had deeply irritated his cousin by positively welcoming Spanish and Sicilian Jews into southern Italy in vast numbers. Following the capture of the kingdom in 1503, Ferdinand rapidly decided to expel the south Italian Jews, as he had those of Sicily and, of course, Spain. His difficulty was that the expulsion decrees in southern Italy were repeatedly deferred or modified by viceroys with their own local priorities. Don Gonzalo de Córdoba was simply not interested in expulsion, disingenuously insisting that the number of Jews in southern Italy was really quite insignificant, while also arguing a contradictory case that their expulsion would have a detrimental effect on the economy, especially since many Jews could be expected to settle in Venetian territory, thus handing Venice great benefit. This was the sort of fiscal argument that often appealed to Ferdinand, and, following representations from the Neapolitan elite, he decided in 1508 to confirm the privileges conferred on the Jews by Ferrante in another return to traditional policies. Even when Ferdinand once again ordered the expulsion of the Jews in 1510, this pragmatism re-emerged as he permitted important exceptions, thereby undermining his own principle of completely suppressing the Jewish religion in all the lands he ruled. Two hundred families were allowed to stay, subject to an annual tribute of 3,000 ducats. Later, Charles V also confirmed Ferrante's privileges, and a final expulsion of Jews did not take place until 1541.

However, it was the war against the Turks that dominated Spanish policy towards southern Italy in the first half of the sixteenth century, when the kingdom of Naples passed under the rule of Ferdinand's eventual successor Charles V. Charles saw the kingdom as a potential, though reluctant, source of cash for the naval war against the Ottomans, and, in 1527, for a renewed land war against the French, who briefly reached Naples itself. The hunt for cash was one reason for allowing Jews to remain until 1541. Certainly the Spanish viceroys had to confront constant complaints that war taxes were too high; their fiscal demands were not matched by growth in the economy, nor by economic initiatives comparable to those under Ferrante. Yet it would be difficult to indict the viceroys as ruthless exploiters of a newly won Spanish colony. Pedro de Toledo, whose name is still commemorated in the main street of Naples, did something to realize Alfonso II's dream of turning the city into a model capital. Relations with the provinces stabilized, after the long period of conflict between the great barons and the monarchy. This was accompanied by some degree of economic growth, as population levels recovered and trade around the kingdom's shores prospered, even if it was Genoese in the Tyrrhenian ports and Venetians in the Adriatic ones who managed the most profitable commerce.

Signs of recovery were also visible in Sicily, which was able to meet the needs of growing population and reviving markets through grain sales. Like southern Italy, the island stood dangerously poised on the frontier with Islam, and Ferdinand, followed by Charles V, tried to protect the island's exposed flanks by seizing cities along the north coast of Africa. Charles also protected the waters south of Sicily by granting Malta, long part of the kingdom of Sicily, to the Order of St John of Jerusalem (the Knights Hospitallers), whose defence of the island against the Turks in 1565 helped ensure that the central and western Mediterranean would not become an Ottoman lake.

The southern Renaissance

The history of southern Italy in this period is thus not simply a story of impoverishment and decay. Energetic kings and viceroys played a significant part in the politics of Italy as a whole. Naples welcomed some of the leading cultural figures of the age: under Robert the Wise, the painter Giotto and the literary giants Petrarch and Boccaccio; under Alfonso the Magnanimous, the sculptor Laurana and the humanist polemicist Valla; and under Ferrante, the sculptor Mazzoni and the humanist Giovanni Pontano. Sicily too was not cut off from cultural developments on the peninsula, even if its greatest artist, Antonello da Messina, was partly trained in Flanders and plied his trade in Naples. Monarchy was not detrimental to the arts: Charles of Anjou was the patron of troubadour poets, and Petrarch selected Robert to examine him and declare him fit for the laurel crown in recognition of his mastery of the art of poetry. To Robert, 'puissant king and pride of Italy, great glory of our age', Petrarch dedicated his epic poem *Africa*. The political thinkers of fifteenth-century Naples mobilized classical texts, such as Seneca's *De clementia*, to extol Alfonso and Ferrante. The study of civil law was promoted, and under Ferrante Naples' reputation as a centre of musical patronage was unrivalled (the king had a large private museum of musical instruments). The library catalogues of the great barons also show an impressive taste for Latin and even Greek culture. Ferrante encouraged the new art of printing for a combination of economic and educational motives; not merely Latin but Hebrew printing flourished, and several illuminated printed books survive from the royal library, illustrating the king and his courtiers. The magnificence of display when Alfonso received Emperor Frederick III in Naples in 1452 astounded contemporaries. Building projects also show how well the South was integrated into the cultural world of Renaissance Italy. The Aragonese summer residence at Poggioreale was modelled on the Medici villa at Poggio a Caiano outside Florence, and the Aragonese arch of the Castelnuovo in Naples brilliantly combined classical features with themes from medieval romance. Both in the early fourteenth and the mid and late fifteenth century, Naples was a place to go to in search of effective and generous patronage: not for nothing was King Robert nicknamed 'the Wise' and King Alfonso 'the Magnanimous'.

In 1500 Naples, a large, beautiful, and desirable city, stood at the hub of Italian politics and attracted the merchants of Genoa and Barcelona, Florence and Augsburg. It also attracted conquerors from France and Spain. The struggles for power damaged but did not wreck the foundations of this Italian kingdom.

Representations of power

Edward Muir

Rulers in Renaissance Italy recognized that power must catch the eye. The evocative representation of power in works of art and public ceremonies has long been recognized as a hallmark of Italian Renaissance culture. Jacob Burckhardt's famous phrase, 'the state as a work of art', epitomized his view that the naked exercise of power so common in Italy from the late fourteenth to the sixteenth century required the legitimation supplied by patronage of the arts and sponsorship of festivals. More recently scholars have remained intrigued by 'the arts of power', the ways in which works of art constituted personal and institutional power relationships, in effect creating as well as representing political networks.[1] Since Burckhardt wrote a century and a half ago, the assessment of power in the Renaissance has broadened to treat the exercise of authority as a kind of public performance, enacted through civic rituals; princely, papal, and episcopal entries; and official rites of passage such as elections and coronations.

The historical problem is to sort out how political and social contexts gave meaning to the stock repertoire of symbols and allegories inherited from medieval Christianity and resurrected from Greek and Roman antiquity, the latter of which became ever more prominent in the fifteenth and sixteenth centuries. The meanings imputed to

---

[1] Jacob Burckhardt, *The Civilization of the Renaissance in Italy* (first published 1860), trans. S. G. C. Middlemore (2 vols., New York, 1958); R. Starn and L. Partridge, *Arts of Power: Three Halls of State in Italy, 1300–1600* (Berkeley, 1992).

specific images and symbols were never simple matters of icono-
graphical translation but always multiple and subject to conflicting
interpretations that reveal not just underlying social tensions but also
the Renaissance love of ambiguity and intellectual play.

The power of perception

Understanding how images and performances formulated and
evoked power requires the examination of two interrelated processes.
The first was the creation of the representation itself, product of a
series of decisions by patrons, theological and humanist advisers,
artists, and masters of ceremonies about how to depict religious or
political power and create an image for those who held that power.
These decisions were based upon an understanding of local history,
scripture, hagiography, and classical mythology as encoded in narratives and iconography. Those who made these decisions became
sophisticated and, in some cases, highly professional image makers,
essential assistants to anyone who wished to acquire and retain
power. The successful management of the representation of power, as
in the case of Cosimo de' Medici or Pope Julius II, propagated a high
reputation among contemporaries and promoted lasting fame.

   The second process involved the perception by viewers of those
representations. Certainly many of those who looked at images or
ceremonies or heard orations and music would have missed much of
the allusive content, especially if they lacked formal theological training or a classical education. Nevertheless, there is ample evidence that
the unlettered were attracted to and impressed by the splendour of
public representations of power, even if they did not fully understand
the nuances of meaning. The educated and 'political' classes
included many keen connoisseurs of artistic representations and
rituals. The diaries and poems of merchants and ordinary citizens,
the diplomatic reports of ambassadors and legates, and the accounts
of humanists and historians provide an instructive record of perceptions. The Florentine wine merchant Bartolomeo del Corazza, for
example, kept a precise account of the ceremonies he witnessed
between 1405 and 1438 and was exceptionally conscious of their symbolic significance. The Venetian diarist and senator Marin Sanudo

recorded and interpreted hundreds of civic ceremonies, diplomatic receptions, and festivals in his copious diaries from 1496 to 1533. Commemorative and descriptive interpretations of great civic ceremonies, especially celebrations of victories and visits of foreign princes, became a staple of the printing industry by the middle of the sixteenth century, a clear indication of strong market demand for them.

The ambiguity of most representations of power allowed considerable room for creative interpretation and manipulation, usually to the benefit of the powerful. The cult of the Magi in fifteenth-century Florence, for example, blended sacred and secular power in a characteristically enigmatic way. The Magi of the biblical story were three wise men who followed a star to the manger in Bethlehem where they worshipped the Christ child. The narrative supplied a metaphor for the spiritual journey of the wise and wealthy towards humble submission to the divine. In post-biblical versions the wise men were transformed into three kings, which metaphorically bonded spiritual power to secular authority. From 1390 to 1470 Florentines mounted a large number of Magi processions, organized by a confraternity that revealingly described itself as 'the republic of the Magi'. Florence lacked a king or prince who could supply a charismatic centre as a focus of civic loyalty, and before 1434 short terms of office and prohibitions against family members succeeding one another in office prevented any individual or family from cultivating the charisma of a prince.

Devotion to the Magi supplied the necessary charisma for Florentine governments, which took a keen interest in the Magi spectacles and plays. A law of 1429 obligated the governing priors to make an offering at the church of San Marco on Epiphany and, together with prominent Florentines who took the parts of the Magi, to accompany in procession images depicting Mary and the infant Jesus. After 1434 Cosimo de' Medici assumed unofficial power over the republic and conspicuously joined the entourage of the Magi during the annual Epiphany procession. Adopting the three kings as a family cult, the Medici commissioned numerous works of art featuring the Magi and exploited the Magi narrative to legitimate their domination of Florentine politics. By inserting themselves and their followers into the annual processions, the Medici presented themselves as worthy companions of kings, prince-like in honour and rank if not in name.

The centrepiece of the Medici association with the Magi became the frescoes in the chapel of the Medici palace that depict Cosimo, his relatives and allies, and the Byzantine emperor accompanying the Magi on their journey to pay homage to the Christ child. Although the intimate chapel was a place for private devotions, Cosimo used it for his social and diplomatic receptions. In 1459, Galeazzo Maria Sforza, the son of Cosimo's most important foreign ally, made an official visit to Florence, and Cosimo received him in the chapel with an elaborate display of affection. During his two-week stay Galeazzo Maria always met Cosimo in the chapel and attended mass there at least six times. This conflation of the sacred and the political was characteristic of Medici representations of power. On another occasion, the Milanese ambassador described a crowd of visitors to the Magi chapel offering allegiance to the Medici: 'It was as if [Cosimo] were holding a church dedication at home.'[2] Recognizing the political significance of the cult of the Magi for legitimating Medici influence, the republic that replaced the Medici in 1494 removed the chapel furnishings, altar, and altarpiece to the Palazzo della Signoria. Whatever Cosimo's intentions had been, others clearly perceived how he employed the Christian symbolism of the Magi to give spiritual sanction to his political power.

Representing and perceiving involved more than interpreting meanings. Contemporary optical theories suggested that the viewers of an object are brought under the influence of what they see through a profusion of material or spiritual emanations from the object itself. The crucial implications were that the viewer receives images passively and that the impressions created in the brain are assimilated as concepts. To see objects or persons was to come under their power through their effect on cognition. On feast days of the Virgin in Siena, for example, images of her were carried in processions through the streets and neighbourhoods in an attempt to maximize the effects of the beneficent emanations from a sacred icon. In the late thirteenth century the city commissioned a series of ever more elaborate and large panels, culminating in the 1308 commission to Duccio di Buoninsegna who painted the huge sixteen by fifteen foot *Maestà*, which was too large to hoist up and carry throughout the streets. The

---

[2] Cited in D. Kent, *Cosimo de' Medici and the Florentine Renaissance: The Patron's Oeuvre* (New Haven, 2000), p. 306.

government had the painting set on the high altar of the cathedral and required citizens to walk by the image rather than have it carried to them. Processing in front of the *Maestà* on the feast of the Assumption became the crucial test of political loyalty since all citizens of Siena and subjects in surrounding villages were obliged to join the procession and make offerings of candles. Criminals who had been deprived of their rights of citizenship were specifically prohibited from appearing. Thus, through a legally defined obligation to join in a procession, the Sienese looked at the Virgin and came under her power.

Princes, popes, and civic officials adopted this religious practice of displaying objects in order to bring people under their power. The prototype of the Renaissance prince in fashioning a self-image in this way was King Robert of Naples (r. 1309–43). He understood the power of public representations in his commissions to prominent artists associating him with King Solomon, and he performed conspicuous acts of piety, especially in support of the Spiritual Franciscans, who enhanced his kingship through religious sanction. Unlike earlier medieval rulers whose fame depended on significant military achievements, Robert cultivated a reputation largely as a cultural project in image making. He achieved his reputation in two ways. One was through the display of his own erudition. He authored, certainly with considerable assistance from advisers, several hundred learned texts, including many sermons. He inserted himself into many public ceremonies by reading his sermons or having them read at mass in the royal chapel and throne hall, but also in monasteries, at the medical school in Salerno, and before visiting ambassadors and foreigners. Robert's other method for cultivating a magnificent reputation was through visual images. He patronized learned men as advisers to artists who decorated Naples with images celebrating the virtues of Robert and his dynasty. Giotto decorated the palace chapel and throne hall (now destroyed) with depictions of illustrious men from the Bible and classical antiquity, thereby associating Robert with the most famous men in history. Simone Martini painted a panel showing angels crowning Robert's brother, Louis of Toulouse, a Franciscan, champion of the dissident Spirituals, and later a saint, who in turn gives Robert the crown of Naples. Robert thus associated himself with sanctity and created the image of a sacred dynasty that had received authority to rule directly from God. Robert's patronage anticipated the style of rule of the Renaissance princes of the fifteenth and sixteenth centuries—the Gonzaga, Este, Medici, and the later Aragonese rulers of Naples itself—who relied on the arts and letters to fashion public images as an instrument of rule.

So pervasive were these associations between displaying objects and representing power that good government was assumed to have visual effects in the sense that its results would be evident to rulers and ruled alike. Those who walked or rode in a procession witnessed the consequences of their public actions; good government was thus mirrored in well-ordered civic spaces and well-mannered citizens. In Ambrogio Lorenzetti's mid fourteenth-century *Allegory of Good and Bad Government* in the Sala dei Nove in the Palazzo Pubblico in Siena, the frescoed walls depicting the effects of good and bad government provided visual models for what the officials who met in the room would see when they walked in a civic procession. If they governed well, they would observe buildings in good repair, commerce thriving, students studying, and young women enjoying the security of a well-policed state. If they governed ill, they would witness urban ruin and streets ruled by armed thugs. On another wall in the room, the constitution of government itself was allegorized with the female figures of Justice, Concord, and the other Christian virtues. Beneath these allegorical figures, the officials of Siena are depicted walking in a procession of mutual concord, as if they were observing the effects of their decisions on the adjacent walls. The power of perception was, therefore, twofold: on the one hand, the arts and rituals created images that brought the ruled under the influence and power of the rulers, and, on the other hand, they provided a pictorial representation of the obligations and duties of rulers, binding them to ideals of good government.

Vocabularies of power

The vocabularies for representing power, whether rhetorical, iconographic, or ceremonial, exhibited the traits of several coherent systems, full of cross-references and borrowings. The most pervasive medieval system of representations invoked the mystical body of Christ. For all Christians the singular fact of history was the incarnation of Christ, his incorporation of the two natures of God and man. All legitimate power on earth partook of this unique bonding of the divine and the human. Other religious figures also suffused the political vocabulary, including the Magi, the Virgin, characters from the Hebrew scriptures such as David and Judith, and the saints whose relics had flowed into the churches of rich Italian cities, especially during the Crusades. The lore of Troy taken from the *Aeneid* and the history of ancient Rome supplied other concepts. Classical mythology provided new motifs derived from the legends of Hercules and Perseus and the myths of the Greek and Roman gods.

In medieval monarchic theory the body metaphor based on Christ's two natures was transformed into the image of two bodies, one mortal and one eternal, that prevailed in the visual, ceremonial, and legal representations of the king's two bodies in France and England. In Italy the most systematic representation of the two-bodies theory of rulership appeared in Venice during the interregnum ceremonies after the death of a doge. In the case of France and England, interregnum rites smoothed the path of dynastic succession, but in Venice, where the doge was an elected official, they blocked any hint of dynastic identification with the office. At news of the doge's death all emblems of his authority—his official gold ring, the stamps for ducal seals, and forms for the ducat coin issued by the Venetian mint—were smashed. Two new silver emblems were quickly produced: one, inscribed with the name of the deceased doge, depicted an enthroned and crowned doge holding the banner of St Mark in his hand; the other was identical to the first except that it lacked the doge's name. Officials smashed the first emblem while the second was presented to the new doge after his election. Venetian political thought explained these ceremonies through the theory of two doges: 'In this alone are they different: that the one is the perpetual head of all, while the other is temporary and governs a single part. Both are equally called the Prince: for being the first, and grandly revered and honoured by all, he represents a truly absolute prince to those who see him in his majesty, with so many ornaments acquired by means of his valour; but in fact he is tied by the laws in a way that his position is not at all different from the other positions of any magistracy.'[3] The objective of the Venetian ducal interregnum

---

[3] Francesco Sansovino, *Venetia città nobilissima et singolare*, with additions by Giovanni Stringa (Venice, 1604), p. 314r.

ceremony was to represent to the doge's family and the political elite this constitutional theory of the two doges: the rites disjoined the mortal, magistrate doge of the first emblem from the eternal, regal doge symbolized by the second. In this fashion Venetian inter-regnum rituals precluded dynastic succession and prevented the subversion of the republican system that required the election of the new doge.

Only Venice among the Italian city–republics adopted a systematic representation of its polity based on metaphors of Christ's body. Without the body of a prince to hang the metaphor on, the body image tended to fragment as much as unify republics. As John Najemy has observed, 'metaphors of the body . . . prove to be a prob-lematic, sometimes inappropriate, and ultimately a structurally con-flicted way of talking about political associations'.[4] He suggests that the Italian humanists attempted to contain the conflicts of the body metaphor by subjecting it to a fantasy of idealized beauty, that digni-fied, harmonious, well-proportioned body borrowed from the ancient Greeks. In a revealingly multivalent fashion, the Florentines attached the signs of power to several different figures represented in sculptures prominently displayed at the seats of civic power.

The locations for the display of two sculptures by Donatello illus-trate how the vocabularies of the human body were adapted to suit the interests of different regimes in Florence. The bronze *David* and *Judith and Holofernes* were first shown for about thirty years in the outdoor spaces of the Medici palace. David and Judith represented parallel narratives: both were underdogs—a boy and a woman—who saved their peoples from tyranny by beheading, respectively, a Philis-tine giant and an Assyrian king. Displayed in the courtyard of the Medici palace, 'together the sculptures conveyed the controversial, self-serving message that the family's role in Florence was akin to that of venerable Old Testament tyrant slayers and saviors of their people, symbolically inverting the growing chorus of accusations that the Medici had become tyrants who had sucked all real power out of the

---

[4] J. M. Najemy, 'The republic's two bodies: body metaphors in Italian Renaissance political thought', in A. Brown (ed.), *Language and Images of Renaissance Italy* (Oxford, 1995), p. 241.

city's republican institutions'.[5] These sculptures created a close metaphorical bond between the Medici and Florence, which had historically depicted itself as a weak yet valiant city surrounded by powerful, tyrannical enemies. The Medici, seen by some Florentines as tyrants, thus sought to create a counter-image of themselves as defenders of Florentine liberty.

In 1495, after the expulsion of the Medici, the republican government dominated by the Dominican friar Savonarola confiscated the *Judith* and placed it on the ceremonial stage in front of the Palazzo della Signoria. The new context inverted the *Judith*'s Medicean meaning by transforming the once dominant family into the tyrants defeated by the republic, which now associated itself with Judith. For Savonarola Judith probably offered a salutary public example of the triumph of virtue over vice. But she did not remain for long as the predominant symbol of the republic. After the fall of Savonarola, the government of Piero Soderini removed the *Judith and Holofernes* from its prominent place in front of the town hall. In 1504 a committee of artists and Florentine citizens decided to replace Donatello's bronze with Michelangelo's newly commissioned giant marble statue of David, which became the powerful, hyper-masculine symbol of the revitalized republic. According to the herald of the Florentine republic, Francesco Filarete, the *Judith* was unsuitable because it was a 'deadly sign' for the republic and because 'it is not good to have a woman kill a man'. As Adrian Randolph has argued, Filarete's hostility to Donatello's *Judith* 'emerged from the peculiar ambivalence of the statue itself', but also from fears about the role of women in a republic.[6] Michelangelo's muscular David, which was such a dramatic contrast to Donatello's slight, adolescent David, became a distinctive emblem emphasizing the need to be vigilant to defend the republic's liberty.

In 1530 the new Medicean principate abandoned the family's old strategy of presenting themselves as first among equals and completely transformed the dynasty's vocabulary for representing power. No longer did the Medici associate themselves with valiant and pious figures from the Bible: the Magi kneeling before the Christ child,

---

[5] S. B. McHam, 'Donatello's bronze *David* and *Judith* as metaphors of Medici rule in Florence', *The Art Bulletin*, 83 (2001), p. 32. For a differing interpretation, cf. Adrian W. B. Randolph, *Engaging Symbols: Gender, Politics, and Public Art in Fifteenth-Century Florence* (New Haven, 2002), pp. 259–60.

[6] Randolph, *Engaging Symbols*, pp. 280–1.

David the slayer of Goliath, Judith the slayer of Holofernes. Instead they imitated the pagan ancients, especially the Roman emperors. Grand duke Cosimo adopted Hercules as a favoured emblem of the dynasty, and decorations at his funeral were designed to transform his passing into an apotheosis, the elevation of his mortal body to the eternal realm of the gods. The message to his Florentine and Tuscan subjects was that succeeding Medici grand dukes were gods-in-waiting. Portraits of family members in paintings, sculptures, and medallions now asserted their individuality as powerful persons rather than their iconic position as stand-ins for Biblical figures. The portrait became the vehicle for representing the idealized bodies of princes and promoting a kind of fame previously denied by the rectitude of republican values in which the elevation of an individual above his fellow-citizens generated political suspicions and envy.

Despite the changing images of power as Florence went from republic to Medicean principate, the seat of government remained the Palazzo della Signoria. This venerable building, which dated back to 1299–1314, provided the concrete symbol of republican power in Florence, even when the Medici actually ruled the city from their private palace. Control of this building, in fact, signified possession of legitimate power, and rebels in 1343 and 1378 concentrated their efforts on occupying it. So vital was its representational force as the locus of power that the statues displayed in front of it were, as we have seen, changed with successive regimes. Despite its symbolism as a bastion of republican Florence, Grand Duke Cosimo I de' Medici refused to tear it down. According to Giorgio Vasari, Cosimo transformed the old town hall into a Medici palace rather than replace it with something more modern because of the respect he had for the republican foundations of his government. The town halls of other cities, such as the Palazzo Pubblico in Siena, similarly symbolized continuity of rulership despite changing regimes.

In Venice where the republic survived without significant changes for 500 years after 1297, the Palace of the Doges embodied historical continuity, not just as a venerable building but in its decorations. On the walls of its major council halls, vast canvases depicted cardinal moments in Venetian history, especially episodes in which emperors and popes recognized the republic's autonomy and liberty. The Palace of the Doges was the setting for important diplomatic receptions and most spectacularly for the coronation of each new doge who was crowned at the top of a magnificent marble staircase that emphasized the majesty of his bearing. In each of the cities that Venice conquered on the mainland, it retained the old town hall as the seat of local government but replaced local symbols with a statue or relief of the winged lion of St Mark, the symbol of Venice. The transfer of sovereignty was conveyed through a change of symbolic labels.

Unlike the new Medicean duchy, the princes of the long-standing principalities felt no compunctions about restructuring their cities to magnify their power. In Milan, Ferrara, and Mantua, the castles and palaces of the ruling princes dominated the city, marking the princely family's power with a huge urban footprint. These palaces made not merely symbolic statements about power; they also created an intimidating physical presence through their size, menacing towers, crenellated walls, and surrounding moats. They left no doubt about who was in charge of the city. None of these princes was more successful in self-representation through architecture than Federico II da Montefeltro (1422–82), duke of Urbino. Through his patronage and cultural activities, Federico fashioned a reputation as the ideal Renaissance prince: a father figure to his subjects, an astute diplomat, brilliant soldier, generous patron, avid collector, and man of learning. Federico's greatest achievement, however, was the building of his vast palace. The project was supervised by the architect Luciano Laurana (c.1420–79), but Federico deserves most of the credit for what remains the single best example of Renaissance architectural ideals in a palace. Because of Federico, the small mountainous duchy of Urbino acquired a cultural importance far greater than its size warranted.

Representing the pope

Representing the papacy created a singular dilemma because the pope was both the universal monarch of all Latin Christendom and the ruling prince of the papal state, a composite role that produced contradictions and innumerable complications. In addition, the popes themselves, almost exclusively drawn from Italian aristocratic families after 1417, were deeply enmeshed in the politics of the peninsula through familial bonds, political alliances, and patronage. In contrast to the prevailing theory of kingship, canon law did not grant the pope two bodies. What remained after the death of a pope were Christ and the Apostolic See, not the fictive body of an eternal Pope. After the popes returned to Rome from Avignon in 1377 and the Council of Constance resolved the Great Schism in 1417, they faced the problem of regaining their hold over the papal state, which proved to be a dirty war-provoking business, while at the same time restoring the dignity and moral stature of the papacy. Resolving this dilemma became the predominant theme of the Renaissance papacy.

Perhaps most crucial were the rituals of the Vacant See, as the interregnum between one pope and another was called. The successful performance of these rituals assisted the Church in maintaining continuity of authority but also in separating the popes' ecclesiastical and princely power. The cardinal chamberlain first ensured that the pope was actually dead by striking the head of the corpse three times with a silver hammer, calling out the deceased's name. The chamberlain then signalled the beginning of the Vacant See by removing from the dead pope's finger the 'ring of the fisherman', which was then broken. The Patara bell signalled to the city that the pope had died. His apostolic authority reverted to Christ. His princely authority over the city of Rome reverted to the Roman commune. Prisoners were released, there were usually popular disorders, and ritual pillages of the former pope's property frequently occurred. The typical objects of ritual pillage were the statues of the deceased pontiff, personal icons of the incumbent's hold on the papal office. After the death of Julius II in 1513, the people of recently conquered Bologna destroyed Michelangelo's bronze statue of the pope, using the traditional ritual pillage as an occasion to protest against Julius's unpopular conquest of their city. In 1559 after the death of Paul IV, the Roman people themselves transformed the traditional ritual into protest by sacking the offices of the Inquisition, decapitating the pope's image erected on the Capitoline, and dragging the head of the statue through the streets of the city for days.

Once a pope was elected, he was dressed in the papal robes, seated on the throne of St Peter, the fisherman's ring was placed on his finger, and the cardinals kissed his hand, foot, and mouth, the usual gestures of obedience. The dual authority of the papacy was re-established through two additional ceremonies: the coronation at St Peter's and St John Lateran's, which conferred the apostolic power over the universal church on the new pope; and the *possesso*, a solemn procession to the Capitol, where the pope took possession of the city of Rome. Riding a white mule (an animal without reproductive capabilities that paralleled the celibate pope's inability to establish a ruling dynasty over the city), he was accompanied by representatives of the various social orders of the city. At the Capitol he received and returned the keys to the city and, like the newly elected doge in Venice, threw money to the crowd. Universal and local rule was re-established, a fact confirmed by the delegations of ambassadors who offered their congratulations.

Much of the pope's time in office was occupied by a continuous round of rituals: the 'audience' in which visitors engaged in an elaborate performance of obedience that culminated in kissing the papal foot, masses, celebrations of the liturgical calendar, the Holy Year eventually held every twenty-five years, entries of foreign dignitaries, canonizations, and absolutions. Some have been tempted to see all this as so much theatre, especially since by the sixteenth century an extensive propaganda bureaucracy was devoted to expressing papal magnificence. As the rituals of the Vacant See make clear, however, these were far more than mere 'representations' of power. They constituted power. Without the proper performance of these rituals, especially the coronation and *possesso*, the authority of the pope did not exist.

It is not surprising that some papal families sought ways to keep a hold on the prestige of the papacy. In Siena cathedral Pintoricchio painted scenes from the life of Pope Pius II (pontificate 1458–64) paid for by Pius's Piccolomini relatives. This humanist pope, a persuasive orator and skilled diplomat, had imaged a revitalized papacy built upon an ideology of universal empire with the pope as its spiritual head. To make this dream a reality, Pius proposed to lead a crusade against the Ottoman Turks, an event memorialized in Pintoricchio's frescoes. But the project died from lack of support from Europe's monarchs and Pius's own premature death. Pintoricchio's images obscure the untidy nature of papal diplomacy and the persistent failure of Renaissance popes to generate sufficient support for a crusade. Pope Julius II personally attempted to guarantee his own fame by commissioning Michelangelo to build a grand tomb. By memorializing the grandeur of Julius's pontificate, the tomb of imperial dimensions compensated for the message embedded in papal rituals that at his death Julius and his family lost all hold on the papacy. The challenge of representing papal power was a daunting task. Living popes had to blur distinctions by somehow creating a seamless web of authority over their multiple roles derived from scripture, tradition, canon law, and local Roman history, but the dead ones received summary treatment as their power was ritually dismantled.

Representing the city

How was the power of the city represented during the Renaissance? Because communes and city–states were the dominant political institutions in northern and central Italy, this question is both the most important and perhaps the most complex to answer. The city can be defined in several ways, each of which had the capacity to function as a part that stood for the whole. Cities were physical spaces, composed of an aggregation of buildings and usually a circumscribing wall; they were legal spaces in which certain statutes applied that defined citizenship, distributed authority among various offices, established how officials would be chosen, and set penalties for criminal offences; they were social spaces in which certain kinds of interactions habitually occurred, such as manufacturing, buying and selling, borrowing, negotiating, studying, gossiping, praying, cooperating, and competing; and they were an idea and a place identified by a name and symbols that conveyed a sensibility called *civiltà*. Writers from Bonvesin da la Riva in late-thirteenth-century Milan to Marin Sanudo in late-fifteenth-century Venice celebrated the marvels of their cities. Painters like Lorenzetti in Siena did so with images, and the invention in the fifteenth century of the bird's eye view of cities created the illusion of civic totality. In representing the city to its inhabitants and visitors, three ritual practices, in particular, reflected changing social and political conditions, modelled ideal arrangements of power, and created opportunities to subvert or redefine power relationships. These practices were the cults of patron saints, regular civic processions, and occasional entries of distinguished visitors.

Civic patriotism evolved out of devotion to patron saints. In fact, it could be argued that an intimate artistic and ritual relationship between the cults of patron saints and the citizenry was the crucial test of civic harmony. The list of lasting patronal relationships is long—St Ambrose in Milan, St Zenobius in Verona, St Mark in Venice, St Nicholas in Bari, St John the Baptist in Florence, and the Virgin Mary in Siena (but also practically everywhere else)—and the absence of a single unified cult, such as the failure of St George to attract the devotion of all Genoese, points to a more fragmented distribution of power. Essential for cultivating an effective civic cult was the possession of relics, the acknowledgement of miracles attributed to those relics, and the reliance of ecclesiastical and civic authorities on the protection of the saint in times of travail. In cities that lacked a princely dynasty, such as Siena, Florence, and Venice, saints' relics supplied the necessary charismatic centre, but even in princely regimes much of a lord's power derived from his conspicuous devotion to patron saints.

Civic processions derived from ecclesiastical processions that displayed relics to the citizens on feast days and during periods of crisis. They were particularly frequent during the liturgically rich season from December to June and ranged from a simple progress through the streets by a confraternity on its patron saint's feast day to an assembly of the entire civic order, both ecclesiastical and political, in which the relics of the saint were accompanied by blazons, symbols, and programmatic floats. Venice's elected officials, especially the doge, completely appropriated the liturgical rites of St Mark to create the most comprehensive state cult of any city–state in Italy. In Florence, as Richard Trexler has shown, urban processions were intimately connected to the changing forms of power. During the fourteenth and early fifteenth centuries, the classical commune represented itself as guided by wise elders, exemplified by the Magi processions, and as borrowing from traditional knightly sources of honour. At first the Medici made no attempt to alter this well-established ritual vocabulary of power. They merely tried to insert themselves into it, as with the Magi processions. But their quiet subversion of the republic's electoral procedures also undermined its symbolic underpinnings, creating a kind of charismatic void at the centre. Under Lorenzo de' Medici the Florentines began to experiment with alternative sources of charisma in what Trexler calls the 'ritual revolution'. A cult of youth and processions of boys substituted for the old ritual order dominated by elders. The trend continued under Savonarola. Both the secular quasi-prince Lorenzo and the pious Dominican friar became charismatic figures who unified the city during periods of symbolic and ritual instability. This ritual revolution can be traced through the changing composition of civic processions.

Cities were most vulnerable, physically and symbolically, at their gates. When foreign diplomats, visiting princes, or new bishops passed through those gates the entry had to be carefully stage-managed. During the fifteenth century entries evolved from a simple formal reception of the visitor by the city fathers to elaborate pageants complete with displays of blazons, expensive tapestries and carpets, painted mottoes, stages with actors pantomiming historical events, and even temporary triumphal arches. The expertise in protocol of masters of ceremonies and heralds was crucial since every statement made and gesture performed, the distance travelled to meet the visitor, the clothing worn, and the gifts presented were carefully read by participants and onlookers as messages of power. Protocol alone was insufficient to control meaning, which is why the pageantry decorations created for sixteenth-century entrances attempted to interpret the event for participants and witnesses. These pageants served as a kind of gloss on the ritual text of the entrance, and they taxed the ingenuity of the humanists, historians, and artists who created them. When King Henry III of France visited Venice in 1574, a committee of nobles, including two well known for their humanistic interests, planned the decorations for the entrance. The architect Andrea Palladio designed a wooden triumphal arch, which was decorated by Veronese and Tintoretto with historical scenes depicting France and Venice as natural allies against Protestant heretics and Turks.

City gates and walls played a metaphoric role similar to the king's bodies in monarchies. They contained and defined the physical limits of the city, but the power of all city–states stretched beyond their walls into the rural *contado* and subject towns, which made the walls an unstable metaphor of civic power. Entries through a city's gates took three forms: receptions for the arrival of formal equals who made no claim of authority over the city; advents that imitated Christ's Palm Sunday entry into Jerusalem and conveyed the image of a spiritual journey appropriate for a bishop or pope; and triumphs, like those of Roman generals, which welcomed visitors as conquerors.

Despite the rigidity of the protocol, entries were important moments in which power relationships could be redefined or subverted, and the impressions made on these occasions might have far more consequence than anything written in a treaty or said in a formal speech. When King Louis XII entered Genoa in 1507 after suppressing a rebellion, he intended to signify the city's loss of liberty by striking the city gate with his sword, but the Genoese attempted to mitigate the consequences of their defeat by lining the entry route with young virgins who begged for mercy on behalf of their elders. Competing rituals of triumph and supplication were employed by both sides in an attempt to define the relationship between the monarch and the city. When the Medici Pope Leo X, who had recently reasserted his family's control over their native city, entered Florence in 1515 he was greeted by seven triumphal arches, each depicting one of the seven Virtues and an eighth that displayed all the Virtues together. Temporary triumphal arches, which emulated surviving arches from imperial Rome, were relatively new. They had not figured in the earlier papal entrances into Florence of Eugenius IV in 1434 and Pius II in 1459. The latter had entered the city surrounded by mercenaries, 'like a tyrant', to the scandal of Florentine sensibilities.[7] The arches for Leo X expanded the authoritarian image of the pope to include the dignity of an imperial triumph, and they were located throughout the city, creating the unmistakable message that all of Florence, not just the traditional Medici strongholds around the family palace, had become Medici territory.

Representing the prince and court

In the principalities, in contrast to the republics, the body politic shrank back from unwieldy metaphors to human size, to the actual physical bodies of the men and women who were lords and ladies. In Milan, Mantua, Ferrara, and Urbino the field for the representation of power was intimate, private, even domestic, consisting of the lord's blazon erected in places subject to him, his palaces, the decorations of their receiving rooms, and especially the many little things revealed by his speech, gestures, manners, and bodily comportment. These

---

[7] Francesco Filarete, as quoted in R. C. Trexler, *Public Life in Renaissance Florence* (New York, 1980), p. 330.

were sites of self-presentation and self-representation, but as in the city, far from merely reflecting the power of the prince, these representations helped constitute and interpret it.

Renaissance courts bore the distinguishing marks of the prince's personality. Princely courts were as circumscribed by protocol and rules of behaviour as the papacy, but they were not as wedded to a strict regime of ritual performances, and princes guaranteed their lasting fame through the ability to perpetuate themselves through dynastic succession and marriage and patronage connections to other noble courts. The sinews of the princely court consisted of aristocratic blood, which irrevocably set the prince's family and court apart from common subjects, and the prince's word, which extended his authority beyond his ability to coerce obedience. It is no little irony, therefore, that courts were in reality places where the talented might find patronage and even social promotion no matter how common their social background and where the arts of dissimulation were most highly cultivated.

Galeazzo Maria Sforza both epitomized and profoundly tested the system. As duke of Milan (1466–76), according to no less an authority than the author of *The Courtier*, Baldassare Castiglione, he presided over 'the most beautiful court of any prince in Italy'[8], one noted for its rigid adherence to ceremony and precedence. But Galeazzo Maria's insensitive behaviour, his mercurial whims, and most of all his obsessive dissimulation, tested his subjects' tolerance. He was assassinated by three of his own courtiers, one motivated by a bad investment the prince had refused to make right and another out of revenge for his sister's seduction by the duke. Galeazzo Maria's compulsion to compete with the grandest courts of Europe, including those of France and Burgundy, led him to maintain a magnificent court that supported thousands of courtiers. He lavished gifts and lucrative stipends on them, and in 1476 the ducal budget devoted almost 200,000 ducats to court expenses, including everything from buildings to musicians. Gregory Lubkin has estimated that 'the duke spent huge sums on food, drink, jewelry, and clothes—as much as half the income of Italy's wealthiest princely state. To his outlay were added all the expenditures of court members who lived outside the walls and

---

[8] Baldassare Castiglione, as quoted in G. Lubkin, *A Renaissance Court: Milan under Galeazzo Maria Sforza* (Berkeley, 1994), p. 3.

spent their own money on sustenance and display.'⁹ The duke himself constituted the centre of power, which emanated outward from his person through the court to the city and dominion of the duchy. The reach of the duke of Milan stretched far beyond the duchy itself through a network of other courts and client states. The careful observance of religious feasts, court entertainments, and cultivation of graceful manners served to consolidate a network of clients under the patronage of the duke. But Galeazzo Maria's cruelty and lust corroded these careful arrangements and subverted his punctilious regard for hierarchy and precedent. Where the body politic actually was the body of the prince, the whole political order was in a sense represented by his behaviour.

Contemporary observers were keenly aware of the contrast between Galeazzo Maria's behaviour and that of one of his princely clients whose comportment carefully maintained an image of honourable rectitude. Marquis Ludovico Gonzaga (r. 1444–78) of Mantua served as the lieutenant general of Milan. When he received Galeazzo Maria's envoys in 1470 to renegotiate his contract, Ludovico welcomed them with a revealing statement about how his commitment to his own word was so deep that it had physical manifestations. He reported that he sweated or shivered when he promised something. Ludovico's commitment to fidelity, such an obvious contrast to Galeazzo Maria's inconstant word, may have been a 'combination of self-staging and crusty directness', but its bodily manifestation in sweat and shivers perfectly encapsulated the task of representing princely power.¹⁰ Ludovico, of course, was the patron and guiding figure behind the most revealing visual representation of an Italian court, Andrea Mantegna's frescoed room (now called the Camera degli Sposi) in the castle of Mantua. A monument to princely fidelity (the dedicatory plaque reads *ac fide invictissimo*), the room served both as a reception hall and as a bedroom. On one wall the court itself was depicted with the seated marquis and marquess presiding over a gathering of elegantly turned out courtiers, and on another the marquis is receiving the entourage of his son who had recently been named a cardinal. Randolph Starn and Loren Partridge have analysed the relationship between the actual court and the painted representa-

---

⁹ Lubkin, *Renaissance Court*, pp. 250–1.
¹⁰ Starn and Partridge, *Arts of Power*, p. 88.

tion of it: 'No doubt the pictures served to communicate, confirm, and commemorate shared experiences that set the court apart from the ordinary world. Together with the illusion of intention and movement commonly attributed to them, they actively constructed a court in their own image. The painted court, in other words, could also be seen as a model for a real one.'[11]

Mantegna's frescoed room grants us access to the complicated, often contradictory effect common to all representations of power. Representations reflected power but transformed it in the process. They established a dialogue about power because they served both as a model *of* power and a model *for* power. As a model of power they revealed the constituted power relationships found 'out there' in the real world of the cities, curia, and principalities. As a model for power they represented idealized constructions of how power should and could be constituted. Through this dialogue the arts and ceremonies in Renaissance Italy helped to create, not just record, the dominion of power.

[11] Ibid., p. 98.

Rethinking the Renaissance in the aftermath of Italy's crisis

Alison Brown

The crisis of 1494 and its impact on Renaissance culture

No one familiar with the histories and chronicles of Italy in the years from 1494 to 1530 can be unaware of the sense of crisis that pervades these writings. According to Francesco Guicciardini, the arrival of the French army in 1494 introduced 'a flame and a plague into Italy' which 'not only overthrew the states but changed their forms of government and the methods of warfare', turning everything 'upside down' and causing the ruin of Italy. Even his more reflective *History of Italy*, written in the late 1530s, described the invasions as 'the calamity of Italy' in introducing years of appalling disasters and fear, which were all the worse because they followed a period of unparalleled prosperity.[1] The 1494 invasion was followed by other French invasions in 1499 and 1515. In 1502 the Spanish invasion of southern Italy

---

[1] Francesco Guicciardini, *The History of Florence*, chs. 10–11, trans. M. Domandi (New York, 1970), pp. 88–9; *The History of Italy*, trans. C. Grayson (Chalfont St Giles, 1966), pp. 85–6.

brought Spain into the country, and then, after Charles V was elected emperor in 1519, the Germans too, whose bloody Sack of Rome in 1527 also awakened fears of Lutheranism and the new Protestant heresies. Each state experienced the crisis at different moments: Florence in a repetitive cycle of Medici expulsions (1494, 1527) and restorations (in 1512 after the sack of Prato by Spanish troops, and in 1530 after the long siege by imperial and papal armies); Milan through conquests and domination by France (1499–1512 and 1515–25) and Spain (from 1525 on); Naples in the initial French onslaught (1494) and subsequent conquest by Spain (1501–4); Venice in a disastrous defeat and temporary dismemberment of its mainland empire (1509); and Rome in the great Sack. Humanists may have exaggerated the part played by these events in transforming the world they knew. Nevertheless, these political upheavals clearly triggered an ubiquitous crisis of confidence in the humanist culture that had created and nourished the distinctive identities of the independent city–states.

Although the focus here will be on the longer-term influence of the invasions on writers and intellectuals, it is important at the outset not to undervalue the violence of the invasions as a factor in the Italians' perception of change. It was the initial defeat of the Neapolitan forces and their allies by the French at Mordano in the Romagna on 20 October 1494 that first demonstrated that the French fought to kill; and shortly after the fortress was destroyed and its inhabitants murdered, reports about 'the cruelty of Mordano' spread terror and consternation among the neighbouring states. Even the territories of the French king's supporters were sacked and pillaged, so it was not surprising that his army was awaited with trepidation throughout Italy, even in cities like Florence, where the king was initially welcomed as a liberator. According to one Florentine chronicler, Charles's polyglot army consisted of 'bestial men, as were the Swiss, Gascons, Normans, Bretons, Scots and men of many other tongues, who not only were not understood by our men, but couldn't even understand each other'.[2] After numerous threatening incidents, Charles left Florence as its unloved conqueror, in receipt of a large indemnity as the price of evacuating his troops from the city.

In Rome, pope Alexander was persuaded to negotiate only by the

---

[2] Bartolomeo Cerretani, *Storia fiorentina*, ed. G. Berti (Florence, 1994), p. 201; cf. 218–20.

sight of Charles's guns paraded through the city; and, after one more massacre at Valmontone, the king achieved his conquest of the kingdom of Naples by the most savage of all his assaults, on the castle and town of Monte San Giovanni, where between 700 and 1000 inhabitants, mostly civilians, were slaughtered. Naples fell after an assault lasting about three weeks. Although it was quickly recaptured after Charles returned to France, his retreat was marked by yet another bloody engagement at Fornovo, in which the marquis of Mantua gave orders to give no quarter, on pain of death, but simply to kill 'for the glory of the Latin name'. By then, the French were as fearful of the Italians as the Italians had been of them on their arrival, 'not like the men who went to Naples, who were fat and rubicund . . . Now their bodies seem emaciated and their clothes in shreds'. So they were relieved to return home, as men (we are told, in another revealing indication of the national prejudice that war intensified) 'who believe there is no other sky, no other pleasures, no other sun except in France'.[3]

Fear and irrational belief in the power of fortune now replaced the humanists' earlier confidence in the power of reason and prudence as guides for the rulers of city–states and became for Machiavelli the bases of a new political morality, as we shall see. The contrast is striking if we compare two writings by Florentine humanists in defence of their city at the beginning and end of the fifteenth century, Leonardo Bruni's 1403–4 *Panegyric* or *Praise of the City of Florence* and Bartolomeo Scala's 1496 *Defence of Florence*, in which Florence was transformed from the resplendent centre of a stable universe to the unstable hub of a fragmenting galaxy. Bruni (later first chancellor of Florence, like Scala) wrote his work just after the city had been saved from attack by the unexpected death of the duke of Milan in 1402. Influenced by Aristides' praise of ancient Athens, the *Panegyric* opens with a confident description of Florence's ordered beauty and magnificence before going on to describe the city's Roman origins, its love of liberty, and its republican institutions. Republicanism was also a theme of Scala's defence of Florence, written after he was reappointed chancellor of the Savonarolan regime that succeeded the Medici in 1494. But in contrast to Bruni's opening praise of Florence

---

[3] Marcello Adriani, Florence, Archivio di Stato, Signori, Dieci, Otto, Legazioni e Commissarie, Missive-Responsive, 4, fol. 81v.

as the stable centre or hub of an orbit whose power radiated out to the periphery, like 'the moon surrounded by the stars', Scala begins with a digression on Lucretian atomism and the power of fortune that can overturn everything at will when it rages against us, as had happened recently, he wrote, when Florence lost her subject cities Pisa and Montepulciano after the French invasion.[4] Openly attributing this new view of the power of fortune to Lucretius, the Roman poet whose recently recovered poem *On the Nature of Things* followed the Greek atomist Epicurus, Scala was careful to say that he was not completely convinced that the world originated in 'the fortuitous clash of invisible atoms', as Lucretius and Epicurus believed. Nevertheless, he declared he was equally sceptical about those who removed fortune 'totally from human affairs', since, without God's dispensation, nothing can deflect nature's impetus when it rages against us, 'as has clearly happened to us now'.

This new view of fortune's destabilizing power was shared by other Italians writing about these years. In a letter written to the king of Naples in 1495 (anticipating his later dialogue *On Fortune*), the king's secretary Giovanni Pontano explained the present crisis as the work of the heavens, which would carry everything in its wake if unopposed, 'like an unbounded river, suddenly swollen with rain and water'. His metaphor in turn influenced the Florentine patrician Bernardo Rucellai's *Commentary on the French Invasion* (written after he had discussed history writing with Pontano in Naples), in which he also compared the invasion to a raging river that would be impossible to control once it had broken across the boundaries of the Alps. And it was then made famous by Machiavelli in his discussion of the power of fortune in chapter 25 of *The Prince*, where he likened fortune to 'one of our destructive rivers which, when it is angry, turns the plains into lakes, throws down the trees and buildings', as had happened, he said, to Italy in his own day.[5] Scala, Pontano, and Machiavelli—as well as Machiavelli's university teacher, Marcello Adriani—were all early readers of Lucretius's poem and of Diogenes

---

[4] Leonardo Bruni, *Panegyric to the City of Florence*, trans. B. G. Kohl in Kohl and R. G. Witt (eds.), *The Earthly Republic* (Philadelphia, 1978), pp. 144–5; Bartolomeo Scala, *Apologia contra vituperatores civitatis Florentiae* (Florence, 1496), in his *Humanistic and Political Writings*, ed. A. Brown (Tempe, Ariz., 1997), pp. 396–7.

[5] All discussed in M. Santoro, *Fortuna, ragione e prudenza nella civiltà letteraria del Cinquecento* (Naples, 1967), esp. pp. 11–21.

Laertius's *Life of Epicurus*, the two texts that helped to circulate Epicurus's radical and subversive ideas about the universe in the fifteenth century. Heretical though these ideas were (the existence of multiple worlds created by the chance clash of atoms within empty space, where life evolved without the support of caring gods or an afterlife), they were given new relevance by the crisis after 1494. The crisis also encouraged the dissemination of new Lutheran and reformist heresies, which destroyed the earlier syncretism that had blended classical and Christian belief in a stable, earth-centred world. Together these challenges led to new thinking not only about the moral basis of politics (reflected in Machiavelli's later radicalism) but also about the structure of the world itself, in which the earth was displaced by Galileo and his contemporaries from the centre of the universe.

So the cultural implications of the crisis were more profound than the initial events suggested. From their earliest days, the communes had promoted the ideal of active citizenship by identifying themselves with ancient republics. Even if the political reality was very different from the ideal, citizen debates and humanist writings in the new lordships and in oligarchies like Florence reveal the continuing vitality of classical republicanism as a language that bonded city-dwellers and gave them a sense of their own cultural past. Although republicanism is not the only defining characteristic of Renaissance culture, it represented a set of distinctive values directly relevant to urban dwellers. To live and share in the social and political life of cities had a civilizing and humanizing effect on individuals, it was believed. The idea that a citizen without his city was only 'a painted image or a form of stone' was widely held, not only by the Dominican preacher Remigio de' Girolami (d. 1319) but by laymen like Dante (d. 1321), who remained immensely influential through his great poem, the *Divine Comedy*. When Dante is asked in Paradise (viii.115–16), 'would man be worse off on earth if he were not a citizen?', he briefly replies, 'yes, and here I ask no proof', because men are born with different abilities that can only be fulfilled in socially mixed and diversified cities. Dante represents an outlook widely diffused at the time, that citizens should participate in governing their cities, ruling and being ruled in turn, as Aristotle put it, and that this constituted their particular 'activity' and 'virtue' as city-dwellers.

Even when many cities fell into the hands of single rulers in the late thirteenth and fourteenth centuries, the debate about government continued. Did 'activity' mean being politically active or simply active as working townspeople, not sequestered from the world in monasteries, 'idle upon their knees', as Machiavelli later put it in his poem *The Golden Ass*? Was 'virtue', as the Roman historian Sallust suggested, a quality that develops through being politically active or was it an inborn quality that made some citizens better rulers than others? And which type of government best protected liberty and equality? These were much-discussed topics in debates and writings addressed both to young nobles in courts like those of Ferrara and Mantua and to citizens of republics. They help to chart the progression from the more egalitarian ethos of communal guild republicanism to the elitism of fifteenth-century civic humanism.

It was not however the progression towards elitism in itself that constituted the essence of the crisis. Debate about the best form of government was central to classical republicanism, and the fact that it continued throughout the fifteenth century and into the sixteenth only serves to demonstrate that one of its key ideals—open argument on both sides of the question—was alive and well. The crisis manifested itself when Italian states began to lose confidence in the relevance of humanist and republican values themselves, in a deconstructive process that began by questioning their validity and ended by destroying the stable Ptolemaic universe that had underpinned them. We can first see this happening in Milan, where republican government was briefly re-established on the death of the last Visconti duke in 1447. The people were summoned to a meeting at which they appointed a government of twenty-four 'captains and defenders of liberty' to preserve 'the grace of liberty' unexpectedly granted to them by God, and this encouraged other cities like Pavia, Lodi, Piacenza, and Parma to follow suit. Only three years later, however, they were all back under the control of a single ruler, Francesco Sforza, who was acclaimed duke by a popular assembly, 'since it was agreed that it was impossible to live in liberty'. Subsequently, the historians of the new Sforza regime helped to undermine republican idealism by pointing out how biased the histories of the famed Leonardo Bruni were in praising Florence at the expense of Milan, for, as another historian put it, 'differing versions . . . are given by the winners and by the losers'. This anticipated Machiavelli, who some sixty years later wrote in his *Discourses on Livy* (ii.5) that all records are prejudiced because they represent only the views of the conquerors and not the conquered. Bruni's republicanism was also undermined by Poggio Bracciolini, the disillusioned ex-chancellor of Florence who, in a eulogy he wrote of Venice in 1459, discredited even Bruni's classical republican models, calling Sparta 'deeply-unhappy', Athens 'perverse', and the greatest of them all, Rome, 'not a republic at all but a den of thieves and a despotism of the cruellest sort'.[6]

Twenty years later there is even clearer evidence that belief in republican values was being undermined in Alamanno Rinuccini's *Dialogue on Liberty*. Rinuccini wrote the dialogue in 1479 during the Pazzi War, fought by Florence to defend its 'liberty' after the abortive conspiracy against the Medici a year earlier. But far from defending the Medici as protectors of Florence's liberty, Rinuccini instead condemned them as tyrants, telling us that 'the fine words and the golden letters', in which the word liberty was inscribed on one of Florence's banners symbolizing its famous love of freedom, 'clash with the facts'. The notion of ideals 'clashing with the facts' alerts us to the extent of Rinuccini's radicalism. By describing Lorenzo de' Medici's 'tyranny' as he had experienced it, Rinuccini defines liberty in Florence in a similarly concrete way: as the rule of law which ensured civil equality, selection of office-holders by lot, and the open and free debate of civic matters in political meetings. This was Bruni's definition of republicanism in his *Panegyric*, but in presenting it as a critique of government in his own day, Rinuccini gave reality to abstract definitions. Justice was no longer equal but favoured those with power and influence; meetings were no longer summoned openly; men were too intimidated by threat of exile and imprisonment to exercise freedom of speech; offices were not drawn by lot but given to satellites, and taxes were spent not on the common good but on 'horses, dogs, birds, actors, sycophants, and parasites'.[7]

It seemed to many that only Venice represented true republicanism in Italy before the events of 1494. But although the city was widely

---

[6] Poggio Bracciolini, *In Praise of the Venetian Republic*, trans. M. Davies in J. Kraye (ed.), *Cambridge Translations of Renaissance Philosophical Texts* (2 vols., Cambridge, 1997), vol. ii, pp. 137–8.

[7] Alamanno Rinuccini, *Dialogue on Liberty*, trans. R. N. Watkins, *Humanism and Liberty: Writings on Freedom from Fifteenth-Century Florence* (Columbia, S.C., 1978), pp. 197, 204–7.

admired as a model of republican government with its carefully elected lifetime doge or duke, its legislative Great Council of hereditary nobles, and its Senate, it always remained a static model, representing stability rather than innovation, as we can see from Venetian analyses of their constitution both before and after their crisis of 1509. Domenico Morosini's treatise *On the Well-Ordered Republic* had already wanted to restrict government to fewer magistracies; and after the defeat stability was praised as the principal virtue of the republican system. Yet, as the Florentine Francesco Vettori pointed out, Venice could also be considered a tyranny in restricting political office to nobles, who constituted only 4 per cent of the population, and the administration to non-noble citizens, who constituted only 5 to 8 per cent. Moreover, its rulers were all old men, the average age of the doges being seventy-five, and its committee members usually over fifty: an inward-looking group, whose attempts to preserve their purity by refusing to marry down ended in paralysis and loss of power. By the mid seventeenth century the nobility were forced to sell membership rights in the Great Council, 'prostituting' their city in the eyes of critics and making a mockery of its much-vaunted republicanism. For this reason, Venice's political thought, 'stubbornly holding on to medieval notions of . . . grace and ancient utopias of perfection',[8] developed in a very different direction from Florence's.

By contrast, Florence's experience of crisis after 1494 was far more dramatic than Venice's. It first overthrew the Medici in favour of more open government in 1494, then restored them to power with Spanish help in 1512, then overthrew them again in 1527, for the last three violent years of Florentine republican government, before finally restoring them to power in 1530 with the help of the emperor Charles V, who established the Medici as dukes two years later. Through this prolonged crisis, in which each change was mediated by foreign invaders, Florentine political thought was transformed. Rejecting utopianism, Florentine writers instead adopted a new realism that destroyed the old consensus about humanist and republican values, thereby helping to undermine these values themselves.

---

[8] J. Sperling, *Convents and the Body Politic in Late Renaissance Venice* (Chicago, 1999), pp. 56–7, 75.

The new political realism

The immediate impact of the French invasion in Florence was to overturn the Medici regime and restore a more open republic. The initial intention of the men from the old elite who helped to overthrow the Medici was to institute a republic on the Venetian model. They were supported by the sermons of the Dominican friar, Girolamo Savonarola, who also recommended imitating Venice. The Great Council he helped to create, however, was quite unlike Venice's, since it consisted not of hereditary nobles, as in Venice, but of a wide mix of oligarchs, middle-class merchants, and artisans (the last two groups being excluded from government altogether in Venice), and also because the Council selected more and more office-holders by lot. So although no populist himself, the reform Savonarola encouraged led to something quite new: the presence of 'almost all Florence in the government'. The radicalism of this reform has been underestimated, perhaps because it did not survive the counter-attack of the old elite and the return of the Medici in 1512. For, as had happened in Milan during the Ambrosian republic, the experience of popular government in the crisis conditions of war and famine alienated the oligarchs, who initially withdrew from government altogether and then returned only after a lifetime head of state was created. Far from ensuring stability, however, these reforms reintroduced endemic factionalism that taught Florentine writers a series of important lessons about politics. Force was more important than legitimacy or ability in exercising power, liberty and equality were delusory ideals, and political necessity overrode religious and moral constraints.

The importance of force was an early lesson learnt by Machiavelli and by Paolo Vettori, the brother of his friend, the diplomat and historian Francesco Vettori. The message that Paolo gave cardinal Giovanni de' Medici (soon to become Pope Leo X) on his return to Florence in 1512 was that, whereas his father Lorenzo and his forebears had maintained power 'more by skilful management than by force', 'you need to use force more than skilful management'.[9] A year

---

[9] Paolo Vettori, 'Memorandum to Cardinal de' Medici about the affairs of Florence', trans. R. Price in Kraye (ed.), *Cambridge Translations*, p. 239.

later, in chapter 6 of *The Prince* (dedicated first to Giovanni's brother Giuliano and then, in 1515, to his nephew Lorenzo), Machiavelli wrote that to be successful a leader needed to be powerful and armed. In his later *Discourses on Livy* (iii.30) he added that a ruler had to be capable of overriding the laws if need be, in order to save the republic, a role that he believed neither the friar Savonarola nor the lifetime head of state, the timorous and law-abiding Piero Soderini, had been capable of playing. By the time the Medici made their final return to Florence in 1530, the argument for the use of force had become explicit. 'Considering how many enemies we have', Francesco Vettori wrote in 1530, 'we have to consider holding the state by force'; for with insufficient money to reward enough citizens with paid offices to ensure their support, 'only one way is open to us, that Alessandro [de' Medici] become the boss and do what he likes, and that the city be left with this empty name of liberty.'[10] Francesco Guicciardini agreed. Believing as he did that 'all states are illegitimate and, excepting republics, inside their own city walls and not beyond them, there is no power whatsoever that is legitimate' (as he wrote in his *Dialogue on the Government of Florence*), Guicciardini accepted unquestioningly the authority of the unpopular Alessandro (who became duke of Florence in 1532), telling the Florentine exiles three years later that, once established, a state has unlimited power. This presumably would have made their heroic stand at Montemurlo in 1537 quite unjustified in his eyes, not a legitimate defence of liberty but 'a mere game of bagatelle', as his brother Luigi called it.[11]

Machiavelli's *Prince* is usually regarded as the most radical statement of the new realism: 'getting at the real truth of the matter, rather than how it is imagined to be', as he expressed it in chapter 15. He provocatively urged new princes whenever necessary to be cruel rather than kind, parsimonious rather than generous, and cunning and deceitful rather than truthful. But his friends Guicciardini and Vettori were equally radical. Guicciardini called the new realism

[10] 'Parere I', in Francesco Vettori, *Scritti storici e politici*, ed. E. Niccolini (Bari, 1972), pp. 306–7.

[11] Francesco Guicciardini, *Dialogue on the Government of Florence*, trans. A. Brown (Cambridge, 1994), pp. 158–9, *Maxim* 48, ibid., p. 172; 'Risposta . . . alle querele de' fuorusciti', *Opere inedite*, ed. G. Canestrini (Florence, 1866), vol. ix, p. 355; Luigi Guicciardini, letter to his son Niccolò, 14 April 1537, in R. von Albertini, *Firenze dalla repubblica al principato*, trans. C. Cristofolini (Turin, 1970), p. 278, n. 2.

'reason of state', which he said would justify cruel and immoral deeds like murdering prisoners of war, if necessary, while Vettori defended his radicalism by saying that he was 'talking about the things of this world according to the truth and without regard for what people will say', in contrast to the utopianism of writers like Plato and 'the Englishman Thomas More'. He defined all governments as tyrannies, not only in Florence, where many citizens wanted to participate in politics but were left 'on the side-lines, to watch the game', but also in Venice, which, although 'the oldest and most stable republic there is', was still a tyranny because 'three thousand nobles hold under more than 100,000 people and no commoner can become a gentleman'. France was equally tyrannical, for despite having a 'most perfect' king, nobles alone possessed arms and paid no taxes, which were paid by poor peasants with no recourse to justice.[12]

Vettori's thoughts on government were clearly influenced by the Sack of Rome and the disastrous, if heroic, last Florentine republic. All these writers were republicans, especially Machiavelli, who 'loved liberty extraordinarily', according to Giovanbattista Busini. Yet they all, in different ways, undermined the old republican ideals of liberty and equality with their new realism about politics. This can be seen most clearly in Machiavelli's and Guicciardini's blueprints for how Florence should be governed after the unexpected deaths of Giuliano and Lorenzo de' Medici left a vacuum in the city. Written at the request of cardinal Giulio de' Medici, cousin of Pope Leo, both Machiavelli's *Discourse on Remodelling the Government of Florence* and Guicciardini's *Dialogue on the Government of Florence* retained a facade of popular republicanism by proposing to reinstate the Great Council and by asserting the merits of Florence's republican tradition. But the reality would have been rather different. According to their plans, the Great Council would no longer appoint all office-holders but merely the less important political offices and the paid administrative ones. Machiavelli even deprived it of its legislative functions, while preserving its role as final court of appeal. And political power would no longer have been exercised by an elected two-monthly priorate and its advisory colleges but by an executive appointed for life and a legislative council to be selected (and

---

[12] Guicciardini, *Dialogue*, p. 159; Vettori, *Sommario della istoria d'Italia*, in *Scritti storici*, pp. 145–6.

controlled) by the Medici in Rome during their lifetimes. Admitting the loss of liberty this would entail, Machiavelli sought to placate the populace by giving them a new passive role as 'witnesses' of what went on in the government palace, with the right to protest against measures they disliked, thereby restoring to them 'a position that resembles what has been taken from them'. In his blueprint, Guicciardini more radically attacked the validity of the concepts of liberty and equality. Through his spokesman, the Medicean new man Bernardo del Nero, he called 'this word "liberty" ' a 'disguise and excuse' to dazzle and conceal rulers' true ambition, since most of those who preached liberty would not hesitate to join a restrictive regime if they thought they would be better off there.[13]

Where Guicciardini and Machiavelli differed was in their admiration for ancient Rome as a model of republican government. Whereas Guicciardini admired Venice more than Rome and thought it was as misguided to quote the Romans all the time 'as it would be to expect a donkey to run like a horse', Machiavelli consistently praised Rome's republican institutions, especially its citizen army, and provocatively declared that the conflict between the social orders had been a good thing because it contributed to Rome's freedom through the creation of the Tribunate of the Plebs. Guicciardini thought this was like 'praising a sick man's disease because of the virtues of the remedy applied to it'.[14] Nevertheless, by the 1520s even Machiavelli had become sceptical about the relevance of ancient republicanism to his times, as we can see from his two last political writings, *The Art of War*, which he began in 1518 and published three years later, and the *Florentine Histories* which he was commissioned to write in 1520 and completed in 1525 for cardinal Giulio de' Medici, by then pope Clement VII. Although they are usually assumed to promote the Roman model for Florence, in fact Machiavelli argues the opposite: Florentine factionalism was so different from Rome's that the latter's political experience was no longer relevant. Nor was its literary culture, which, instead of strengthening Italy, had in fact contributed to its defeat.

The Art of War is thought to represent Machiavelli's most

[13] Guicciardini, *Dialogue*, pp. 35–7, 38–9; cf. *Maxim* 66, ibid., p. 172.
[14] Guicciardini, *Maxim* 110 and *Considerations on Machiavelli's Discourses* in his *Selected Writings*, trans. M. Grayson (London, 1965), pp. 30, 68.

persuasive attempt to reintroduce ancient Roman ideals through its leading speaker, the renowned *condottiere* Fabrizio Colonna. But although Fabrizio begins the dialogue by claiming that it is 'not impossible' to reintroduce ancient ways of fighting according to the model of 'my Romans', his view is immediately challenged by another speaker who asks him why as a professional soldier he has not himself reintroduced the ancient methods he praises. To this Fabrizio's defence is that times have changed, for, whereas ancient culture unified citizens and soldiers in love of the common good, in the Italy of his day the culture of civilians was totally divorced from military life, in dress, customs, and language. At the end of his pains-taking analysis of ancient military techniques, Colonna in fact con-cludes that, far from offering a working model for reform, they were totally impractical for present-day armies, whose lack of training, religion, and discipline made them incapable of doing what the Romans had done. How could soldiers be trained all day long as the Romans trained theirs? How could they be made to abstain from the gaming, lasciviousness, blasphemy, and rudeness that they dem-onstrate every day? 'By which God or which saints shall I get them to swear on oath, by those they adore or by those they curse . . . how can those who scorn God revere men?' Their leaders were just as bad, valuing a ready wit, gold, gems and wanton pleasures more than military valour: hence 'the incredible fear, rapid retreats and amazing losses' that came about in 1494.

In the *Florentine Histories* Machiavelli elaborates on the Italians' failure to learn from the Romans. After describing in book i (chapter 5) how Italy had failed to preserve the common culture that it had enjoyed under the Romans (the same 'laws, customs, way of life, religion, language, dress and names') he proceeds to denounce (in the introductory chapters of books ii–vi) Italy's other failures. Instead of using law to protect liberty and ending the conflict between the nobles and the people by sharing honours between them, as the Romans did, the Italians perpetuated conflict by resorting to fighting and exile. Instead of using war to build new colonies and to enrich the public fisc, the Italians gave away ransoms and booty to their mercenary captains. And unlike the Romans, they failed to use war to purge the vices of leisure. This last criticism at the beginning of book v provides the greatest insight into Machiavelli's loss of confidence in the relevance of ancient culture to present-day Italy. Since the endemic small-scale warfare of the fifteenth century was a state neither of settled peace nor of open war, Machiavelli wrote, Italy was unable to follow the ancient cycle from war to peace to war again, whose purgative effect prevented soldiers from being corrupted in periods of prolonged peace by learning or 'letters'. Modern war had by contrast failed to purge this learned culture that undermined its soldiers' ethos, thereby bringing about the barbarian invasions of 1494 and Italy's re-enslavement. As we know from his criticism in *The Art of War* of the culture of Italy's military leaders, who spent their days in their studies thinking up witticisms and writing letters, decorating themselves with gems and gold, and sleeping and eating more splendidly than others, the leaders Machiavelli had in mind were princely *condottieri* from families such as the Gonzaga, Este, and Montefeltro, whose courts were centres of classical learning. Is Machiavelli attacking the very qualities that for us today epitomize what we define as the Renaissance? To attempt to answer this question, we must turn in the concluding section to the culture of these courts to see the extent to which even there classical civilization was beginning to seem irrelevant to post-1494 Italy.

Renaissance culture in Italian courts

Italian courts were based in cities that had nearly all once been free communes. The communes had first revived ancient republicanism, inspiring their citizens with ideals of patriotism and active citizenship. Even when cities ceased to be self-governing, classical literature continued to be taught and cultivated by humanists in the new courts. At the Gonzaga court in Mantua and the Este court in Ferrara, the new 'liberal arts' schools of Vittorino da Feltre and Guarino da Verona provided models for humanist educators throughout Italy. As professional publicists, humanists also continued to debate the best form of government in the language supplied by classical republicanism, supporting either Scipio or Caesar according to whether their employer was a republic or a prince. And even in cities controlled by a single ruler republican ideology remained alive. Although the 'dangerous' word 'popolo' had been forbidden since 1385 under the lordship of the Visconti, the republic of 1447–50 shows that civic and republican ideas survived. Duke Galeazzo Maria Sforza was murdered in 1476 by students, we are told, of Sallust's *Catiline Conspiracy*, 'who wanted to copy those ancient Romans and be liberators of their country'. And when his brother Lodovico 'il Moro' was ejected from the city by the French in 1499, an abortive attempt was again made to re-establish a republic. Although these attempts failed, even the overlordship of the Habsburg emperors in the 1550s did not succeed in extinguishing the aspirations of Milan's citizens to recover their lost freedom.

Classical culture also helped to justify the growing splendour and magnificence of fifteenth- and sixteenth-century courts, whose de facto power was legitimized with the gloss that antiquity gave them. When Sigismondo Malatesta of Rimini buried medals of himself in the foundations of his most important buildings, he explained that this would give him glory in the same way that coins 'representing antiquity' glorified the names of ancient builders. For similar reasons the Gonzaga claimed that Mantegna's *Triumph of Caesar* paintings gave their family 'glory in having them in the house', and we may guess that the Este rulers of Ferrara believed that their collection of ancient gems, statues, and books did the same for them as they did for the aspiring prince, Lorenzo de' Medici, whose antiques helped to give him the cultural status he lacked as a banker in the still overtly republican Florence.

The legitimizing role of classical culture seems to have continued almost unbroken until at least the eighteenth century, making it difficult to identify a moment of crisis similar to the one experienced by the Florentine republicans. Yet if we look closely at the description of court life in Baldassare Castiglione's famous dialogue about the court of Urbino, *The Courtier*, we find that it betrays the same loss of confidence in Renaissance culture as do Machiavelli's later writings. Castiglione's dialogue was begun in 1507, revised in 1516 when Urbino was swallowed up by Leo X and given to his nephew Lorenzo, and finally printed in 1528. Its discussion of the virtues needed by the perfect courtier purports to admire a culture deeply imbued with classical values. The courtier should ideally be a man of noble birth and skilled not only in arms but also in the liberal arts, that is, in literature, oratory, music, and painting, as Castiglione reveals himself to be in the numerous *exempla* drawn from classical writings that pepper the text. But at the end of the first two books, we are told that this paragon 'never was, nor perhaps ever could be'. Castiglione not only undermines the importance of military valour by presenting the duke as an impotent cripple, who 'rarely succeeded in what he undertook'; he also undermines the value of the courtier's learning by giving women the role of critical commentators who twice interrupt the discussion telling the men that their debate has become 'too protracted and tedious' and too academic, and urging them to 'speak in a way that you can be understood'. According to one of the disputants, Cesare Gonzaga, this man of virtue and learning seems more like a 'good schoolmaster' than a noble courtier, whose task should instead be to encourage magnificence and splendour on the model of the Mantuan court of Francesco Gonzaga, the duchess of Urbino's brother, 'who in this regard seems more like King of Italy than the ruler of a city'.[15]

This, it seems, is the model of the future, according to the later discussion in book iv about whether a prince or a republic was more likely to restore a Golden Age. This last book of *The Courtier* is prefaced by 'bitter thoughts' about how 'Fortune frustrates our weak and feeble plans, sometimes wrecking them even before we sight harbour', thoughts occasioned by the deaths of three of the speakers in the dialogue during its long gestation, who would have provided clear proof, we are told, of the brilliance of the court of Urbino. But it was not just this that embittered Castiglione, nor even Urbino's loss of independence in 1516. It was also the fact that by the time the book was completed, none of its few surviving protagonists was still living in Urbino. As Carlo Dionisotti memorably put it, 'the fragile splendour' of Guidobaldo's court was dimmed by the shadow of another society that was overhanging it, the ecclesiastical society of the papal curia in Rome.[16] In this context, Castiglione's answer to the question of who best could restore a Golden Age was predictable: not the republic praised by another speaker, the Venetian Pietro Bembo, but a prince enjoying 'kingly and civic' powers and ruling in the image of God who controls the universe. The princes in whom future hope of success rested, according to Castiglione, were not even

[15] Baldesar Castiglione, *The Book of the Courtier*, trans. G. Bull (London, 1967), pp. 202, 41, 84, 221, 310, and 281–2, below.

[16] Carlo Dionisotti, 'Chierici e laici', in *Geografia e storia della letteratura italiana* (Turin, 1967), p. 70.

Italians (with the sole exception of Francesco Gonzaga's son Federigo, whose nimble politics had enabled him to survive unscathed into the new imperial age), but the sons of the kings of France, England, and Spain, their task not to rescue Italy but to subjugate the 'infidels' to Christianity.[17]

By the early sixteenth century, papal Rome was the principal centre of courtly culture. As the nerve centre of religious and political patronage, it was the place where every lesser court kept a cardinal to represent its interests, as well as the hub of international diplomacy during the years of foreign invasions. Thanks to the extensive patronage of Julius II and the Medici popes, cultural life flourished after 1494, sodalities and games keeping alive a semblance of ancient practices and values. It was there that the most ambitious artistic projects were undertaken, such as Raphael's frescoes in the new papal apartments (or *Stanze*) and his tapestries for the Sistine chapel, Bramante's cloister for S. Maria della Pace, Michelangelo's planned tomb for Julius II and his Sistine ceiling. Yet in 1527 even Rome was attacked by the barbarian invaders. The sack of the city by German and Spanish mercenaries and the imprisonment of the pope finally shattered the myth of Rome as *caput mundi*, home and centre of Christendom and of the ancient Roman republic and empire. In the diaspora of artists and writers from the city, one painter, Sebastiano del Piombo, even wondered if he was the same man he had been 'before the Sack'.

By then, Christian Europe was being threatened not only by the Muslims, but also by the heretical Lutherans, whose ideas were beginning to spread in reformist or *spirituali* circles throughout Italy, both in large cities like Naples and Venice and in ducal courts. The French wife of Ercole d'Este, for example, was a Protestant and introduced the new ideas to the court of Ferrara, while aristocratic women such as Giulia Gonzaga and Vittoria Colonna worked at the centre of personal networks to disseminate reforming beliefs to other cities and courts in Italy. Faced with schism in the Church, the Papacy embarked on a period of reform that brought to an end the close and unselfconscious identification of scholars with ancient Rome, the 'homely confidence' in classical literature and the sense of continuity with the past that they had previously experienced there. The Council of Trent (1545–63) and its *Index of Prohibited Books* imposed an

---

[17] Castiglione, *The Courtier*, pp. 296–9, 310, 312–13.

authoritarianism that increased people's awareness of the distance between classical and Christian culture, sending authors like Lucretius and Epicurus back underground again after their very brief airing, and Galileo Galilei (for being influenced by them and other new ideas about the universe) to prison.

The new religious controls also represented what has been called 'Italy's new investment in the values of social surveillance and reform', which in turn encouraged a return to the ordered, hierarchical society that had begun to be challenged. This was a direct response to anxiety about loss of social control created by almost continuous invasions that led to a perception among prominent cultural spokesmen of an Italy rendered 'effeminate' in its political helplessness. It also encouraged the displacement of discussion about political order and values to discussion about sexual and domestic matters in the private sphere, where it 'fueled the reappearance of the *querelle des femmes*' in many Renaissance writings.[18] The 'language debate' also revived in the sixteenth century. Pietro Bembo's success in imposing Petrarch and Boccaccio as archaizing models for modern Italian (in his 1525 *Prose della volgar lingua*) was in part a result of the political crisis: perhaps a common, standardized language could unify an increasingly fragmented country. The language debate was also sustained by the establishment of new literary academies that attempted to bring writers under political control. One academy made its members agree in 1546 that 'to avoid any murmuring, no one may debate the Holy Scriptures'. The transformation of humanism as a result of these controls also undermined the civic culture that had originally helped to create the political ethos of humanism. Italian was increasingly used in the law courts instead of Latin, and local laws and statutes were now written in Italian; so too were plays and histories, and also funeral addresses, which became informal homilies delivered by friars instead of formal orations by humanists.

Thus change was not limited to politics but extended widely to the whole of Italian civic life. At the beginning of the sixteenth century, even the clothing of republican citizens had begun to change. The patrician youth of Florence 'cast off their togas' (the traditional long magisterial gowns) and adopted a new kind of dress, 'neither the sort

---

[18] D. Shemek, *Ladies Errant: Wayward Women and Social Order in Early Modern Italy* (Durham, N.C., 1998), pp. 31–2.

worn by their fathers nor in keeping with the style appropriate to citizens but flaunting their grandeur and magnificence'. Despite the Florentines' admiration for 'civilian dress and familiar manners', the Medici adviser Lodovico Alamanni thought it would be easy to get the next generation to 'adopt a [courtly] cape in place of a [republican] hood', as easy as adopting the habit of a monk, because 'they will renounce the republic and profess themselves in [the duke's] order'.[19] By the mid sixteenth century, Torquato Tasso (1544–95) denounced the ancient republican 'hood of the Florentines' and the 'Venetian toga' as outdated garments fit only to be dressing-up or Carneval clothes for the princely councillor of his dialogues, *Malpiglio or about the Court* and *Il Gianluca or about the Mask*. These dialogues suggest that even the ostensibly republican and Ciceronian role Castiglione had ascribed to his courtier could no longer be translated to the courts of Tasso's day, where the garments worn by Florentine and Venetian republicans served only as masks for Carneval time, not proud symbols of ancient ideals.[20]

If it is possible to define a moment when ideas catch on and seem relevant, then it must also be possible to define moments when they lose relevance. Sometimes we describe this as 'the end of an era'. But without necessarily thinking of the Renaissance as an era (as historians have tended to do for a long time), we can, I think, chart the erosion of belief in the political and cultural values we associate with the Renaissance in Italy. What better emblem of this new world from which to survey the old than Galileo Galilei (1564–1642). Born and educated in Pisa, Galileo taught mathematics in the university there for three years before moving to the university of Padua in the Venetian dominions. Although he made his name there for the astronomical discoveries through his telescope, he returned to Tuscany in 1610 to work freely for the Medici grand dukes, declaring that a republic like Venice could not offer the sort of legitimation he sought and that he desired to serve only a princely patron. The change in values represented by his move was predicated on the assumption that to serve a single patron brought purity because it was a monogamous

---

[19] Jacopo Nardi to A. Lapaccini, 20 October 1501, in A. Verde, *Lo Studio fiorentino*, iii, 1 (Pistoia, 1977), p. 411; L. Alamanni, *Discorso*, 25 November 1516, in von Albertini, *Firenze dalla repubblica al principato*, p. 383.

[20] Incisively analysed by V. Cox, 'Tasso's *Malpiglio overo de la corte*: The Courtier revisited', *The Modern Language Review*, 90 (1995), pp. 897–918, esp. 911–14.

relationship instead of one of prostitution to an open and arbitrary market.[21] So it was to the new stable centre of Florentine patronage, the Medici grand dukes, and not to the open market forces of a republic, that Galileo offered his telescopes and his revolutionary books, *The Starry Messenger* describing his four newly discovered satellites around Jupiter, dedicated to Cosimo II, and *The Dialogue concerning the Two Chief World Systems, Ptolemaic and Copernican,* dedicated to Ferdinand II. Trying in vain to procure a copy of *The Dialogue* a year after its publication in 1632, Thomas Hobbes percipiently told his patron that in Italy they were saying it was 'a booke that will do more hurt to their religion than all the bookes have done of Luther and Calvin'.[22] It is perhaps paradoxical that Galileo opted for a stable ducal patron as the centre of his universe at the same time that he displaced the earth from the stable centre of the old Ptolemaic system. But in so doing he showed that the civic culture that had made his achievement possible ended with the collapse of republicanism in the course of the sixteenth century.

[21] M. Biagioli, *Galileo, Courtier: The Practice of Science in the Culture of Absolutism* (Chicago, 1993), p. 29.

[22] Thomas Hobbes to William Cavendish (26 January 1633), cited in *La Corte, il mare, i mercanti* (Florence, 1980), p. 232 (9.26).

Further reading

For bibliography on the medieval background to Italian history in the Renaissance, see the suggestions for further reading in the preceding volume of the series, *Italy in the Central Middle Ages*, ed. David Abulafia (Oxford, 2004), pp. 255–70.

Chapter 1

The standard account of education and literacy in Renaissance Italy is P. Grendler, *Schooling in Renaissance Italy: Literacy and Learning, 1300–1600* (Baltimore, 1989). P. Gehl, *A Moral Art: Grammar, Society, and Culture in Trecento Florence* (Ithaca, 1993) focuses on schoolbooks in fourteenth-century Florence. A useful survey of educational institutions throughout Italy is P. Denley, 'Government and schools in late medieval Italy', in T. Dean and C. Wickham (eds.), *City and Countryside in Late Medieval and Renaissance Italy: Essays Presented to Philip Jones* (London, 1990), pp. 93–107. W. K. Percival has published fundamental studies of Italian grammar textbooks, including 'Renaissance grammar: rebellion or evolution?' in G. Tarugi (ed.), *Interrogativi dell'umanesimo* (3 vols., Florence, 1976), vol. ii, pp. 73–90, and 'The place of the *Rudimenta grammatices* in the history of Latin grammar', *Res publica litterarum*, 4 (1981), pp. 233–64. R. Black relates the humanist school curriculum to traditional medieval teaching in *Humanism and Education in Medieval and Renaissance Italy: Tradition and Innovation in Latin Schools from the Twelfth to the Fifteenth Century* (Cambridge, 2001) and contrasts the differing approaches to education adopted by various Tuscan towns in 'Humanism and education in Renaissance Arezzo', *I Tatti Studies*, 2 (1987), pp. 171–237. A controversial but provocative treatment of humanist education is A. Grafton and L. Jardine, *From Humanism to the Humanities: Education and the Liberal Arts in Fifteenth- and Sixteenth-Century Europe* (Cambridge, Mass., 1986). A recent translation of humanist educational treatises is C. W. Kallendorf, *Humanist Educational Treatises* (Cambridge, Mass., 2002). A case study of humanism in one city is M. King, *Venetian Humanism in an Age of Patrician Dominance* (Princeton, 1986). R. G. Witt offers an account of the origins and development of Italian humanism up to the early fifteenth century in *'In the Footsteps of the Ancients': The Origins of Humanism from Lovato to Bruni* (Leiden, 2000). A recent anthology of studies on humanism is R. Black (ed.), *Renaissance Thought: A Reader* (London, 2001). The best short introduction to early printing in Italy is V. Scholderer, 'Printers and readers in Italy in the fifteenth century', in his *Fifty Essays in Fifteenth- and*

Sixteenth-Century Bibliography, ed. D. Rhodes (Amsterdam, 1966), pp. 202–15. Further studies include S. H. Steinberg, *Five Hundred Years of Printing*, 2nd edn (Harmondsworth, 1961); M. Davies, 'Humanism in script and print in the fifteenth century', in J. Kraye (ed.), *The Cambridge Companion to Renaissance Humanism* (Cambridge, 1996), pp. 47–62; E. Eisenstein, *The Printing Press as an Agent of Change* (2 vols., Cambridge, 1979) and, also by Eisenstein, *The Printing Revolution in Early Modern Europe* (Cambridge, 1983); L. Febvre and H.-J. Martin, *The Coming of the Book: The Impact of Printing 1450–1800*, trans. D. Gerard, eds. G. Nowell-Smith and D. Wootton (London, 1984); R. Hirsch, *Printing, Selling and Reading, 1450–1550*, 2nd edn (Wiesbaden, 1974); and M. Lowry, *The World of Aldus Manutius: Business and Scholarship in Renaissance Venice* (Oxford, 1979) and, also by Lowry, *Nicholas Jenson and the Rise of Venetian Publishing in Renaissance Europe* (Oxford, 1991).

Chapter 2

The starting point for the study of Italian Renaissance humanism remains Jacob Burckhardt's work (1860), available in English as *The Civilization of the Renaissance in Italy*, trans. S. G. C. Middlemore (New York, 1958). P. O. Kristeller, *Renaissance Thought and its Sources*, ed. M. Mooney (New York, 1979), provides a widely accepted definition of humanism. The most comprehensive recent introduction is *Renaissance Humanism: Foundations, Forms, and Legacy*, ed. A. Rabil, Jr (3 vols., Philadelphia, 1988), esp. vol. i. W. J. Bouwsma, 'The two faces of humanism: Stoicism and Augustinianism in Renaissance thought', in his *A Usable Past: Essays in European Cultural History* (Berkeley, 1990), pp. 19–73, builds on Kristeller to explore the main intellectual conflicts within humanism. The religious thought of the humanists is explored by C. Trinkaus, *In Our Image and Likeness: Humanity and Divinity in Italian Humanist Thought* (2 vols., Chicago, 1970). R. Fubini, *Humanism and Secularization: Petrarch to Valla*, trans. M. King (Durham, N.C., 2003) connects new ways of reading classical authors with developments in humanist ethical thought. A. Grafton and L. Jardine, *From Humanism to the Humanities: Education and the Liberal Arts in Fifteenth- and Sixteenth-Century Europe* (Cambridge, Mass., 1986), highlights the gap between humanist educational claims and practices. J. Kraye (ed.), *The Cambridge Companion to Renaissance Humanism* (Cambridge, 1996) and C. Nauert, *Humanism and the Culture of Europe* (Cambridge, 1995) relate Italian to European humanism as they introduce the movement's essential features. D. Kelley, *Renaissance Humanism* (Boston, 1991) and especially T. Davies, *Humanism* (London, 1997) place Renaissance humanism in a broader intellectual context, as did Ernst Cassirer in his foundational *The Individual and the Cosmos in Renaissance Philosophy*, trans. M. Domandi (Philadelphia, 1963). E. Garin, *Italian Humanism: Philosophy and Civic Life*, trans. P. Munz

(New York, 1965) brings together the literary and political dimensions of humanism, as does S. Jed in her thought-provoking but controversial *Chaste Thinking: The Rape of Lucretia and the Birth of Humanism* (Bloomington, Ind., 1989).

Hans Baron's influential *The Crisis of the Early Italian Renaissance*, 2nd edn (Princeton, 1966), links humanist thought to political events. J. Hankins, 'The Baron thesis after forty years and some recent studies of Leonardo Bruni', *Journal of the History of Ideas*, 56 (1995), pp. 309–38 and the essays in his edited volume *Renaissance Civic Humanism: Reappraisals and Reflections* (Cambridge, 2000) analyse the impact and significance of Baron's ideas. See also M. Jurdjevic, 'Civic humanism and the rise of the Medici', *Renaissance Quarterly*, 52 (1999), pp. 994–1020. Exemplary general studies of humanism outside Florence include J. F. D'Amico, *Renaissance Humanism in Papal Rome: Humanists and Churchmen on the Eve of the Reformation* (Baltimore, 1983) and M. L. King, *Venetian Humanism in an Age of Patrician Dominance* (Princeton, 1986). P. Fortini Brown, 'Renovatio or Conciliatio? How Renaissances happened in Venice', in A. Brown (ed.), *Language and Images of Renaissance Italy* (Oxford, 1995), pp. 127–54, and V. Cox, 'Rhetoric and humanism in Quattrocento Venice', *Renaissance Quarterly*, 56 (2003), pp. 652–94 highlight how local factors shaped the development of humanism.

L. D. Reynolds and N. G. Wilson, *Scribes and Scholars: A Guide to the Transmission of Greek and Latin Literature*, 2nd edn (Oxford, 1974), outlines the Renaissance recovery of classical texts; see pp. 108–46. A. Grafton, *Commerce with the Classics: Ancient Books and Renaissance Readers* (Ann Arbor, 1997) analyses humanist reading practices through case studies. J. Hankins, *Plato in the Italian Renaissance* (Leiden, 1994) studies all aspects of the reception of one ancient author. R. Witt, *'In the Footsteps of the Ancients': The Origins of Humanism from Lovato to Bruni* (Leiden, 2000) defines humanism in terms of literary imitation and traces its emergence and development from Padua to Florence. P. Godman, *From Machiavelli to Poliziano: Florentine Humanism in the High Renaissance* (Princeton, 1998) examines a crucial later period. T. M. Greene, *The Light in Troy: Imitation and Discovery in Renaissance Poetry* (New Haven, 1982) offers a brilliant interpretation of Renaissance hermeneutics, and M. L. McLaughlin, *Literary Imitation in the Italian Renaissance: The Theory and Practice of Literary Imitation in Italy from Dante to Bembo* (Oxford, 1995) surveys changes in humanist literary strategies. D. Marsh, *The Quattrocento Dialogue: Classical Tradition and Humanist Innovation* (Cambridge, Mass., 1980), J. M. McManamon, *Funeral Oratory and the Cultural Ideals of the Italian Renaissance* (Chapel Hill, N.C., 1989), and G. McClure, *Sorrow and Consolation in Italian Humanism* (Princeton, 1991) examine important humanist genres. D. Quint, 'Humanism and modernity: a reconsideration of Bruni's *Dialogues*', *Renaissance Quarterly*, 38 (1985), pp. 423–45 and V. Kahn, 'Virtù and the example of Agathocles in Machiavelli's *Prince*', *Representations*, 13 (1986), pp. 63–83 explore attitudes towards the classical past in two central texts. On humanist historiography, see N. Struever, *The Language of History in the Renaissance: Rhetoric and Historical Consciousness in Florentine Humanism* (Princeton, 1970); E. Cochrane, *Historians and Historiography in the Italian Renaissance* (Chicago, 1981); E. B. Fryde, *Humanism and Renaissance Historiography* (London, 1983); and G. Ianziti, *Humanistic Historiography under the Sforzas: Politics and Propaganda in Fifteenth-Century Milan* (Oxford, 1988). And for the humanists' reactions to the expansion of Islam in the east, see N. Bisaha, *Creating East and West: Renaissance Humanists and the Ottoman Turks* (Philadelphia, 2004).

Sample studies of individual authors or texts include: C. Quillen, *Rereading the Renaissance: Petrarch, Augustine, and the Language of Humanism* (Ann Arbor, 1998); R. Witt, *Hercules at the Crossroads: The Life, Work, and Thought of Coluccio Salutati* (Durham, N.C., 1983); *The Humanism of Leonardo Bruni: Selected Texts*, trans. and eds. G. Griffiths, J. Hankins, and D. Thompson (Binghamton, N.Y., 1987); G. Ianziti, 'Bruni on writing history', *Renaissance Quarterly*, 51 (1998), pp. 367–91; C. S. Celenza, *Renaissance Humansim and the Papal Curia: Lapo da Castiglionchio the Younger's* De curiae commodis (Ann Arbor, 1999); A. Grafton, *Leon Battista Alberti: Master Builder of the Italian Renaissance* (New York, 2000); and J. M. Najemy, *Between Friends: Discourses of Power and Desire in the Machiavelli–Vettori Letters of 1513–1515* (Princeton, 1993).

English translations of humanist texts not already cited include: E. Cassirer, P. O. Kristeller, and J. H. Randall, Jr (eds.), *The Renaissance Philosophy of Man* (Chicago, 1948); B. Kohl and R. Witt (eds.), *The Earthly Republic: Italian Humanists on Government and Society* (Philadelphia, 1978); Francesco Petrarca, *Letters on Familiar Matters*, trans. A. S. Bernardo (Baltimore, 1975–85), and *Letters of Old Age*, trans. A. S. Bernardo, S. Levin, and R. S. Bernardo (Baltimore, 1992); Leon Battista Alberti, *Dinner Pieces: A Translation of the Intercenales*, trans. D. Marsh (Binghamton, N.Y., 1987). The many translations of Machiavelli make it superfluous to cite any one in particular. An increasing number of Latin texts by Italian humanists are becoming available in bilingual editions from the I Tatti Renaissance Library; volumes to date include works by Boccaccio, Bruni, Alberti, Manetti, Ficino, and Renaissance educational treatises. Writings by women humanists are being published in the series *The Other Voice in Early Modern Europe*, eds. M. L. King and A. Rabil, Jr. Published volumes include: Laura Cereta, *Collected Letters of a Renaissance Feminist*, trans. and ed. D. Robin (Chicago, 1997); Moderata Fonte, *The Worth of Women*, trans. and ed. V. Cox (Chicago, 1997); Tullia d'Aragona, *Dialogue on the Infinity of Love*, trans. and eds. R. Russell and B. Merry (Chicago, 1997); Veronica Franco, *Poems and Selected Letters*, trans. and eds. A. R. Jones and M. F. Rosenthal (Chicago, 1998); and Cassandra Fedele, *Letters and Orations*, trans. and ed. D. Robin (Chicago, 2000).

Chapter 3

The burgeoning literature is surveyed by D. S. Peterson in 'Out of the margins: religion and the Church in Renaissance Italy', *Renaissance Quarterly*, 53 (2000), pp. 835–79. E. Duffy summarizes the work of Pastor, P. Partner, B. McClung Hallman, and others in *Saints and Sinners: A History of the Popes* (New Haven, 1997), pp. 115–61. C. L. Stinger delineates Roman culture in *The Renaissance in Rome* (Bloomington, Ind., 1985). R. Brentano's survey of local institutions applies to much of the Renaissance: *Two Churches: England and Italy in the Thirteenth Century* (first published 1968) (Berkeley, 1988). More recent studies of bishops are by D. J. Osheim, *An Italian Lordship: The Bishopric of Lucca in the Late Middle Ages* (Berkeley, 1977) and G. Dameron, *Episcopal Power and Florentine Society, 1000–1320* (Cambridge, Mass., 1991).

The most concise portrait of a civic religious context remains G. A. Brucker, 'The Church and the Faith', in *Renaissance Florence* (first published 1969) (Berkeley, 1983), pp. 172–212. For the countryside, see J. S. Grubb, 'Spirituality and religion', in *Provincial Families of the Renaissance: Private and Public Life in the Veneto* (Baltimore, 1996), pp. 185–215. R. C. Trexler's challenging analysis of religious ritual, *Public Life in Renaissance Florence* (first published 1980) (Ithaca, N.Y., 1989) has been a seminal work. E. Muir offers a comparative synthesis in *Ritual in Early Modern Europe* (Cambridge, 1997). The groundbreaking work on confraternities in Venice and Florence by B. Pullan, *Rich and Poor in Renaissance Venice: The Social Institutions of a Catholic State to 1620* (Cambridge, Mass., 1971) and R. F. E. Weissman, *Ritual Brotherhood in Renaissance Florence* (New York, 1982) has been followed by numerous studies: see C. F. Black, *Italian Confraternities in the Sixteenth Century* (Cambridge, 1989); N. Terpstra, *Lay Confraternities and Civic Religion in Renaissance Bologna* (Cambridge, 1995); J. Henderson, *Piety and Charity in Late Medieval Florence* (Oxford, 1994); and K. Eisenbichler, *The Boys of the Archangel Raphael: A Youth Confraternity in Florence, 1411–1785* (Toronto, 1998). On popular religious movements, see D. Bornstein, *The Bianchi of 1399: Popular Devotion in Late Medieval Italy* (Ithaca, N.Y., 1993); and, on women and religion, the translations of selected articles by A. Benvenuti, G. Zarri, and others in *Women and Religion in Medieval and Renaissance Italy*, trans. M. J. Schneider, eds. D. Bornstein and R. Rusconi (Chicago, 1996). On saints, besides D. Weinstein and R. Bell, cited in note 12, see D. Webb, *Patrons and Defenders: The Saints in Italian City-States* (London, 1996) and A. Vauchez, *Sainthood in the Later Middle Ages*, trans. J. Birrell (Cambridge, 1997).

Points of entry into vernacular religious literature are offered by K. Gill, 'Women and the production of religious literature in the vernacular, 1300–1500', in E. A. Matter and J. Coakley (eds.), *Creative Women in Medieval and Early Modern Italy: A Religious and Artistic Renaissance* (Philadelphia, 1994), pp. 64–104; and D. Kent, 'Compilations and the corpus of texts' in *Cosimo de'*

Medici and the Florentine Renaissance (New Haven, 2000), pp. 69–93. Among numerous studies of mendicant preaching, see C. L. Polecritti, *Preaching Peace in Renaissance Italy: Bernardino of Siena and His Audience* (Washington, D.C., 2000); D. Lesnick, *Preaching in Medieval Florence: The Social World of Franciscan and Dominican Spirituality* (Athens, Ga., 1989); A. Thompson, *Revival Preachers and Politics in Thirteenth-Century Italy* (Oxford, 1992); F. Mormando, *The Preacher's Demons: Bernardino of Siena and the Social Underworld of Early Renaissance Italy* (Chicago, 1999); B. Paton, *Preaching Friars and the Civic Ethos: Siena, 1380–1480* (London, 1992); P. Howard, *Beyond the Written Word: Preaching and Theology in the Florence of Archbishop Antoninus, 1426–1459* (Florence, 1995); and N. Ben-Aryeh Debby, *Renaissance Florence in the Rhetoric of Two Popular Preachers: Giovanni Dominici (1356–1419) and Bernardino of Siena (1380–1444)* (Turnhout, 2001). On the monastic orders, see B. Collett, *Italian Benedictine Scholars and the Reformation: The Congregation of Santa Giustina of Padua* (Oxford, 1985).

The classic work on humanism and religion remains C. Trinkaus, *In Our Image and Likeness: Humanity and Divinity in Italian Humanist Thought* (2 vols., Chicago, 1970). See also G. Holmes, *The Florentine Enlightenment 1400–50* (London, 1969), esp. ch. 4, pp. 106–36. O. Niccoli's *Prophecy and People in Renaissance Italy*, trans. L. G. Cochrane (Princeton, 1990) captures the religious and apocalyptic expectations of the high and late Renaissance. Savonarola's long-lived influence is studied by L. Polizzotto, *The Elect Nation: The Savonarolan Movement in Florence, 1494–1545* (Oxford, 1994). E. G. Gleason captures the contradictions of Catholic reform in *Gasparo Contarini: Venice, Rome, and Reform* (Berkeley, 1993). On ideas of reform in Rome, see J. W. O'Malley, *Praise and Blame in Renaissance Rome: Rhetoric, Doctrine, and Reform in the Sacred Orators of the Papal Court, 1450–1521* (Durham, N.C., 1979). J. Martin, *Venice's Hidden Enemies* (Berkeley, 1993) analyses the Italian response to Lutheranism.

Chapter 4

Three collections of essays provide an episodic overview of family and marriage: *La famiglia e la vita quotidiana dal '400 al '600* (Rome, 1986); D. I. Kertzer and R. P. Saller (eds.), *The Family in Italy from Antiquity to the Present* (New Haven, 1991); T. Dean and K. J. P. Lowe (eds.), *Marriage in Italy 1300–1650* (Cambridge, 1998).

On demography, see M. Barbagli, *Sotto lo stesso tetto: mutamento della famiglia in Italia dal XV al XX secolo* (Bologna, 1984); M. Ginatempo and L. Sandri, *L'Italia delle città. Il popolamento urbano tra medioevo e Rinascimento (secoli XIII-XVI)* (Florence, 1990). On the impact of the plague, see R. Comba, G. Piccini, and G. Pinto (eds.), *Strutture familiari, epidemie, migrazioni nell'Italia medievale* (Naples, 1984).

D. Herlihy's and C. Klapisch-Zuber's pioneering investigation of the Florentine Catasto of 1427 is the crown jewel of Renaissance family demography: *Les Toscans et leurs familles* (Paris, 1978); an abbreviated English edition appeared as *Tuscans and their Families: A Study of the Florentine Catasto of 1427* (New Haven, 1985). For an incisive assessment of their research, see R. M. Smith, 'The people of Tuscany and their families in the fifteenth century: medieval or Mediterranean?', *Journal of Family History*, 6 (1981), pp. 107–28. Herlihy's influential essays on marriage and the family are published in *Cities and Society in Medieval Italy* (London, 1981) and *Women, Family and Society in Medieval Europe: Historical Essays, 1978–1991*, ed. A. Molho (Providence, R.I., 1995). For Klapisch-Zuber's dazzling ethnographic explorations of family and marriage rituals, see her *Women, Family, and Ritual in Renaissance Italy*, trans. L. G. Cochrane (Chicago, 1985) and *La maison et le nom. Stratégies et rituels dans l'Italie de la Renaissance* (Paris, 1990).

A large, ever growing, and diverse body of social history studies devoted to the family, marriage, and dowries in late medieval and Renaissance Italy, but especially Florence, is available. In addition to the studies of Herlihy and Klapisch-Zuber cited above, see, for Florence, R. A. Goldthwaite, *Private Wealth in Renaissance Florence* (Princeton, 1968); F. W. Kent, *Household and Lineage in Renaissance Florence: The Family Life of the Capponi, Ginori and Rucellai* (Princeton, 1977); P. Gavitt, *Charity and Children in Renaissance Florence: The Ospedale degli Innocenti, 1410–1536* (Ann Arbor, 1990); L. Fabbri, *Alleanza matrimoniale e patriziato nella Firenze del '400. Studio sulla famiglia Strozzi* (Florence, 1991); A. Molho, 'Deception and marriage strategy in Renaissance Florence: the case of women's ages', *Renaissance Quarterly*, 41 (1988), pp. 193–217; and his magisterial *Marriage Alliance in Late Medieval Florence* (Cambridge, Mass., 1994); the essays of F. W. Kent, R. Bizzocchi, T. Kuehn, S. Strocchia, and L. Pandimiglio on the patrician family in fifteenth-century Florence, in *Palazzo Strozzi: metà millennio, 1489–1989* (Rome, 1991), pp. 70–158; A. Crabb, *The Strozzi of Florence: Widowhood and Family Solidarity in the Renaissance* (Ann Arbor, 2000). For trends beyond Florence, see G. Motta, *Strategie familiari e alleanze matrimoniali in Sicilia nell'età della transizione (secoli XIV–XVII)* (Florence, 1983); G. Delille, *Famille et propriété dans le Royaume de Naples* (Rome, 1985); P. Jansen, *Démographie et société dans les Marches à la fin du Moyen Âge: Macerata au XIVe et XVe siècles* (Rome, 2001); E. Grendi, 'Profilo storico degli alberghi genovesi', in his *La repubblica aristocratica dei genovesi* (Bologna, 1987); A. Barbero, *Un'oligarchia urbana. Politica ed economia a Torino fra Tre e Quattrocento* (Rome, 1995); J. S. Grubb, *Provincial Families: Private and Public Life in the Veneto* (Baltimore, 1996); D. Romano, *Patricians and Popolani: The Social Foundations of the Venetian Renaissance State* (Baltimore, 1987); A. Bellavitis, *Identité, marriage, mobilité sociale. Citoyennes et Citoyens à Venise au XVIe siècle* (Rome, 2001);

and D. Rheubottom, *Age, Marriage, and Politics in Fifteenth-Century Ragusa* (New York, 2000).

On women and gender, see M. T. Guerra Medici, *L'aria di città. Donne e diritti nel comune medievale* (Naples, 1996); J. C. Brown and R. C. Davis (eds.), *Gender and Society in Renaissance Italy* (London, 1998); S. Chojnacki, *Women and Men in Renaissance Venice* (Baltimore, 2000); A. Jacobson Schutte, T. Kuehn, and S. Seidel Menchi (eds.), *Time, Space and Women's Lives in Early Modern Europe* (Kirksville, Mo., 2001); I. Chabot, 'Widowhood and poverty in late medieval Florence', *Continuity and Change*, 3 (1988), pp. 291–311.

On law, see, for a general orientation, M. Bellomo, *The Common Legal Past of Europe, 1000–1800* (Washington, D.C., 1995). On the indispensable Roman legal background, see B. Rawson (ed.), *The Family in Ancient Rome: New Perspectives on the Family* (Ithaca, N.Y., 1986); and A. Arjava, *Women and Law in Late Antiquity* (Oxford, 1996). For the Renaissance, one should begin with N. Tammasia, *La famiglia italiana nei secoli decimoquinto e decimosesto* (Milan, 1910). For a convenient guide to recent scholarship, see G. Di Renzo Villata, 'Persone e famiglia nel diritto medioevale e moderno', in *Digesto, civile*, UTET, 13 (Turin, 1996), pp. 457–527.

For socio-legal approaches, see the studies of T. Kuehn, *Law, Family, and Women: Toward a Legal Anthropology of Renaissance Italy* (Chicago, 1991), and *Illegitimacy in Renaissance Florence* (Ann Arbor, 2002); and those of J. Kirshner, 'Materials for a gilded cage: non-dotal assets in Florence (1300–1500)', in Kertzer and Saller (eds.), *The Family in Italy from Antiquity to the Present* (cited above), pp. 184–207; '*Li Emergenti Bisogni Matrimoniali* in Renaissance Florence', in W. J. Connell (ed.), *Society and Individual in Renaissance Florence* (Berkeley, 2002), pp. 79–109.

On dowries, M. Bellomo, *Ricerche sui rapporti patrimoniali tra coniugi. Contributo alla storia della famiglia medievale* (Milan, 1961) remains fundamental, as does L. Mayali's *Droit savant et coutumes. L'exclusion des filles dótees XIIème–XVème siècles* (Frankfurt am Main, 1987).

On marriage disputes, clandestine marriages, and marital separation, see two excellent volumes of essays edited by S. Seidel Menchi and D. Quaglioni, *Coniugi nemici: la separazione in Italia dal XII al XVIII secolo* (Bologna, 2000); and *Matrimonio in dubbio: unioni controverse e nozze clandestine in Italia dal XIV al XVIII secolo* (Bologna, 2001). On dowry assistance to poor girls, A. Esposito, 'Le confraternite del matrimonio: carità, devozione e bisogni sociali a Roma nel tardo Quattrocento', in L. Fortini (ed.), *Un'idea di Roma: società, arte e cultura tra Umanesimo e Rinascimento* (Rome, 1993), pp. 7–51.

On last wills and inheritance, see A. Romano, *Famiglia, successioni e patrimonio familiare nell'Italia medievale e moderna* (Turin, 1994); D. O. Hughes,

'Struttura familiare e sistemi di successione ereditaria nei testamenti dell'Europa medievale', *Quaderni storici*, 11, n. 33 (1976), pp. 929–52. On Siena, S. K. Cohn, Jr, *Death and Property in Siena, 1205–1800* (Baltimore, 1988); G. Lumia, 'Morire a Siena: devoluzione testamentaria, legami parentali e vincoli affettivi in età moderna', *Bullettino senese di storia patria*, 103 (1996), pp. 103–285; on Florence, T. Kuehn, 'Law, death and heirs in the Renaissance: repudiation of inheritance in Florence', *Renaissance Quarterly*, 45 (1992), pp. 484–516. On women's last wills, L. Guzzetti, *Venezianische Vermächtnisse: die soziale und wirtschaftliche Situation von Frauen im Spiegel spätmittelalterlicher Testamente* (Stuttgart, 1998); M. L. Lombardo and M. Morelli, 'Donne e testamenti a Roma nel Quattrocento', *Archivi e cultura*, 25/26 (1992/3), pp. 25–130. On the vexed issue of disinheritance, J. Kirshner, 'Baldus de Ubaldis on disinheritance: contexts, controversies, consilia', *Ius commune: Zeitschrift für Europäische Rechtsgeschichte*, 27 (2000), pp. 118–214.

Chapter 5

On the body as a microcosm, see L. Barkan, *Nature's Work of Art: The Human Body as Image of the World* (New Haven, 1975); for body metaphors in political thought, J. M. Najemy, 'The republic's two bodies: body metaphors in Italian Renaissance political thought', in A. Brown (ed.), *Language and Images of Renaissance Italy* (Oxford, 1995), pp. 237–62; and on Alberti and the proportionality of bodies, buildings, and the cosmos, see J. Gadol, *Leon Battista Alberti: Universal Man of the Early Renaissance* (Chicago, 1969); and A. Grafton, *Leon Battista Alberti: Master Builder of the Italian Renaissance* (New York, 2000).

On plagues: S. K. Cohn, Jr, *The Black Death Transformed: Disease and Culture in Early Renaissance Europe* (London, 2002); D. Herlihy, *The Black Death and the Transformation of the West*, ed. S. K. Cohn, Jr (Cambridge, Mass., 1997); and A. G. Carmichael, *Plague and the Poor in Renaissance Florence* (Cambridge, 1986). The cultural effects of the plagues are treated in D. Williman (ed.), *The Black Death: The Impact of the Fourteenth-Century Plague* (Binghamton, N.Y., 1982). On syphilis see A. Foa, 'The new and the old: the spread of syphilis (1494–1530)', in E. Muir and G. Ruggiero (eds.), *Sex and Gender in Historical Perspective* (Baltimore, 1990), pp. 26–45.

For medicine and the state of medical knowledge: N. Siraisi, *Medieval and Early Renaissance Medicine: An Introduction to Knowledge and Practice* (Chicago, 1990); also by Siraisi, *Taddeo Alderotti and His Pupils: Two Generations of Italian Medical Learning* (Princeton, 1981); and K. Park, *Doctors and Medicine in Early Renaissance Florence* (Princeton, 1985). D. Biow discusses reactions to the plague and provides a subtle analysis of Fracastoro's treatise on syphilis in *Doctors, Ambassadors, Secretaries: Humanism and Professions in Renaissance Italy* (Chicago, 2002). On hospitals in Florence and Tuscany:

J. Henderson, *Piety and Charity in Late Medieval Florence* (Oxford, 1994); and G. Pinto (ed.), *La società del bisogno: povertà e assistenza nella Toscana medievale* (Florence, 1989). On the Innocenti and its foundation by Francesco di Marco Datini: P. Gavitt, *Charity and Children in Renaissance Florence: The Ospedale degli Innocenti, 1410–1536* (Ann Arbor, 1990).

Recent Italian scholarship on the Jews is presented in depth in *Storia d'Italia: Annali* 11. *Gli ebrei in Italia*, ed. C. Vivanti (Turin, 1996). For an assessment of the scholarship, see C. Vivanti, 'The history of the Jews in Italy and the history of Italy', *Journal of Modern History*, 67 (1995), pp. 309–57. Overviews in R. Bonfil, *Jewish Life in Renaissance Italy*, trans. A. Oldcorn (Berkeley, 1994); and A. Foa, *The Jews of Europe after the Black Death* (Berkeley, 2000). On Roman Jews: K. Stow: *Taxation, Community, State: The Jews and the Fiscal Foundations of the Early Modern Papal State* (Stuttgart, 1982); Stow, 'Marriages are made in Heaven: marriage and the individual in the Roman Jewish ghetto', *Renaissance Quarterly*, 48 (1995), pp. 445–91; and Stow, *Theater of Acculturation: The Roman Ghetto in the Sixteenth Century* (Seattle, 2001). On Jewish bankers and the papacy: L. Poliakov, *Jewish Bankers and the Holy See from the Thirteenth to the Seventeenth Century* (London, 1977). For Florence's Jews, in addition to the older and still valuable works by U. Cassuto, *Gli ebrei a Firenze nell'età del Rinascimento* (Florence, 1918), and M. Ciardini, *I banchieri ebrei in Firenze nel secolo XV e il Monte di Pietà fondato da Girolamo Savonarola* (first published 1907) (Florence, 1975), see A. Gow and G. Griffiths, 'Pope Eugenius IV and Jewish money-lending in Florence: the case of Salomone di Bonaventura during the chancellorship of Leonardo Bruni', *Renaissance Quarterly*, 47 (1994), pp. 282–329. The authorization by the Florentine government in 1399 of a moneylender in Arezzo is analysed and published by A. Molho, 'A note on Jewish moneylenders in Tuscany in the late Trecento and early Quattrocento', in A. Molho and J. Tedeschi (eds.), *Renaissance Studies in Honor of Hans Baron* (Florence, 1971), pp. 99–117. The volume *La cultura ebraica all'epoca di Lorenzo il Magnifico*, eds. D. L. Bemporad and I. Zatelli (Florence, 1998) contains valuable essays on Jewish participation in Renaissance intellectual life (including one in English by M. Idel, 'Jewish mystical thought in the Florence of Lorenzo il Magnifico', pp. 17–42) and an important essay on Jewish moneylending and public loan banks by R. Fubini, 'Prestito ebraico e Monte di Pietà a Firenze (1471–1473)', pp. 101–55. On Jews in Venice: B. Pullan, *Rich and Poor in Renaissance Venice: The Social Institutions of a Catholic State, to 1620* (Cambridge, Mass., 1971), part III, 'Venetian Jewry and the Monti di Pietà', pp. 429–625.

On Bernardino and the Jews, see F. Mormando, *The Preacher's Demons: Bernardino of Siena and the Social Underworld of Early Renaissance Italy* (Chicago, 1999), which also contains illuminating chapters on Bernardino's crusade against witches and sodomites. Bernardino's dialogues with his listeners are analysed by C. Polecritti, *Preaching Peace in Renaissance Italy: Bernardino of Siena and his Audience* (Washington, D.C., 2000). On the perceived link between Jews and prostitutes, see D. O. Hughes, 'Distinguishing signs: ear-rings, Jews and Franciscan rhetoric in the Italian Renaissance city', *Past and Present*, 112 (1986), pp. 3–59. On the emergence of the *monti di pietà*, in addition to the work of Pullan (above), see C. Bresnahan Menning, *Charity and State in Late Renaissance Italy* (Ithaca, N.Y., 1993). The alleged murder in Trent in 1475 and its consequences are treated by R. Po-chia Hsia, *Trent 1475: Stories of a Ritual Murder Trial* (New Haven, 1992).

On Florentine prostitutes: M. S. Mazzi, *Prostitute e lenoni nella Firenze del Quattrocento* (Milan, 1991); and R. C. Trexler, 'Florentine prostitution in the fifteenth century: patrons and clients', in Trexler, *Dependence in Context in Renaissance Florence* (Binghamton, N.Y., 1994). Some comments on government supervision of prostitution in Venice are in G. Ruggiero, *The Boundaries of Eros: Sex Crime and Sexuality in Renaissance Venice* (Oxford, 1985). The life and writings of Veronica Franco and the figure of the cultivated courtesan are described in M. Rosenthal, *The Honest Courtesan: Veronica Franco, Citizen and Writer in Sixteenth Century Venice* (Chicago, 1992). Government policy toward sodomy in Florence is the subject of the excellent study by M. Rocke, *Forbidden Friendships: Homosexuality and Male Culture in Renaissance Florence* (Oxford, 1996).

Chapter 6

On the more than fifty-year-old debate on the Renaissance economy, see C. M. Cipolla, 'The trends in Italian economic history in the later Middle Ages', *Economic History Review*, s. II, 2 (1949), pp. 181–4; R. S. Lopez, 'Hard times and investment in culture', in *The Renaissance: A Symposium* (New York, 1953), pp. 29–54; W. K. Ferguson, 'Recent trends in the economic historiography of the Renaissance', *Studies in the Renaissance*, 7 (1960), pp. 7–26; R. S. Lopez and H. A. Miskimin, 'The economic depression of the Renaissance', *Economic History Review*, s. II, 14 (1962), pp. 408–26; R. Romano, *Tra due crisi: l'Italia del Rinascimento*, (Turin, 1971); G. Cherubini, 'La "crisi del Trecento": bilancio e prospettive di ricerca', *Studi storici*, 15 (1974), pp. 660–70; J. C. Brown, 'Prosperity or hard times in Renaissance Italy?', *Renaissance Quarterly*, 42 (1989), pp. 761–80; S. R. Epstein, *Freedom and Growth: The Rise of States and Markets in Europe*, 1300–1750 (London, 2000), esp. ch. 3

For demographic developments on the peninsula and in the cities, see the works of J. C. Russell, *Late Ancient and Medieval Population* (Philadelphia, 1958) and *Medieval Regions and Their Cities* (Bloomington, Ind., 1972); M. Ginatempo and L. Sandri, *L'Italia delle città. Il popolamento urbano tra Medioevo e Rinascimento (secoli XIII–XVI)* (Florence, 1990); L. Del Panta, M. Livi Bacci, G. Pinto, and G. Sonnino, *La popolazione italiana dal Medioevo a oggi*, (Rome, 1996); P. Malanima, 'Italian cities 1300–1800: a quantitative approach', *Rivista di storia economica*, 14 (1998), pp. 91–126.

A general picture of the transformations of the Renaissance urban economy, with particular reference to the larger cities, can be assembled from the following: J. Day, *The Medieval Market Economy* (Oxford, 1987), pp. 185–224 ('Crises and trends in the late Middle Ages'); M. Luzzati, 'La dinamica secolare di un "modello italiano"', in R. Romano (ed.), *Storia dell'economia italiana*, vol. i, *Il Medioevo: dal crollo al trionfo* (Turin, 1990), pp. 5–114; M. Aymard, 'La fragilità di un'economia avanzata: l'Italia e le trasformazioni dell'economia', ibid., vol. ii, *L'età moderna: verso la crisi*, (Turin, 1991), pp. 5–137; R. A. Goldthwaite, *Wealth and the Demand for Art in Italy 1300–1600* (Baltimore, 1993), esp. pp. 13–40; C. F. Black, *Early Modern Italy: A Social History* (London, 2001), esp. chs. 5–6; P. Malanima, *L'economia italiana. Dalla crescita medievale alla crescita contemporanea* (Bologna, 2002); and from the volume *Italia 1350–1450: Tra crisi, trasformazione, sviluppo* (Pistoia, 1993), the essays by M. Ginatempo, B. Dini, A. Molho, and G. Pinto. On the southern kingdom, see E. Sakellariou, *The Kingdom of Naples under Aragonese and Spanish Rule: Population Growth and Economic and Social Evolution in the Late Fifteenth and Early Sixteenth Century*, Ph.D. thesis, University of Cambridge, 1996. For a study of a smaller city, see J. C. Brown, *In the Shadow of Florence: Provincial Society in Renaissance Pescia* (New York, 1982).

On merchants and banking, see F. C. Lane, *Andrea Barbarigo, Merchant of Venice, 1418–1449* (Baltimore, 1944); also by Lane, *Venice: A Maritime Republic* (Baltimore, 1973); I. Origo, *The Merchant of Prato: Francesco di Marco Datini* (London, 1957); R. de Roover, *The Rise and Decline of the Medici Bank, 1397–1494* (Cambridge, Mass., 1963); A. Sapori, *The Italian Merchant in the Middle Ages* (London, 1970); B. Z. Kedar, *Merchants in Crisis: Genoese and Venetian Men of Affairs and the Fourteenth-Century Depression* (New Haven, 1976); R. A. Goldthwaite, 'Local banking in Renaissance Florence', *Journal of European Economic History*, 14 (1985), pp. 5–55; E. Otte, 'Il ruolo dei Genovesi nella Spagna del XV e XVI secolo', in A. De Maddalena and H. Kellenbenz (eds.), *La repubblica internazionale del denaro tra XV e XVII secolo* (Bologna, 1986), pp. 17–56; S. R. Epstein, *An Island for Itself: Economic Development and Social Change in Late Medieval Sicily* (Cambridge, 1992); E. S. Hunt, *The Medieval Super-Companies: A Study of the Peruzzi Company of Florence* (Cambridge, 1994); R. C. Mueller, *The Venetian Money Market: Banks, Panics, and the Public Debt, 1200–1500* (Baltimore, 1997).

Works on the chief areas of production include M. F. Mazzaoui, *The Italian Cotton Industry in the Later Middle Ages, 1100–1600* (Cambridge, 1981); B. Dini, 'L'industria tessile italiana nel tardo Medioevo', in S. Gensini (ed.), *Le Italie del tardo Medioevo* (Pisa, 1990), pp. 321–59; H. Hoshino, 'The rise of the Florentine woollen industry in the fourteenth century', in N. B. Harte and

K. G. Ponting (eds.), *Cloth and Clothing in Medieval Europe: Essays in Memory of Professor E. M. Carus-Wilson* (London, 1983), pp. 184–204; F. Franceschi, 'Florence and silk in the fifteenth century: the origins of a long and felicitous union', *Italian History and Culture*, 1 (1995), pp. 3–22; L. Molà, *The Silk Industry of Renaissance Venice* (Baltimore, 2000); R. A. Goldthwaite, *The Building of Renaissance Florence: An Economic and Social History* (Baltimore, 1980); R. C. Davis, *Shipbuilders of the Venetian Arsenal: Workers and Workplace in the Preindustrial City* (Baltimore, 1991), mostly on the seventeenth century, but useful for the earlier period as well; M. J. C. Lowry, 'La produzione del libro', in S. Cavaciocchi (ed.), *Produzione e commercio della carta e del libro (secc. XIII–XVIII)* (Florence, 1992), pp. 365–87 (which, despite the title, is actually in English); and M. Fantoni, L. C. Matthew, S. Matthews-Grieco (eds.), *The Art Market in Italy (15th–17th Centuries)* (Ferrara, 2003), esp. section 2 and the article by R. A. Goldthwaite.

For the origins of 'proto-industry' and the development of economic regions, see P. Malanima, 'Politica ed economia nella formazione dello Stato regionale: il caso toscano', *Studi veneziani*, n.s., 11 (1986), pp. 61–72; M. Mirri, 'Formazione di una regione economica. Ipotesi sulla Toscana, sul Veneto, sulla Lombardia', ibid., pp. 47–59; S. R. Epstein, 'Cities, regions and the late medieval crisis: Sicily and Tuscany compared', *Past and Present*, 130 (1991), pp. 3–50; and Epstein's *Freedom and Growth*, cited above.

On the organization of work and the role of the guilds, see R. Greci, 'Forme di organizzazione del lavoro nelle città italiane tra età comunale e signorile', in his *Corporazioni e mondo del lavoro nell'Italia padana medievale* (Bologna, 1988), pp. 129–55; S. A. Epstein, *Wage Labor and Guilds in Medieval Europe* (Chapel Hill, N.C., 1991) (a general treatment, but with considerable attention to Italy); D. Degrassi, *L'economia artigiana nell'Italia medievale* (Rome, 1996); G. Pinto, 'L'organizzazione del lavoro nei cantieri edili (Italia centro-settentrionale)', in *Artigiani e salariati. Il mondo del lavoro nell'Italia dei secoli XII–XV* (Pistoia, 1984), pp. 69–101; P. Massa Piergiovanni, 'Technological typologies and economic organisation of silk workers in Italy, from the XIVth to the XVIIIth centuries', *Journal of European Economic History*, 22 (1993), pp. 543–64; *The Art Market in Italy (15th–17th Centuries)*, cited above; R. de Roover, 'Labour conditions in Florence around 1400: theory, policy and reality', in N. Rubinstein (ed.), *Florentine Studies: Politics and Society in Renaissance Florence* (Evanston, Ill., 1968), pp. 277–313; R. Mackenney, *Tradesmen and Traders: The World of the Guilds in Venice and Europe, c.1250–c.1650*, (Totowa, N.J., 1987); and F. Franceschi, *Oltre il 'Tumulto'. I lavoratori fiorentini dell'arte della lana fra Tre e Quattrocento* (Florence, 1993), part II, pp. 81–231.

On the distribution of wealth and trends in living standards, see R. A. Goldthwaite, 'The Renaissance economy: the preconditions for luxury consumption', in *Aspetti della vita economica medievale* (Florence, 1985), pp. 659–75; also Goldthwaite's *Wealth and the Demand for Art*, cited above, esp. pp. 40–67; P. Malanima, *L'economia italiana*, cited above; D. Herlihy and C. Klapisch-Zuber, *Tuscans and their Families: A Study of the Florentine Catasto of 1427* (New Haven, 1985); D. L. Hicks, 'Sources of wealth in Renaissance Siena: businessmen and landownwers', in *Bullettino senese di storia patria*, 93 (1986), pp. 9–42; D. Romano, *Patricians and Popolani: The Social Foundations of the Venetian Renaissance State* (Baltimore, 1987), ch. 2. On the workers of the textile industry in Florence, see G. A. Brucker, 'The Ciompi revolution', in Rubinstein (ed.), *Florentine Studies*, cited above; and F. Franceschi, *Oltre il 'Tumulto'*, cited above, part III, pp. 235–334.

Finally, on the urban uprisings, see V. Rutenburg, *Popolo e movimenti popolari nell'Italia del '300 e '400* (Bologna, 1971); J. M. Najemy '*Audiant omnes Artes*: corporate origins of the Ciompi revolution', in *Il tumulto dei Ciompi. Un momento di storia fiorentina ed europea* (Florence, 1981), pp. 59–93; S. K. Cohn, Jr, *The Laboring Classes in Renaissance Florence* (New York, 1980); and also by Cohn, 'Florentine insurrections, 1342–1385, in comparative perspective', in R. H. Hilton and T. H. Aston (eds.), *The English Rising of 1381* (Cambridge, 1984), pp. 143–64.

Chapter 7

Valuable general studies that deal with the period of the popolo's rise to political prominence include J. K. Hyde, *Society and Politics in Medieval Italy: The Evolution of the Civil Life, 1000–1350* (London, 1973); D. Waley, *The Italian City–Republics* (first published 1969) (London, 1978); J. Larner, *Italy in the Age of Dante and Petrarch, 1216–1380* (London, 1980); L. Martines, *Power and Imagination: City–States in Renaissance Italy* (first published 1979) (Baltimore, 1988); E. Occhipinti, *L'Italia dei comuni. Secoli XI–XIII* (Rome, 2000); and J.-C. Maire Vigueur, *Cavaliers et citoyens. Guerre, conflits et société dans l'Italie communale, XIIᵉ–XIIIᵉ siècle* (Paris, 2003).

On the early popolo in the context of the evolution of the communes, see the magisterial synthesis of P. J. Jones, *The Italian City–State from Commune to Signoria* (Oxford, 1997), esp. ch. 4, part IV, 'The century of the popolo', pp. 485–521. Also J. C. Koenig, *The Popolo of Northern Italy (1196–1274): A Political Analysis*, Ph.D. thesis, University of California at Los Angeles, 1977; and E. Artifoni, 'Tensioni sociali e istituzioni nel mondo comunale', in *La storia. I grandi problemi dal medioevo all'età contemporanea*, vol. ii, *Il medioevo* (Turin, 1986), pp. 461–91.

On the popolo and the guilds, see the old but still useful work of G. De Vergottini, *Arti e 'popolo' nella prima metà del sec. XIII* (Milan, 1943); also R. Greci, *Corporazioni e mondo del lavoro nell'Italia padana medievale* (Bologna, 1988), esp. ch. 3, 'Corporazioni e politiche cittadine: genesi, consolidamento ed esiti di un rapporto (qualche esempio)', pp. 93–129; E. Artifoni, 'Corporazioni e società di "popolo": un problema della politica comunale nel secolo XIII', *Quaderni storici*, 25, n. 74 (1990), pp. 387–404; and A. I. Pini, *Città, comuni e corporazioni nel medioevo italiano* (Bologna, 1986).

The literature on the magnates is extensive, not all of it directly relevant to the popolo. But see the collection of papers in *Magnati e popolani nell'Italia comunale* (Pistoia, 1997); and, on the anti-magnate legislation authored by the popolo, G. Fasoli, 'Ricerche sulla legislazione antimagnatizia nei comuni dell'alta e media Italia', *Rivista di storia del diritto italiano*, 12 (1939), pp. 86–133 and 240–309. On magnates and popolo in Florence, the classic work of Gaetano Salvemini is still valuable: *Magnati e popolani in Firenze dal 1280 al 1295* (first published 1899) (Milan, 1966). For modern treatments of the Florentine anti-magnate legislation, see C. Lansing, *The Florentine Magnates: Lineage and Faction in a Medieval Commune* (Princeton, 1991), esp. pp. 192–211; and A. Zorzi, 'Politica e giustizia a Firenze al tempo degli Ordinamenti antimagnatizi', in V. Arrighi (ed.), *Ordinamenti di Giustizia fiorentini. Studi in occasione del VII centenario* (Florence, 1995), pp. 105–47.

Studies on the popolo in specific contexts are available. Perugia: J.-C. Maire Vigueur, 'Il comune popolare', in *Società e istituzioni dell'Italia comunale: l'esempio di Perugia (secoli XII–XIV)* (Perugia, 1988), vol. 1, pp. 41–56; and J. P. Grundman, *The 'Popolo' at Perugia, 1139–1309* (Perugia, 1992). Siena: W. M. Bowsky, *A Medieval Italian Commune: Siena under the Nine, 1287–1355* (Berkeley, 1981); V. Wainwright, 'Conflict and popular government in fourteenth-century Siena: il Monte dei Dodici, 1355–1368', in *I ceti dirigenti nella Toscana tardo comunale* (Florence, 1983), pp. 57–80; also by Wainwright, 'The testing of a popular Sienese regime: the *Riformatori* and the insurrection of 1371', in *I Tatti Studies: Essays in the Renaissance*, 2 (1987), pp. 107–70. Genoa: G. Petti Balbi, 'Genesi e composizione di un ceto dirigente. I "populares" a Genova nei secoli XIII e XIV', in G. Rossetti (ed.), *Spazio, società, potere nell'Italia dei comuni* (Naples, 1986), pp. 85–103. Rome: J.-C. Maire Vigueur, 'Il comune romano', in A. Vauchez (ed.), *Roma medievale* (Rome, 2001), pp. 117–57; and two new studies on Cola di Rienzo and his Roman revolution, A. Collins, *Greater than Emperor: Cola di Rienzo (ca. 1313–54) and the World of Fourteenth-Century Rome* (Ann Arbor, 2003); and R. G. Musto, *Apocalypse in Rome: Cola di Rienzo and the Politics of the New Age* (Berkeley, 2003). Venice: D. Romano, *Patricians and Popolani: The Social Foundations of the Venetian Renaissance State* (Baltimore, 1987); and G. Rösch, 'The *Serrata* of the Great Council and Venetian society, 1286–1323', in J. Martin and D. Romano (eds.), *Venice Reconsidered: The History and Civilization of an Italian City–State, 1297–1797* (Baltimore, 2000), pp. 67–88. Milan and the Ambrosian Republic: M. Spinelli, 'Ricerche per una nuova storia della Repubblica Ambrosiana', *Nuova rivista storica*, 70 (1986), pp. 231–52, and 71 (1987), pp. 27–48. See also E. Artifoni, 'I governi di "popolo" e le istituzioni comunali nella seconda metà del secolo XIII', *Reti medievali Rivista*, 4 (2003) (online at http://www.storia.unifi.it/_RM/rivista/saggi/Artifoni.htm).

For the popolo in Florence, in addition to the works cited above by Salvemini, Lansing, and Zorzi on the magnates, see, on the influence of the popolo on electoral institutions and the composition of the office-holding class, J. M. Najemy, *Corporatism and Consensus in Florentine Electoral Politics, 1280–1400* (Chapel Hill, N.C., 1982); and on the popolo's impact on the elite, Najemy, 'The dialogue of power in Florentine politics', in A. Molho, K. Raaflaub, and J. Emlen (eds.), *City–States in Classical Antiquity and Medieval Italy* (Ann Arbor, 1991), pp. 269–88. On the guild community and its 'corporate values', G. Brucker, *The Civic World of Early Renaissance Florence* (Princeton, 1977), pp. 14–59; and on the 'new men', M. Becker, *Florence in Transition*, vol. II, *Studies in the Rise of the Territorial State* (Baltimore, 1968), pp. 93–149; also by Becker, 'Some aspects of oligarchical, dictatorial, and popular *signorie* in Florence, 1282–1382', *Comparative Studies in Society and History*, 2 (1960), pp. 421–39; on courts and public order, A. Zorzi, 'Contrôle social, ordre public et répression judiciaire à Florence à l'époque communale: éléments et problèmes', *Annales E.S.C.*, 45 (1990), pp. 1169–88.

For the revival of popular republicanism in Florence after 1494, see, in addition to the many studies on Savonarola, R. Pesman Cooper, 'The Florentine ruling group under the "*Governo Popolare*", 1494–1512', *Studies in Medieval and Renaissance History*, 7 (1985), pp. 69–181; and G. Cadoni, *Lotte politiche e riforme istituzionali a Firenze tra il 1494 e il 1502* (Rome, 1999). On the last republic of 1527–1530, see the classic narrative by C. Roth, *The Last Florentine Republic* (first published 1925) (New York, 1968); and J. N. Stephens, *The Fall of the Florentine Republic, 1512–1530* (Oxford, 1983), 203–55.

Chapter 8

A useful recent general and comparative account of politics and government in many Renaissance states is D. Hay and J. Law, *Italy in the Age of the Renaissance, 1380–1530* (London, 1989). D. Herlihy and C. Klapisch-Zuber, *Tuscans and their Families: A Study of the Florentine Catasto of 1427* (New Haven, 1985), is a mine of information on the population of Florence and her dependencies, including wealth and its sources, and patterns of marriages, births, and deaths, constrasting the experience of the elite with the rest of society.

Much of the literature on elites, and especially the idea of nobility, is in Italian. However, English-speaking scholars have made many of the attempts to identify or measure the ruling elite or *reggimento* for the two best-documented states, Florence and Venice. On Florence see: G. Brucker, *The Civic World of Early Renaissance Florence* (Princeton, 1977), especially ch. 5;

D. Kent, 'The Florentine *reggimento* in the fifteenth century', *Renaissance Quarterly*, 28 (1975), pp. 575–638; R. Pesman Cooper, 'The Florentine ruling group under the "*Governo Popolare*," 1494–1512', *Studies in Medieval and Renaissance History*, 7 (1985), pp. 71–181; R. B. Litchfield, *Emergence of a Bureaucracy: The Florentine Patricians 1530–1790* (Princeton, 1986), ch. 1; D. Herlihy, 'The rulers of Florence, 1282–1530', in *Women, Family and Society in Medieval Europe: Historical Essays, 1978–1991* (Providence, R. I., 1995), pp. 353–80. For a definition of the elite solely in terms of wealth, see A. Molho, *Marriage Alliance in Late Medieval Florence* (Cambridge, Mass., 1994). On Venice, see S. Chojnacki, 'In search of the Venetian patriciate', in J. R. Hale (ed.), *Renaissance Venice* (London, 1973), pp. 47–90.

Among the most stimulating studies of issues particularly concerning the ruling classes of individual cities, see: N. Terpstra, *Lay Confraternities and Civic Religion in Renaissance Bologna*, (Cambridge, 1995); T. Dean, *Land and Power in Late Medieval Ferrara: The Rule of the Este, 1350–1450* (Cambridge, 1988); N. Rubinstein, *The Government of Florence under the Medici (1434–1494)*, 2nd edn (Oxford, 1997); J. M. Najemy, *Corporatism and Consensus in Florentine Electoral Politics, 1280–1400* (Chapel Hill, N. C., 1982); H. C. Butters, *Governors and Government in Early Sixteenth-Century Florence, 1502–1519* (Oxford, 1985); D. O. Hughes, 'Kinsmen and neighbors in medieval Genoa', in H. A. Miskimin, D. Herlihy, and A. L. Udovitch (eds.), *The Medieval City* (New Haven, 1977), pp. 95–112; C. Meek, *Lucca 1369–1400: Politics and Society in an Early Renaissance City–State* (Oxford, 1978); M. E. Bratchel, *Lucca 1430–1494: The Reconstruction of an Italian City–Republic* (Oxford, 1995); D. M. Bueno de Mesquita, 'Ludovico Sforza and his vassals', in E. F. Jacob (ed.), *Italian Renaissance Studies* (London, 1960), pp. 184–216; S. Blanshei, 'Population, wealth and patronage in medieval and Renaissance Perugia', *Journal of Interdisciplinary History*, 9 (1979), pp. 597–619; C. F. Black, 'The Baglioni as Tyrants of Perugia, 1488–1540', *English Historical Review*, 85 (1970), pp. 245–81; B. Kohl, *Padua under the Carrara, 1318–1405* (Baltimore, 1998); W. J. Connell's study of Pistoia, *La città dei crucci. Fazioni e clientele in uno stato repubblicano del '400* (Florence, 2000); W. M. Bowsky, *A Medieval Italian Commune: Siena under the Nine 1287–1355* (Berkeley, 1981); P. J. Jones, 'The end of Malatesta rule in Rimini', in Jacob (ed.), *Italian Renaissance Studies*, pp. 217–55; A. Ryder, *The Kingdom of Naples under Alfonso the Magnanimous: The Making of a Modern State* (Oxford, 1976); S. Carocci, 'Una nobiltà bipartita: Rappresentazioni sociali e lignaggi preminenti a Roma nel Duecento e nella prima metà del Trecento', *Bullettino dell'Istituto Storico Italiano per il Medio Evo e Archivio muratoriano*, 95 (1989), pp. 71–122; D. Queller, *The Venetian Patriciate: Reality versus Myth* (Urbana, Ill., 1986); D. Romano, *Patricians and Popolani: The Social Foundations of the Venetian Renaissance State* (Baltimore, 1987); J. Martin and D. Romano (eds.), *Venice Reconsidered* (Baltimore,

2000); on Verona, P. Lanaro Sartori, *Un'oligarchia urbana nel Cinquecento veneto. Istituzioni, economia, società* (Turin, 1992); J. Grubb, *Firstborn of Venice: Vicenza in the Early Renaissance* (Baltimore, 1988).

On the personal ties that bound the elites: C. Klapisch-Zuber, *Women, Family and Ritual in Renaissance Italy* (Chicago, 1985), especially the essay on 'Kin, friends, and neighbors: the urban territory of a merchant family in 1400', pp. 68–93. On the family: F. W. Kent, *Household and Lineage in Renaissance Florence: The Family Life of the Capponi, Ginori, and Rucellai* (Princeton, 1977); D. Herlihy, 'Family and property in Renaissance Florence', in Miskimin *et al.* (eds.), *The Medieval City*, pp. 3–24. On instrumental friendship and patronage: R. F. E. Weissman, 'Taking patronage seriously: Mediterranean values and Renaissance society', in F. W. Kent and P. Simons (eds.), *Patronage, Art, and Society* (Oxford, 1987), pp. 25–45; D. Kent, *The Rise of the Medici: Faction in Florence 1426–1434* (Oxford, 1978); R. Finlay, *Politics in Renaissance Venice* (New Brunswick, 1980). On neighbourhood: D. V. and F. W. Kent, *Neighbours and Neighbourhood in Renaissance Florence* (Locust Valley, N.Y., 1982); D. O. Hughes, 'Domestic ideals and social behavior: evidence from medieval Genoa', in C. E. Rosenberg (ed.), *The Family in History* (Philadelphia, 1975). On women, men, and the law: T. Kuehn, *Law, Family and Women: Toward a Legal Anthropology of Renaissance Italy* (Chicago, 1991); J. Kirshner, 'Materials for a gilded cage: non-dotal assets in Florence, 1300–1500', in D. I. Kertzer and R. P. Saller (eds.), *The Family in Italy from Antiquity to the Present* (New Haven, 1991), pp. 184–207; S. Chojnacki, *Women and Men in Renaissance Venice: Twelve Essays on Patrician Society* (Baltimore, 2000).

On magnates: C. Lansing, *The Florentine Magnates: Lineage and Faction in a Medieval Commune* (Princeton, 1991); C. Klapisch-Zuber, 'Honneur de noble, renommée de puissant: la définition des magnats italiens (1280–1400)', *Médiévales*, 24 (1993), pp. 81–100. On elites and the state, see particularly J. Kirshner (ed.), *The Origins of the State in Italy 1300–1600* (Chicago, 1995); and W. J. Connell and A. Zorzi (eds.), *Florentine Tuscany: Structures and Practices of Power* (Cambridge, 2000).

Chapter 9

For comparative work, the essays in J. Kirshner (ed.), *The Origins of the State in Italy, 1300–1600* (Chicago, 1995) are a good place to begin: P. Schiera on 'Legitimacy, discipline, and institutions'; G. Chittolini on 'The "private", the "public", the state'; A. Mazzacane on 'Law and jurists'; E. Fasano Guarini on 'Center and periphery'; A. Molho on 'The State and public finance'; T. Dean on 'The courts'; R. Bizzocchi on 'Church, religion, and State'; and R. Fubini on 'The Italian League and the policy of the balance of power'. Four volumes of studies comparing Florence with Milan and Venice contain valuable essays on government and state structures: *Florence and Venice: Comparisons and Relations*, vol. 1, *Quattrocento* (Florence, 1979); vol. 2, *Cinquecento* (Florence, 1980); *Florence and Milan: Comparisons and Relations* (2 vols., Florence, 1989). Despite its title, the collection of essays in A. Molho, K. Raaflaub, and J. Emlen (eds.), *City–States in Classical Antiquity and Medieval Italy* (Stuttgart, 1991) contains much on the Renaissance, including the idea of the city, citizenship, politics, urbanism, rituals, and territorial expansion and diplomacy. The best single-volume overview of the period is L. Martines's *Power and Imagination: City–States in Renaissance Italy* (first published 1979) (Baltimore, 1988). For the city–states up to 1300, see P. J. Jones, *The Italian City–State: from Commune to Signoria* (Oxford, 1997) and Jones's still provocative essay, 'Communes and despots: the city–state in late medieval Italy', *Transactions of the Royal Historical Society*, 5th ser., 15 (1965), pp. 71–96. And for an overview of recent scholarship, see J. M. Najemy, 'Politics and Political Thought', in J. Woolfson (ed.), *Palgrave Advances in Renaissance Historiography* (London, 2005).

Naples

On Angevin government, see the excellent new study by S. Kelly, *The New Solomon: Robert of Naples (1309–1343) and Fourteenth-Century Kingship* (Leiden, 2003). A. Ryder provides a magisterial analysis of Aragonese government in *The Kingdom of Naples under Alfonso the Magnanimous* (Oxford, 1976), and J. H. Bentley illuminates royal patronage and humanist political ideas under Ferrante in *Politics and Culture in Renaissance Naples* (Princeton, 1987).

Rome and the states of the Church

P. Partner's *The Papal State under Martin V* (Rome, 1958) is still indispensable. Partner also provides an overview in *The Lands of Saint Peter: The Papal State in the Middle Ages and the Early Renaissance* (Berkeley, 1972); a study of the bureaucracy of papal government in *The Pope's Men: The Papal Civil Service in the Renaissance* (Oxford, 1990), and an investigation of papal finances in 'The "budget" of the Roman Church in the Renaissance period', in E. F. Jacob (ed.), *Italian Renaissance Studies* (London, 1960), pp. 256–78. On Cola di Rienzo and his Roman revolution, see R. Musto, *Apocalypse in Rome: Cola di Rienzo and the Politics of the New Age* (Berkeley, 2003) and A. Collins, *Greater than Emperor: Cola di Rienzo (ca. 1313–1354) and the World of Fourteenth-Century Rome* (Ann Arbor, 2002). The example of Orvieto in Albornoz's state-building is from D. Foote, 'In search of the quiet city: civic identity and papal state building in fourteenth-century Orvieto', in P. Findlen, M. M. Fontaine, and D. J. Osheim (eds.), *Beyond Florence: The Contours of Medieval and Early Modern Italy* (Stanford, 2003), pp. 190–204. J. Larner's *The Lords of*

Romagna (Ithaca, N.Y., 1965) illuminates the origins of the *signorie* in the papal Romagna. P. J. Jones has studied in depth one city of the papal domains and its ruling family in *The Malatesta of Rimini and the Papal State: A Political History* (Cambridge, 1974). On the early-sixteenth-century papal government of Rome and the papal states, see C. Shaw, *Julius II: The Warrior Pope* (Oxford, 1993). For the financial aspects of papal government under Popes Leo and Clement, see M. M. Bullard, *Filippo Strozzi and the Medici: Favor and Finance in Sixteenth-Century Florence and Rome* (Cambridge, 1980).

Florence

On electoral institutions and the evolution of the office-holding class, see J. M. Najemy, *Corporatism and Consensus in Florentine Electoral Politics, 1280–1400* (Chapel Hill, N. C., 1982); N. Rubinstein, *The Government of Florence under the Medici, 1434–1494,* 2nd edn (Oxford, 1997); and R. Pesman Cooper, 'The Florentine ruling group under the "*Governo Popolare*", 1494–1512', in *Studies in Medieval and Renaissance History,* 7 (1985), pp. 71–181. G. Brucker's fundamental studies, *Florentine Politics and Society, 1343–1378* (Princeton, 1962) and *The Civic World of Early Renaissance Florence* (Princeton, 1977), which covers the period 1378–1430, skilfully analyse government and political conflicts up to the Medici. The formation of the Medici regime in the structures of patronage is analysed by D. Kent, *The Rise of the Medici: Faction in Florence, 1426–1434* (Oxford, 1978). The fundamental studies of fiscal institutions, the Catasto, and the public debt are by E. Conti, *L'imposta diretta a Firenze nel Quattrocento (1427–1494)* (Rome, 1984) and A. Molho in *Florentine Public Finances in the Early Renaissance, 1400–1433* (Cambridge, Mass., 1971) and, for comparative perspective, Molho, 'Tre città–stato e i loro debiti pubblici: quesiti e ipotesi sulla storia di Firenze, Genova e Venezia', in *Italia 1350–1450: tra crisi, trasformazione, sviluppo* (Pistoia, 1993), pp. 185–215. The Florentine communal army is studied by D. P. Waley, 'The army of the Florentine Republic from the twelfth to the fourteenth century', in N. Rubinstein (ed.), *Florentine Studies: Politics and Society in Renaissance Florence* (Evanston, Ill., 1968). On law and the courts, see L. Martines, *Lawyers and Statecraft in Renaissance Florence* (Princeton, 1968); L. Ikins Stern, *The Criminal Law System of Medieval and Renaissance Florence* (Baltimore, 1994); A. Zorzi, *L'amministrazione della giustizia penale nella Repubblica fiorentina* (Florence, 1988); and S. K. Cohn, Jr, *Women in the Streets: Essays on Sex and Power in Renaissance Italy* (Baltimore, 1996). The structures of the Florentine territorial state under the republic are analysed in the excellent essays in W. Connell and A. Zorzi (eds.), *Florentine Tuscany: Structures and Practice of Power* (Cambridge, 2000); and for the early principate, see E. Fasano Guarini, *Lo stato mediceo di Cosimo I* (Florence, 1973). The chancery has been expertly studied in works on two prominent chancellors by A. Brown, *Bartolomeo Scala, 1430–1497, Chancellor of Florence: The Humanist as Bureaucrat* (Princeton, 1979) and R. Black, *Benedetto Accolti and the Florentine Renaissance* (Cambridge, 1985). The government of the post-Medicean republic is perceptively treated in G. Cadoni, *Lotte politiche e riforme istituzionali a Firenze tra il 1494 e il 1502* (Rome, 1999) and H. Butters, *Governors and Government in Early Sixteenth-Century Florence, 1502–1519* (Oxford, 1985). The succeeding Medici regime and its collapse are analysed by J. N. Stephens, *The Fall of the Florentine Republic, 1512–1530* (Oxford, 1983).

Venice

A good introduction is F. Lane's *Venice: A Maritime Republic* (Baltimore, 1973). See also two collaborative volumes separated by a generation: J. R. Hale (ed.), *Renaissance Venice* (London, 1973), especially the important essays by S. Chojnacki on the patriciate in the fourteenth century, M. Mallett on Venice and its *condottieri*, D. E. Queller on ambassadors and their *relazioni*, and G. Cozzi on law and political power; and J. Martin and D. Romano (eds.), *Venice Reconsidered* (Baltimore, 2000), with valuable contributions by G. Rösch and Chojnacki on the patriciate, E. Muir and E. G. Gleason on the Venetian state and political thought in the crisis of the early sixteenth century, and J. Grubb on the 'citizens'. Grubb has also studied the Venetian territorial state from the vantage point of the subject city of Vicenza in *Firstborn of Venice: Vicenza in the Early Renaissance State* (Baltimore, 1988). The inner workings of government are treated by R. Finlay, *Politics in Renaissance Venice* (New Brunswick, 1980). Venice's military history is thoroughly dissected by M. Mallett and J. Hale in *The Military Organization of a Renaissance State: Venice, c. 1400 to 1617* (Cambridge, 1984).

Milan

D. M. Bueno de Mesquita's *Giangaleazzo Visconti, Duke of Milan (1351–1402)* (Cambridge, 1941) is still the best introduction in English to the chief architect of the Visconti state. Also valuable is his analysis of 'The privy council in the government of the dukes of Milan', in *Florence and Milan*, vol. 1 (cited above), pp. 135–56, and his overview of the growth of the *signoria* in Milan in 'The place of despotism in Italian politics', in J. R. Hale, J. R. L. Highfield, and B. Smalley (eds.), *Europe in the Late Middle Ages* (Evanston, Ill., 1965), pp. 301–31. The important studies of J. W. Black illuminate the struggle between the extravagant claims for, and the legal restraints on, the personal power of the Visconti and Sforza rulers. In addition to the unpublished paper cited in n. 3, see 'The limits of ducal authority: a fifteenth-century treatise on the Visconti and their subject cities', in P. Denley and C. Elam (eds.), *Florence and Italy: Renaissance Studies in Honour of Nicolai Rubinstein* (London, 1988), pp. 149–60; and '*Natura feudi haec est:* lawyers and feudatories in the duchy of Milan', *English Historical Review*, 109 (1994), pp. 1150–73. On the nature of the Sforza principate, see two essays by D. M. Bueno de Mesquita: 'The Sforza prince and his state', in Denley and Elam (eds.), *Florence and Italy*, pp. 161–72; and 'Lodovico Sforza and his vassals', in Jacob (ed.), *Italian Renaissance Studies*, pp. 184–216. On the Sforza court, see the lively treatment by G. Lubkin, *A Renaissance Court: Milan under Galeazzo Maria Sforza* (Berkeley, 1994). The studies of G. Chittolini on the Sforza state are particularly important: see his 'L'onore dell'officiale', in *Florence and Milan*, vol. 1, cited above, pp. 101–33. Milan under French rule is the focus of the essays in L. Arcangeli (ed.), *Milano e Luigi XII. Ricerche sul primo dominio francese in Lombardia (1499–1512)* (Milan, 2002), in which, on law and the courts, see C. Storti Storchi, ' "*Acciò che le cause passino più consultamente e con minor rechiamo"*: Nodi della giustizia nei primi anni del dominio di Luigi XII a Milano', pp. 147–65; see also L. Arcangeli, *Gentiluomini di Lombardia. Ricerche sull'aristocrazia padana nel Rinascimento* (Milan, 2003), pp. 3–67. On the Milanese state in the sixteenth century, see the classic work of Federico Chabod, *Lo stato e la vita religiosa a Milano nell'epoca di Carlo V* (Turin, 1971).

Valuable studies of government in other cities and states

Mantua and Ferrara: D. S. Chambers and T. Dean, *Clean Hands and Rough Justice: An Investigating Magistrate in Renaissance Italy* (Ann Arbor, 1997). Genoa: C. Shaw, 'Counsel and consent in fifteenth-century Genoa,' *English Historical Review*, 116 (2001), pp. 834–62; and S. A. Epstein, *Genoa and the Genoese, 958–1528* (Chapel Hill, N.C., 1996). Siena: W. M. Bowsky, *A Medieval Italian Commune: Siena under the Nine, 1287–1355* (Berkeley, 1981); and W. Caferro, *Mercenary Companies and the Decline of Siena* (Baltimore, 1998). Padua: B. G. Kohl, *Padua under the Carrara, 1318–1405* (Baltimore, 1998). Lucca has been particularly well studied in English: on its early *signoria*, see L. Green, *Castruccio Castracani: A Study on the Origins and Character of a Fourteenth-Century Italian Despot* (Oxford, 1986); two books by C. E. Meek, *The Commune of Lucca under Pisan Rule, 1342–1369* (Cambridge, Mass., 1980), and *Lucca 1369–1400: Politics and Society in an Early Renaissance City–State* (Oxford, 1978); and M. E. Bratchel, *Lucca 1430–1494: The Reconstruction of an Italian City–Republic* (Oxford, 1995).

Government paternalism

The Florentine government's prosecution of sodomy is illuminated by M. Rocke, *Forbidden Friendships: Homosexuality and Male Culture in Renaissance*

Florence (Oxford, 1996). For its policy on prostitutes, see M. S. Mazzi, *Prostitute e lenoni nella Firenze del Quattrocento* (Milan, 1991). And on the management of dowries and the government dowry fund, see A. Molho, *Marriage Alliance in Late Medieval Florence* (Cambridge, Mass., 1994). The interventions of Venetian government to control crime and sexuality are the focus of two studies by G. Ruggiero: *Violence in Early Renaissance Venice* (New Brunswick, 1980) and *The Boundaries of Eros: Sex Crime and Sexuality in Renaissance Venice* (Oxford, 1985). On sumptuary legislation, see the comparative survey by C. Kovesi Killerby, *Sumptuary Law in Italy, 1200–1500* (Oxford, 2002). On crime and the law, see also the essays in T. Dean and K. J. P. Lowe (eds.), *Crime, Society and the Law in Renaissance Italy* (Cambridge, 1994).

Chapter 10

A stimulating point to begin is Benedetto Croce's classic *History of the Kingdom of Naples*, trans. F. Frenaye (Chicago, 1970), with its thoughtful arguments about the nature of baronial power and the obstacles that prevented the kingdom from becoming a coherent nation state. For an overview of political and economic developments in the region, see D. Abulafia, *The Western Mediterranean Kingdoms, 1200–1500: The Struggle for Dominion* (London, 1997), with a fuller bibliography than is possible here, organized by period and theme. On individual rulers, see J. Dunbabin, *Charles I of Anjou: Power, Kingship and State-Making in Thirteenth-Century Europe* (London, 1998); there is also much to be enjoyed in S. Runciman's classic *The Sicilian Vespers: A History of the Mediterranean World in the Later Thirteenth Century* (Cambridge, 1958). The old work of St Clair Baddeley, *Robert the Wise and his Heirs, 1278–1352* (London, 1897) still has some virtues, but, having been withdrawn by the publisher after threats of a libel suit, it remains a rarity. It has at last been overtaken by the brilliant book of S. Kelly, *The New Solomon: Robert of Naples (1309–1343) and Fourteenth-Century Kingship* (Leiden, 2003). For his Aragonese rival, see C. Backman, *The Decline and Fall of Medieval Sicily: Politics, Religion and Economy in the Reign of Frederick III, 1296–1337* (Cambridge, 1995). N. Housley, *The Italian Crusades: The Papal–Angevin Alliance and the Crusades against Christian Lay Powers, 1254–1343* (Oxford, 1982) is also very helpful on the politics of the house of Anjou.

Two books by A. Ryder greatly enhance our understanding of the Aragonese period: *Alfonso the Magnanimous, King of Aragon, Naples and Sicily, 1396–1458* (Oxford, 1990), and his earlier *The Kingdom of Naples under Alfonso the Magnanimous: The Making of a Modern State* (Oxford, 1976). For the reign of Ferrante, see C. Kidwell, *Pontano: Poet and Prime Minister* (London, 1991). A collection of essays dealing with various aspects of the French invasion of Italy in 1494 is in D. Abulafia (ed.), *The French Descent into Renaissance Italy, 1494–95: Antecedents and Effects* (Aldershot, 1995); see also V. Ilardi, *Studies in Italian Renaissance Diplomatic History* (London, 1986). Later developments can be traced in C. Shaw, *Julius II: The Warrior Pope* (Oxford, 1993), and in F. Baumgartner, *Louis XII* (New York, 1994). For the early sixteenth century, see A. Calabria and J. Marino (eds.), *Good Government in Spanish Naples* (New York, 1990).

On the economy, S. R. Epstein's *An Island for Itself: Economic Development and Social Change in Late Medieval Sicily* (Cambridge, 1992) is a counterblast against H. Bresc, *Un monde méditerranéen. Économie et société en Sicile, 1300–1450* (2 vols., Rome, 1986). For the mainland, see E. Sakellariou, *The Economy of Naples under Aragonese and Spanish Rule* (forthcoming); also J. Marino, *Pastoral Economics in the Kingdom of Naples* (Baltimore, 1988), particularly for the late fifteenth and sixteenth centuries.

A good introduction to the cultural history of the Aragonese period is J. Bentley, *Politics and Culture in Renaissance Naples* (Princeton, 1987). For Alfonso as a Spanish Roman emperor, see P. Stacey, *The Royal Ideology of Renaissance Naples, 1442–58* (forthcoming). Other aspects of cultural life are treated in A. Atlas, *Music at the Aragonese Court of Naples* (Cambridge, 1985), and in G. Hersey, *The Aragonese Arch at Naples, 1443–1475* (New Haven, 1973) together with his *Alfonso II and the Artistic Renewal of Naples, 1485–1495* (New Haven, 1969). On recent historiography, see D. Abulafia, 'The diffusion of the Italian Renaissance: southern Italy and beyond', in J. Woolfson (ed.), *Palgrave Advances in Renaissance Historiography* (London, 2005).

The literature in Italian also has notable gaps. Fortunately, there is a masterly and massive survey of the period in G. Galasso, *Il Regno di Napoli. Il Mezzogiorno angioino e aragonese (1266–1494)* (Storia d'Italia UTET, Turin, 1992), with a further volume by the same author in preparation on later developments. On Sardinia, see F. C. Casula, *La Sardegna aragonese* (2 vols., Cagliari, 1990); and, for Sicily, P. Corrao, *Governare un regno: potere, società e istituzioni in Sicilia fra Trecento e Quattrocento* (Naples, 1991) and (in Spanish) J. Vicens Vives, *Fernando el Católico, príncipe de Aragón, rey de Sicilia, 1458–1478* (Madrid, 1952). The outstanding work on the economy is by M. del Treppo, *I mercanti catalani e l'espansione della Corona d'Aragona nel secolo XV*, 2nd edn (Naples, 1972). The collection of essays on *Good Government* mentioned above contains translations of excellent essays by Italian historians, beginning with a splendid piece by Galasso on Naples under Charles V.

Chapter 11

For a general introduction to the representation of power in early modern Europe, see E. Muir, *Ritual in Early Modern Europe* (first published, 1997) (Cambridge, 2005), the most comprehensive comparative analysis of rituals. The methods for studying historical rituals are most fully explored in the work of R. C. Trexler, especially, 'Florentine religious experience: the sacred image', *Studies in the Renaissance*, 19 (1972), pp. 7–41; 'Ritual behavior in Renaissance Florence: the setting', *Medievalia et Humanistica*, n. s., 4 (1973), pp. 125–44; and 'Ritual in Florence: adolescence and salvation in the Renaissance', in C. Trinkaus and H. Oberman (eds.), *The Pursuit of Holiness in Late Medieval and Renaissance Religion* (Leiden, 1974), pp. 200–64.

The contemporary understanding of how people came under the influence of the images and rituals just by witnessing them has been studied with regard to late medieval theories of sight. R. Scribner's 'Ways of seeing in the age of Dürer', in D. Eichberger and C. Zika (eds.), *Dürer and his Culture* (Cambridge, 1998), pp. 93–117, is a useful summary of the late medieval theories of sight and their implications for how contemporaries understood the power of images. An especially stimulating view of the relationship between theories of sight and the power of images is in L. P. Wandel, 'The reform of the images: new visualizations of the Christian community at Zürich', *Archiv für Reformationsgeschichte*, 80 (1989), pp. 105–24, and her *Voracious Idols and Violent Hands: Iconoclasm in Reformation Zurich, Strasbourg, and Basel* (Cambridge, 1995). For an examination of the relationship between theories of sight and the experience of participating in or witnessing public processions, see E. Muir, 'The eye of the procession: ritual ways of seeing in the Renaissance', in N. Howe (ed.), *Visual Life in the Renaissance* (Notre Dame, forthcoming). On the veneration of religious images as a test of civic loyalty, see B. Kempers, 'Icons, altarpieces, and civil ritual in Siena Cathedral, 1100–1530', in B. A. Hanawalt and K. L. Reyerson (eds.), *City and Spectacle in Medieval Europe* (Minneapolis, 1994), pp. 89–136.

The vocabularies of power available to Renaissance humanists, artists, and masters of ceremony were quite vast. The beginning point is the two-body theory of royal power; see the classic analysis by E. H. Kantorowicz, *The King's Two Bodies: A Study in Medieval Political Theology* (Princeton, 1957). A more recent analysis is S. Bertelli, *The King's Body: The Sacred Rituals of Power in Medieval and Early Modern Europe*, trans. R. B. Litchfield (University Park, Pa., 2001). The changing vocabularies of power have been most thoroughly traced for the various governments of fifteenth- and sixteenth-century Florence. The first exploration of the Florentine cult of the Magi is R. Hatfield's 'The Compagnia de' Magi', *Journal of the Warburg and Courtauld Institutes*, 33 (1970), pp. 107–61. Later work on the Magi has been built upon this pathbreaking study. For how Cosimo de' Medici employed the Magi motif and other themes in the arts to fashion a self-image, see the masterful study by D. Kent, *Cosimo de' Medici and the Florentine Renaissance: The Patron's Oeuvre* (New Haven, 2000). R. C. Trexler's *The Journey of the Magi: Meanings in the History of a Christian Story* (Princeton, 1997) is a comprehensive study of the cult of the Magi across history.

Other scholars have studied the use of the arts as representations of power in Florence. S. B. McHam demonstrates how the Medici depicted themselves as defenders of Florence's liberties in 'Donatello's bronze *David* and *Judith* as metaphors of Medici rule in Florence', *Art Bulletin*, 83 (2001), pp. 32–47. This article should be consulted in conjunction with the study of the public uses of art in fifteenth-century Florence by A. W. B. Randolph, *Engaging Symbols: Gender, Politics, and Public Art in Fifteenth-Century Florence* (New Haven, 2002). For later periods see M. Fantoni, *La corte del granduca. Forma e simboli del potere mediceo fra Cinque e Seicento* (Rome, 1994). For a revealing examination of how the Medici gave away paintings to convey diplomatic messages, see J. Cox-Rearick, 'Sacred to profane: diplomatic gifts of the Medici to Francis I', *Journal of Medieval and Renaissance Studies*, 24 (1994), pp. 239–58. Cox-Rearick has examined the artistic context of Medici patronage during the early sixteenth century in *Dynasty and Destiny in Medici Art: Pontormo, Leo X, and the Two Cosimos* (Princeton, 1984).

The fundamental dilemma involved in representing the pope is outlined in P. Burke, 'Sacred rulers, royal priests: rituals of the early modern popes', in *The Historical Anthropology of Early Modern Italy: Essays on Perception and Communication* (Cambridge, 1987), pp. 168–82. Focusing on the late medieval period, A. Paravicini-Bagliani demonstrates how important the representation and treatment of the actual physical body of the pope was for understanding the nature of the papacy itself in *The Pope's Body*, trans. D. S. Peterson (Chicago, 2000). On papal interregnum rituals, see L. Nussdorfer, 'The Vacant See: ritual and protest in early modern Rome', *Sixteenth Century Journal*, 18 (1987), pp. 173–89. On ritual pillages after the death of a pope, see 'Ritual pillages: a preface to research in progress', by the Bologna Seminar coordinated by C. Ginzburg, in E. Muir and G. Ruggiero (eds.), *Microhistory and the Lost Peoples of Europe* (Baltimore, 1991), pp. 20–41. For an examination of the revival of classical imperial triumphs in Renaissance papal Rome, see C. L. Stinger, '*Roma triumphans*: triumphs in the thought and ceremonies of Renaissance Rome', *Medievalia et Humanistica*, n.s., 10 (1981), pp. 189–201. For a fascinating study of how the public image of a Renaissance pope was fashioned, see R. Starn and L. Partridge, *A Renaissance Likeness: Art and Culture in Raphael's* Julius II (Berkeley, 1980).

The best-studied cities of Renaissance Italy with regard to representations of power are Florence and Venice. R. C. Trexler, *Public Life in Renaissance Florence* (New York, 1980) is a pathbreaking study for Florence of the relationship between public rituals, politics, and private lives that serves as a model for how to study other cities. For Venice, see E. Muir, *Civic Ritual in Renaissance Venice* (Princeton, 1981), a study of the rituals of Venetian public life with an emphasis on the representation of the republic and its doge. Building on these studies, M. Casini in *I gesti del principe: La festa politica a*

Firenze e Venezia in età rinascimentale (Venice, 1996) has produced a systematic comparison between the civic rituals of the two cities. For representations of political ideas in town halls, see the comparative study that focuses on Siena, Florence, and Mantua by R. Starn and L. Partridge, *Arts of Power: Three Halls of State in Italy, 1300–1600* (Berkeley, 1992), and also Starn's *Ambrogio Lorenzetti: The Palazzo Pubblico, Siena* (New York, 1994). For a fascinating, original analysis of the gendered construction of the image of a city in prints, see B. M. S. Wilson, *The World in Venice: Print, the City, Early Modern Identity* (Toronto, 2004). For entrances into towns, G. L. Gorse, 'Between empire and republic: entries into Genoa during the sixteenth century', in B. Wisch and S. S. Munshower (eds.), *'All the World's a Stage . . .': Art and Pageantry in the Renaissance and Baroque,* (University Park, Pa., 1990) pp. 188–257, and J. Shearman, 'The Florentine *Entrata* of Leo X, 1515', *Journal of the Warburg and Courtauld Institutes,* 38 (1975), pp. 136–54.

On the representation of the prince and his court, S. Kelly, *The New Solomon: Robert of Naples (1309–1343) and Fourteenth-Century Kingship* (Leiden, 2003); G. Lubkin, *A Renaissance Court: Milan under Galeazzo Maria Sforza* (Berkeley, 1994); and C. M. Rosenberg, 'The use of celebrations in public and semi-public affairs in fifteenth-century Ferrara', in M. de Panizza Lorch (ed.), *Il teatro italiano del Rinascimento* (Milan, 1980), pp. 521–35.

Chapter 12

On the crisis of 1494 and its impact on Renaissance culture, three collections of essays written in connection with the quincentenary offer up-to-date introductions: D. Abulafia (ed.), *The French Descent into Renaissance Italy, 1494–95* (Aldershot, 1995), esp. C. Clough, pp. 191–215; J. Everson and D. Zancani (eds.), *Italy in Crisis, 1494* (Oxford, 2000), esp. A. Brown, pp. 3–40; and S. Fletcher and C. Shaw (eds.), *The World of Savonarola: Italian Elites and Perceptions of Crisis* (Aldershot, 2000), esp. L. Martines, pp. 5–21, and the section 'Italian states and their elites', pp. 128–81. On the theme of fortune, see M. Santoro, *Fortuna, ragione e prudenza nella civiltà letteraria del Cinquecento* (Naples, 1967), esp. 11–21 ('L'invasione francese e il tema della fortuna'); A. Brown, 'Lucretius and the Epicureans in the social and political context of Renaissance Florence,' *I Tatti Studies,* 10 (2001), pp. 11–62; and pp. 23–6 of Brown's essay in *Italy in Crisis* (above).

On republicanism, two classic works are still indispensable: H. Baron, *The Crisis of the Early Italian Renaissance: Civic Humanism and Republican Liberty in an Age of Classicism and Tyranny,* 2nd rev. edn (Princeton, 1966); and J. G. A. Pocock, *The Machiavellian Moment: Florentine Political Thought and the Atlantic Republican Tradition* (Princeton, 1975). The best recent assessment is the volume of essays edited by J. Hankins, *Renaissance Civic Humanism: Reappraisals and Reflections* (Cambridge, 2000), esp. J. Najemy, J. Hankins, A.

Brown, and A. Moulakis, pp. 75–104, 143–222. Also useful is the volume *City–States in Classical Antiquity and Medieval Italy*, eds. A. Molho, K. Raaflaub, and J. Emlen (Ann Arbor, 1991) (see below for individual contributions). On the survival of republicanism in Milan: G. Ianziti, *Humanistic Historiography under the Sforzas* (Oxford, 1988); E. Welch, *Art and Authority in Renaissance Milan* (New Haven, 1995); and the Treccani *Storia di Milano*, vols. vi–viii (Milan, 1955–7), which is still the best overall account. On Florence: J. Najemy, in *Renaissance Civic Humanism*, cited above, and Najemy, 'The dialogue of power in Florentine politics' in *City–States in Classical Antiquity*, cited above, pp. 269–88; D. Herlihy, 'The rulers of Florence, 1282–1530', ibid., pp. 197–221; R. Fubini, 'From social to political representation in Renaissance Florence', ibid., pp. 223–39. For Venice and its influence as a republican model: F. Gilbert, 'The Venetian constitution in Florentine political thought', in N. Rubinstein (ed.), *Florentine Studies* (London, 1968), pp. 463–500, and Gilbert, 'Venice in the crisis of the League of Cambrai', in J. R. Hale (ed.), *Renaissance Venice* (London, 1973), pp. 274–92; also L. Libby, 'Venetian history and political thought after 1509', *Studies in the Renaissance*, 20 (1973), pp. 7–45; J. Sperling, *Convents and the Body Politic in Late Renaissance Venice* (Chicago, 1999); M. King, *Venetian Humanism in an Age of Patrician Dominance* (Princeton, 1986); E. Muir, 'Was there republicanism in Renaissance republics?', in J. Martin and D. Romano (eds.), *Venice Reconsidered: The History and Civilization of an Italian City–State, 1297–1797* (Baltimore, 2000), pp. 137–67; and the classic work of W. Bouwsma, *Venice and the Defense of Republican Liberty: Renaissance Values in the Age of the Counter Reformation* (Berkeley, 1968).

On the new political realism, one can begin with three essays on Savonarola and political change in Florence in *The World of Savonarola*, cited above, by A. Brown, N. Rubinstein, and L. Polizzotto, pp. 22–64. On the revolution in political thinking, see A. Brown, 'Demasking Renaissance republicanism', in *Renaissance Civic Humanism*, cited above, pp. 179–99; A. Moulakis, 'Civic humanism, realist constitutionalism, and Francesco Guicciardini's *Discorso di Logrogno*', ibid., pp. 200–22; and H. C. Mansfield, 'Bruni and Machiavelli on civic humanism', ibid., pp. 223–46; cf. A. Brown, 'Changing perceptions of city and citizen in late medieval Italy', in *City–States in Classical Antiquity*, cited above, pp. 93–111; and J. N. Stephens, *The Fall of the Florentine Republic, 1512–1530* (Oxford, 1983), pp. 203–55.

General books on the culture of the fifteenth-century courts include S. Bertelli, F. Cardini, and E. Garbero Zorzi, *The Courts of the Italian Renaissance* (London, 1986); A. Cole, *Virtue and Magnificence: Art of the Italian Renaissance Courts* (London, 1995). There are several studies of individual courts. Milan: E. Welch, *Art and Authority in Renaissance Milan*, cited above, is the best-illustrated account of the Sforza court; G. Lubkin, *A Renaissance Court: Milan under Galeazzo Maria Sforza* (Berkeley, 1994) gives a microscopic account of court life under a single ruler. Rimini: J. Woods-Marsden, 'How Quattrocento princes used art: Sigismondo Pandolfo Malatesta of Rimini and *cose militari*', *Renaissance Studies*, 3 (1989), pp. 387–414. Ferrara: W. Gundersheimer, *Ferrara: The Style of a Renaissance Despotism* (Princeton, 1973). Mantua: D. Chambers and J. Martineau (eds.), *Splendours of the Gonzaga* (London, 1981), esp. C. Elam, 'Mantegna and Mantua', pp. 15–25; and C. Mozzarelli, *Mantova e i Gonzaga* (Turin, 1987). Urbino: G. Gerboni Baiardi, G. Chittolini, and R. Loriani (eds.), *Federigo da Montefeltro: lo stato, le arti, la cultura* (Rome, 1986). On the unofficial court of Lorenzo in Florence: F. W. Kent, *Lorenzo de' Medici and the Art of Magnificence* (Baltimore, 2004). Rome: C. Stinger, *The Renaissance in Rome* (Bloomington, Ind., 1985); I. Rowland, *The Culture of High Renaissance Rome: Ancients and Moderns in Sixteenth-Century Rome* (Cambridge, 1998); and T. C. Price Zimmerman, *Paolo Giovio Historian and the Crisis of Sixteenth-Century Italy* (Princeton, 1995). On the Sack, see Stinger, cited above, pp. 320–32; A. Chastel, *The Sack of Rome, 1527*, trans. B. Archer (Princeton, 1983); K. Gouwens, *Remembering the Renaissance: Humanist Narratives of the Sack of Rome* (Leiden, 1998).

On the intellectual crisis and later developments, there is an excellent overview by A. Prosperi, 'Intellettuali e chiesa all'inizio dell'età moderna', in *Storia d'Italia. Annali* 4 (Turin, 1981), pp. 159–252. On the 'feminization' of Italy, D. Shemek, *Ladies Errant: Wayward Women and Social Order in Early Modern Italy* (Durham, N.C., 1998). For the language debate, see the entry 'Questione della lingua' in the recent *Oxford Companion to Italian Literature*, eds. P. Hainsworth and D. Robey (Oxford, 2002), pp. 495–6. On academies, K.-E. Barzman, *The Florentine Academy and the Early Modern State* (Cambridge, 2000); and R. S. Samuels, 'Benedetto Varchi, the *Accademia degli Infiammati*, and the origins of the Italian academic movement', *Renaissance Quarterly*, 29 (1976), pp. 599–634. And on Galileo, M. Biagioli, *Galileo, Courtier: The Practice of Science in the Culture of Absolutism* (Chicago, 1993).

Chronology

1282	Sicily rises against French rule (the 'Sicilian Vespers')
1282	Establishment of the priorate and guild-based government of Florence
1287–1355	Rule of the Nine in Siena
1293	Ordinances of Justice bar Florentine magnates from major offices
1294–1303	Pontificate of Boniface VIII
1296	Construction of new cathedral begun in Florence
1297	First stage in the Serrata (closing) of the Venetian patriciate enlarges the Great Council but makes future additions more difficult
1298	Bankruptcy of the Sienese Company of the Bonsignori
1299	Construction of Palace of the Priors begun in Florence
1300	First Jubilee in Rome
c.1300	Tolomeo of Lucca writes *On the Government of Rulers*
1301	Charles of Valois invades Florence in support of Black Guelfs
1302	Dante Alighieri (1265–1321) is banished from Florence; writes the *Divine Comedy* in exile
1302	Pope Boniface issues *Unam Sanctam*
1303	Boniface is humiliated by French troops at Anagni
1308	Duccio di Buoninsegna commissioned to paint the *Maestà* in Siena
1309–43	Reign of Robert of Anjou, king of Naples
1309–77	Popes reside in Avignon
1310	Council of Ten instituted in Venice
1310–13	Emperor Henry VII (d. 1313) fails to revive imperial power in Italy
1314	Emigration of skilled workers from Lucca disseminates methods of silk production
1316–34	Pontificate of John XXII; issues *Ex debito*, 1316, on benefices; *Cum inter nonnullos*, 1323, condemns Spiritual Franciscan doctrine of apostolic poverty

1324	Marsilius of Padua completes *The Defender of Peace*
1328	Padua succumbs to the rule of the Carrara lords
1328–9	Florentines devise electoral system of scrutinies and sortition
1329	Azzone Visconti acquires imperial vicariate over Milan
1338–9	Ambrogio Lorenzetti paints the *Allegory of Good and Bad Government* in the Palazzo Pubblico in Siena
1339	Genoese elect Simone Boccanegra 'doge for life'
1340	Construction of Palazzo Ducale begun in Venice
1341	Francesco Petrarca (Petrarch, 1304–74) crowned Poet Laureate in Rome
1342–3	Brief *signoria* of Walter of Brienne, duke of Athens, in Florence
1343	Cola di Rienzo in Avignon representing Roman popular government; meets Petrarch
1343–8	Popular government of the guilds in Florence consolidates public debt into the *Monte comune*, funds it in 1345
1343–6	Bankruptcy of the great Florentine trading and banking companies of the Bardi, Peruzzi, Acciaiuoli and many smaller ones
1345	Petrarch recovers Cicero's *Letters to Atticus* in Verona
1347	Cola di Rienzo leads revolution in Rome, is declared 'Tribune'
1347–50	First outbreak of plague kills 3.5 million people (slightly less than 30 percent of Italy's population); subsequent major epidemics in 1363, 1374, 1400, 1417, 1422–5, 1430, 1457, 1479, 1497, 1527
1348–51	Giovanni Boccaccio (1313–75) writes the *Decameron*
1353–67	Cardinal Gil Albornoz sent by Innocent VI to reimpose papal control over the papal state; issues *Constitutiones Egidianae*, 1357
1353	Petrarch moves definitively to Italy, lives in Milan until 1361, thereafter in Venice and Padua
1355	Anti-noble conspiracy uncovered in Venice; its leader, doge Marin Falier, is executed along with many others
1368	Petrarch defends the religious value of humanism in *On his Own Ignorance*
1370–5	Revolts by woolworkers in Perugia and Siena

1375–1406	Coluccio Salutati (1331–1406) chancellor of Florence
1375–8	War of the Eight Saints between Florence and papacy of Gregory XI
1376–7	Catherine of Siena (1347–80), Dominican tertiary, exhorts Pope Gregory XI to reform the Church and return to Rome
1378	Revolt of the woolworkers (Ciompi) in Florence
1378–82	Popular government of the guilds in Florence introduces fiscal reforms
1378–81	Victory of Venice over Genoa in the War of Chioggia gives the Venetians commercial supremacy in the eastern Mediterranean
1378–1417	Papal schism; rival popes in Rome, Avignon, and later Pisa
1385	Giangaleazzo Visconti seizes sole power from his uncle Bernabò, forbids use of the word 'popolo'
1386	Construction of new cathedral in Milan begun
1390	Raymond of Capua (1330–99), inspired by Catherine of Siena, founds Observant Dominicans
1390–1402	Series of wars between Milan and Florence
1395	Giangaleazzo Visconti acquires the title of duke of Milan from the emperor; the title is extended to all Visconti territories in 1396
1397	Foundation of the Medici Bank by Giovanni di Bicci de' Medici
1397	Manuel Chrysoloras invited to Florence to teach Greek
1398	Pope Boniface IX reimposes papal sovereignty over the commune of Rome
1401–2	Lorenzo Ghiberti wins competition against Filippo Brunelleschi for commission to sculpt bronze doors of baptistery in Florence
1402	Giangaleazzo Visconti dies; the Visconti state disintegrates
1403–8	Leonardo Bruni (1370–1444) writes the *Panegyric to the City of Florence* and the *Dialogues to Vergerio*
1404	Giovanni Dominici (c.1356–1419) condemns humanism in *The Glowworm*
1406	Florence conquers her ancient rival Pisa
1408	Establishment in Genoa of the quasi-public Banco di San Giorgio
1409	Council of Pisa elects Pope Alexander V (1409–10) but fails to end the schism

1409–14	Wars between Florence and Ladislas of Naples
1412	Filippo Maria Visconti recognized as duke of Milan
1414–18	Council of Constance ends the papal schism, electing Oddone Colonna as Pope Martin V (1417–31); council declares its superiority over the pope in the decrees *Haec Sancta* (1415) and *Frequens* (1417)
1415	Ermolao Barbaro writes treatise *On Wifely Duties*
1415–44	Bruni writes the *History of the Florentine People*
1420–36	Brunelleschi designs and directs construction of the dome of Florence Cathedral
1421	Genoa submits to Filippo Maria Visconti
1424–40	Another series of wars between Milan and Florence
1425	Venice allies with Florence against Milan
1425	Government dowry fund (*Monte delle doti*) introduced in Florence
1425–8	Masaccio and Masolino paint frescoes in Brancacci Chapel in Florence
1425–7	Bernardino of Siena (1380–1444), Observant Franciscan, preaches in Florence and Siena
1427	First Catasto (tax survey) in Florence precisely measuring population and assets through self-assessment by all households in the city and its Tuscan dependencies
1427–44	Leonardo Bruni chancellor of Florence
1431–3	Leon Battista Alberti (1404–72) drafts the first three books *On the Family*
1431–47	Pontificate of Eugenius IV (Gabriele Condulmer)
1431–49	Council of Basel challenges Pope Eugenius and reissues *Haec Sancta* (1431)
1432	Florence institutes the Officials of the Night to control and penalize sodomy
1433	Cosimo de' Medici banished from Florence by Albizzi faction
1434	Cosimo recalled, controls Florence until his death in 1464
1435	Genoa rebels against the Visconti
1435–6	Alberti writes treatise *On Painting*
1437	Florence grants contract (*condotta*) to Jewish bankers

1438–9	Cosimo de' Medici and Pope Eugenius IV host Council of Ferrara–Florence; *Laetentur coeli* (1439) reunites Greek and Latin churches
1440	Lorenzo Valla (1407–57) completes *On the False Donation of Constantine* and *On the Profession of the Religious*
1441	Francesco Sforza marries Bianca Maria Visconti, daughter of Filippo Maria
1442	Alfonso of Aragon conquers the kingdom of Naples
1444	Cosimo de' Medici begins building family palace in Florence
1444–72	Federico da Montefeltro commissions construction of Palazzo Ducale in Urbino
1444–78	Ludovico Gonzaga marquis of Mantua
1445	Alfonso begins construction of Triumphal Arch in Naples
1446–59	Antoninus (Antonino Pierozzi, b. 1389), reforming archbishop of Florence
1447	Death of Filippo Maria Visconti, duke of Milan
1447–55	Pontificate of Nicholas V (Tommaso Parentucelli); plans restoration of Rome, begins Vatican Library
1447–50	Ambrosian Republic in Milan
1450	Francesco Sforza becomes duke of Milan
1452	Borso d'Este of Ferrara acquires title of duke of Modena and Reggio from the emperor
1452	Alfonso gives lavish welcome to Emperor Frederick III in Naples
1452–3	Giannozzo Manetti (1396–1459) completes *On the Dignity and Excellence of Man*
1454	The Peace of Lodi ends decades of war among all the states of Italy
1455	The *lega italica* recognizes the spheres of influence of the five major regional states (Milan, Venice, Florence, Rome, Naples)
*c.*1455	Valla completes *Annotations on the New Testament*
1458	The Observant Franciscans James of the Marches (1393–1476) and Bernardino da Feltre (1439–94) begin founding *monti di pietà*
1458	Death of Alfonso, succeeded by his son Ferrante as King of Naples

1458–63	Genoa submits to French rule (1458), expels the French and reasserts its independence (1461), falls to Francesco Sforza (1464)
1458–64	Pontificate of Pius II (Aeneas Sylvius Piccolomini, b. 1405); issues *Execrabilis* (1460), condemning doctrine of conciliar supremacy in the Church
1459	Pius II convenes the Congress of Mantua to exhort the Italian states to organize against the Ottoman Turks
1459	Benozzo Gozzoli paints the Procession of the Magi in the chapel of Palazzo Medici
1463–70	Italian merchants move en masse from the fairs of Geneva to those of Lyon
1464	Cosimo de' Medici dies; in 1465–6 his former lieutenants attempt to prevent his son Piero from 'succeeding' to the leadership of their faction; political confrontation ends in victory in 1466 for the Medici who fill the city with troops
1465	First books printed in Italy at Subiaco, near Rome
1465–74	Andrea Mantegna paints the Camera degli Sposi in Mantua
1466	Francesco Sforza dies, succeeded by his son Galeazzo Maria Sforza
1468	Niccolò Perotti's *Rudimenta grammatices*
1469–74	Marsilio Ficino (1433–99) composes *Platonic Theology: On the Immortality of the Soul*
1469	Lorenzo de' Medici assumes leadership of Medici regime
1471	Borso d'Este acquires title of duke of Ferrara from the pope
1471–84	Pontificate of Sixtus IV (Francesco Della Rovere); builds Sistine Chapel, founds the Datary to regulate sale of church offices and indulgences
1472	Volterra sacked and hundreds killed as Lorenzo de' Medici orders Federico da Montefeltro to attack the subject city in a dispute over control of an alum mine
1475	Jews accused and burned for the ritual murder of Simon of Trent
1476	Assassination of Galeazzo Maria Sforza by Milanese aristocrats
1478	Federico da Montefeltro acquires title of duke of Urbino from Sixtus IV
1478	Pazzi Conspiracy against Lorenzo de' Medici; his brother Giuliano is killed

1478–80	Pope Sixtus IV and King Ferrante of Naples declare war and invade Florentine territory
1479	Alamanno Rinuccini's *Dialogue on Liberty* denounces Lorenzo as a tyrant
1480	Lodovico il Moro seizes power in Milan from the widow of Galeazzo Maria and the powerful ducal secretary Cicco Simonetta
1480	The Ottoman Turks attack and occupy Otranto
1485–6	Revolt of the Barons against King Ferrante of Naples
1486	Giovanni Pico della Mirandola (1463–1494) composes *Oration on the Dignity of Man* and the 900 theses
1489	Pope Innocent VIII (1484–92) promotes thirteen-year-old Giovanni de' Medici, Lorenzo's son and the future Pope Leo X, to the cardinalate
1492	Death of Lorenzo de' Medici
1492–1503	Pontificate of Alexander VI (Rodrigo Borgia)
1494	First French invasion of Italy under Charles VIII; fall of the Medici regime and expulsion from Florence of Lorenzo's sons; establishment of a new Great Council under the influence of Fra Girolamo Savonarola (1452–98); Pisa throws off Florentine rule
1495	Naples conquered by Charles VIII; Charles leaves Italy after the battle of Fornovo in July
1495–8	Leonardo da Vinci paints *Last Supper* in Santa Maria delle Grazie in Milan
1496	Bartolomeo Scala publishes his *Defence of Florence*
1497	St Catherine of Genoa (1447/8–1510) and Ettore Vernazza found Oratory of Divine Love
1498	Trial and death at the stake in Florence of Savonarola
1498	Niccolò Machiavelli appointed head of second chancery in Florence
1499	Second French invasion of Italy by Louis XII, who occupies Milan and expels Lodovico Sforza
1499–1503	Cesare Borgia, son of Pope Alexander, creates a Borgia state in the Romagna, dispossessing most of the region's *signori*, including the duke of Urbino (1502)
1500	Milan rebels against French rule; Lodovico Sforza returns briefly but is then taken prisoner by the French

*c.*1500	Domenico Morosini of Venice writes *On the Well-Ordered Republic*
1501	Naples conquered by Louis XII of France and Ferdinand of Spain
1502	Piero Soderini elected lifetime Standard bearer of Justice in Florence
1503–4	Spain drives France from Naples, occupies the Kingdom
1503–13	Pontificate of Julius II (Giuliano Della Rovere); he begins rebuilding St Peter's basilica, has Michelangelo paint the Sistine Chapel ceiling and Raphael paint the Vatican Stanze
1504	Michelangelo's *David* erected in front of the Palace of the Priors in Florence as a symbol of republican strength
1505–7	Machiavelli invents, organizes, and recruits the Florentine militia
1506	Pope Julius reconquers and enters Bologna
1506	The Venetian 'Golden Book' compiled to register the patriciate
1506–7	Popular revolt in Genoa crushed by the French
1509	Venice defeated by Julius II's League of Cambrai, temporarily loses its mainland dominions
1509	Florence reoccupies Pisa
1510–11	Julius II organizes the Holy League against France
1512	At the battle of Ravenna the French are victorious; but when the Swiss invade Lombardy, the French leave Italy; Spanish troops invade Tuscany and restore the Medici; fall of the republic; exile of Piero Soderini; removal of Machiavelli from his posts
1513	Machiavelli arrested and tortured for suspected involvement in an anti-Medici conspiracy; he writes *The Prince* and intends to dedicate it to Giuliano de' Medici, the pope's brother
1513–21	Pontificate of Leo X (Giovanni de' Medici)
1515	Third French invasion under Francis I; French occupy Milan; Concordat of Bologna between Francis and Pope Leo; Leo makes formal entrance into Florence
1516	First enclosure of Jews in Italy in Venice's 'Ghetto'
1516	Machiavelli dedicates a second version of *The Prince* to Lorenzo de' Medici the Younger, the nephew of Leo X
1516	Leo X removes Francesco Maria Della Rovere as duke of Urbino and replaces him with his nephew Lorenzo

1516–18	Machiavelli writes the *Discourses on the First Ten Books of Titus Livy*
1517	Pope Leo X adds thirty-one cardinals to the college
1519	Charles V elected emperor
1520	Machiavelli writes the *Discourse on Remodelling the Government of Florence*
1520	Leo X issues *Exsurge Domine* condemning Luther's teaching
1521	Machiavelli's *Art of War* printed
1521–4	Guicciardini writes the *Dialogue on the Government of Florence*
1523–34	Pontificate of Clement VII (Giulio de' Medici)
1521–5	Machiavelli writes the *Florentine Histories*
1525	French defeated by imperial forces at Pavia
1527	Sack of Rome by German and Spanish troops; restoration of republican government in Florence; Machiavelli dies in June; Francesco Vettori begins his *Sommario della istoria d'Italia*
1528	Baldassare Castiglione (1478–1529) publishes *The Book of the Courtier*
1530	Florence surrenders to papal and imperial forces after a ten-month siege; Medici restored by order of Charles V
1532	Florence's republican government formally terminated and a principate proclaimed; Alessandro de' Medici made duke
1532	Revolt of the Straccioni in Lucca
1534–49	Pontificate of Paul III (Alessandro Farnese)
1536–41	Michelangelo paints *Last Judgement* in Sistine Chapel
1537	Alessandro de' Medici assassinated, succeeded by Cosimo I as duke of Florence
1537	Gasparo Contarini (1483–1542) presents the *Consilium de emendenda ecclesia* to Paul III
1537–40	Guicciardini writes his voluminous *History of Italy* covering the period from 1490 to 1534
1540	Paul III approves the Society of Jesus (the Jesuits)
*c.*1540	Effects of the price revolution, in part caused by the arrival of American silver, begin to be felt
1541	Expulsion of the Jews from Spanish Naples
1542	Papal, Roman Inquisition established

1543	Gasparo Contarini's *On the Magistrates and the Republic of the Venetians*, written over twenty years, is published
1545–63	Council of Trent
1550	Giorgio Vasari publishes first edition of his *Lives of the Artists* (second, expanded edition in 1568)
1555	Duke Cosimo I of Florence conquers Siena and incorporates it into his dominions
1555–9	Pontificate of Paul IV (Giovanni Pietro Carafa); establishes the Jewish ghetto in Rome (1555)
1559	Peace of Cateau-Cambrésis recognizes Spanish hegemony in most of Italy
1559	Creation of Pauline Index of Prohibited Books
1564	Tridentine Index of Prohibited Books

Map section

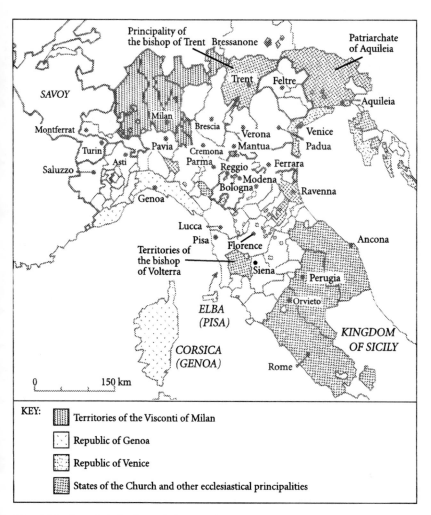

Map 1 Northern Italy in the early fourteenth century
Source: Robert S. Lopez, *Naissance de l'Europe* (Librairie Armand Colin, Paris, 1962), p. 276.

1. Marquisate of Monferrato
2. County of Asti
3. Territory of the Malaspina
4. Marquisate of Mantua
5. Dominions of the Este
6. Republic of Lucca
7. Duchy of Piombino

Map 2 Italy in the mid-fifteenth century
Source: Brian Pullen, *Early Renaissance Italy* (Allen Lane, London, 1973), p. 344.

Map 3 The papal state and central Italy in the fifteenth century
    Source: David Abulafia ed., *The French Descent into Renaissance Italy,*
    1494–95 (Variorum–Ashgate, Aldershot, 1995), p. xiv.

Map 4 Italy, 1500
Source: Paul Grendler ed., *Encyclopedia of the Renaissance.*
Charles Scribner's Sons. © Charles Scribner's Sons 2000.
Reprinted by permission of The Gale Group.

Map 5 Italy, 1559
Source: Paul Grendler ed., *Encyclopedia of the Renaissance.*
Charles Scribner's Sons. © Charles Scribner's Sons 2000.
Reprinted by permission of The Gale Group.

Index